THE MOTHER OF GOD

THE MOTHER OF GOD

LUNA TARLO

PLOVER PRESS

To Ernesto Cuevas,
with much love and gratitude

Acknowledgements

Sandra Brand, Josh Cohen, Ernesto Cuevas,
Patricia Duffy, Laura Glenn, Richard Grabel, Leslie Kean,
Donna Moylan, Patricia Newcastle, John and Nomi Stadler,
Rosalind Palermo Stevenson, Julie Thayer, and Bertha Workoff

The names of some people in this book
have been changed to respect their privacy.

Plover Press
c/o Autonomedia
POB 568 Williamsburgh Station
Brooklyn, New York
11211-0568 USA

Phone & Fax: 718-963-2603
World Wide Web: http://www.autonomedia.org

Printed in the United States of America

"What is this flesh I purchased with my pains,
This fallen star my milk sustains,
This love that makes my heart's blood stop
Or strikes a sudden chill into my bones
And bids my hair stand up?"

From "The Mother of God"
William Butler Yeats (1932)

"Adulation … has an addictive quality difficult to resist. Being the focus of such attention would activate the excitation levels of any sentient being on the receiving end of it. Whether for a guru or a rock star, this can be a more powerful experience than the strongest drug. It is also one of the greatest seductions of power."

From *The Guru Papers*
Masks of Authoritarian Power
By Joel Kramer and Diana Alstad

"After breakfast, at Andrew's request, I read a few pages from my diary. I was sure it would be boring, and up until now, hadn't given it a glance. But Andrew said he found it interesting, and added, *'It might make a nice little book someday.'*"

From Chapter 6
The Mother of God

PROLOGUE

IN 1983, MY SON ANDREW SET OFF FOR INDIA TO SEEK enlightenment. After two years there he invited me to visit him. The following is based on a diary I kept from December 1985 to May 1989. It was recorded in school notebooks, on bits of paper, stenographer's pads—whatever I could find while travelling with Andrew. Not a scrap was ever lost. I don't know where the impulse to keep a diary came from. I'd never kept a diary before. But without it this book could never have been written.

The story began six years before, when Andrew, twenty-two at the time, and already practicing karate and studying Eastern philosophy, started giving me books to read about Yoga and Buddhism. I remember how he used to hand them over with that ambiguous expression of his, ironic but somehow hopeful, because he knew how skeptical I was about 'religion.' I'd been brought up in an atheistic Jewish household and I had certainly never been interested in Eastern philosophy. He knew that.

Nevertheless, much to my surprise, those books intrigued me and had an effect on me, probably because of all the recent deaths in my family. When my mother died I was so frozen with grief that for a long time I couldn't shed a tear. Two years later my husband died of a brain tumor. Then my father died. Three deaths in four years. In each case I was the one on whom the responsibility fell to clean up the debris of a life.

Those books gave me useful suggestions on how to deal with death and loss and how to go on living. I remember discussing a lot of questions they raised with Andrew. He was pleased at my interest and although we had always been close, it brought us even closer than we had been before. I felt that the road along which he seemed to be travelling might help me too. So when he went on his first retreat to a meditation center in Massachusetts, I impulsively decided to join him.

I would not have felt impelled to write so intimate an account of what follows if I did not believe that it stood for something more consequential and universal.

1

AT EXACTLY MIDNIGHT THE PILOT OF THE AIR India 747 announced that we were about to land in New Delhi. The cabin lights went out. I fastened my seat-belt, leaned back and closed my eyes, gritty with fatigue. I couldn't relax. I was too excited about meeting my son Andrew, whom I hadn't seen for two years.

A little breathless, I was the first one out of the plane door and down the metal landing stairs. I stopped for a moment on the tarmac to sniff the smoky, spicy darkness. After the damp winter cold of New York, the warm air felt desert dry and enticingly alien. With a quiver of anticipation, I turned and hurried towards the terminal.

The terminal was a flimsy barn-like affair constructed, it seemed, entirely of dirty white wallboard. It suggested the possibility of collapsing at any moment. The floor was covered with a worn reddish carpet and bits of debris lay everywhere.

Hundreds of people, the women for the most part in brightly colored Saris, stood in ragged noisy lines next to mountains of huge bulging suitcases. Apparently a few planes had landed at approximately the same time. I watched everything going on about me curiously and after answering endless queries from what seemed to me inordinately suspicious immigration authorities and customs officers, I was escorted by some functionary, a sullen-looking man in a soiled white jacket and a faded green turban, to a door that led into the neon gloom of yet another enormous, crowded, implausibly rundown room. It was the airport waiting room.

A sea of black eyes gripped mine instantly. I was confronted by a waiting horde that had congregated at the entry. I didn't see Andrew. Somewhat fearful, clutching my suitcase tightly and pressing my shoulder bag against my chest, I tried to push my way through and met a surprising amount of resistance; no one wanted to give up their place near the door.

Once clear, I looked about anxiously. Where was Andrew? A river of enormously laden passengers and their families and friends streamed slowly towards the exit doors at the other end. My heart began to pound. Where in the world was Andrew?

All at once I saw him. He was running towards me. A tall, lean, clean-shaven, dark-haired boy in a clean T-shirt and jeans. As he approached his face gradually condensed into the dear familiar configuration I remembered; the round, dark eyes, the prominent nose, the well-shaped jaw and chin. Then he was there, in front of me, grabbing me in a tight, loving hug. We separated and stood for a while grinning and looking one another over. I noticed that the pale thinness of his New York self, the shadow of discontent behind his eyes, seemed to have vanished. He had even put on a little weight.

"Luna," he said, "I want you to meet someone." He turned to the woman he'd been with for the past year and who was now standing slightly behind him. She came forward smiling. "Luna," Andrew said, "this is Alka Aurora, I wrote you about her. And Alka," he smiled at her, "this is Luna."

Her shoulder-length hair was worn loosely, Western style, and she had on a spotless white pajama and kurta. She was a slight, small-boned woman and looked to be in her middle twenties. Her face, though somewhat sharp-featured, was pretty, and behind her horn-rimmed spectacles I saw large slightly protruding dark eyes. She stepped forward and embraced me warmly.

"You have a lovely name," I said.

She smiled at me shyly.

An ancient taxi transported us to the city. The driver pressed his horn constantly. On the way there wasn't much I could see except for the blinding undimmed lights of oncoming traffic. I sat on one side of Andrew, and Alka on the other.

"We're going to see the Taj Mahal tomorrow," Andrew said, squeezing my arm.

I'd been presented with so many photographs of the Taj Mahal during my life and had heard so much about this 'seventh wonder of the world' that I felt I had already seen it. Andrew must have sensed my lack of enthusiasm because he said, "It's not what you think, Luna."

"Yes, truly," Alka echoed, leaning forward to nod at me.

"But won't there be millions of tourists?" I said.

"Yes, it's as commercial as hell." Andrew squeezed my arm again. "But it's worth it."

"You won't be sorry Luna," Alka said, leaning forward again. "It's very amazing. Very beautiful."

"Trust us," Andrew said.

I got the impression that they had taken the time to make careful plans for my trip and I felt very touched.

We were staying at separate hotels. Andrew told me he had reserved a room in a more luxurious one for me. But the 'more luxurious one' turned out to be very rundown with scratched furniture, stained rugs and low-watt lighting. The mattress was a thin cotton pad laid over a panel of wood. I couldn't imagine what *their* place was like.

Although I'd been flying for countless hours it took me a long time to get to sleep. I wanted Andrew nearby. From his letters, I knew that he'd spent all his time in India visiting ashrams and meeting assorted holy men and yoga teachers. Now I wanted to hear from his own lips his feelings about it all, and ask him what he had gained here during the past two years. I was dying to speak to him alone. I was feeling lonesome.

When my eyes finally closed I was thinking about my mother, and how astonished and fascinated she would have been to hear about Andrew's search for enlightenment and my trip here to visit him. She was a shy, unsure woman who nonetheless possessed a lively curiosity. I missed my mother.

It took three hours by train to get to Agra to see the Taj Mahal. I was still suffering from jet lag and dozed most of the way. We disembarked into a dissonance of shouting peddlers. We passed stands that sold every kind of merchandise imaginable—tape players, batteries, cigarettes, candles, shawls, blankets, cotton shirts, soap, and even toilet paper. We were closely followed by people holding out for our perusal post-cards, pictures of saints, statues of the Buddha, miniature versions of the Taj, etc. Ragged children tugged at us begging for coins.

In a narrow alley leading to the Taj Andrew called, "Just a second, wait!" I hesitated. "You have to see it as I did for the first time," he said, and came from behind and put his hands over my eyes. He led me forward a few paces and turned me left. "Now," he said, "now you can look."

I was standing before a small archway and straight ahead, filling the archway from one side to the other, from top to bottom, there appeared, as if in a dream, a shimmering white vision. I took a moment to catch my breath and then stepped through into what I later realized was a vast walled garden. At first the white marble mausoleum held my entire attention.

Domed and solid, it stood exquisitely balanced by four minarets at its four corners that appeared to lift against gravity and float in the light blue sky. Andrew told me that it had been built in the seventeenth century by a Mogul emperor for himself and a wife he cherished above all the others, who had died before he did. It was as close to perfection as any architecture I'd ever seen.

We remained in the garden until dark in order to see the Taj by moonlight. Most of the tourists were gone by then. Sitting on a bench in front of the reflecting pool we watched, enchanted, as a full moon rose slowly in the sky and gradually bathed the Taj in a luminous silvery glow, bequeathing it a kind of radiant hazy delicacy.

A flush of tears rose to my eyes.

At some point Andrew took out his walkman and offered to let us hear a tape of some strange, leaping music. I was stunned at how precisely it mirrored in sound the spirit of the splendor before us.

On our way back on the train Andrew told me that he and Alka had decided to take me to all the holy places they'd been to in the south of India, all the places of pilgrimage and all the places where the great saints had lived

"We can stay at their ashrams," Alka said.

"Really?" I found the idea fascinating.

"And there are many beautiful old temples," Alka said.

"Older than anything in Europe," Andrew said. "Tomorrow night we'll take a train for Madras, that's the main city in south India."

I felt I was at the beginning of a great adventure. "How long does it take to get to Madras?" I asked.

"Two nights and one day," Andrew said.

"Two nights and one day!" I was aghast. "Can't we fly there?"

"Its expensive," Alka said.

"I'll pay for the three of us," I said. "I'll be glad to."

Andrew looked a little flustered at my impetuous offer. He knew I didn't have much money. But I insisted. Anyway, I wanted to pay for some of the luxuries they couldn't afford while I was here. India was cheap, and apart from the plane fares I figured it wouldn't amount to a lot.

When we got to New Delhi we went directly to my hotel for something to eat. Andrew said it had an American dining room, meaning, I found out, that it served pizza and hamburgers. But he was complaining so much about a pain in his back that Alka offered to give him a deep muscle massage on the floor of my room first. She was trained to give a rare type of Indian massage. That was how she earned her living.

I lay on my bed watching her sitting astride Andrew's back, a strong slender figure, kneading him with powerful narrow hands. She appeared to be in her element, cool and confident. When Andrew groaned in pain she laughed and kneaded him harder.

"Good," he said, "Don't pay attention to me, don't stop."

He groaned again. She smiled down at his naked back and worked the muscles even harder. She was obviously mad about him.

When she was through, Andrew got to his knees and turned to her. He said he felt much better and then they exchanged a long look so intimate that it embarrassed me.

In the morning we missed our Air India plane to Madras! No one had informed us how much time in advance of the flight you were obliged to be at the airport and we'd assumed it was the usual one hour for domestic travel, but no, it was two. When we arrived we were no longer allowed on the plane and the money for the tickets would not be returned. Nor would we be issued new tickets. That was the rule. I'd lost it all. Furthermore there were no vacant seats on planes going to Madras for at least a week.

We raced to the railway station by taxi where Alka took over. Somehow or other she pushed her way through a crush of people in front of the wicket and demanded three tickets to Madras. The ticket seller, taking his own sweet time, riffled through a small stack of papers with lists on them. When finally he looked up, he barely glanced at Alka but slowly scanned the crowd behind her and made the announcement that the train was full and not only that, it would be full every night for a week.

Since nothing further could be done, and to compensate for our disappointment, I decided that we should treat ourselves to a good hotel. We went to the Hotel Marina in Connaught Circus and took one room with three single beds for the night. Alka had bargained down the price. She seemed genuinely concerned that I not spend much money.

Andrew and I decided to try the elegant hotel dining room for dinner. We found the atmosphere quite lively. Indian musicians on a stage at the far end of the room were slapping conical-shaped drums with the palms of their hands and plucking at globular bulging stringed instruments and singing what Andrew told me were the popular songs of the day. Many of the customers wore colored turbans. Andrew informed me that they were Sikhs, members of a reformed Hindu sect who were regarded as the 'Protestants' of India.

Although it was a long time since we'd all eaten, Alka had remained behind, saying she wasn't hungry, Andrew said Alka often needed to be by herself. He didn't explain further and for some reason I felt constrained from asking why that was. But I was happy to be able to talk to him alone at last. He ordered the food and for a few minutes we sat listening to the music and sipping mango juice. Then I asked him if he missed New York.

"New York?" He grinned at me. "Not a bit."

"Not at all?"

"Not really, Luna. Don't you remember that I'd been wanting to leave New York for years? The one thing I wanted to do was leave."

"But you didn't when you could, when you had the money."

"I know. I know. The only thing I wanted to do was leave and I was still there. I couldn't believe, with all the freedom at my disposal I still hadn't left. I couldn't accept it. I was miserable."

"What held you back?" He shrugged his shoulders and turned to gaze at the musicians.

After an interval I said, "But finally you did leave—"

He looked back at me. "Yeah, and when I did and came here, I told you, I know I wrote you, a great upheaval took place inside me. I found myself letting go of the past for long periods of time and experiencing amazing depths of insight and joy. All I wanted to do was meditate." He paused to take a sip of his drink. "Then I decided to study Hatha Yoga. I'd always wanted to try it. And after that, as I told you, I got involved with Alka—"

The waiter placed steaming bowls of soup before us.

15

"It's Sambar soup," Andrew said, "beans and vegetables."

I tasted it. "Delicious," I said. I swallowed another spoonful. The soup had a most unusual, delectable flavor. It contained spices I'd never tasted before.

"She seems very much in love with you," I said.

"Alka? Yeah, she's great isn't she?"

He had written from India: 'I have met an Indian girl/person with depth, spiritual depth... the more time we spend together only brings us closer... there is a growing sense of trust between us, and a wonderful feeling of peace...'

"You're lucky to have met her," I said.

"I am." He looked at me. "Y'know it's hard to explain, but as my meditation practice deepened I began to realize how much we believe we are separate isolated individuals instead of seeing how we are interconnected with every other human being." He took a few spoonfuls of soup and added, "I saw how really unimportant all my preoccupations with my own little life really were. I saw that life was something much greater than my own success or failure."

The wisdom of his words surprised and moved me. We finished our soup in silence. Then he leaned his elbows on the table and gazed at me with an earnest expression. "I know you're worried, I know I'll have to do something practical soon."

"I'm not really worried," I said, "but I wonder, are you thinking of going back to music?"

Andrew had had a serious ambition to be a musician and he used to practice twelve to seventeen hours a day on his drum-set in a Broadway loft he rented or at home on a practice pad. He was so driven about practicing that it made me uneasy. I didn't know much about music or musicians and imagined that maybe all serious musicians were equally driven and practiced equally long hours, but then suddenly he had given up the drums because, as he put it, "I don't have the right stuff to get to the top."

The fact that he had the notion that he had to be either number one or nothing came as a disagreeable revelation to me. I'd never noticed this aspect of his personality before.

"What are you going to do now?" I'd asked him at the time.

He said he didn't know. He took a few odd jobs to get by and then his grandmother died and left him a small inheritance, so for a time it seemed he could postpone any decision about a career. When he told me he was going to India, I didn't interfere. I felt he needed time to explore.

The Indian musicians at the end of the room finished their song to loud, enthusiastic applause. Andrew waited until the noise subsided and then he said, "No, I'll never go back to music."

Very early the next morning, at the railroad station, we were told again there were no seats for the evening train. We decided to go to the central office of Air India.

After four hours of being sent from wicket to wicket and cubicle to cubicle beseeching help, Alka suggested that I pull rank as an outraged respectable foreign lady, make a big fuss, and demand to see the manager. Which I did, reluctantly. The result was that I was granted three new tickets for the next day for an extra twenty-five percent of the fare. We were told by an amazed ticket seller that we'd been incredibly lucky. Usually the ticket manager, who has to deal with hundreds of desperate people daily, refused everyone point blank. We'd been fortunate to see him when he was for some reason in a good mood, he said.

In the afternoon I went shopping for a shawl with Alka. Around the corner from my hotel, in front of a jewelry shop, an entire family was living on the pavement on a spread of dirty blankets. The mother, in rags, and looking much older than she probably was, walked up to us with a baby in her scrawny arms. She pointed to some children asleep on the blankets behind her and held out her hand wailing pitifully.

"Give her two rupees," Alka said.

I handed the note to the mother, but the baby, who appeared no more than one year old, in a sudden unexpected movement, reached out a tiny hand and snatched it from my fingers and stuffed it down the front of its soiled wrapper. Then, asking for more, it put its own hand out, and wailing pitifully in imitation of its mother, stared at me so intently, its black eyes so stark, that I was forced to glance away, overwhelmed not so much by compassion as by the recognition of a wee fellow-creature's ferocious will to survive.

Alka tugged at my arm and we moved on down the street.

"Did you see that, Alka? Good God, did you see that?"

There was a silence, then Alka said, "You see everything in India."

I turned to glance at her. She was wearing western clothes now. Her long black hair moved like silk against the collar of her clean blue cotton shirt. She seemed unmoved. I realized that she must have experienced such scenes of wretched penury all her life and had somehow become inured to them.

After visiting numerous shops and fingering many stacks of shawls Alka finally pointed to one she approved of and looked at me questioningly. It was made of very fine woven wool, delicately tinted in shades of cream and beige and the palest brown. I wrapped it around my shoulders and the shopkeeper held up a mirror. "It's perfect," I said. Alka examined it again and patiently negotiated the seller down to what seemed to me an absurdly low price.

Exhilarated at my beautiful bargain, I followed her down a long flight of wooden steps to the street and at the bottom, I said, "You were terrific, Alka. Thanks so much." Alka seemed pleased.

Five minutes later, crossing an enormous dusty racketing thoroughfare, I felt something strike me on my right side and I fell down. I heard a motorbike roar away. The traffic continued unabated on either side of us. Alka helped me get up, and steering me between the vehicles that continued to race heedlessly in our direction, got me to the sidewalk. I was breathless with fright. Alka had remained calm. She gingerly touched the arm I had fallen on.

"How is it?" she asked.

"I guess I'm okay," I said. No bones seem to be broken."

However my elbow ached and was bleeding. Alka got out a clean handkerchief and began to wrap it. It was then that I noticed a policeman watching impassively from a nearby corner. He made no attempt to come over but stayed where he was.

"Do you see that Alka?" I cried, "The policeman over there is looking at us. He must have seen it all. And he doesn't move!"

Alka shrugged with what I took to be an expression of resignation.

"I don't understand it, Alka. I just don't understand."

I continued to express my outrage as we went carefully along the cracked pavement towards our hotel. Alka didn't say anything. She made no attempt to explain why such things happened in India and her silence made me pause about asking. Would I be insulting her with a direct question that insinuated criticism of her country? I didn't know. After a few days together I knew nothing more about her than I had that first moment we'd met.

Andrew told me some time afterwards that Alka actually hated India. I was astonished. He also told me that Alka had never trusted a single soul until she met him.

On the third day after my arrival I was informed by Andrew that after we completed a two week tour around India we were all going to a Vipassana meditation retreat held every year at this time in Bodh Gaya by an Englishman, Christian Travers. It was at this same retreat that Andrew and Alka had met a year ago.

"We're going to spend a month at a retreat?" I was appalled.

"You'll love it," Andrew said.

"But a month? I didn't come all the way to India to go to a retreat. I can do that at home."

"It's different going to a retreat here," he said.

"But I've already been to a few of Christian Travers' retreats in Massachusetts. What can be different here?" I asked.

"The place. The atmosphere. It's closer to the source."

"Anyway," I said, "I don't like Travers. I've told you before…"

Andrew cut me off sharply. "I don't agree," he said.

There was a silence.

"He's affected," I said. "I don't trust him."

"You're being negative, Luna. That's always been your tendency." He gave me a sarcastic smile. "Why don't you just drop your opinions for a change and see what happens?"

Was Andrew really talking to me like this in front of someone I'd just met? I felt my cheeks burning. Alka was listening intently. I looked from her to Andrew and then I looked away.

We arrived in Madras, taxied through blind unlit streets and disembarked in a black alley. Electricity was out due to a recent cyclone and the small lobby of the Hotel Broadlands was lit by a few flickering candles. The middle-aged Indian woman behind the reception desk greeted Andrew warmly. It seemed she remembered him from past visits. A few shadowy figures were sitting in chairs along a wall, chatting softly in English, their faces almost invisible.

I was given a lit candle and led up two steep flights of creaking wooden stairs to a small stuffy room. I put the candle on a shelf next to the bed, took off my clothes, and too exhausted to wash or brush my teeth, lay down and closed my eyes. I was hearing Andrew's words again, resonating inside my head. "You're being negative, Luna. That's always been your tendency. Why don't you just drop your opinions for a change and see what happens?"

I opened my eyes and stared at the shadows trembling on the window wall. Perhaps I should have stopped to think before I criticized Christian Travers. I knew Andrew revered him and considered him a flawless teacher. I knew he wanted to emulate him in every way. Perhaps I should have been more careful. But to have defended Travers by demeaning me in front of another person seemed, at the moment, more than I could bear.

Not that defending his teacher should have come as a total surprise. I should have expected it. The truth was, Andrew had idolized all his spiritual teachers, one after the other, even though he suffered painful disillusionment in each case. Travers was his latest ideal. It was as simple as that.

Nevertheless it was the first time he had ever spoken to me

so rudely, and with such contempt. Tears filled my eyes and ran down my sweating cheeks. He had suddenly seemed like—like what?—like someone I didn't know—had never ever known. . .

A barely perceptible drift of air from the window blew out the candle. My eyes closed again. A few moments later I was gripped by the most awful loneliness—a strange and terrible sensation accompanied by a stinging memory.

I saw myself in my father's bedroom packing his clothes into giant black plastic garbage bags. It was a hot muggy summer night. My father had died three days before. I opened a closet and saw, hanging in a row, about a dozen of his shirts, all perfectly ironed and all in the light blue shade he favored. They seemed animated somehow, as if they were waiting for him. All at once a curious cry splintered the silence of the room. At first I didn't know what it was. It sounded like an animal. But it was me.

That night in Madras, tired as I was, I barely slept.

In the morning I had a shower in a spotless wooden stall. The hotel, although extremely modest, was well-cared for, an exception in India. When I returned to my room I found a beautiful Indian boy waiting with a thermos of coffee. Andrew had told me that south India was famous for its coffee. It was delicious. I sipped the steaming brew looking out the window at a sun-filled garden of palm trees and bright tropical blossoms and began to feel cheerful again. An hour later Andrew knocked on my door and came in smiling. Then he stood looking out at the garden.

"This is nice," he said, and, after a pause, "how about an early lunch?"

"Sure, I'm starving."

"I know a place called Woodlands, it's air-conditioned."
"Great," I said.

He turned from the window. "Alka's not coming," he said, "she felt like reading in bed."

I'd discovered that Alka read mainly teen-age romances.

"How can she read that stuff?" I asked. "It's just junk for kids."

The funny thing was, Andrew didn't mind my question. Instead he grinned and said, "Alka's an odd person I guess." He started for the door. "Hey, let's go before it gets too hot."

I wondered what he meant about Alka being odd, but once again experienced a subtle inner pressure to refrain from questioning him further.

We took a taxi along shabby blocks of buildings. The streets were teeming with cows and dogs and masses of people most of whom were darker-skinned and shorter in stature than those in Delhi. Madras was the third largest city in India but most of the buildings were only a few stories high. When we got out of the taxi I noticed, in the narrow street next to the restaurant, a hand-driven water pump where women and children were soaping up and bathing and brushing their teeth with bare twigs.

As in the past Andrew was an entertaining, responsive companion and on this day he seemed more engaging than ever. Talkative and happy, I sat opposite him eating delicious dishes I had never eaten before and whose components I couldn't for the life of me have named, allowing myself to be utterly charmed. Last night's misery seemed no more than a bad dream.

After lunch we took a four-and-a-half-hour bus ride to Pondicherry, ninety miles south. It had been part of France's once extensive holdings in India and French was still widely spoken there. The town was the home of the Sri Aurobindo International Education Center and was occupied to a large extent by the French followers of the Indian saint Sri Aurobindo and 'Mother,' a French woman who'd become Aurobindo's assistant and ultimately his partner in teaching. Both were now dead. Andrew told me 'Mother' had been responsible for making the saint's ashram famous.

We stayed at the new Sri Aurobindo Ashram Guest House, where my spacious room fronted on a grey and glistening sea. I unpacked and then, on the floor below mine, found Alka in the large tiled shower stall of an equally spacious room in the process of washing all the dirty clothes she and Andrew had accumulated. Andrew, looking at her fondly, said, "She loves washing clothes and playing in the water." I turned to him, curious. His tone seemed to imply that here at last was a simple natural woman doing your simple natural thing. It didn't sound like him at all.

Andrew and I had dinner alone again, this time at a Chinese restaurant. I was beginning to feel uneasy about Alka's absences at meals. Was it my presence that kept her away?

On the way the thong of my rubber sandal broke. I was horrified at the idea of walking on these roads without shoes, so Andrew gave me his sneakers and he went barefoot. A few minutes later we stopped at a shoe repair. A small, gaunt, bearded man squatting beside the road on a square of burlap fixed my sandal with a cleverly-placed safety pin. Andrew told me the man mended nothing other than rubber sandals. "It's his specialty," he said, and I marvelled that India must be the only place in the world where men make a living repairing rubber sandals that sell for less than one U.S. dollar.

The next night, since it was Christmas eve, we elected to go to twelve o'clock Mass at a nearby Catholic church. On the way we passed a small rundown hospital and saw lots of people lying asleep on blankets near the entrance. Andrew told me they were relatives of the patients inside and sometimes stayed there for weeks until the patient was well again or died.

The entire face of the church sparkled with ropes of multicolored lights. There was no space inside so we listened to the Mass out on the plaza. The men wore suits. A good number of them seemed to have come alone. Most of the women wore brilliant silk saris trimmed in gold and had shining sheaths of oiled black hair braided down their backs and festooned with fresh flowers. For the entire duration of the Mass everyone stood facing the church in silence.

Christmas day I had the urge to go alone to the Aurobindo ashram and meditate near the tombs of Aurobindo and 'Mother'. I mounted a bicycle rickshaw for the first time. The driver was a small slight man. His frail back hunched over the handle-bars and his thin stringy spindle legs pumping away filled me with shame. When I mentioned to Andrew that all rickshaw drivers seemed to have the same bodies, he said, "They don't live for long."

Covered with blankets of many-hued marigolds, the two crypts lay under a green canvas canopy on a dais in an open court-yard. People in western and eastern dress were kneeling and stretching both their arms forward over the flowers and closing their eyes. I sat on the grass and watched them for a while. Then I closed my own eyes. The air was heavy with floral perfume and the smell of incense. After a while my body grew still, and in that silence, broken only by the rustling of clothing and the padding of naked feet, I was aware of feeling totally present for the first time in months. It was heaven.

On the way out I passed what had once been 'Mother's' room and was now a shrine. I peeked in. It was quite tiny, dominated by a narrow bed with a white satin coverlet. At the head of the bed lay a heap of white satin pillows, some of them edged with lace. A smell of camphor came from the room that was suffocating.

Looking back now, I realize that I was accumulating painting-like images of India that seemed discrete at the time but eventually came together in my mind as a single sweeping vision of a fascinating, puzzling, complex country as unlike my own country as it was possible to be.

We went to Tiruvannamalai, the locale of the ashram of Ramana Maharshi, a famous saint who had died in 1950. As the train approached the town Andrew and Alka excitedly pointed out the holy mountain, Arunachala, to which Ramana Maharshi had been irresistibly drawn after his enlightenment. He had lived on the mountain itself or in its proximity for the rest of his life. The story was that when he was sixteen years old, an imagined experience of his own death had ended in his permanent enlightenment.

We took a rickshaw to the ashram. Along the road people stood in clouds of dust selling platters of cooked food, sweet buns, dried beans, nuts, candy, cigarettes and flowers, and on the road itself, impeding the rickshaw's progress were countless cows, dogs, pigs, water-buffalo and children running to and fro, baby girls with gold earrings and silver ankle chains, and baby boys with great dark eyes outlined in kohl. The sense of explosive energy was exciting.

The ashram was a compound of a number of buildings, the most elaborate, the one that housed the twin shrines of the saint and his mother, the simplest, a hut with a thatched roof. The grounds were planted here and there with dusty bushes and a few trees. Since all the rooms available for visitors had been taken, we proceeded to the 'best' hotel in town, a ramshackle, seedy place, but my cell-like room with its dirty faded blue walls was redeemed by possessing an electric fan and the luxury of a private toilet— although it was no more than a hole in the concrete floor.

When we returned to the ashram, we went to the small hall where Ramana Maharshi had lived, slept, and held court. On a platform guarded by a low gate was a soiled couch, and on its frayed seat stood an enlarged photograph of the saint reclining on this self-same couch. His body, clothed only in what looked like a diaper, was shapeless, as if it were no longer wholly functional, but his eyes gazed forth with an expression of sublime compassion. There were about forty people sitting in meditation and we joined them.

Dinner was served on the cement floor of a large assembly hall. Brahmin cooks wearing white loin cloths patrolled the aisles of seated devotees and visitors and scooped curried vegetables and rice and yogurt from pails onto 'plates' made of two palm leaves sewn together. Andrew whispered to me that the cooks were actually priests who'd dedicated their lives to serving others. "They're very clean," he said. "They bathe from head to toe each day before entering the kitchen."

The food was spicy, delicious and plentiful. There were no

utensils. I crouched over my leaves resting one hand on the floor and eating with the other while gobs of food dropped on my clothes.

We walked home on a lightless road packed with traffic and mobs of chattering people. Loud screeching noises issued from loud-speakers along the way. Alka explained it was temple music in honor of some religious holiday.

Saturated with sense impressions, I was relieved to be back alone in my ugly little room.

December twenty-eighth, Ramana Maharshi's birthday, we spent the morning walking up his holy mountain. Andrew and Alka removed their shoes because the saint had said that walking on the mountain barefoot strengthened your spiritual life. I felt silly about it but I took off my shoes too and as a result I got a thorn in my sole and had a lot of trouble getting it out.

The crush of people trying to get into the ashram for Maharshi's birthday lunch scared me to death. I found myself one of three thousand people pushing or being pushed to get through a solitary narrow gate of entry. Andrew told me later that it was hard for people to line up for anything in India because there was not enough to go around. Consequently people went crazy trying to get their share.

Sometime during the celebrations Andrew found the person who, unbeknownst to me, he had come here to meet, Manny Rivers, a Canadian homeopath who was staying temporarily at the ashram with his sari-clad Australian wife, Spirit, and nine-year-old daughter. Manny, who looked attractive and at ease in his well-fitting cream-colored kurta and pajama, was very knowledgeable about teachers and meditation centers in India. He told Andrew about a guru who had been enlightened by Ramana Maharshi, Hari Lal Poonja of Lucknow, and gave Andrew Poonja's address. Andrew was ingratiating towards Manny as if he wanted to impress him.

At seven o'clock the next morning we left for the ashram to say good-bye to the director and thank him for his hospitality. But before we could utter a word the director demanded a donation. I handed him two hundred rupees, an amount suggested by the experienced Manny as more than generous. The director sat regarding the money I had placed on his desk with disdain. He didn't thank me, he didn't look up, he didn't say anything. As we went through the outer gate a Brahmin cook came running towards us. He held out his hand, panting. "A tip, a tip," he cried.

Alka seemed shocked. "Don't give him one single rupee!" she said in an angry tone.

So much for Brahmin cooks who are really priests dedicating their lives to serving others! We turned and left feeling terribly disillusioned with the whole place.

In Ranchipurnam, one of the oldest towns in India, after a late lunch at an Indian tourist hotel catering to English visitors —soft-boiled eggs, white toast, butter, strawberry jam, and a huge pot of English tea—we went to visit an ancient temple Manny had told us about.

We left our luggage stowed in two bicycle rickshaws outside the temple gate. The train for our next sight-seeing stop left in two hours, at six o'clock.

Inside the temple, throbbing through the smoky, incense-scented dimness, came a chain of strangely syncopated unearthly sounding drum beats that made the hair on the back of my neck stand up. Andrew whispered that the sounds suggested the creation of the universe.

As we were about to enter a huge stone archway a priest stopped us and said only Alka, because she was Indian, was allowed to enter. We separated and arranged to meet outside at five o'clock. Andrew and I meandered on. For a while we sat beside the temple pool watching some women washing clothes by pounding them with stones. They smiled at us from time to time.

When we returned to the rickshaws Alka hadn't arrived. We waited. At five-fifteen Andrew left to investigate, saying, "That's not like Alka. She's usually very prompt." About ten minutes later he came running back. He hadn't been able to find her.

"She's probably in the forbidden section," I said.

"But it's so late, we'll miss our train!" He shook his head. "I don't get it." He raced back. After a few more minutes he returned perspiring, his face bleak. "I still can't find her!"

At that very moment Alka emerged. She gave us an expressionless glance and, without a word, proceeded unhurriedly to get into the rickshaw closest to her.

"Is something wrong?" I asked Andrew.

"Let's go," he said. We climbed into the other rickshaw, and, moving along, Alka in front, ourselves behind, Andrew said grimly, "She'll start crying soon. She'll feel sorry." I remained silent. Something was happening and I had no idea what it was.

We arrived in Navaballiporam in the dark. I was disappointed to see that it seemed just another rundown random sort of place. Rooms being scarce, we had to stay at separate hotels. That night, New Year's Eve, we went to eat in a large noisy restaurant next to the sea. There were only westerners present. I ordered a grilled local lobster. Andrew and Alka, strict vegetarians, had spaghetti with tomato sauce, a novelty in India. Alka sat next to Andrew, stony and withdrawn. Her mood cast such a pall over everything that I felt tense and had trouble swallowing my lobster, which in any case had arrived dry and tasteless. We went to bed early.

The next day we walked on the beach. The sand was dark brown and the bay a dirty grey. We passed a section where fishermen and their families lived and here the sand was strewn with their feces and you had to watch every step you took. Further on, where the beach seemed clean, Andrew and Alka decided to go swimming. I leaned against a tree and flipped through an Indian magazine.

The first to come out was Alka shrieking and hugging her chest as if she were freezing. In the still air her laughter sounded unusually shrill. When Andrew appeared they started chasing each other until Andrew caught Alka and wrestled her to the ground. They lay on their backs for a few minutes catching their breath and then got up and started doing yoga asanas (yoga postures) together. They seemed happy again.

What had happened to change things? Had they made love? They were concealing something from me, I could sense it. I began to speculate what it was that had attracted Andrew to Alka. She was so unlike any of his previous girl-friends—less worldly, secretive, and moody. I had tried to feel relaxed with her, but there was a masked quality she had, a kind of armor that held you at bay.

We flew north from Madras and arrived in Calcutta at nine-thirty the next evening. Andrew had written that Calcutta was a 'real' city in the sense that New York was a 'real' city. I'd been very curious to see it. As soon as our taxi got past the suburbs I was immediately disheartened by the sight of endless lonely underlit boulevards containing huge decaying European style buildings. Against the walls, in small groups, lay clumps of sleeping bodies. It was a dismal spectacle. The taxi came to a halt in front of a crumbling entranceway. My heart sank. I was dead tired. I hadn't had a hot shower since my arrival in this country. I had picked a five star hotel because by now I craved an escape from the dirt and decrepitude and disarray of India, and I was willing to splurge. We passed through a long tacky hall lined with jewelry and antique shops and I dreaded what I would find at the other end.

But lo and behold, I found myself all at once in a vast soaring heavenly space—the great lobby of the elegant, opulent, five star Oberoi Hotel! Pillars of marble, overstuffed brocade-covered sofas, polished wood tables, deep blue gold-bordered carpets and masses of fresh flowers in gigantic shiny ceramic bowls. The transition was stunning. And the marvel of this exorbitant luxury in the midst of the dreary destitution I'd just witnessed was such a relief, so delicious, so comforting, that I was filled with a kind of crazy gratitude that made me want to hug the slender, soft-spoken, silken, sari-clad Indian woman who signed me in.

Once in our room—we were sharing one because of the expense—a sumptuous meal was ordered from room service—three different vegetable casseroles, lemon rice, dal soup with slices of carrot floating on its golden surface, chapatis, yogurt salad, coconut chutney, two mango shakes and one beer. We lolled on our soft beds eating and grinning at one another with pure pleasure.

Around four o'clock the following day I was taken to the temple of Kali, a black goddess of stupendous power, whose specialty, I was informed, was killing demons.

To get there we had to drive through dusty roads full of potholes, the taxi darting like an insect between buses, trucks, people, bullock carts, bicycles, and all sorts of rickshaws, even some pulled directly, without the aid of bicycles, by human beings, whose bare feet slapped rhythmically, like nerveless machines, along the filthy macadam.

I was upset and appalled at the sight.

In the temple complex on the Ganges the air was thick with a loud cacophony of bells ringing, drums hammering and cymbals crashing. At one shrine everyone was bowing to a small black mythic face surrounded by a wreath of flowers. Alka said it was the image of Kali.

The great saint Ramakrishna who died in 1886 had been a priest in this temple. He believed all religions were paths to a common goal—Samadhi or God-consciousness.

We'd been meditating in the saint's modest book-lined bedroom for some time when I remembered we were to meet our taxi at seven o'clock. It was now six-fifty. I tapped Alka, who was sitting next to me. She didn't move. My legs were aching from sitting cross-legged on the floor so I got up and went outside. At seven o'clock I returned, and since I couldn't reach Andrew, who was hemmed in on the other side of her, I tapped Alka's shoulder once more. She didn't move. I shook her gently, and then more vigorously. I waited. With incredible slowness she raised open seemingly sightless eyes in my direction, paused for a moment, then closed them, lowered her head and became still once more. An uncanny sensation crept across my scalp. She can't wake up, I thought. Suddenly Andrew looked over and saw me. I pointed to my watch and went outside again. A few minutes later they both appeared and we ran to find our driver.

On the way back, under a flickering street lamp, I saw goats standing on their hind legs eating paper ads off the walls of buildings. Apparently nothing was ever wasted in this wretchedly poor country.

We picked up our luggage at the Oberoi and went to Howrah station, a hellish stinking cavern where, in the perennial half-light, masses of people slept on the floor or squatted eating, or just huddled together while others rushed about madly in search of God knows what aid or service. The entire enormous space of the station had an air of hectic desolation.

Our first class compartment turned out unsurprisingly to be a foul unsanitary hole. There were many ranges of first class. This must have been the bottom of the barrel. We lay our sleeping bags on the seats and stretched out and tried to sleep.

We were on our way travelling north-west, to Christian Travers' retreat in Bodh Gaya.

2

A T SIX IN THE MORNING WE ARRIVED IN GAYA, poor, grey, and dreary. It was freezing. We took a motorized rickshaw to Bodh Gaya and entered a lighter airier world swarming with two hundred thousand Tibetans who had come because the Dalai Lama was here on a visit for the first time in many years. No preparations had been made for them and the sanitary conditions in the village were catastrophic; the fields and rivers had become open toilets.

We breakfasted at a famous gathering place for Westerners. The restaurant consisted of a few old benches and tables and a raised cooking stall. But the porridge tasted wonderful and so did the chai (sweet spiced tea). Most of the Westerners were young with long hair and bland peaceable expressions. Andrew commented that the majority of them looked as though they had "no balls," a favorite expression of his at this time.

Since Bodh Gaya was the site of the Buddha's enlightenment, every denomination of Buddhism was represented by its own temple. We reserved two huts at the Thai temple where the retreat was to be held. They were small cubicles, each containing two wood slatted beds without mattresses. But we located some straw later and made mattresses out of that. For a reason I can't remember, the retreat was going to be delayed and would not begin for nine days. Christian Travers, however, was to arrive in two. That was good enough for Andrew. But what was I going to do here for nine days?

In the evening we went to the main temple in the town. At the center of a complex of buildings and stupas (memorial shrines) stood a Bodhi tree reputed to be a descendant of the original under which the Buddha had decided to sit no matter how long—to this day no one actually knows how long—until he was enlightened.

Surrounding the complex, a circular walk had been constructed, and along it, in an incredibly extravagant display of faith, chanting and prostrating flat down on the ground every few steps, the Tibetans moved like a slow river, leaving in their wake, on the balustrades, thousands of lighted candles. It was a fantastic scene. It was a scene I'll never forget. But it puzzled me.

"Don't you think there's something weird about the way the Tibetans abase themselves with all those prostrations?" I asked Andrew the next morning at breakfast. "Who do you think they're bowing to? The Buddha? I thought the Buddha didn't believe in God and certainly didn't think of himself as God."

"It's symbolic," Andrew explained. "They're expressing gratitude for the Buddha's teaching."

I'd heard this before but it seemed to me, observing them, that they really were bowing to the Buddha himself and that they believed the Buddha *was* God. Besides, I'd gotten the impression long ago that people don't mind bowing to anything they perceive as more powerful than themselves because it makes them feel safe. Andrew went on. "Don't you think it's amazing that the Tibetans don't bear the slightest grudge against anyone even though their relations were massacred and they were robbed of their country?"

"It is amazing," I said. It was true. They went about everywhere somewhat tattered but enormously cheerful.

More than any other place I longed to see Benares, the holiest city in India and Andrew had promised me at the beginning of our trip that we would definitely visit there after this retreat was over. It was a few hours by train to the northwest. Since the retreat had been postponed, he agreed reluctantly to go to Benares for two days. He told me, without saying why, that Alka didn't want to come.

The following day I bought a meditation blanket, mosquito netting and a roll of toilet paper (one American dollar per roll).

Travers arrived in the late afternoon, handsome and elegant in his slender British fashion. He wore an open shirt with a silk paisley neckerchief knotted at the throat. A group of us had dinner with him and as I remembered from the past, people were edgy in his presence because he never seemed able to relax at such informal get-togethers.

We left the next morning and travelled second class to Benares and arrived at eleven-thirty. After a breakfast of idlis (Indian pancakes) and coffee we headed for the famous burning ghat (cremation place) on the Ganges.

A pall of smoke hung over the area. We stood on the outskirts of a small crowd of Westerners and watched. Carried on a stretcher by family members, the body arrived wrapped in a bright sari and was dipped into the holy river before being laid on a wooden pyre. More logs were placed on top of the body and a Brahmin priest, naked except for a loin-cloth, sprinkled the logs with a mixture of herbs and spices. I was told that this was the reason that there was no smell of scorched hair or flesh. The pyre was lit from below with a clump of burning straw and there was an immediate obscuring conflagration. In a few minutes the fire had burned through the sari and blackened skin became visible. I watched a leg burn and saw a foot fall off. On another pyre—I pointed it out to Andrew—perhaps due to a contraction of burning muscle, a hairless charred featureless head rose slowly on a charred neck as if the body were trying to rise from its own ashes.

"He doesn't want to go," Andrew said, laughing.

I didn't think it was funny. It was terribly eerie, but it wasn't funny. The whole scene seemed implausible and unreal. Emaciated dogs sniffed about, some attempting to mount each other, and pretty little girls and handsome little boys scampered between the corpses, gathering smoldering bits of leftover wood in baskets for their families' cooking stoves. From time to time they ran to cool their feet in the scummy water below. Priests flitted from pyre to pyre. Nothing was supposed to remain of the dead, only ashes. As wood was expensive, this rule was not always observed and occasionally a priest removed what was left of a body, some black still smoking chunk that had not been consumed by the flames, and going down to the river, threw it in. Water was then poured on the embers by the men who tended the fires, the lowest caste, the untouchables, and another pyre was set up for cremation.

That evening we ate at a restaurant near the ghat. When we started home, the electricity suddenly went off in the streets and you couldn't see a thing. But as if he had the eyes of a cat, Andrew unhesitatingly guided me down a few frighteningly narrow steps to the walkway along the river and up again to a shopping area lit by candles and oil lamps. It struck me, not for the first time, how at home Andrew felt in India.

The next day, I felt I was getting a cold. I bought two blankets for the one a.m. train ride back and returned to the hotel and went to bed to rest. Suddenly I was freezing. I piled the two new blankets on top of the threadbare one the hotel offered.

Andrew woke me at 10 p.m. to eat and pack my things. I felt very hot and my chest ached.

"I think I'm too sick to travel," I said.

Andrew frowned.

"I'm sorry." I said.

"It's only a five-and-a-half hour ride," Andrew said. His desire to get back to Travers had evidently obliterated every other consideration. My feelings were hurt and I had the thought that at the moment his spiritual quest seemed just as selfish as any material one.

"I'm sorry," I repeated.

Andrew turned away and gazed out the window. He was silent for a time. "Do you want something to eat?" he asked finally.

"No," I said, "I couldn't."

He turned back and gave me a tense little smile. "I'd better go and have something then."

He's angry, I thought. "Close the light on your way out," I called after him and I heard my voice tight with indignation.

I lay, now bathed in sweat, staring into the motionless dark, wondering, as I had many times before, whether Andrew's idealization of his teachers had something to do with the early loss and idealization of his father.

Andrew had loved his father very much. A couple of months before his death his father had become blind and at times would fall to the floor and urinate helplessly. In his confusion and suffering he'd become abusive and irrational and I'd been dismayed that Andrew, a young teenager at the time, should be witness to such scenes. His father and I had separated a year before, and since Andrew's grandmother and a nurse were in attendance, I implored Andrew to leave his father and come and stay with me at a friend's apartment. But Andrew said he would not abandon his father and I couldn't help but admire his courage and loyalty.

Andrew's father, far from the ideal Andrew seemed to be searching for in others, had nevertheless adored him, and had shown a strong preference for him over his brother Joshua, five-and-a-half years older.

Joshua had taunted Andrew incessantly when they were children. "You're a dumbbell, you're stupid! Stupid! Dumb! Dumb! Dumb!" And Joshua had repeated these words over and over, a refrain that Andrew took to heart. And no matter what we did to try to ameliorate the effect of this assertion, Andrew grew to believe he really was stupid. His father loved him. I loved him. Joshua hated him. What to do? We sent him to a child analyst. Nothing doing. We sent Joshua to an analyst. The war between them continued unabated and Andrew had trouble learning to read.

Above all else Andrew yearned for his brother's respect. I don't know that he ever really got it. I asked Joshua recently if it was because of jealousy that he was so rejecting of Andrew. Joshua replied that he couldn't remember what it was.

Respect remained a dominating passion in Andrew's life. When he finally found his 'true' guru, he wrote me: "What I have felt coming from this man makes up for lifetimes of not being recognized—"

So while his brother went through the Lycee Francais and graduated completely bilingual with honors, Andrew stumbled through a progressive school in Greenwich Village that he later claimed taught him nothing, not even how to spell. But he did learn how to read.

I couldn't get out of bed the next morning either, so it wasn't until the day after that we departed for Bodh Gaya.

I arrived back with a temperature of one hundred and two degrees and a queasy stomach and promptly went to bed again. Andrew stopped in to see me in the afternoon, chipper once more, and gave me an Indian magazine with an article on, of all people, Hugh Hefner. Feeling a little improved the next morning, I walked to the post-office to have some stamps marked so they couldn't be stolen off my post-cards and then I went to have tea across from the Thai temple where the retreat was to start the next day. Since men and women were separated for the duration, Alka and I had arranged when we'd first arrived to share a hut.

The owner of the tea stall had elephantiasis. Coughing and spitting, he was rinsing glasses in a pail of water. As I sipped the oversweet drink from my thermos cup a mouse ran under my bench and I leapt up and ran out, spilling the hot tea over myself. It burned and I pulled my T-shirt away from my chest. Next to the Thai temple, in a garbage-strewn field, a man was defecating. I shut my eyes.

The rules of the retreat were no eye-contact with fellow meditators and absolute silence except for an occasional private chat with Travers in his hut. However that didn't prevent you from giving people surreptitious glances; you were always curious about who came to these affairs and why. Mostly they were young, between twenty-one and thirty-five and mostly they were white middle-class people

from Europe or America. Probably they came for the same reasons
that had drawn me to meditation retreats—to find some kind of inner
strength, some transcendent meaning that would get you through the
pain of life. They all seemed ordinary enough, as they always do,
with a few exceptions. There was one I'll never forget, a tall thin
dark-haired Israeli girl in her late twenties. During a group session
with Travers at which people were invited to ask questions, she
demanded to know what gave Travers the right to be a teacher. At the
time I wondered what lay behind her audacity. Months later I heard
she'd been caught a few days after our retreat ended running naked
down the street of some Indian village, masturbating!

For the first few days I continued to feel unwell and what
aggravated my condition was the physical discomfort which at
times was extreme. There were innumerable flies, and mosquitoes
so thick, I often had to cover my face with a kerchief during the
nightly meditation session; there was nowhere to sit or to lie down
except on something hard; there was no way to bathe except by
pouring tins of cold water over yourself; the toilets, the standard
stinking holes in the ground, frequently overflowed and no toilet
paper nor any kind of paper was provided. In India amongst the rich
and poor, people used their left hands and water to clean themselves. So, on the positive side, the food at the retreat was said to
be safe because great care had been taken to see that the cooks were
trained to wash their hands before preparing each meal!
Surprisingly, the food was quite good.

To a true believer it was all worth it.

"But why am I here?" I asked myself more than once. Apart
from wanting to appease Andrew, did I really believe meditating
amidst this squalor would bring me closer to freedom?

The only gain for me from what amounted to thousands of
hours of meditation during the last few years was some modest
though important knowledge of how the mind works.

I discovered that in spite of the fact that meditating occasionally calmed and occasionally relieved me, for short periods,

from the burden of thought, basically my mind continued to chatter endlessly, repeating painful memories, repeating useless associations, repeating orders to itself etc. etc. etc. The latter is particularly astonishing because it can go on all your life without you ever being aware of it. For example, since I had nothing to take care of on a retreat besides things like washing my socks, the first time I sat down in the meditation hall I told myself at least fifty times in ten minutes that I had to wash my socks. It was a great discovery. I later called this phenomenon the washing of the socks syndrome.

The third day, while I was sitting on a stone ledge near the kitchen having the usual vegetables and dal and rice for lunch, something happened which at the time seemed inexplicable. Alka was crossing diagonally in front of me looking down at the ground as if she were preoccupied, and, as she came closer, I was suddenly struck by a sharp visceral aversion for her that seemed to come from nowhere and was so powerful, that I was left shaken. I threw my food into a garbage pail and returned to my hut. When Andrew came around later for a chat—he didn't seem to care about the no-talking rule—I didn't mention my experience at lunch regarding Alka. I didn't understand it; it scared me. Instead I found myself complaining about the poor sanitary conditions.

"You're being negative again," Andrew said. "And it's always got this nasty sting to it. One wants to get away from you." He'd said it softly, even apologetically, but on my way to the evening meditation session I felt so depressed that the sight of a Thai monk kindly patting a little ragged Indian boy on the head brought on a gust of tears.

A few days later, after having had a bath, I returned to the hut to find Alka sweeping the floor. As I put a foot through the doorway she suddenly started to sweep so furiously in my direction that I had to back away. I took another step in on the other side of the entrance and she immediately started to sweep furiously in that direction. I backed up again and stood watching her. She didn't raise her head.

Was it possible that she didn't see me? I tried to enter a third time and for a third time she swept me back. Was she trying to keep me out? I couldn't believe it. It was too insane. I walked in.

By dinnertime I'd succeeded in forgetting all about it. I'd succeeded in dismissing it as some erroneous interpretation on my part of what had occurred. But after I'd gone to bed, curling up towards the wall with my back to the door, I heard Alka enter and suddenly imagined her standing over me with a dagger in her raised hand.

In the morning Andrew came in to visit again and sat down beside me on my bed, gave me a hug, and started to gossip a bit. I had the impression that he was trying to make up for his sharp words of the day before. Alka was stretched out on her bed, silent, her eyes closed, frowning, as if she had a headache. On an impulse, I reached over and put my hand around her ankle. I wanted to include her in the conversation. I didn't know what was happening, I wasn't sure what was real, and I couldn't bear it. I thought that maybe I was imagining things, that maybe I was losing my mind.

I felt her tense under my touch. She stopped frowning but didn't move and remained silent, stiff as a corpse.

It was the night of the full moon, January twenty-six, the anniversary of the Buddha's enlightenment. To celebrate the occasion we were going to the Bodhi tree for Travers' nightly talk. Refreshments were being brought and as Alka was carrying some of the supplies, I put my arm around her shoulders and asked, with a gesture, if she could add my thermos top, which I used as a cup, to her sack. I was trying to behave as if everything were normal. Since she and I were following the rule of silence I didn't know what else to do. She snatched the thermos top from my fingers and abruptly turned away and hurried off. My heart was pounding. She hates me, I thought, aghast at this realization, but why, in God's name, why?

I didn't find Travers' sermon on the Buddha's enlightenment very enlightening. He seemed distracted and I couldn't help thinking that with his impassioned tone and rolling r's he should have been an actor. Furthermore I was very distressed by what had happened. At one point, Alka, who sat to my right, turned and smiled in my direction. Thinking at first that the smile was meant for me, I smiled back, but Alka's gaze, fixed on a man just to my left, never wavered one iota and I felt myself blushing.

When I reached home I got into bed with all my clothes on.

Alka arrived soon after and as she came through the door I froze and again had the crazy sensation that in the next moment I would feel a dagger in my back.

The following day after lunch I signalled to Andrew, who had all the accoutrements for making coffee in his hut, that I would like a cup, and he signalled for me to come. While he prepared the coffee there was a knock on his door. He told me to open it. Alka was outside, Andrew's soap dish in her hand. Her hair was wet. Apparently she'd just bathed. She proffered the soap dish, but as if suddenly realizing it was to me and not to Andrew, as I reached out my hand, she grabbed the dish back, gave me a vicious look, and stalked off.

"What's going on?" Andrew asked.

"She hates me!" I burst out, convinced now that it was true.

Andrew didn't seem surprised. "She's done this before," he said, "I'm sick and tired of it," and he left his coffee fixings and ran out after her.

I turned to go, trembling. Done what before? What had he meant? She was jealous, that was it, that was the mystery. She was jealous of *me*! I couldn't believe it.

Neither Andrew nor Alka appeared for the rest of the day. About two a.m. I woke up to the sound of weeping and I listened without pity, my heart dead.

The following afternoon Alka approached me and said she wanted to talk. We sat down on the steps of our hut. "I identify with India," she said, and she bulged her eyes at me, a habit she had that she used for emphasis, "and I couldn't stand your negativity towards it because I share the same attitude."

That might be true, I thought, but considering the extremity of her behavior, her enmity towards me, what she said sounded ludicrous. I turned to watch a mangy cat, patches of crusty skin showing, chewing something under the tree in front of the hut. I was sure Andrew had been at her to apologize. She's the one that's crazy, I thought, not me.

The next morning as I left the hut for the first meditation session I saw Andrew sauntering along towards me. He was grinning. He came over and hugged me and I suddenly burst into wild uncontrollable crying.

Andrew looked shocked. "People will hear you," he said. "Let's go inside."

"No!" I cried.

He started to pull me towards the door.

"No! *She's* in there!" I yanked away from him. He grabbed my arm. We grappled for a while as I tried with all my might to pull away but finally I was forced to yield and let myself be dragged back inside.

Andrew pushed me gently onto my bed and sat down beside me. I was sobbing. He put an arm around my shoulders. "Tell me about it," he said.

"I feel awful," I said, "awful."

"Why?" he asked.

"Lots of things, the way you acted in Benares for one. Lots of things." The tears overflowed again and Andrew got up to get my box of Kleenex.

"I'm really sorry," he said sitting down again and squeezing my shoulder.

Alka sat on her bed looking at me with an icy expression.

I stared at her for a few moments. "And then I was picking up all this stuff, this hatred," I said, "poisonous hatred, and I didn't know it was hatred, I didn't know what was going on." I took a choking breath. "I thought it was me! Me! I thought I was going crazy. It was horrible."

Andrew laid his head on my shoulder. I closed my eyes. After a minute or two I felt Alka's hand on my knee and heard her mumble what I took to be another apology. I opened my eyes and looked down at her. She was squatting at my feet her head bent towards the floor.

"You think I can forgive you?" I said. "I can't forgive you." I heard myself saying lines from a soap opera, but I couldn't stop. "Maybe I can forgive you someday," I went on, "but not now." I turned to Andrew whose head still rested on my shoulder and imagined that I saw a tear running down his cheek. This is the most insane situation I've ever been in my life, I thought.

Later Andrew took me out through the temple gates breaking another rule that no one was to go outside until the retreat was over. He admitted, when I inquired, that he had asked Alka to apologize. So that's why he was grinning when we met in the morning!

We were walking into the countryside. It was like walking into an ancient world. Far away I saw litters being carried single file across what seemed a wasteland leading nowhere. Andrew said invalids were being transported to a hospital. A ragged sadhu (itinerant holy man) came towards us his eyes riveted straight ahead as if on some invisible destination. I watched him pass by, thinking that he probably wants nothing from this world. He doesn't need to be loved, he isn't afraid of rejection, he doesn't need to be important or secure, he isn't jealous. I couldn't imagine him as a parent or as somebody's child, or even somebody's friend. I gazed at his receding back. He belonged to no one and I envied him.

"We planned your trip so carefully, we wanted you to have a good time," Andrew said, "I'm really sorry." He gave me a sad little squeeze. "I've seen Alka jealous a few times before but never like this."

"The awful thing was," I said, "I didn't realize before it was jealousy, I didn't know what it was, and that made it even more horrible."

"I'm sorry." He shook his head. "I'm really sorry."

I didn't ask him what he was going to do about it but I knew he'd do something.

Just before the evening meal Andrew came over and whispered that he wanted me to meet him on the other side of the compound, behind the nearest monk's hut, where we could talk unobserved.

He arrived before I did. "He wants to speak to you," he said.

"Who?"

"Travers."

"Why? What's going on?" I asked

"He wants to hear your side of the story."

"He wants to hear my side? Why? Has he heard hers?"

"No."

"Then why does he want to speak to me before he speaks to her?"

"I don't know." he said in an strained tone. "He must have his reasons. Trust him."

"Did he say anything to you?"

"Nothing much. He just said he wants to speak to you and Alka first."

I was perplexed by this. When I went to Travers' hut after dinner he listened quietly to my side of the story.

"Trust your feelings," he said, nodding sympathetically.

I was glad that he seemed to understand and suddenly felt sure he'd find a way to solve the difficulty between Alka and myself.

"Do you think it might be beneficial for Alka to get some professional help?" I asked.

He hesitated, then he said, "I'll see what I can do," and gave me a reassuring smile.

As soon as I stepped out the door Andrew was at my side. "What happened?" he asked.

"He told me to trust my feelings. He was nice." I said.

"He'll take care of it," Andrew said.

Enormously relieved, I took a slow walk around the compound stopping for a moment to gaze at a coil of human excrement on my path and marvelling that the body knew how to extract nourishment from food and squeeze out the rest so tidily.

It was the last day of the retreat. We were whispering behind the monk's hut. Andrew was sweating heavily. He said, "Alka saw him and then I saw him but Alka didn't tell him anything about being jealous. She didn't tell him anything!"

"Why?"

"I don't know." A look of anguish crossed his face. "She said she'd tell him the next time."

"The next time, there'll be no next time," I said, exasperated, "the retreat's over."

He shrugged his shoulders in a forlorn gesture. "He told her to trust her feelings, that's all."

"Trust her feelings! That must be his line. Trust your feelings! Regardless of the situation everybody, just trust your feelings!"

"He was angry that we'd talked about your interview, Andrew said."

"Why?"

"Jesus, I don't know. And then he said, listen to this, he said whenever he hears someone suggest that another person needs psychiatric help he wants to throw them out the window."

"He said that?" I was furious.

"I know, I know." Andrew stood shaking his head from side to side. "He pretended to agree with you, I know. He pretended to be sympathetic. I told him he was a hypocrite."

"Good for you!" I gave him a quick hug.

Then, in a breaking voice, Andrew continued. "He said even though I'd known Alka for a year I couldn't possibly know her as he did. He said her spiritual experiences were so deep I couldn't even begin to imagine what they were like."

"God!"

During the retreat last year Alka had meditated for three days and three nights without sleep and that had impressed Travers as a sign of profound spirituality. In Calcutta, in Ramakrishna's bedroom, I'd seen for the first time with my own eyes how Alka seemed to actually disappear into deep cavity inside herself and was able to remain there fixed and immobile with her legs folded under her, hardly breathing, for a long time. But the more I observed her, the more I wondered whether she was only hiding in there.

"Travers is full of shit," I said.

"He never once asked how I was feeling."

"He doesn't give a damn about you," I said.

I went to dinner with Andrew's room-mate, Sidney Schell, an American who was presently working as a translator in Thailand. We ate at the Buddha's Belly, a vegetarian restaurant run by Westerners, and returned to the temple around midnight and sat looking up at the stars. Most people had moved out and the compound already had a forsaken aspect. At one o'clock I stood up. "I'm dead, Sidney," I said, "I'm sorry, but I have to go to bed."

A noise awakened me. It was still dark. I looked over at Alka's bed. It was empty. I got up and went out on the porch and looked at my watch in the light of the moon and saw that it was five o'clock. A small group had gathered in front of Travers' hut to bid him farewell and Alka was amongst them. When Travers emerged, bag in hand, he shook hands with a few people and then went over and embraced her.

I went back to bed and lay with my eyes open. Alka came in. I listened to her undress, bristling with dislike. If Travers crooked his finger, I thought, she'd leave with him right now. She's weird. Weird. I was still at a loss to figure her out. The moment a glimmer of light showed outside I pulled on my clothes and went to Andrew's hut. The door was open. Both he and Sidney were gone. It was barely dawn but I left the temple compound and started on the road to the village. Normally I would have been afraid to walk alone at this hour, however none of the people sleeping along the sides of the road seemed to notice me. There was a small deer park just before the village, and as I neared it I saw Andrew and Sidney, unshaven and rumpled, coming towards me. They looked exhausted.

"We've been up all night talking," Andrew said.

"After you went to bed," Sidney said, "I went back to my hut and found my suitcase missing."

"Gee, that's awful," I said. "What was in it?"

"Most of my stuff, clothes, books, two cameras and a walkman." Sidney's plain good-natured face showed deep lines.

"They didn't take any of my things, I was lucky," Andrew said.

"Travers came to our hut when he heard about the robbery," Sidney said, "and—"

"I told him how I felt about everything," Andrew broke in, "Alka, everything, and we almost got into a fight." Andrew was unusually pale.

"Travers insisted Andrew was giving Alka a hard time," Sidney said."

"He doesn't give a damn about me or you," Andrew burst out bitterly. "He just cares about Alka."

I sat down by the side of the road. They squatted next to me. "Was she there?" I asked.

"Alka? Sure Alka was there, she'd promised to tell Travers that he had insulted me and had been disrespectful to you. But she didn't open her mouth, so I told her, 'Go on Alka, tell him what you think, go on!'"

There was a silence.

"She said nothing?" I asked.

"She said she had nothing to say. How could she do this to me?"

"Travers said Andrew couldn't hold a candle to Alka spiritually," Sidney said. "That's when they almost came to blows."

"The way he said it was insulting," Andrew said. "But he backed off. I'm sorry he backed off."

"You mean you actually had your fists up?" I laughed. There was something hilarious about two spiritual seekers prepared to settle their differences by hitting each other.

"Yeah. We were going for it," Andrew said.

"What happened?"

"Travers just put his hands down and said he didn't think it was a good idea," Andrew said.

I told him about Alka getting up at dawn to bid Travers good-bye.

"That's it," he said, "I'm through." He stared at the ground. "But what will she do?"

"What do you care?" Sidney said.

"I've got to have it out with her."

"You've been having it out with her all week," Sidney said.

Andrew looked up. "I can't get through to her. She just cries." He looked as if he might cry himself. "I have to see her one more time," he said.

Horrified, I realized he was still tied to her hand and foot. Tied to a madwoman. He seemed mad too.

Sidney said someone in the Burmese Bihar (temple) had a suitcase for sale and he was going over to take a look. We all stood up. Andrew said he was going home to rest.

I walked with Sidney to the village. He told me that after the incident with Travers, Andrew had lain down on his bed and said, "I'm going to have a break-down."

He turned to me. "Do you know that Alka's been forcing him to make a choice between the two of you?"

"No, I didn't know that."

"I heard her say more than once, 'Why do you always have to include *her*?'"

"But he invited me here."

"What can you do, she's jealous." We walked for a while in silence, then Sidney added, "A few days ago we had a talk. 'I love him,' she said, 'what hold does his mother have on him? Why can't he let go of her? Why does he have to accompany her to Calcutta when she leaves?' Then she cried."

I wondered, did she really expect me to go to Calcutta alone?

On the way back to the temple I saw her coming towards me wrapped in her shawl. Her hair hung loose as if she'd just washed it and she was wearing her new green trousers. I crossed to the other side of the road.

A lady from Bombay invited me to join her for an early dinner, and when I returned to the hut I lay down to read an Indian magazine she'd given me that contained an expose of Baghawan Rajneesh. Suddenly Andrew burst in, followed by Sidney.

"Can you be ready to leave in ten minutes?" Andrew was breathing heavily. "I want to go now!"

I jumped up.

"Take my new suitcase," Sidney said to Andrew. "You won't have to pack. Just throw everything in."

"What happened?" I asked.

"She doesn't know what she's doing," Andrew gasped.

"Get going," Sidney urged.

"She complained you avoided her on the road."

"What does she expect?" I said.

"She doesn't understand anything."

"C'mon, c'mon," Sidney said.

I flung everything in sight that was mine into my bag and ten minutes later we were in a bicycle rickshaw on our way to the village. It turned out that I'd left half my things behind. People followed us out of the temple asking what had happened but we didn't explain. Our tickets were for tomorrow night and Sidney wished us luck in finding space on the train. I bent down from the rickshaw to squeeze his hand. "You've been wonderful. I'll write to your Boston address," I said.

When we reached the motorized rickshaw stand we transferred our luggage and waited for the rickshaw to fill. It held about eight people. Andrew didn't stop ranting, reviewing everything that had happened over and over again. Suddenly he leapt down. "I've got to find her," he said.

My heart sank. "Why? What for?"

"I promised to meet her in Puri in two weeks. It's too soon."

"Write her," I said.

"No, I have to tell her face-to-face. I have to act like a man."

He was obsessed!

"We'll miss our train," I cried, as he dashed off left towards the Buddha's Belly. So he hadn't let go at all. I waited with a sense of foreboding. The rickshaw was half full.   He was back in three or four minutes dripping with perspiration.

"She wasn't there!"

I stared down at his white sweating suffering face. I'd never seen him in such a state. He was beside himself. A wrenching pity tore at me.

"I'm going to the main temple." He raced off to the right but I didn't call after him this time.

After five minutes I stood up in the rickshaw about to debark with the luggage when he came running back, yelling for us to wait. He sprang up beside me panting terribly. "She was meditating under the Bodhi tree," he gasped, as the rickshaw roared into life and started for Gaya.

When his breath had calmed Andrew said, "I told her I'd write and let her know when we could meet. I told her I needed time." He was silent for a while and then he cried, "I forgot to leave her some money!"

"She has no money?"

"Not enough! God!"

"She can borrow from someone."

"Who can she borrow from? A lot of people have left."

"She can wire her parents. They have money. Good heavens, can't you forget her for now?"

"She'd hate to do that. Jeeze, I feel like a real shit."

"Forget her for Pete's sake."

But he couldn't. He was as involved as ever and rattled on frantically all the way to Gaya.

At the station a great bull roamed the railroad tracks eating discarded banana and mango peels. The train was going to be late. Andrew sat morosely on his luggage with his eyes closed. It was clear by now that he hadn't really wanted to leave and that we could have waited until tomorrow after all and not had all this tension and this worry about our tickets.

Near us a young girl from the retreat came over. She told me her name was Dvora and that she had a berth in second class.

"We're in first class," I told her, "but our tickets are for tomorrow. I hope we can get the conductor to accept them for tonight."

"Maybe you will be lucky," she said, "normally there is no room." She was from Israel. She was short and plump with a lot of black curly hair and an angelic smile. "If you cannot get a place you can share with me," she added. "We can sit together on my bed for the night."

I considered the offer unusually generous, and during the next hour she repeated her invitation several times to make sure we believed her. Although Andrew hadn't spoken and had seemed lost in reverie, he later said, "She asked five times, did you notice Luna? It wasn't just an empty gesture,"

We were lucky after all. A lavish bribe to the conductor got us berths in first class.

The next morning we met Dvora on the train platform and had breakfast with her at a place Andrew knew that served delicious fresh fruit salad and yoghurt. Dvora, who was a second year law student, told us she wrote her family daily and called them every two weeks so that they wouldn't worry about her. She seemed a very likeable down-to-earth girl.

Before we parted—Andrew and I to the Oberoi hotel, and Dvora to a youth hostel—I invited her for lunch the next day.

Immediately after we checked in Andrew took off for the barber shop for a shave, shampoo and massage and I proceeded to the beauty parlor and had my hands manicured and my feet pedicured and my hair washed and blow-dried. We met in the softly lit bar afterwards and sat on padded bar stools and drank draughts of Courvoisier from huge glinting brandy snifters. After what I'd been through it was as if some huge enveloping mother presence had gathered me to her soothing, healing bosom.

Andrew talked and talked and talked and I listened and listened and listened. He went on talking right through the next two days until my plane left for New York. I told him a couple of times that I would faint if he didn't stop, but he went on and I didn't faint, although I honestly thought I would. Once, his face ugly with murderous rage, his eyes mad, he addressed a chair as if Alka were virtually in it, and accused her of betrayal and stupidity and blindness and cruelty.

It was clear that Alka had remained a magnetic force, but I believed that all the talking and venting of emotion was releasing him from his agony and that he was beginning to understand enough to never see her again.

Only during our lunch with Dvora did he exert some control over his tongue. It so happened that both of them were going to Puri at the same time and he asked her if she would buy his train ticket when she bought hers.

"A trip to the station means at least half a day and I want to spend the time with my mother," Andrew said. "She's leaving tomorrow."

Dvora gave him one of her most angelic smiles. She said she was happy to oblige.

My flight was delayed. Andrew waited with me at the airport still raving. In the wan light from the neon tube that flickered above us I studied his thin haggard face. His eyes looked stark. I had to struggle to keep my composure when I said, "I don't want to leave you like this. I don't have to leave now. Do you want me to stay? I could stay, it doesn't matter to me. . ."

"I'll be all right."

"Sure?"

"I'll be fine."

"What are you going to do in Puri?" I asked.

"Take a rest. Swim. There's a beach."

"And then-?"

"Maybe I'll check out that guru Manny told me about."

"What guru?"

"A guru. A man called Poonja, remember?" The old guy

Manny told me about. He lives in Lucknow." He shrugged, "Not that I want another goddam teacher. I don't really want to go. I probably won't. I'll see."

I reached over and stroked his cheek. "I thought you might be coming home soon," I said.

"Yeah. I don't know. I'll see." He smiled for the first time in days. "Don't worry about me. I'll be okay."

"Be sure and write," I said. "I'll be anxious."

"I promise."

A voice announced it was time to go.

We hugged each other and I joined the queue to the exit gate. When I turned he waved, smiling his dear familiar smile of old.

He would never seem familiar to me again.

3

New York

URING THE NEXT FOUR MONTHS THERE WERE many letters from Andrew which were, without exception, unexpectedly cheerful. He'd decided to see Alka again and wrote that although a lot of what I said about Alka was true, "Alka is a person with tremendous potential and Travers did recognize her *mostly hidden depth* and... I do feel she could change..."

Then a startling letter arrived from Lucknow dated May 3, 1986 addressed to both me and Joshua.

"Something clicked on my very first meeting with Poonja," Andrew wrote. "I spent two-and-a-half weeks with him, usually eight hours a day... all the questions which had troubled me greatly were answered... I have stepped out of this world into the unknown... and let go of *everything*."

He went on to say that he'd gone to Bombay and had a reconciliation with Alka who owned up to all her sins. But, he assured me, "I have made no commitments."

He'd then returned to Lucknow where Poonja informed him their WORK was over and he wanted Andrew to accept responsibility for it. Which meant, in Poonja's own words, to take his teaching out into the world and "start a revolution amongst the young!"

So he'd let go of everything! Everything except Alka. But the big news was his enlightenment and that overwhelmed all my other thoughts. I was very excited. *Everything*. What did he mean by that? All his conditioning, that's what he meant. That's what I'd read enlightenment was all about. He was no longer controlled by his past. In his own words, from a book he wrote later called *Enlightenment Is a Secret,* he explained that enlightenment was a state where you were free of "any trace of self-interest of any kind in any form", it was "the end of the struggle to become anyone or anything," it was "coming finally to rest, here and now, in this life," it was "the conscious realization of perfect happiness."

When Andrew first wrote me about his enlightenment, my years of meditation had already acquainted me with the notion. Even though I couldn't imagine what it was like, I longed for it—who wouldn't long for perfect happiness—but I never let myself presume for the fraction of a second that such a miracle could ever happen to me or anyone I knew. It was too preposterous. Still, when I read Andrew's letter and he told me it had happened to him, I believed it immediately. It was too enchanting a prospect to resist.

In his next letter Andrew related that one day, in New Delhi, while looking at his passport photo, he'd exclaimed to Dvora, without thinking and referring to himself, "*He* isn't here anymore!"

This final letter thrilled me to the marrow of my bones. I felt as if I'd won some kind of cosmic lottery. My son had transcended his conditioning and had become an *enlightened* man! From what I'd learned, he had reached the loftiest human possibility!

I read the letters to whomever among my friends I thought would comprehend what had happened to Andrew, and each time I rejoiced anew that I was the mother of such a son. Did the Virgin exult in the same way in the face of her own Son's godliness? Believe it or not, at that time, I was capable of seriously considering such an idea! It was the thundering unlikelihood of it all. It was the strange glamour. Or perhaps it was my grasping at a fairy-tale when I was having trouble writing and my life seemed unusually dry. I don't know. But I was ecstatic. What had happened to Andrew was more spectacular to me than if he had won the Nobel prize for the cure of cancer. Or had become president of the United States. Or been crowned king of England.

Sometime around the beginning of June I got a telephone call from India. The voice at the other end was blurred and very distant. I had to strain to hear it. It was Andrew. "Come back to India," he said. "Interesting things are happening."

"What—? Say that again?"

"Interesting things are happening here. Come back!"

"Now?"

"Now!"

"It's summer! The heat!"

Why did I hesitate? I was dying to go.

"Forget the weather! Just come!"

4

New Delhi

ANDREW MET ME AT THE AIRPORT IN NEW DELHI appearing marvelously healthy, his narrow face suntanned, his cheeks ruddy. We hugged each other and then I stepped back and took a long curious look at him.

"Do I seem different?" he asked, smiling.

His eyes held me for a few moments; they were unusually lustrous and had an incredible soft, knowing, melting expression.

"Yes," I said, with a sense of shock.

He took my luggage and I followed him out of the airport into the morning sunshine to the taxi stand. Even his stride seemed new, more certain, more unequivocal. There was no question that something had happened to him. I knew it then, right away.

He took me to an ancient hotel situated near his teacher, Poonja, who was staying, for the time, at the home of his daughter. Our room, alleged to be air-conditioned, was quite hot, but the cool delivered by the air-conditioner was so slight and it made so much noise, that we turned it off.

Andrew ordered toast and tea and we sat down opposite each other at a small table. "How do I seem different?" he asked eagerly.

"You seem—?" I examined his face again. He'd always been a somewhat anxious person but every sign of that seemed gone.

"You seem terribly confident, very sure of yourself," I said, and I looked away uneasily.

"Why do you think that?" he asked.

"I don't know, you just don't seem the same."

"That's true, I'm not the same. I *am* different." he said.

The absoluteness of his answer shook me. I looked back at him. "It's all very odd," I said, intimidated by his tone.

"It sure is, Luna," he said, and he laughed.

He'd stopped addressing me as 'Mom' when he'd begun his spiritual journey years before. It had probably been his way of diminishing my influence over him.

The food arrived and we ate and drank and talked while I tried to adjust to the changed state of the one person in the world I had thought I knew best.

I didn't know what to make of it. It was a miracle. What else could it be? People don't change in a twinkling, just like that. But in the space of the four months since I'd last seen Andrew, he had become a new man.

I gazed at him. He was calmly sipping tea from his cup. He put the cup down and looked back at me. And then I began to feel a peculiar sense of detachment, as though I were disengaging from my usual consciousness. And after a few moments I heard myself say, "It's funny Andrew, but right now, this second, for some reason I feel very far away from you; I feel as if I don't care about anything or anybody. I don't even care about you."

I had no idea why I was saying this. Or where it was coming from.

Andrew gave me an enigmatic smile. "It's beginning," he said.

"What do you mean? It's beginning?"

"Your mood isn't accidental. It's because of my presence."

"What mood exactly?"

"Not caring. Not being bothered about anything. That's the real you, Luna." He smiled at me with immense approval. And he added, "There are no accidents."

His confidence was flabbergasting. But for a few moments

I had felt as if someone had untied my hands; I'd felt free.

The next morning Poonja knocked on the door of our room at about eleven a.m. He was unusually tall with strong features and intense dark eyes. As soon as Andrew introduced us, Poonja pointed at him, looked at me, and announced, "He is *my* son!"

His remark and his tone were aggressive and confused me for an instant, but in the next instant I was so moved by the fact that this man felt close enough to Andrew to consider him his son, that I experienced a surge of gratitude. I knew how much Andrew missed his real father who had loved Andrew more than he had loved anybody else in the world. When Andrew was a little boy his father would catch him up in his arms as he came through the door each evening after work, and throw him up in the air, and catch him. And Andrew would fling his own arms, thin as matchsticks, around his father's neck and embrace him tightly, squealing with joy. During his father's funeral he cried so broken-heartedly, and for so long, that I thought he'd never be able to stop. Afterwards he was depressed for months.

We all sat down and chatted a bit. Poonja treated me with such extreme deference that I had continually to control the impulse to look behind to see if he were addressing someone else. It made me uncomfortable, yet I was flattered by the attention. When he left Andrew asked me what I thought.

"He has a lot of charisma," I said, "and he seems a very powerful man, but we were together for only half an hour. I don't know him."

"Believe it or not Poonja and I might be the only two people in the whole world doing the work we're doing," Andrew said.

This was so dumbfounding I couldn't react to it. *The only two?*

The pretension of it all sounded quite mad. Still, I have to admit, part of me wanted to believe it, crazy as it seemed. Part of me wished Andrew to be the extraordinary man he seemed to have become overnight.

In the evening we went to Poonja's daughter for dinner. She and her family lived above their photography shop in a dingy apartment that, Andrew had told me, was full of beds. Even the room we dined in was dominated by a double bed. Poonja and Andrew sat on the floor in front of the bed and I was given a chair and a small table. The meal had to have required considerable labor. It consisted of numerous courses. I had no idea what I was eating but each dish tasted more exquisite than the last. After she'd served us, Poonja's daughter, a plain looking, shabbily dressed woman, sat at another table at the other end of the room as if she were a servant and not on an equal footing with us. The rest of the family was out of sight. Andrew had informed me that Poonja's daughter had been enlightened by Ramana Maharshi years before.

We ate in silence.

"You say she's enlightened?" I asked Andrew later.

"Yes, I told you."

"But she acts like a maid. And she works like a dog, as far as I can see."

"She doesn't mind. It's her life. She accepts it."

I didn't say anything. I didn't know what to say. I was aghast at my once tender-hearted son saying that it was all right for Poonja's daughter to live like that.

RISHIKESH

We took off the next afternoon for Rishikesh, a holy town in the foothills of the Himalayas where Andrew and a few other people had taken rooms on the roof of a temple beside the Ganges river. There we would await Poonja, he explained, who was to arrive in a few days and stay with us for a while as our teacher. It sounded very glamorous—a group of sincere spiritual seekers getting together in a remote Indian village to sit at the feet of a holy man who had access to the wisdom of the ages. I felt incredibly lucky to be in on such a grand adventure.

We hired a taxi for the ride. The driver kept his fist on the horn all the way. We couldn't talk so we sat wired to Andrew's walkman that had two head-phones.

It was still daylight when we arrived. We stepped out onto a dusty road and, carrying our luggage, went down a flight of very steep stone steps that led to a narrow suspension bridge across the Ganges. The bridge moved under our feet, and in the towers above it, monkeys squawked and made threatening gestures. At the other end of the bridge we took an unpaved track along the river to the temple. I was enthralled by how primitive everything was. A precipitous stony footpath beside the temple led up to our rooms on the roof.

Two men came to welcome us. I was immediately taken aback by their attitude of homage towards Andrew. One was the forty-year-old Manny Rivers whom I'd met on my last trip to India and who had introduced Andrew to Poonja. The other was a student of Sanskrit and Hindi from the University of California. Both of them embraced Andrew warmly. A moment later Dvora appeared. She gave Andrew a big hug and then she greeted me. Her manner was vastly different from what it had been four months ago. She didn't seem girlish anymore. Andrew had told me in New Delhi that Dvora and Manny had both been enlightened by *him* and not by Poonja.

There were a few other men living on the roof whom I'd meet later. I was introduced to one of them, Bud Rivers, at dinner, and found him a tall, skinny, nice-looking, sandy-haired young man. He was a philosophy student from Johns Hopkins University. He treated me in such an inordinately respectful manner as the mother of Andrew, that this brought home again the realization that Andrew wasn't just a spiritual instructor to these people. No, Andrew was a fully realized guru!

I was curious about how other people, apart from Dvora and Manny, had discovered Andrew. I was told that foreign seekers in India go to all the same famous ashrams and there they exchange gossip about who's teaching what and where.

The house on the roof was a long structure consisting of four rooms in a row, two large and two small. Manny and Dvora each had a small room of their own. One large room was occupied by the other men and another by Andrew and myself. In front of the rooms ran a wide corridor where the group collected to talk in the evening. At one end it opened up into a kitchen no one used except to make tea. To get to the toilets you had to climb over two roofs and down some stairs. At night you needed a flashlight because you could fall to your death in the abyss between the roofs! Water for tea and cleaning your teeth and face came from a single pipe jutting from a wall outside the house. I'd brought a water filter with me the others made fun of, but as it turned out, I was the only one who didn't get sick. Baths were taken at night (for privacy) behind a huge tank, also on the roof. You dumped pails of cold water over yourself and it ran off down a drain.

The rooms were unfurnished except for a few rusting lamps and some ancient electric fans that made loud scratching noises. In spite of the heat they were often turned off in order to hear what was being said. Everyone slept on the floor on paper thin mattresses on top of which they placed their sleeping bags. As soon as the sun went down clouds of insects invaded the unscreened rooms. Nevertheless the place was spacious and isolated enough to be able to stay up all night talking without disturbing anyone.

After unpacking we went for a dip in the Ganges, or Ganga, as they called it. A dangerous current kept us close to the bathing ghat. The muddy swirling water was opaque, and so icy, you could have sworn it had just spurted from the glacier high above.

That night the group gathered in Manny's room. I was very tired and could barely follow what people said but I was aware that Andrew was the magnetic center of everyone's attention and that he seemed born to his amazing confidence and stunning clarity of speech.

I went to bed around midnight, dizzy with undigested new impressions. Apart from Andrew's incredible poise and assurance, I realized he'd been transformed in yet another fashion. My son, who had been fairly articulate but certainly not a master of verbal communication, now had a silver tongue. Words with meanings precisely fitted to what he wanted to convey flowed forth exact and sparkling. It seemed to me his vocabulary had quadrupled, as if he had now at his disposal every single word he'd ever heard or read in the past!

Nothing, not even his letters, had prepared me for what I'd found when I stepped off the plane in New Delhi two days ago.

In the morning I went out alone—everyone was still asleep—and walked to a nearby chai shop, a lean-to with tables and benches, and I sat, glancing down every now and then at the racing river below, and drank tea and wrote in my diary. My thoughts were racing too. My son seemed to belong to them; he seemed strangely distant from me. But I felt as if I might be on the edge of a new and wonderful life for myself and the hope that filled my breast was intoxicating.

Dvora joined me. She said they'd all gone to bed at dawn. "Andrew told Bud to leave." she said.

"Leave? What do you mean, leave?"

"To get out."

"Get out?"

"He went to a hotel in the village."

A sudden misgiving made me lower my gaze.

"He wasn't taking Andrew's teaching seriously enough," she said.

"Were his feelings hurt?" I asked.

She came back like a shot. "Andrew was right."

I looked up at her again. She'd become forceful and I didn't like it. As if sensing my withdrawal she said, "But it's okay, Bud is allowed to spend his days and evenings with us anyway."

I left Dvora writing in Hebrew in her own diary and ambled through the part of town on this side of the river called Laxman Jhula.

The rainy season was coming and heavy humid heat poured from the sky. Color blazed everywhere, from mythic figures on the walls of shrines and from the cloth of women's saris. I saw two men in gaudy make-up imitating Hanuman (elephant-headed god) and a scrawny fellow lying peacefully on a bed of nails. It was a wondrously alien world.

When people who'd gathered for the night's meeting were waiting for Andrew to begin and sat regarding him humbly and expectantly, I was surprised by the tears that filled my eyes. They believed in him. It was unbelievable, but they believed. And his power affected me too. I suppose I identified with it.

Instead of bathing in the Ganges, one day we walked into the flower-scented jungle nearby and followed a path to a small waterfall and stood under it and let the cool water bless us. Dvora, the only other woman present besides myself, looking somewhat chunky, but full and ripe, her large breasts swinging freely under her bra-less nylon and lycra bathing suit, frolicked unselfconsciously with the men. Her angelic smile was there for everyone. They seemed to regard her as a kind of earth mother and except for Andrew, seemed half in love with her. Manny said he could imagine her one day as an old lady in Tel Aviv, knitting in her parlor while dispensing wisdom to seekers who came from far and near to sit at her feet. A Golda Meier type, but spiritual.

On the way back, though people jostled to be near him, I managed to walk beside Andrew for a few minutes.

"Are you having a good time?" he asked.

"I woke up today feeling unusually calm," I said.

"That's because you're in tune with me," he said.

I looked at him, touched by the same qualm I'd had before at the absoluteness of his conviction about himself. "Anyone who loves me," he continued, "is guaranteed enlightenment."

It bothered me when he said things like that. How did he know? Why was he so sure? I couldn't ask. To ask was to be negative, the sin of sins. And besides, something in me, something still tiny, a little worm of a thing, wanted it to be true.

After a long silence I asked "What does it mean to let go?"

"It means you doing nothing and letting me do the work." He grinned at me.

"Well, I don't feel like doing anything anyway. I'm in this funny mood where I don't want to write or think or anything." I pointed to a black heifer lying on the path ahead. "I feel like that cow," I said.

"Are you happy?" Andrew asked. "Is it okay with you to feel like a cow?"

"It's weird but it's okay." I said.

We sat down to rest on some rocks and Manny joined us.

"That's all there is to it." Andrew winked at Manny. "My mother's on her way," he said.

"The trouble is, it sounds like a fairy-tale," I said.

"It is a fairy-tale," Manny said, looking lovingly at Andrew

The others came and sat down near us. They started asking Andrew questions. At some point I began to tell the story I'd just read of a man who'd been too shy to speak to Ramana Maharshi and instead had thrown a note at his feet saying, 'Save me.'"

"Do you want to be saved?" Andrew asked sternly.

Startled, I hesitated. I was aware of being bulldozed, but I nodded.

"Say it then!" Andrew said.

"Say what?" I said.

"Say save me."

I hesitated again, then I said, "Save me," and felt myself blushing.

That night Bud Rivers was given permission to move back into our house.

For some reason Poonja had not arrived. No one knew why. Rooms had been reserved for him days ago. Meanwhile Andrew was interpreting my dreams for me, interpreting almost everything I said. I was afraid to open my mouth. I remember one morning after I'd had a bad dream, he suggested we have lunch—just he and I—on the other side of the river. We had to climb the same treacherous cramped stone steps we'd descended with our luggage when we arrived. Now the steps were lined with moaning begging lepers holding out half-eaten hands or shoving noseless faces at us. Andrew amazed me by joking with them while he tossed some coins. They amazed me even more by joking back.

When we were seated in a restaurant and had ordered, Andrew returned to my bad dream.

"You are attached to the terror in your dream," he said, "because underneath, it's what you really believe. You believe in terror. It comes from the past. It's your known." He looked at me for a few seconds, then he said, "Luna, give me your terror, and give me the fear in letting it go." He said it as if it were a simple matter of choice, like deciding to take three aspirins instead of two. How could I do it? How could anyone do it?

He was pushing me hard. He was becoming my teacher and I didn't want him to be my teacher. It scared me.

He drew an envelope from his pocket and took out two letters. He handed one to me. It was from Alka. I glanced through it quickly feeling my throat tighten. She wanted to come in person to apologize to me.

"No!" I said, looking up at him. Had he put her up to this?

"But she admits she was out of control," he said.

"I don't care."

"Listen, Luna, there was never any relationship between you and Alka. It was between your neurosis and her neurosis. Crazy as it sounds she saw *you* victimizing *her*."

"I don't care," I repeated.

"And you experienced her anger as a victimization of you," he went on calmly, "and it opened an old wound. Deep down you've always had the conviction that in spite of being innocent you would always be regarded as guilty."

There was a silence.

"I don't want to see her now," I said quietly. "I don't want her to come."

"Luna, she's leaving to work for six months as a manager in a Vipassana meditation retreat in England. Give her a chance. You can't refuse someone who is willing to travel two thousand extra miles to apologize."

"I don't want to see her," I repeated, "it's too soon."

"Besides," he went on implacably, "you and Alka should be grateful to each other. Although you didn't know it, you were helping each other demolish your past histories.

He was determined to get me to accept her again.

"She's coming in three days to stay for a week," he said.

I sat there choking on this information. I tried to reason with myself. If a person changed, I told myself, what was there to keep on being angry at? I tried to remain calm.

But after dinner I fell into a fit of intense melancholy and sought Andrew out intending to tell him the truth, that I was afraid to go on opposing him about Alka. I wanted assurance that his love could withstand any differences between us. I wanted desperately for him to understand how, for the first time in my life, I felt bound hand and foot by my fear of losing him. However, when we were sitting on a bench together near the front of the roof, I was over-come suddenly by a strange emotion. I felt as if my mind were dying, as if I were being swallowed up by some horrible disinte-grating force. I heard myself whisper, "I'm slipping away. I'm frightened. I'm slipping, slipping—" I saw the river speeding blackly below and began to cry. In a wild sort of way. Andrew put his arm around my shoulders. After a few minutes, when I could speak again, I said, "I don't know who I am anymore. You've con-vinced me my life, my experience, mean nothing. Nothing. I am nothing." Andrew squeezed my shoulder. "I feel loathsome. I want to kill myself," I said. It was true. A devil inside me craved to get up and jump off the roof. I looked at Andrew. He was smiling!

"The pain comes from comparing the present with the past," he said.

"Who cares. The present is a night-mare."

"If you stand nowhere, without the past, what then?"

"I don't care! I don't care!"

"Come on Luna—"

"But it's true! I don't care. The pain is unbearable."

"Go and tell the others," he said.

"What? Tell them what? God!"

"Tell them what just happened."

"What happened?"

"Just tell them." He pulled me off the bench.

"No! I can't!"

"Yes you can, you can."

"I don't want to."

"Who doesn't want to?"

"I. Me. I don't want to."

He gave me a little shove toward the stairs that led from the roof to our house. People were sitting on the steps waiting for Andrew to begin the night's session.

Self-consciously, sobbing at times, I repeated what I'd said to Andrew. When I finished everyone was smiling. I bowed my head. I felt I'd lost everything. I had no background, no experience, no knowledge, no intrinsic quality, nothing, and before this benignly smiling encouraging group I felt I had removed my clothes and had revealed the naked, pathetic, impotent, unlovable creature that at bottom, I'd always suspected I was.

This was what Andrew had accomplished in less than a week.

At dawn Bud threw all his philosophy books into the Ganges. Everyone was there but me. I was sleeping. When I woke up I felt as if last night's experience had been another bad dream.

During the afternoon, at a tea stall with Andrew and Dvora, Andrew told me I was enlightened. I looked back at him blankly. "It's true, you're already enlightened," he said.

"That's ridiculous," I said. "I don't believe it."

Andrew nodded at me. "I told Manny last night. My mother is enlightened," I said.

"It was the same for me at the beginning," Dvora said, "I didn't believe it either."

"I don't feel changed," I said. "I feel worse than before."

"It takes time to get used to it," Dvora said.

That evening, for the first time since I'd arrived, we gathered in the hallway for our meeting. It was ten p.m. Someone lit a couple of candles and placed them in front of Andrew who sat with his legs folded leaning against a pole and smoking a cigarette. In the candlelight he looked vibrant and beautiful.

I was lying on my stomach on a straw mat supporting myself on aching elbows and staring at the candles. Thick circles of insects buzzed around the two flickering flames. Andrew put his cigarette out in a saucer and said, "Think of this image for a moment. You are in a vast space. A bit of matter catches your eye and consumes all your attention. This is how we live." It was a brilliant image. And it was true.

Walking with Bud one afternoon in Laxman Jhula, I became aware of feeling a queer sense of distance from the lively and vivid surroundings. I tried to describe it to Bud.

"Everything's sort of muffled right now, sort of far away, know what I mean Bud?"

He nodded. "Yeah, I feel the same way. Sort of stoned."

"It's like seeing and smelling and feeling but with a sense of not really seeing and smelling and feeling at all."

"Yeah," Bud said. I looked at him. He was dreadfully gaunt. He'd been sick for months and was unable to digest anything but rice and yogurt. But he'd balked at every suggestion that he go back to America. Maybe he was too young to believe he'd ever die.

Suddenly I was breathless. I had an intuition that Bud was breathless at that same instant too. The machinery of my body felt as if it were decelerating. I was moving in slow motion. I bought a roasted corn and it took me the entire walk home to finish it.

After that, for a while, I felt very close to Bud. I felt our brains had been stormed. Or washed. Or something. Together. But he never returned the feeling and kept his distance.

When I told Andrew about my experience he was pleased. He said I'd been seeing directly and not comparing.

"But there was this separation from everything, this veil," I said.

"The sense of dullness, the muffled quality, is just something you're going through," he said. "It will pass."

The monsoon had come. I awoke one morning to a shrieking wind. Outside it was pouring. As I ran along the flooding path to an indoor tea-shop nearby I passed a woman standing still in a pool of water. Once under the shop's eaves, I looked back. The woman had dropped her clothing and was standing naked, her hair streaming over her shoulders, her arms extended, staring up at the roiling eddying sky. Her body was young and beautiful, her face a ravaged mask. In a holy town like this her nakedness had to be a violent visual shock. But no one looked at her. People who passed kept their eyes averted. She knelt down in the water and bowed her head in her arms and remained, again, motionless. I stood gaping at her. It was a biblical scene in its stark simplicity. I felt profoundly moved. She was probably deranged. But how sane was I? Staying on in this wild Indian place with my wild guru son and his—what should I call them?—his apostles?!

By mid-afternoon the rain had stopped. Andrew and Manny and Dvora had gone off together for a farewell lunch. Manny was leaving the next morning at five a.m. for Totnes, an alternative lifestyle type of town in Devon, England, to prepare the way for Andrew as a teacher. Manny had introduced Andrew to Poonja, had been his mentor at first, and had ended as his disciple. I thought of him as Andrew's John the Baptist and was sure he planned to spend the rest of his life at Andrew's side as chief aide. The two men appeared to love one another and were always conferring together. For some reason I didn't trust Manny. He was quick and smart but I didn't feel comfortable with him. He seemed to look through me not at me whenever we were alone together, as if unwilling to be altogether present with someone not his equal. I thought he was a spiritual snob who considered himself specially endowed to fathom things esoteric. At the same time he had a nice guy image that I sensed was very important to him.

I was in my room reading a Dick Francis mystery when Alka arrived. I was expecting her but nevertheless was startled when I looked up and saw her in the doorway, her color high, her eyes shining. She dashed in and embraced me awkwardly, chatted for a few moments as if nothing had ever happened, and then dashed out. Her entry had seemed a kind of trespass. What I'd guessed, and I now intuited to be true, was that she had not come to straighten out the situation between the two of us because she still felt justified in her resentment against me. She was doing what she was doing only to appease Andrew. And I realized I still couldn't forgive her.

I was given Manny's room and Alka moved in with Andrew.

We all met Orit Sen Gupta at our usual tea stall next to the river. She was an Israeli woman in her late twenties who had married an Indian man and was now divorced. Bud, who'd brought her, told us she was a superb yoga teacher and was presently translating Patanjali's Yogasutras from sanskrit into Hebrew. (Patanjali was the father of yoga.)

She sat opposite Andrew, small, freckled, red-haired, her pretty face tense and suspicious, asking and answering questions very articulately, but gradually growing less and less assured. She subsequently told me that she had come to demolish this Jewish boy from New York, this upstart, but was almost immediately taken aback by the power and simplicity of what he had to say.

We all moved on to the river together where people went swimming. I sat quietly in an absent, vacant mood, still very slowed down. Even now I'm not sure what I was going through. I'd been feeling anaesthetized for days. Near me an ancient woman sanyasi (wandering renunciate) sat alone looking to her left down the river. She was all skin and bones and big dark liquid Indian eyes. I examined her curiously. A woman who roamed alone, drawn here and there by hazard—alone. Did she feel safe? Or was she too old and too poor to attract anyone's attention? I would have loved to have gone and sat beside her and asked her a thousand questions.

At some point Alka ran over and hugged me. "Thank you, thank you," she cried.

I said nothing. I felt nothing. At breakfast Andrew had said, "The change in Alka since Bodh Gaya is nothing less than a miracle."

But I didn't see that she'd changed at all.

On the way home, walking beside me, Andrew confided,

"As I was going down to the river I stopped and looked around. I realized I was completely happy. This is Nirvana, I thought." He gave me a slow smile that sent a pang to my heart. I knew he hadn't been happy much in his life.

At tea I complained about my lumpy mental state. "It's really boring," I said.

"Give into it," Andrew said, "and stop comparing anything with the past!"

Once again, his insistence that you could will yourself into different mental states bewildered me. How could you do it? But I knew it was pointless to ask. He'd just repeat the same words and smile.

I went home and washed my hair, a great accomplishment in the sluggish mood I was in, and collapsed in my room for the rest of the afternoon eating mangoes and reading Dick Francis. It was terribly muggy and the room hummed with the noise of flies. I turned on the fan. There was a night that I forgot to turn on the fan and awoke to find myself and the floor and the chair and my suitcases covered with dead insects!

One evening a strange event took place that remains etched in my memory as if in stone.

We were on our way home from dinner. Andrew walked without talking, plugged into his Walkman. Alka and I, on either side of him, exchanged a few desultory remarks. During her visit we had never gotten beyond this level of exchange. Not a word had been spoken that referred to the past.

Alka turned to Andrew. "When was the last time you heard from Poonja?" she asked. He didn't answer. She raised her voice and repeated the question. When he removed his ear-phones she said, "You're being rude, you know."

"I'm tired and I'm trying to relax before the evening's session," he said quietly. He clamped on the earphones again.

We went the rest of the way in silence, careful of the dim humps of sleeping cattle on our path.

Once home I went and sat in Dvora's room. It was more comfortable than mine. She had fixed it up quite prettily with Indian shawls and floor pillows. A custom had developed that allowed us to wander into each other's rooms without explanation and sit or lie on the floor or simply stare at the wall. Since we were all accustomed to going through powerful unforseen moods and feelings, it was one of the consolations of being with this group that you could even put your head down on the table in a restaurant and close your eyes and no one would ask what you were doing or why.

Bud came in. He said Orit had been very affected by Andrew and would probably come to stay with us. Dvora looked pleased. Suddenly Andrew appeared at the doorway. "Luna, come to my room," he said in a rather peremptory tone.

Alka was sitting on the floor under the window. Andrew indicated that I should sit on a pillow against the opposite wall. Then he lit a cigarette and lay down on his bed and leaned back. There was a long hush. He turned to Alka.

"Something must be made very clear between you and me," he said in a slow measured tone. "Things are not what they used to be." He puffed on his cigarette and then, "I am in a different position now and I won't tolerate your impatience and disrespect any longer." He paused and took another drag on the cigarette. "Do you understand?"

After a long pause, as if wrung from her, in a thin strangled voice, Alka asked "What did I do?"

"On the way home you told me in front of other people that I was rude. I can't be treated that way now by you or anyone else. It shows no respect. It's not acceptable."

Her eyes opened wide, bulging slightly. "Oh," she said. She looked thunderstruck.

"Do you understand?" Andrew repeated.

"I'm sorry," Alka said softly. "I didn't know, I—"

"Being sorry isn't enough," he broke in, and in a slow even voice he continued, "much as I care about you Alka, I don't need you." He paused and repeated, "I don't need you. Understand?"

Still as a statue, Alka stared at him as if hypnotized.

"You're welcome to stay, but only on my terms," Andrew lit another cigarette. His fingers were steady. He blew out the match and dropped it in his ash-tray. "This relationship can't be an ordinary one, Alka. I am no longer an ordinary man leading an ordinary life. And from now on, no one will spend time with me unless they treat me with respect."

An interminable time passed during which nothing was said. I sat paralyzed, barely breathing, watching the tableau before me. Alka's stare remained fixed while Andrew went on smoking, looking straight ahead, his face expressionless. Slowly Alka bowed her head. I bowed mine as well. In spite of how I felt about Alka, I cringed for her.

A sudden movement on Alka's part made me look up. I saw her rising to her feet. She started to move, sinuous, deliberate, floating towards him, her eyes soft, fastened on his eyes again. Upon reaching the bed, she embraced him about the waist in one fluid sinking stooping motion, and gradually folded down, her eyes closing, and lay her head on his chest.

I felt I was transgressing on some sort of intimacy stripped so bare it was positively indecent to remain in that room one moment longer. I got up quietly and went to my own room and lay down. I felt terribly sorry for Alka. I felt ashamed for Alka and horrified at what had been done to her by my son. He'd been vicious. How can you be a guru if you have no compassion? His belief in himself and the inviolate correctness of his behavior seemed nothing more than presumptuous arrogance. It repelled me. I was ashamed for him too.

The next morning Andrew said, "I asked you to come into the room because I wanted to remind you that I was not committed unconditionally to Alka."

He was showing me his control over the situation. He was showing me his power. He had humiliated her and had used my presence to humiliate her further.

That very same evening Orit arrived, shy, hesitant, but with all her belongings.

During the late candlelit session in the hall I was suddenly oppressed with the meaninglessness of life.

"Maybe I should go home," I burst out.

Andrew looked me in the eye. "It takes determination and endurance to bear enlightenment," he said.

"I'm not enlightened," I said, "I'm scared."

"Why are you scared?" he asked.

"I don't know. Andrew. I don't know."

"You don't trust me enough, Luna, that's the trouble. You must trust me totally. Totally."

Why, I thought, why should I trust him? Why trust anyone totally? Why?

"Dependency scares me," I said.

"Not dependency," Andrew corrected, "surrender."

"Surrender scares me. I want to understand, not surrender."

"My dear," he said, "trying to understand is the opposite of surrender." Andrew sighed. "Tell me Luna, what if this conviction of meaninglessness never goes?"

"I'd want to die." I said. I looked at him. Candlelight glinted across his cheeks.

"Why is meaning so important to you?"

"I don't know. I really don't know"

"What can you do," he asked, "to make life more meaningful?"

"I don't know. Nothing, I guess."

"That's right. You can do nothing."

I waited a minute, then I said, "So are you telling me I'm helpless?"

"Yes."

"I have no control?"

"No control."

I watched the circuit of insects wheeling about the flames of the candles. Meaningless.

"Are you relieved to know you have no control?" Andrew asked.

"Relieved? I don't know. Maybe," I said finally.

These exchanges with Andrew were always mind-boggling to me.

On July seventh, at five a.m., Alka left for Bombay. I had no strong feeling about her departure. Apart from that one spell-binding horror scene I had witnessed between her and Andrew, it was as if she hadn't been here. In fact, we'd barely exchanged a word. It was now unequivocally plain to me that her arduous journey across India in the heat of midsummer had not been because she *wanted* to apologize to me, but because to apologize to me, which she never actually did, was to secure the bond with Andrew. Andrew didn't seem to understand this.

The issue that began to dominate my days was boredom. It was raining a lot, sometimes all day and all night *continuously*. I didn't have enough to do. I didn't have enough to read. There was nowhere to go. I was spending a lot of time alone while Andrew went off with someone or other to have private talks.

"Boredom," Andrew said, "gives you a sense of security because then there's another possibility, another hope—the diversion from boredom. It's wanting to do something else that prevents you from knowing what is going on now." Wise words, but what was going on now was that I was bored and there was nothing I could do about it. The image that had surfaced so powerfully during my 'enlightenment' experience, the portrait of myself as a pathetic foolish insignificant unlovable woman, a nothing person with no identity, still turned and flickered inside me like a tattered loop of film. It would come into focus the moment I was alone. I wanted more of Andrew's time, I wanted him to reassure me that I was really not that woman, that the image was just some garbage left over from my childhood, that it was a delusion. I wanted him to love me in the old sweet way—as my son.

I began to feel depressed.

At last he invited me to walk with him to the post-office in Laxman Jhula, just the two of us. After the post-office we went to a tea shop and ordered orange sodas that arrived lukewarm and too sweet. I told him I was feeling depressed.

He said, "You're still trying to understand. You think when you understand you'll jump up and shout 'aha!' Give up trying to understand." I gazed at him, hopeless at this command to do something I couldn't do.

At a certain moment he gave me a teasing look and said, "There's only one thought that separates the state of bondage from the state of enlightenment."

My heart alerted. Was he going to disclose the secret? I couldn't believe it. I leaned toward him expectantly. "What is it?" I whispered. But I knew as soon as I'd asked that he wouldn't tell me.

His lips pursed, he eyed me ironically. "It's for me to know and you to find out," he said, and he laughed.

On the way back along the river I told him that these last few days, whenever I got depressed, I thought of killing myself.

"Go on, do it then," he said, laughing, and pushing me in the direction of the river.

At night around the candles Andrew said, "Time doesn't exist, so what is there to worry about?"

What was there to worry about? Time still existed for me all right.

"There is only the moment." Dvora added portentously.

"Doesn't time have something to do with death? What about death?" I asked.

"It's not relevant," Dvora said. She was twenty-three years old.

"No, actually, the real problem is fear," Andrew said.

"If you live in the moment there is no fear," Dvora said.

"But you can't decide to live in the moment just like that!" I said, irritated. "You have to have seen deeply into something first don't you?"

"Maybe it has to see you," Andrew said enigmatically.

I went to bed at five a.m. The rest remained with Andrew. When I awoke six hours later they were all still up. No one had gone to bed. I was told Orit had flung her manuscript on Patangali into the Ganges at seven. Andrew had persuaded her that her ego had been too identified with it!

I was surprised to find myself alone again with Andrew the next evening. We were on our way home after dinner. The others had gone on ahead without demonstrating their usual propensity to manoeuver as much as possible to be near him.

I told him I couldn't shake the depression I'd fallen into. "Maybe I should leave!" I flung these words at him like a challenge.

"You're acting like a baby," he said in an unusually harsh voice. "You're not serious Luna. All the others are serious. But not you!"

My worst night-mare was coming true. My son was going to send me away! We walked through the darkness in a silence that lasted many minutes. Several times I glanced over at him. He was a dark shadow on the lightless road.

"I arranged this talk," he said, finally, "because I decided it was time to be very hard on you, as I am with the others." His voice was stiff, artificial. "But since you're my mother," he gave a sharp laugh, "I can't do it."

We crossed the suspension bridge side by side. It was swaying in a sudden gust of wind and I held onto the steel cable that ran along its sides. Above us the monkeys were screaming.

Poonja had never been hard on him, I thought. He'd had it easy. Tears started to my eyes. Didn't he know how much he could wound? By the time we reached the other side of the river I was sobbing.

"I won't support your suffering," he snapped.

We walked home without another word. I went trembling all the way.

The next day Andrew and Manny left to meet Poonja's train. They returned at six p.m. Poonja wasn't coming. No one told me why he'd changed his mind. Andrew, Orit, Dvora, Bud and I were going to leave tomorrow for Hardwar. The others had left for their own destinations days before.

5

HARDWAR

WE ARRIVED IN HARDWAR AROUND NOON AND took rooms at the Tourist Bungalow, a motel-type establishment run by the Indian government. Andrew and I shared one room, the other three the room next door. The Tourist Bungalow faced on the Ganges, which looked swifter here and more menacing than in Rishikesh. Poonja lived on the other side of the river. If we squinted we could actually see him at times out on his veranda.

After lunch we crossed the bridge over the river and found him dressed in a white kurta and pajama, sitting cross-legged on a cot in a long narrow room. I was surprised to see that he was sharing his room with a pretty, blond chic Belgian woman and her child, a girl of thirteen. The girl, perhaps bored with what was going on, was sitting on her mattress on the floor reading *Gone with the Wind* in French. I was told the Belgian lady had been enlightened by Poonja and was here to thank him.

Poonja greeted me effusively. "You look completely changed," he said.

I didn't feel changed. But I felt less strained than usual. Andrew reported later that Poonja had asked him if I'd accepted my enlightenment and Andrew had said no, not yet! They both really believed I was enlightened no matter what I said. I guessed that they wanted me to be enlightened—it would be a feather in their caps. That's the way I saw it and it was fun, in a way. It made me feel important.

I found out why Poonja hadn't come to Rishikesh. He'd decided that Andrew should teach on his own right away. He considered Andrew ready to start a revolution amongst the young right there and then after two-and-a-half weeks of instruction. I'd never heard of anything like it. How could you take on the huge responsibility of altering other people's minds with so little training? I was puzzled by Poonja. Where did he get his authority? He was not part of a tradition that educated teachers. He claimed, simply, to have been enlightened by Ramana Maharshi. (Maharshi, I was to find out later, had never authorized anyone's enlightenment or sanctioned anyone to teach in his name.)

The next morning Poonja came to visit us at eleven a.m. He sat quietly for a while looking into space, his large balding head swaying slightly. We were beginning to feel self-conscious and intimidated by his silence when suddenly he asked each of us to write down, in three words or less, the state we were in.

I hesitated, not sure, then I wrote one word.

He asked what I'd written. "Happy," I said, relieved that I felt unambiguous about my inner state, at least for the moment. I knew it was what he wanted to hear.

He gave me a great warming smile and said, "Welcome!" At that moment I experienced a strange humming sensation that started in my chest and arms and I heard a buzzing in my head. It grew stronger and stronger until I thought I'd burst with it. Abruptly it subsided. I was still sweating as I related the episode a few minutes later.

"It's inner music," Poonja said. "It means that you are at the periphery of the Self."

Did that mean that I wasn't really enlightened but merely at the edge of it? Could you be almost enlightened, I wondered? A little enlightened? A quarter enlightened? Half enlightened? The whole business confused me. Nevertheless I was left dazed and excited at the amazing effect Poonja had produced in me. After he left Andrew looked upset. He said he couldn't understand why Poonja's manner had been so formal. "Why can't he just hang out with us like he did with me in Lucknow?" he wanted to know. He lit a cigarette. "Poonjaji claims the Belgian woman is enlightened, but she still seems to suffer from duality as far as I can see. And her daughter is a pain in the neck! Anyway," he went on in a hurt voice, "I feel Poonjaji didn't want us to come here right now."

I had a quick sly thought that I squelched as soon as it appeared. Did Poonja want to be alone with the Belgian woman?

Andrew was troubled enough to bring the subject up again twenty minutes later. "Why is he so protective of her?" he said. "He hasn't told her anything about me. I don't understand it. He hasn't even told her that he's made me a teacher." He paused. "Maybe he thinks she'll feel jealous if he tells her. They're old friends you know," and, as if this explained things, "they met in Rishikesh years ago,"

I thought Andrew was jealous.

Much much later on I found out that the Belgian woman's daughter had been fathered by Poonja!

July twenty-first was Guru's Day—a day to honor gurus. We arrived at Poonja's at nine a.m. laden with flowers.

Poonja sat on his cot looking more festive than usual in an elegant white silk collarless shirt and garlands of flowers draped around his neck. A number of people I'd never seen before were already there. With a beautiful welcoming gesture Poonja invited Andrew to sit beside him on the cot as an equal. Andrew rose from the floor his face flushing, overwhelmed at the tribute.

The Belgian woman suddenly bent from the waist and prostrated before Poonja, her chest and forehead on the floor, her arms stretched out in front, hands palm to palm. She thanked him over and over again for her enlightenment which, I found out, had occurred recently, in Brussels one night, when she was alone, and thousands of miles away. Was it possible that Poonja could have been an influence at such a distance? Or was it that like myself, she didn't realize she was enlightened for a long time and then suddenly, poof!—it happened?

We had tea and cookies and other sweets I didn't recognize, and afterwards Poonja ceremoniously placed a spot of red powder on the foreheads of his disciples, including Andrew, but not on me, Dvora, Orit or Bud, underlining his acknowledgement that we were Andrew's and not his followers.

Oddly enough, it was the day after, while swallowing a thick fragrant luscious mouthful of mango shake at a roadside stand that I had one of my most striking experiences in India. An idea, coming from I know not where, suddenly appeared at the center of my consciousness. I suddenly knew that at any moment freedom was possible! It seemed as if I'd opened to a stupefying truth and I grabbed Andrew's arm and pulled him aside.

"I know something," I whispered, "something incredible. I know that all I have to do is choose to be free!" I stared at Andrew lifted up on a wave of exaltation..

His eyes gleamed with satisfaction. "Congratulations!" he said.

The same evening Andrew left by himself to visit Poonja. The rest of us went to the main ghat of Hardwar where we saw thousands of people, women fully clothed, men naked except for bathing trunks, and children, plunging into the Ganges up to their chins. It was a family scene, a holiday scene—great masses of people purging themselves in the holy river.

Andrew returned from Poonja overcome with emotion. "He's the only one who can affect me like this," he said. "He's the only one." His sadness had been replaced by joy.

I asked myself why his transformed mental state didn't include an indifference to his teacher's attitude towards him? Hadn't I read in the scriptures that enlightenment was serene detachment, an indifference to all external influence? Why did Andrew care so passionately about whether Poonja wanted him here right now or not?

Most of the time my head was buzzing like a hive of bees. Something was definitely happening to me. The buzzing in my head was probably a sign. A sign of what? A sign that I was enlightened?

Andrew had gotten into the daily habit of going off alone to see Poonja. One morning, before leaving, he informed Dvora that her enlightenment was complete. At lunch she sat opposite me, aglow and beautiful. For her the struggle was over. I was filled with envy. If I could accept that I was enlightened too would I look like that? Would I feel as wonderful, as blessed, as she seemed to feel? I waited for an answer but none came.

By late afternoon Andrew hadn't returned so we went down to the river to wait for him there and meditate.

I'd been sitting on a low slab of rock feeling cramps in my legs for some time. But I was deep in meditation and didn't want to budge. All at once the cramps vanished. I opened my eyes. The river, the houses lining the opposite bank, and the crowds of people milling in front of them, appeared peculiarly slanted, out-of-kilter, misshapen and flecked by tiny lights moving in jerks like cells under a microscope. My heart pounded. I closed my eyes again and kept them shut for a few minutes. When I opened them the scene before me had returned to normal.

I had experienced an altered way of seeing. Another sign!

I looked down below at the near shoreline, my heart still hammering away. People were setting tiny paper boats, each holding a single candle, in the water. The candles were lit and the miniature vessels, soon picked up by the current, swept downstream— tiny offerings of light to the river god, a manifestation of the divine.

In the Tourist Bungalow after dinner, Bud and Andrew left to take a walk together. I borrowed Andrew's walkman and sat on the terrace outside my room and listened to Jimi Hendrix and stared up at the sky feeling over-excited and tense. Something was going on. Inside me. Outside me. The sky itself was exploding with more stars than I'd ever seen before.

When Andrew and Bud returned, Andrew announced that

Bud didn't need him anymore. "He's a free man!" Andrew announced triumphantly. At that moment Orit started laughing uncontrollably. She laughed for hours. I thought she was losing her mind. Or that she might die. But Andrew was unconcerned; he said it was cosmic laughter.

Everyone was speeding ahead of me. I was being left behind.

Late at night, Andrew invited me to take a walk with him along the Ganges. The shore, electric lit, was covered with human bodies, all male, as far as I could see, some reclining, some huddled around small fires, cooking, some sitting in meditation, some squatting at the water's edge washing themselves or their clothes. Wandering sanyasi. Most wore orange robes, largely in tatters. Andrew told me not all of them were holy men. Some, because of personal failure, had dropped out of society. They watched us pass with what seemed like aimless curiosity. One old gentleman lay sleeping. We stopped to stare because of his uncommonly refined aristocratic features. He might have been a rajah. His white beard rested on his chest rising and falling peacefully amidst the tumult.

Near the end of our stroll we sat down on a stone step that led to the river. After a long silent interlude Andrew said, "I want to repeat that you really are enlightened whether you know it or not. And," he added, "it will never stop. It will be forever new." I was as dumbfounded as when he'd said it the first time.

"I hope you're right," I said in a fervent voice.

"I am right," he said, "trust me." He squeezed my hand.

Our last evening Poonja invited us to join him for dinner in a restaurant. We arrived at his room early and found him sitting on his cot with his eyes half-closed, looking slightly cross-eyed. As soon as I entered I felt waves of power radiate from him and enter my body.

Walking back from the restaurant at his side, the buzzing strong in my head, I gushed, "A miracle has happened!" He gave me a brilliant glance. "It's all so astounding," I said, "Andrew is so astounding, I can't believe what has happened to him." I stopped short, choked by tears.

"Yes, yes," he said, turning to face me and putting his hands on my shoulders. "It is true," he said, "It is true." We walked on. "Oh yes," he continued, "I have been waiting for Andrew for seventy-five years." He regarded me for a moment with his dark, penetrating eyes. "I will tell you that before Andrew came, I thought I would have to take the fire to the grave with me."

These momentous words took my breath away. I stopped again and looked up at him. What was this wonderful old sage telling me? That he was handing over his mantle to my son Andrew? I lowered my gaze and once more we moved on.

At his door he hugged me and then bent and kissed the top of my head. I told him haltingly, because such extravagant words of gratitude and affection don't come easily to me, I said, "Poonjaji, "I promise I will never, ever, ever forget you!"

Following this scene, as if Poonja's respect and loving acceptance validated my unique importance as the mother of Andrew, and comparing me half-humorously, half seriously to the mother of Christ, that very night, the others began to refer to me the *unvirgin* Luna!

The oscillation I was experiencing all along between wanting to believe in enlightenment and my suspicions about it, had a desperate quality because I already knew that my relationship with Andrew depended wholly on my having faith at least in *his* enlightenment. If I allowed my skepticism to show too much, sooner or later I knew I would lose him. I was being pulled in two directions and it made me feel muddled. It made me seem stupid, as if I had no center. I felt my identity jeopardized.

NEW DELHI

We arrived in New Delhi totally exhausted. Andrew and I took a taxi to the Taj, a five star hotel, where we had a reservation.

We looked so worn out and ragged and dirty from our bus ride that at first we were refused a room. So I decided to tell a big lie. I told the chief of reception, a tall, handsome, intimidatingly elegant man wearing a gorgeous pink satin turban, that if I didn't get a room immediately I would expose him for turning away an American tourist with a legitimate reservation. I would expose him, I said, in the travel section of The New York Times, a newspaper for which I worked as a journalist.

After a long pause, he asked for my journalist's I.D. And I had the gall, because I was so wretchedly weary, to say that I never travelled with my I.D. I always travelled as an ordinary tourist, incognito! Amazingly, it worked.

We were taken to an immense, richly carpeted room containing two twin-sized beds, two brocaded sofas, two velvet lounge chairs and various mahogany coffee and side tables. Our windows looked down upon a shimmering azure swimming pool surrounded by palms.

The others had gone looking for cheap accommodations. They had come to India with a few hundred dollars earned at odd jobs at home or donated by their parents, and it had to last as long as they wanted to stay.

An hour later they arrived to take baths and they revelled in the unlimited supply of hot water in our huge sky-blue tiled bathroom.

We had dinner in the hotel, a gift from Bud. He must have been feeling delirious about his enlightenment to have offered to pay the bill because he was running low on money.

The dining room was filled with upper-class Indians. The women, resplendent in sumptuous saris, glittered with jewels. Some of the older men had unusually refined delicate faces. A few wore white jackets with Nehru collars. There was an air of sophistication and wealth I hadn't encountered in India before. We all enjoyed ourselves thoroughly.

In the morning Andrew said he didn't want to see any of the others that day and he suggested that we stay in and watch movies on TV.

Over a breakfast of scrambled eggs and toast I felt a strange energy begin to stream through me. My head became thick, filled with the now familiar buzzing, and my lids grew heavy and wanted to close. I described my sensations to Andrew.

"It's no accident," he said, and he gave me a long loving smile. I smiled back at him happily. Then I went to the beauty shop and had my hair done and had a manicure and a pedicure and returned blithely to the hotel room and climbed back into bed.

Soon after, there was a knock on the door. Dvora, looking miserable and mumbling apologetically, dragged herself in. Her customary high color was gone. Her curly hair was limp. She looked sick. She said she was feeling extremely disturbed after talking on the phone to her parents. They wanted her to come home.

Without a word Andrew turned off the TV and sat down on the floor opposite her. "You don't tell them the truth," he said. She nodded gloomily. "You're afraid to hurt them." Dvora's head, still nodding, sank slowly to her chest. She began to weep.

"You're a hypocrite." Andrew said calmly.

"I'm not a hypocrite!" Dvora lifted her head and looked Andrew in the eye but in the next moment her head began to wobble and then sink again, very slowly, to her chest. Her nose was running, dribbling onto her flowered T-shirt.

"You're a hypocrite, a liar, and a prostitute," Andrew said in cool measured cadence and he got up, and went to his bed and lay back, and turned on the TV.

Nothing more happened for a few minutes. I couldn't bear to look at Dvora. Instead I inspected the golden dragon woven into the midnight blue carpet at my feet. Then I heard her get up. She ran to a sofa, flung herself onto it, and began to sob and laugh hysterically. I glanced at Andrew.

Imperturbable, he watched the television screen.

After a while Dvora stood up. She was smiling! She looked silly suddenly. Or crazy. Without uttering a syllable she left the room shutting the door silently behind her. Andrew didn't turn a hair. I gaped at him from my chair near the window. My former happiness had dissipated. The scene I'd just witnessed made my insides ache. It reminded me of the one with Alka in Rishikesh. Andrew had displayed the same stony ruthlessness then. It was a trait I'd never seen in him before his enlightenment.

I later learned that disciples of gurus name this kind of cruelty *skillful means* and assume, no matter how humiliating or abhorrent it is, that in the hands of the masters it has a divine purpose—to turn the disciple in the direction of enlightenment.

It was at Poonja's urging—most likely he wanted to be rid of us—that we left the next evening at eight-thirty for Dharamsala, the home of the Dalai Lama. We had to wait one-and-a-half hours in the suffocating heat and darkness of the bus yard because some passenger had reported a stolen briefcase containing forty thousand rupees.

6

DHARAMSALA

AFTER TWELVE TORTUROUS HOURS WE ARRIVED in Dharamsala and started off on foot along a narrow muddy dirt road carrying our luggage and looking around us at the lush mountains that were veiled in a light rain. To me they appeared otherworldly and mysterious, perhaps because I knew this stretch of land, donated by the Indian government, was the refuge of the famed Dalai Lama.

We found accommodations in a simple primitive hotel. Andrew and I shared a room again, and the three others, another. We gave our laundry out to wash and went to the dining room. After all the over-spiced food we'd eaten, the Tibetan food, fresh western style bread and plain stir-fried vegetables and noodles, tasted delicious.

Later we walked up a steep winding road to the Tibetan Meditation Center. From the bushes along the way monkeys screamed and gesticulated at us fiercely. I was afraid of them because I'd heard that the monkeys occasionally attacked people.

The Center was entirely enveloped in a cloud. It was eerie and beautiful. At the entrance to the meditation hall we met Rebecca, a young girl in her early twenties, who had been at Christian Travers' retreat in Bodh Gaya. She was wearing a Tibetan woman's outfit, a wrap-around floor-length jumper made of heavy dark cotton and a short-sleeved blouse. She told us she was staying at the Center and invited us into the hall.

The moment I sat down I felt sucked into a deep velvety silence and for an hour sat motionless, completely relaxed for the first time since I'd come to India. I hadn't realized how tense I'd become trying to adjust to the altered relationship with my son. To all intents and purposes we were changing roles. Our parts were reversing; he was emerging as the parent, the one who knew, and I was becoming more and more the confused vulnerable youth he had been before meeting Poonja.

We sat for awhile in Rebecca's room talking about self-criticism. Rebecca kept staring at Andrew, obviously incredulous at his having become a teacher. She'd known him only slightly in Bodh Gaya.

At some point I said, "There are times when I know I'm being totally selfish and I can't stop. But afterwards I feel like a monster."

"If you feel bad about your selfishness," Andrew said, "go on feeling bad and don't want to feel not bad. Don't want anything." He looked around at the others who, apart from Rebecca, seemed half asleep, and then back at me. "You're the only one who wants to learn today," he said smiling. It was the first time he'd compared me favorably to the others and I felt an instant melting towards him. But I was confused by his advice to not *want* anything, and on the other hand, saying, as if it were a compliment, that I was the only one who *wanted* to learn. It sounded contradictory. However it was the kind of thing I'd stopped asking him to explain because it would be seen as picky, and an example of my stubborn refusal to just go along.

Our laundry was returned very damp. Apparently there was no way to get clothes completely dried during the rainy season. There were no electric dryers, only ancient irons warmed on ancient stoves. The only way to rid your garments of the clamminess that remained was body heat.

Though the fog and the rain were continuous, the atmosphere everywhere was pleasant and optimistic and safe. The

Tibetans went about as smiling and as cheerful as they had in Bodh Gaya. One day, stepping gingerly down an almost vertical path, an incredibly aged Tibetan lady took my arm to help me. The warm-heartedness of these people was hard to believe.

One night we had dinner at a candle-lit restaurant down the road. Leaning back in my chair I looked around the table slowly, and realized with particular pleasure, just how very comfortable I was feeling with this group of people. We were bonded together in a mystic search for truth beyond the confines of ordinary life. We felt special, we felt unique. We had each other and we needed no one and it was cozy and it was fun.

Andrew and I lingered in the restaurant after the others had left. Outside, on the dark road, it was difficult to see ahead, and before we thought of turning on our flashlights, my sandal caught on something and I tripped and fell headlong into an open sewer. Luckily I didn't hurt myself, but horrified with disgust, I sloshed about madly trying to get a foothold in the slimy stinking groove of water. Andrew pulled me out, laughing. I was freezing and had lost my eye-glasses. We turned on our flashlights and peered into the sewer. The glasses were gone.

Shuddering with cold and revulsion, and holding my clothes away from my body as best I could, I went home groaning all the way. When we arrived Andrew drew me into the others' room and displayed me as if it were all a great joke. They roared. I looked at Andrew. He was still chuckling, pointing at splotches of muck on the front of my jacket. Somehow I felt demeaned by him.

There was no hot water so I had to stand cringing under a bitingly cold shower soaping and re-soaping my stricken flesh.

Then I searched frantically through my luggage. Ah yes! There they were. The extra pair of glasses I'd brought from New York!

The sun was shining in the morning. Andrew and Bud and Dvora went for a farewell walk. Andrew had promised in Hardwar to spend some time alone with me in Dharamsala. He had suggested that Bud and Dvora and Orit visit Kashmir and said he would join them later in Bangkok. I was elated at the prospect and hoped it would be an opportunity to rediscover our old easy companionship. However he changed his mind about Orit and said she could stay. I was miserably disappointed.

I started having unpleasant dreams but I tried to let it not matter. Whenever I awoke I told myself how happy I was to be in this rain-misted mountain village with Andrew. Unsurprisingly one night I dreamt I fell into a pit of slime and all day afterwards I fought the impulse to draw from that dream the darkest conclusions about myself. But Andrew, who seemed to read my mind said, "Forget it. Leave the past behind you."

"I want to but I can't," I said.

"Don't think of your story personally," he said, "think of it as human suffering, think of it in a big way. Force yourself to give it up. Do it for others, not yourself. Be an example."

I sat on my bed and regarded him sitting across from me on his bed and pondered this. He was saying wonderful things. He was urging me to rise above my petty self and become larger than life, and it kindled a feeling of exaltation and nobility in my heart. "I'll try," I said solemnly.

"You know, Luna, very few people like me exist in the world. I can destroy a person's karma," he said, referring to the ethical consequences of a person's actions endured by him through many re-incarnations until he has achieved spiritual liberation. "If you trust me, I have the power to completely destroy your past."

The buzzing in my head grew stronger. It had never really stopped. It had been vibrating there like a soft tranquillizing pulse, like blood, since it began. It was a reminder of what was possible. I stared back at Andrew as if in a trance. He looked very beautiful, very pale, his skin almost translucent. I imagined I could see the faint outline of bones in his face. He seemed more spirit than flesh.

"I'll try," I repeated.

Rebecca was spending more and more time in our company. Her resistance to our belief in Andrew as an enlightened teacher made her bristle at almost everything we said. Meals with her were positively unpleasant. I suggested to Andrew that he ask her to stay away. But he didn't. To me, she said, "I just don't believe he is what he says he is. He's too young, too inexperienced."

"Experience has nothing to do with wisdom," I said. I can't imagine where I got this idea. Probably from Andrew himself. But it appeared to hit her like a jolt of lightning. She didn't speak again for a long time. She stayed around us looking angry all day. She even had dinner with us, and finally, unexpectedly, decided to sleep over in Orit's room.

"She's falling under your spell," I told Andrew.

At eleven-thirty p.m. she knocked on the door and asked to borrow my flashlight. She looked worn out. "I couldn't sleep," she said. "I'm going back up to the center."

I imagined it was a long perilous walk alone at this hour. Thinking of the monkeys and the pitch black dark and who knew what might be haunting those hills at night, I tried to stop her.

"This late?" I said. "You're out of your mind."

"It's okay. It doesn't bother me."

I could see she was resolved to get away from us.

We spent most of the next day trekking up and down the mountains' spectacular precipitous downy green slopes. Here and there streams of water cut through miniature emerald valleys creating diminutive foaming rivers—all consequences of the interminable rain. On the way home we got caught in a long heavy downpour and arrived back at the hotel tired and soaked. Andrew found a note from Rebecca that had been slipped under the door. It said she wanted to talk to him.

"She's hooked," I said. Andrew frowned at me. He didn't seem to like the way I'd put it. But as I'd predicted, Rebecca came early the next morning looking terribly wan, to tell Andrew she was ready to commit herself to his teaching. He said she was welcome to join us the following day when we returned to Delhi and she accepted the invitation eagerly.

On my part there was a most extraordinary feeling about the future. No plans. No worry. Everything was going to be all right. I wondered vaguely whether I'd ever write again. Although writing had always been my dominant aspiration, at the same time it had been a source of anxiety and self-doubt, and at times, torture. I wondered whether I'd give it up.

After a dirty all-day rattling bus ride to New Delhi—I felt nauseated most of the way—we took a taxi through streets crawling with the poor and the wretched to the Marina Hotel. As I went up the stairs to the lobby I was achingly aware of how lucky I was to be able to afford this material succor. And, resting after a shower, lying between clean sheets on a soft bed in an air-conditioned room, I reflected that coming down from Dharamsala was descending from Tibet into India, from stability and sanity into chance, into unconsciousness, into scrabbling survival.

BRINDAVAN

Since Andrew had promised to spend some time alone with me in Dharamsala, and it hadn't happened, he now offered to take me alone to Brindavan, yet another holy city in India, for two days. We boarded the Taj Express, an air-conditioned train possessing every conceivable luxury and service. I had never seen anything to match it. You could demand whatever you wanted to eat and they would telephone the order ahead and pick it up at a coming train stop.

In Brindavan we took a taxi to the Hari Krishna Guest House. After lunch and a rest, we went on a bumpy bicycle rickshaw tour of the famous temples. Our first stop was a great hall filled with women in white saris. They were destitute widows who received protection from some local organization. Not all of them were old. Most of them looked vacant, as if their bodies were uninhabited. They sat row upon row chanting "Krishna, Rama, Krishna, Rama," etc. We were told they chanted like this eight hours every day. To me they represented the dregs of a culture that had no use for women without men.

Brindavan was a destination for religious tourists who came to worship Krishna (one of the principal Hindu gods). It was a pilgrim's city and pilgrims of every belief, of every age and color and nationality, could be seen. The streets were fantastic: flaming saris on women from Raghistan, old grizzled sanyasis with painted faces, families decked out in their finest on holiday, beggars, impish children with smears of kohl under their eyes, wandering cattle—one bull with a missing foot limping along with the rest—starving dogs,and bristly grey pigs either rummaging in the garbage that littered the streets or lying along the roadside looking as if they were smiling in their sleep.

The next morning I awoke to what sounded like howling voices coming from below. A minute went by before I realized it was the sound of chanting rising from the temple.

After breakfast, at Andrew's request, I read a few pages from my diary. I was sure it would be boring, and up until now, hadn't given it a glance. But Andrew said he found it interesting, and added, *"It might make a nice little book someday."*

We wandered around the city for the rest of the day and once again I realized how astonishing India was. The potency, the vehemence of it, was everywhere—a great ruthless flood of life—pagan, mystical, superstitious, unstoppable, and still existing, for the most part, outside the scientific mechanical industrial reach of the west.

In the evening, we took the Taj Express back to Delhi. I had spent two precious days feeling tranquil and close to Andrew.

New Delhi

During a breakfast of tea and toast back at the Marina Hotel, Andrew suddenly said, "Luna, the problem with you is that you have a strong sense of what you dislike." He buttered a slice of toast slowly as I watched, apprehensive as to what might come next. I was thinking that I also had a strong sense of what I liked and thought that should balance things out somehow.

Andrew gave me one of his old winsome smiles. "Not that your criticisms aren't usually correct," he said. "I even agree with most of them. But it's the way you cling to them, the way you identify with them." He paused. "To experience enlightenment," he went on, "it's necessary to have no opinions, none, to know nothing, and this is particularly important in your case because playing with ideas is an old habit of yours." He paused once more and then, in a melancholy tone, added, "It's too bad Luna, that you still don't get who I really am."

As we started out for British Airways to make my reservation to return to New York, he told me that Alka, who was already working at the meditation retreat in England, would meet me upon my arrival in Heathrow where I planned to stay overnight at an airport hotel. "She feels a little lonely," he said, "and she wants to hear the latest from here."

"But she'll have to travel for five hours. Five hours," I repeated, "to get from Denbury to Heathrow. It isn't worth it."

"She wants to meet you," he said. "She's anxious to see you again."

One thing was certain. I did not want Alka to meet me at Heathrow. But there was nothing I could think of saying to prevent it.

We stayed in for the rest of the day because I was coming down with a cold. Orit and Rebecca came to visit. Andrew was in a giddy mood and at some point decided to ring up Poonja. A second or two after he made contact, he handed me the phone. "He wants to speak to you," he said.

I took the receiver and began nervously, "Poonjaji, I want to thank you from the bottom of my heart—"

"Yes, yes," Poonja broke in, "I'm glad you're going home madam," he laughed, "in good health," he laughed again, "madam." I took this to mean that he thought I was going home in a radically changed psychological state, i.e., enlightened, and he was very glad of that. At this point the Belgian woman took the phone at the other end and said, "My dear Luna I want you to know that I was very very happy to meet you. Poonjaji and I talk about you and the miracle of your enlightenment all the time." I couldn't help but feel flattered, but it was all too unreal. Who were she and Poonja talking about? Some fictional creature. Not me.

Afterwards, when Orit and Rebecca had left, I told Andrew that now he had everything he'd ever wanted—a true teacher, inner freedom, and the love and respect and friendship of many others.

"I'm blessed," he agreed.

By evening my cold had developed and Andrew had discovered an infected sore on his left ankle.

At dawn we left for the airport. Andrew's infection looked bad and he had a temperature of one hundred and two degrees. But he could not be persuaded to let me go alone in a taxi at such an hour. He promised to see a doctor the minute he returned to Delhi.

I arrived in Heathrow sneezing and coughing and not having slept a wink on the plane. My ears hurt horribly from the pressure shift involved in landing. Alka met me with a big hug and we went to the Penta Hotel where we were to share a room. I immediately climbed into bed incapable of washing or even taking off my clothes, and there I remained as though drugged for most of the next twenty-four hours. I surfaced from time to time and ordered meals from room service, but once the food arrived, found I was too nauseated to eat and soon sank into a heavy drowse again, leaving Alka to finish her own meal watching television.

At eight a.m. I woke up feeling worse than when I'd arrived. My throat was raw. I could see how anxious Alka was for news from India. But even after I drank two cups of black coffee in the hope that it would keep me focussed enough to talk for a bit, I couldn't resist the dazed stupor that immediately took over again. Alka was constrained once more to watch TV until it was time for me to depart for New York. On the way to the plane I apologized for the state I was in and managed to tell her a few of the things she wanted to know.

7

NEW YORK

BACK IN NEW YORK I FELT DISORIENTED. AT TIMES my head throbbed with buzzing sensations so strong, I thought it would explode.

Nevertheless, it was a relief to be on my own again. I enjoyed just being home. I enjoyed the privacy of my apartment and the luxury of making choices unnoticed and therefore uncriticized by anybody. I enjoyed the familiarity of the streets. But suddenly I had nothing to do. I didn't feel like writing. I didn't feel like doing anything. My old friends seemed far away from me. No one, not even Joshua, seemed more than superficially interested in what had gone on in India. When I told people Andrew was now a guru they didn't seem to comprehend what that meant or if they did, it seemed to them some kind of suspect role as a teacher of Eastern gobbledygook. Of course I didn't tell anyone that Andrew said I was enlightened. That would be stretching their patience too far.

For the first time I began to consider the possibility of living life in a brand new way. I began to imagine myself at Andrew's side, as an aide-de-camp or something, helping to propagate the wisdom he had so miraculously achieved.

On August twenty-first I wrote to Bangkok and told him my life in New York seemed to be over.

On August twenty-seventh, Andrew called from Thailand to say all was well.

On September twenty-eighth Andrew called from Totnes, England to say that Manny Rivers had everything organized and meetings would begin in a few days. "I'm very busy," he said in a happy voice, "many people are waiting to see me."

On October ninth Andrew telephoned again. He sounded excited. "It's really happening!" he said, "people are coming from all over!" Then he told me he'd spoken to Christian Travers and it was possible that they might become friends. I thought that highly unlikely but I didn't say so. Last, but most important, he invited me to England for a month.

On October fourteenth he called once more. "It's all really happening," he repeated. He said he was feeling more confident than he had been in India and was conscious of an even greater inner power. "My body feels like an electric generator," he said.

On October eighteenth Andrew called and said he was on fire!

I was thrilled.

On November seventh I departed for England.

8

THE HOUSE, A FEW MILES FROM TOTNES, WAS A small but luxurious two-story, three-bedroom English stone country house. Bud and Dvora and Orit were sharing a bedroom so that I could have a room of my own. Andrew told me they had suggested it, not him. It was kind of them and I was grateful for the privacy.

From the windows of my room I could see grazing horses and sheep and miles of green rolling hills. Due to the constant wet weather the roads were so muddy, you had always to walk out in rubber boots. I found it all charming and very English.

The first evening I was amazed to see twenty people arrive. They sat on the floor of the living room on pillows and Andrew sat at the far end against the wall in an upholstered lounge chair facing them. Someone asked him what method he taught.

"I don't teach any method," he answered, "I only try to make people understand that you don't have to make any effort and there's nothing for you to practice. Practice implies a future result, and the very act of seeking this result strengthens your ego and therefore separates you from the result you are seeking, namely enlightenment." He glanced slowly around the room. "You don't have to believe in anything. The truth will come to you. It's always waiting. The important thing is an attitude of earnestness and humility and the readiness to let everything go. So stop seeking the future. The time is right now."

Everyone seemed dazzled at these words. Two of those present were Manny and his wife, Spirit.

Before going to bed, when Andrew and I were alone in the kitchen, he looked at me frowning, and said, "I feel you've come back with your old attitude of 'I know' and I don't like it."

I looked back at him flustered. Was it true? What had I said to give him that idea? I tried to think back. I was sure I hadn't said anything.

"I'm sorry," I said.

The following evening Andrew requested that people not ask questions but instead sit in silence and move as little as possible for the entire meeting or *satsang*, as it was called. The satsang lasted for about one-and-a-half hours and when it was over I sensed that everyone had been deeply moved, although not a syllable had been uttered. After they left I asked Andrew what had been going on.

"People are being enlightened," he said.

"Just sitting there?" I asked.

"Yes, Luna, just sitting there, as you put it, in my presence."

"Do you see them privately at all?" I asked, dumbfounded by the possibility that people could be enlightened merely by sitting in the same room as Andrew.

"Sometimes," Andrew said. Then he gave me an exultant smile. "Tell me the truth," he said, "did you ever in your life hear of anything like this happening before?"

"No, I haven't," I said, mortified that I'd been feeling bored while mysterious metamorphoses had been taking place around me.

On the way back from a walk in the soft, delicate, misty Devon moors, we were forced to stop the car—an old wreck someone had given Andrew—because part of a flock of sheep was on the road. The rest were billowing out in all directions. The sheep were being herded by two big rust-colored dogs who raced frenziedly

THE MOTHER OF GOD

back and forth trying to get them off the road and at the same time keep them in some sort of order. I found the intensity of the dogs and their concern to do their duty poignant and stirring. And that night, although I didn't enjoy the repeated silent sitting with Andrew, and hadn't enjoyed it the night before either, I understood that like those dogs, he was trying to keep me from billowing out in all directions; he was trying to guide me toward some sort of order. And I wished that in all my unconscious and semi-conscious and indeed, conscious little ways, I could stop resisting and allow him to do what he no doubt regarded as *his* duty.

I got up the next morning after a wretched dream of being chased by a huge slavering German shepherd dog. Below, in the living room. I found Dvora and Orit sitting on the floor in front of the coffee table having tea and cookies. I poured myself a cup of tea and asked, in a irritated tone, how they were feeling. Before they could answer, I said, "I feel rotten!" and took a gulp from my cup and sat down. "How can you surrender to someone you can't be sure is always right?" I asked them. They were used to questions that seemed to erupt out of nowhere and I knew they wouldn't be taken aback by the suddenness of this particular question. In one form or another it was *the* question for all of us.

Orit smiled and took another cookie from the plastic container on the table and said, "The point is, Lunaji, the real issue, is to be able to surrender to someone who *isn't* necessarily always right. The point is to surrender." She popped the cookie into her mouth.

I must have made a face, because both Israeli girls watched me with amused expressions, indicating how familiar they were with the conflict I was experiencing. I drank some more tea and ate a couple of cookies and considered what Orit had just said. I didn't like it. At the first opportunity, I repeated the identical question to Andrew. "How can you surrender to someone you can't possibly be sure is always right?"

Andrew was sitting on the widow-seat in my room smoking and teasing the landlord's parrot who stood on the sill outside pecking at the lock and trying to get in. Without looking around at me Andrew asked, "When as a teacher did you ever think I was wrong?"

"You say people are getting enlightened during those long silent sessions. But asking them not to move is something you told me you disapproved of."

Andrew rattled the window against the parrot who made a raucous outcry and pounded on the glass with his beak. "It's usually okay to move," he said. He rattled the window again and the parrot squawked and flew off. "I was only attempting to emphasize the importance of stillness," he said, turning around at last to face me.

He hadn't answered the question I'd asked and I wanted to say more. But in addition to the nervousness I always felt when I expressed some reservation about his teaching, I sensed an indifference to my criticism and that silenced me.

But at dinner Andrew looked up from his food and straight at me and without a preamble or explanation to the others, said, "What goes on here has nothing to do with democracy, it has to do with surrender!"

Andrew, Alka and I drove to Torquay in the rain to do some shopping. (Alka took the wheel. Andrew had never learned how to drive.) I had asked Andrew if I could join them saying I'd always wanted to see Torquay because it turned up in a lot of English murder mysteries I'd read. Andrew accepted this as a reasonable wish on my part and had agreed, though rather grudgingly. Alka's wooden demeanor during our outing gave evidence in no uncertain terms that she resented my presence. I didn't blame her. She wanted to be alone with him on the rare day he took off from seeing people.

No one else would have dared to ask to go, but I felt driven to insist on my rights as Andrew's mother in order to assuage my growing anxiety about being discarded. It was a dangerous game; it was playing the edge with Andrew.

The next evening, as we were finishing our dessert he said something I thought pretty peculiar to say in front of all of us. He said, "The relationship that exists between Alka and myself is exquisite." *Exquisite*. The adjective was startling. It sounded so showy. What was he telling us? Me?

My unpleasant feelings about Alka had persisted. She was silent a good deal of the time, purposefully moving about the house, cleaning, dusting, tending the plants, re-arranging things, and doing everything perfectly, as was her way. But sometimes her large patrolling eyes caught mine and then blinked away, leaving me with a sense of having been obscurely assaulted.

Hordes of people, as many as seventy or eighty were beginning to arrive on weekends. Some claimed they'd been enlightened by Andrew after only one or two evenings with him. One psychotherapist defined his experience of enlightenment by stating, "I feel that nothing in my life ever really happened, and that includes all my experiences of fear, of low self-esteem, even of love. It all seems like a dream now, unreal." After this he sat back gazing worshipfully at Andrew.

"The past is like looking continuously into a mirror," Andrew said to the psychotherapist. "You've thrown the mirror away." Andrew was explaining to the man that once you cut yourself off from your past you were an enlightened man, or at least you were on your way.

One woman described her non-enlightened state as one of waiting, always waiting, for a happiness that never came.

"Waiting," Andrew said, "is the avoidance of life. Waiting is the future. Life is the present." And, of course, according to Andrew, the singular path that led to living in the present was through surrender to him!

All at once Bud broke into a sort of mad laughter, and in the next second Dvora joined in. It was the same hysterical hilarity that had struck Orit in Hardwar. Everyone turned to stare at them. They were trembling all over and took long frightening gasping breaths between outbursts. Like the last time, Andrew seemed unconcerned. "This morning," he said, "Bud and I had a long talk about letting go." Everyone laughed. "Nights are not usually like this," he added, to more laughter.

Bud and Dvora went on giggling and shaking uncontrollably. Someone said, "If I hadn't been here before, I would think you were all nuts."

"We are," Andrew said.

Later, I complained to Andrew, "Everyone is having experiences except me. Tell me again what not knowing means."

"It means having no opinions and not worrying and leaving everything up to me," he said.

"I have to hear these things over and over again," I said tearfully. "All I seem to do is flounder about here scared to death."

Andrew looked me in the eye. "Good," he said, "then die!"

I woke up in a mood of miserable discontent and at lunch suddenly heard myself address Andrew as 'master' in a sarcastic tone. It simply sprang from my tongue, like a snake, unplanned, unstoppable—a black flash from the unconscious. For a moment I stood revealed as the enemy. Andrew's pained expression made it clear that he felt much more than displeased.

When satsang was over I told Orit in the kitchen how ill-at-ease and moronic I felt, that I didn't know what I was doing from one minute to the next. She said she felt the same way, that her brains had been scrambled for days. "We are uncomfortable because we have such a strong habit of knowing," she said, and gave me a hug.

Bud and Dvora joined us. They admitted they'd been feeling weird and awkward too. Orit said she thought a deepening and refining process was going on inside us all.

"Do you think Andrew is doing this?" Dvora asked. We looked at each other curiously, in awe at the possibility.

It's conceivable," Bud said.

Then we wandered into the living room where a film on reincarnation was showing on the video. When it was over Andrew asked me to guess what I thought our relationship had been in a former life. I shrugged my shoulders. "We definitely knew each other," he said. "Maybe we were the same person."

I didn't believe in reincarnation but my heart leapt at the thought that such an idea had occurred to him. "No," I joked, "not the same person, but twins, maybe."

I had written Poonja a note expressing my gratitude for what had happened to Andrew. This morning I received an answer.

Delhi 11-11-86
Sri Luna Mata Jee,
    My excitement and joy stood in my way to read your letter at one reading. My eyes welled into ocean drops to see your words one after the other.
    O Divine effulgence, the Mother of the universe, to give Birth to the Enlightened One, I send you my Love, Blessings, and gratitude on behalf of my own Self and all Seekers after Truth.
    You were a born Sidha, on the very first glance in a Delhi hotel I could smell that something was to happen through your own Self. It is a miracle converted into a stable reality. I am sure your presence will help all those who go to your close proximity knowing or unknowing. I congratulate you holy Ma! Hip Hip Hurrah. Enjoy the Life as it happens. You are a FREE MAN. Doubt NOT.
    I have read a letter just now, who invited me to go to NY on Jan 87 and also I have an invitation from Hawaii and Darwin and Buenos Aires and Rio-de-Janeiro, Roma and Paris.
    I have local commitments and therefore I cannot leave India. I leave for Hardwar 18-11-86.
    Your own Self.

H W L Poonja

Divine effulgence? Mother of the universe? My head reeled with these flaming grandiose phrases that were supposed to apply to me!

"Is he crazy?" I asked Andrew.

He laughed. "Yes," he said.

I didn't feel complimented or honored by the letter because Poonja had assumed all sorts of goofy things about me that were simply not true. Moreover, referring to me as 'a free man' seemed comical and was probably a tad of unconscious chauvinism.

During a rare walk with Bud one late afternoon, he remarked out of the blue, that Alka was the only person in the house he felt uneasy with. At the next opportunity I asked Andrew to come to my room and told him about Bud's remark. "Whenever I'm alone with her I feel uneasy too." I said. There's something about her silence that feels really hostile."

Andrew didn't say anything.

"For some reason she keeps herself separate from the rest of us," I went on. All at once I remembered the night in Rishikesh again, when Andrew had laid down the law to Alka. "And she acts like your slave," I blurted out. She doesn't feel she has a right to object to anything any more, to differ with you in any way!"

"You're misjudging the situation," Andrew answered calmly, and after a long interval, he said in a sad tone, "She would be devastated if she knew what you thought."

He was protecting her again. At that moment I divined that from then on he would always protect her, and when, a few moments later, he got up to leave and said defensively, "You don't understand Luna, it's just that Alka is very unusual, in some ways she's unique," I was afraid I'd said too much. In fact after the door closed behind him, I was so nervous about it that I ran out of my room and caught up with him in the foyer.

"I'll try harder with Alka," I said.

Andrew gave me a smile that succeeded in washing away a bit of my fear. "And I'll think about what you said," he replied.

That evening at satsang Andrew said, "Any view, any opinion, is egotism. We have to give up the idea that anything is not the way it should be, that the world feels wrong. We must accept it all. Acceptance means we're no longer demanding that anything be any particular way."

I was sure that what he said was the result of our exchange in the afternoon.

Anyway Andrew was always talking about giving things up. It wasn't news to me that sooner or later, if I remained with him, I'd have to take a giant step and give up every last one of my ideas, which meant giving up all of my past. And the bottom line was—I knew it in every cell of my body by now—the bottom line was, I'd have to give him up as my son.

A few days later he came to my room again and sat down on the window seat and lit a cigarette and said, "I disagree with you about Alka. I've considered everything you said carefully and I've come to the conclusion that you are wrong. You are misreading her behavior." He took a long drag on his cigarette and craned around to stare out the window for a minute. Then he turned back to me. "I've talked to Bud," he said. "I've explained things to Bud."

"What did you say?" I asked.

"Bud changed his mind. He understands now."

I began to feel tense.

"Isn't it sufficient for you that I'm happy with Alka?" Andrew asked. "If you love me, that should be enough for you."

Now he was making a son's appeal to his mother. But he wouldn't let me be his mother. And I don't know what came over me. I exploded. "Alka hasn't changed at all!" I cried. "You think she's changed? She hasn't! There's the same old withholding, the same old expression on her face that makes me feel rebuffed whenever I look at her!" I was appalled at what I was saying but I couldn't stop. "She hasn't got one close friend here. Nobody knows her!"

He was quiet for a few moments, then, referring to our last talk, as if to mollify me, he said, "Do you think I wouldn't notice if she was my slave? If she was, she'd bore me."

I sat on my bed, fearful, exhausted by my tirade, looking at him. Maybe I was wrong. After all, what did I know of myself?

What do any of us know of ourselves? Maybe I was wrong about the whole affair.

Andrew lit another cigarette and leaned forward towards me and said slowly—and I don't know why he chose this moment to say it—an attempt at further appeasement?—he said, "I'm going to tell you something that I've told no one but Poonjaji," he paused to take a puff, and then, "You know Luna sometimes I feel like a god." He stared at me. "*Your son is dead,*" he said.

I heard this in a sort of chill.

"Do you see him anymore?" he asked.

I hesitated, confused for a moment. "No," I said, "only in little things sometimes." I could feel my lips quivering.

"But don't you realize you are with me more now than you were before? And that you're welcome to come wherever I am forever?"

"It doesn't feel that way to me," I said, beginning to cry. "I'm glad he's dead," Andrew said.

Orit and I had a luxurious tea (scones and strawberry jam and clotted cream) in the village of Totnes. She told me I was beautiful, that an enormous change had come over me. When I got home I ran up to my room and looked in the mirror. I saw a few new lines around my eyes. But I didn't see any other change. I saw myself growing older, that's all.

Some Rajneesh devotees began coming to satsang. Rajneesh, a notorious Indian guru, had operated with colossal popular and financial success in Antelope, Oregon, until it was discovered that he'd been involved in illegal activities regarding drugs and arms. He was subsequently expelled from the U.S. and died shortly afterwards in India. One woman who'd been a follower of Rajneesh told Andrew, almost in tears, that although her pain was less now, the disillusionment she still felt burned like acid inside her.

"Before I met Poonjaji," Andrew responded, "I'd had three teachers all of whom I felt had betrayed me. But after I met Poonjaji I realized I couldn't really blame them. Actually, I'd gotten a lot from all three. A tremendous amount of learning. We get hurt because we hang around our teachers too long even though our hearts tell us otherwise. We don't take enough responsibility and leave." Our hearts? Surely he meant our rational minds!

Ironically, this was a warning from Andrew's own lips that I should have taken seriously. But at the time I was incapable of 'hearing' it.

Christian Travers, who lived in Totnes, had been invited to dinner and satsang by Andrew. One evening he materialized at the back door, saw me in the kitchen, came over and embraced me and kissed me on the cheek. Why this display of affection? I was sure he didn't like me. Perhaps it was a sign of nervousness at coming face-to-face with his erstwhile adversary.

During satsang a lively exchange occurred between Andrew and Travers, the latter taking a patronizing tone, his eyes continuously darting about, seeking confirmation from the others. The subject of discussion was the role of memory. It went on for about twenty minutes and concluded with:

Andrew: "The interest in the past, once one is aware of the unknown, no longer serves any purpose. A preoccupation with the *other* takes over."

Travers: "So it's the relationship to memory that changes, not that memory dies."

Andrew: "Yes, but the past is no longer constantly there. Rapture and delight in the present take over. It's like being in love. Always in love with the *other*."

I wasn't sure that I could follow the debate completely, but I was impressed at how courageous Andrew appeared in this verbal duel with a man he had revered and probably had feared as well. Despite some tension showing in his voice, he'd spoken eloquently, and with confidence, and had held his ground. I remembered that not long ago Andrew had said that Christian Travers was his last hurdle, so afterwards, when Andrew was sitting with us in front of the fire looking more peaceful than usual, I said, half in jest, "You seem to be completely relaxed tonight. Is it because your last obstacle, Christian Travers, has been overcome?"

Andrew gave me one of his recently inscrutable smiles. I imagined he was granting me credit for being accurate.

"Don't be silly," Dvora burst out, "that's not true!"

"You don't think he's more relaxed?" I asked, baffled at her reaction.

"No," Dvora said. She gave me a hard look. "Andrew can't be affected by Travers, he can't be affected by anyone. Andrew is always the same!" She was sitting at Andrew's feet. She lifted her head and gave him an adoring smile, but Andrew, remarking about something to Alka, didn't notice.

When I had a moment alone with him I said, "Don't you think Dvora is becoming a bit arrogant?"

"She does have that tendency," Andrew agreed, "but it's under control now. She's an incredible girl, don't you think? She's really brilliant."

"She's still in love with you," I said.

"No, no, I told you that ended long ago," he said."

"Did you see the look she gave you before?" I asked.

"No. What look? Anyway you're probably reading things into it."

In describing Dvora as arrogant I wasn't being precise enough. I should have added fanatic, but I knew Andrew didn't regard an excess of ardor on the part of his followers as anything to be criticized unless, of course, they began to behave like raving maniacs. When one did, from time to time, he or she became an embarrassment and he asked them to leave.

While everyone else watched a movie until the wee hours I went up to my room and read *Chasm of Fire* by Irina Tweedie. It was the story of a woman who had spent years in India being reviled and degraded by a Sufi master, an Islamic mystic, until she was enlightened. It turned my stomach. Would I ever sink to that level? I looked up from the page and stared at the wall. How could humiliating a person be the path to enlightenment? It went against your nervous system, your very nature.

The next day we watched five movies. Andrew frequently had a yen to do nothing but watch movies, one after the other, on his rest day. To tell the truth, it was fun giving into the extravagance of it all. The greatest charm of living with Andrew and his group was that there was no schedule for anything except meals and satsang hours. Spontaneity was the rule.

The last movie we watched was French, with subtitles. I can't remember the name. Dvora had chosen it and had called it a masterpiece. After it was over people ventured their opinions. The first few said they enjoyed it. I said I felt the film was pretentious. When Andrew immediately agreed with me, Dvora was so offended, that her face turned crimson. She closed her eyes and sat motionless, a stance that I interpreted as a reproach to our insensitivity to what she considered art.

The room suddenly hushed. Andrew was sitting near the open door puffing on a cigarette and blowing the smoke outside. After a couple of minutes he looked over at Dvora and exclaimed, "Dvora!" She kept her eyes shut and didn't answer. We all stared at her, aghast. Andrew threw away his cigarette and repeated her name two more times. Finally she opened her eyes. He leaned forward in his chair. "Dvora, you are egotistical and defensive," he said in a low threatening tone. "I want you to know that I can't have people acting like that around me." After a few moments of deathly silence Dvora bowed her head and broke out into loud terrified sobs.

It's true that one persons's anger can poison a whole roomful of people, and I thought Dvora deserved some criticism, but Andrew's public castigation of her and the distinct underlying warning that if she didn't shape up she'd be shipped out, made me shiver.

The next morning after breakfast, Andrew called me to his room and got down on his knees. "You were right about Dvora's arrogance," he said, "I promise, I'll never distrust your judgement about people again." It was done facetiously, but I was very pleased at his acknowledgement that at least one of my opinions deserved respect. Nonetheless, as I looked down at him kneeling at my feet and grinning, I wanted to say, but what about your arrogance, my son?

Needless to say, I didn't utter a word.

As Christmas approached, Andrew and Alka decided to marry right away. They said it was because of the constant visa problems with Alka's Indian passport. By then I didn't have much feeling about it one way or the other. I had already concluded that their marriage was in the cards whether I liked it or not. They settled on New Year's eve for the date of the wedding, even though they knew I wouldn't be present because I was due in Taiwan on December twenty-fifth for Joshua's wedding. Joshua had elected to get married in Taipei where he had a lot of friends—he'd been in business there for a number of years—and where the celebrations would be more exotic than at home and, according to him, a lot more fun.

Before Andrew resolved so suddenly to marry right away, he had been planning to go to Joshua's wedding. Then he changed his mind. Joshua was very hurt by this. Andrew actually suggested that I not go to Taipei but stay in Totnes for his wedding instead. Not that he made too much of it, but it revealed to me that the old competition with his brother was still alive and still showing its effects. He seemed totally unconscious of what was motivating this shabby behavior.

Of course I refused to stay.

On the thundery evening before my departure, after satsang, Andrew told our group the story of his death. We were all grouped around the hearth eating a chocolate cake someone had donated and drinking Italian coffee, one of Andrew's addictions. In the future, people would frequently bring him gifts of coffee, either imported from

Italy or brought directly by the Italians who became his disciples.

Andrew was stretched out on the floor leaning on his elbow and gazing at the crackling fire. "After two-and-a-half weeks with Poonjaji," he began, "I would experience, on and off during the day, the presence of something Other. I knew for sure there was something in my hotel room with me. At the same time I was experiencing these explosions in my body. Both were part of the same thing, a tremendous energy I can only think of as love. I was being consumed by this Otherness and imagined that if it went on long enough, there'd be nothing of me left. But simultaneously, something was opening up, something infinite and vast, with no past in it. One day I realized that all my fears and my sense of unworthiness were gone and in their place had come an awareness of this Otherness that was now present all the time. My entire relationship with time had changed. I felt removed from it and yet at the center of it more than before."

Andrew sat up and reached for his cup of coffee, "That was my experience of death," he concluded.

Everyone sat spellbound, their eyes glued to his face on which the rosy flames of the fire were reflected. No one spoke for some time.

Orit accompanied me to London. Out of curiosity we were going to look up Irina Tweedie, the author of *Chasm of Fire*. I was on my way to Taiwan for Joshua's wedding. During the bus ride Orit astonished me by saying that she and Dvora and Bud all felt that Andrew had no right to speak to me as disrespectfully as he did.

I received this information as if it were a live grenade. I couldn't afford to consider it for more than a second. It was the truth I couldn't face and it threatened to blow everything to pieces.

"It doesn't mean what it sounds like," I responded quickly. "Andrew doesn't intend to be disrespectful." Orit looked dubious and I added, lamely, "We're used to having an egalitarian relationship."

Orit didn't pursue the subject. That night, in bed, I lay in bed twisting and turning and feeling very apprehensive. My breath seemed unnaturally shallow. There was a bitter taste in my mouth. Alone, separated from Orit by the dark, I was haunted by what she had said.

In the morning I wrote a long letter to Andrew hinting at some of my uncertainties.

9

A S THE PLANE DRIFTED OVER THE ALPS, BARE lunar peaks passed slowly under me. Not far down I could discern a number of villages nestled in the crooks of hills from where lilliputian streaks of smoke were rising. They looked cozy amidst all the wild white splendor. I used to think I'd like to live in the north country of Canada, but now this glimpse of that old dream seemed insubstantial. I was not attracted to it as I once had been.

In spite of my reservations about Andrew's behavior and teaching techniques, a part of me had gotten hooked to the same conviction he had, that perfect, permanent happiness was possible in this life. And I was convinced that I'd been given a golden opportunity through the special access I had to my own son who had become a guide to the illumination I sought. There was no question but that for the moment, I thought my life had meaning at his side and nowhere else.

In Taipei I experienced a kind of holiday, a happy diversion from my often painful obsession with Andrew.

Joshua and his wife Pat had surrendered completely to the arrangements of their Chinese friends for a traditional Chinese wedding. Pat looked beautiful in the various ceremonial and ball gowns she was required to wear. Joshua looked handsome and dig-nified in his own outfits and appeared very pleased at the goings-on. Everyone was Chinese except for a six foot seven blond American who was an old Taipei friend of Joshua's, my brother and his wife, and an old school chum of mine. I had never encountered a more amiable, congenial, generous group than those Chinese people from Taipei.

I stopped in Bangkok on the way back to New York and on New Year's Eve I telephoned Andrew. He and Alka were already married and were preparing to go to their wedding party.

Andrew said, "It's clear from your last letter that you still think I have it in for you." From his voice I gathered that he was disturbed by the idea. After what Orit had said in the bus going to London, the idea certainly disturbed me.

"It isn't true," Andrew said. "You must stop thinking it's true. You still don't trust me enough."

Would he still insist I was enlightened? Or had he developed some rationalization for why I was behaving in a manner he considered so recalcitrant? In any case I wasn't going to query him about that on his wedding day.

The last leg of this journey around the world took me to California where I stopped to see a friend. On the plane to New York I sat staring down at the low rosy chunky expanse of the Rocky Mountains. The snow lacing their peaks glittered like drifts of diamonds in the afternoon sun. The world was beautiful, I thought. We shit on it.

10

I ARRIVED IN AMSTERDAM AT THE BEGINNING OF May to find that in the flat Andrew's group had rented, I had a room to myself again and was very thankful for it. Satsang was held in a disciple's (a Dutch harpsichordist) studio. Once more I saw faces of worship, of wonder, of awe, all turned towards Andrew. There were at least three times as many people as I'd seen in Devon. And for the first time I saw Andrew's chair banked on either side by vases of flowers—offerings from his followers.

The next day, alone with Andrew in the living room, I asked him if during the last twenty-four hours he'd noticed whether I was more humble now than when he'd last seen me. Without bothering to answer, he shouted, "Satsang is beginning!" To my horror he was summoning Dvora and Bud and Alka to witness something humiliating to me. I was sure of it, and I waited, quaking in my boots. He would hardly yell for people to come immediately so he could pay me some sort of tribute. He wasn't in the habit of praising me in front of others.

When they arrived and had sat down he looked at me for a long instant. His face had turned hard. "Either you give way to me or our relationship cannot continue!" he said slowly, enunciating each syllable with uncharacteristic precision.

I hadn't expected anything as conclusive as this. I was shocked, and felt a sick sensation start up in my stomach.

"You have never surrendered," he said. "You're frightened of me."

I lowered my head.

"It's your ego that's afraid!"

My ego? Whatever it was, I had no control over it. "I'm still scared of losing my place with you," I muttered, back to the old familiar misery of it all.

Orit was my favorite person amongst Andrew's disciples. She'd been one of Andrew's sturdiest and most intelligent supporters. I was therefore shocked to hear that she'd fallen away from him and hadn't wanted to come to Amsterdam. I was told that Andrew was so upset by her defection that he'd telephoned Jerusalem and had entreated her to make the trip so that they could talk and clear up her 'confusion.' She had agreed to come.

The first chance I got I called her up and invited her to dinner. Sitting opposite her in a vegetarian restaurant, I asked, "What happened?"

"I don't know," she said. She seemed despondent.

"Did something happen?"

"No. Nothing happened."

"But something must have happened."

"No." She took a sip of apple juice. " I don't know. I can't explain it." She looked away from me at the crowded restaurant. "This is a really nice place," she said.

She looked back at me. "It's good to see you again Lunaji. I missed you." The food arrived.

Either Orit had nothing further to say about the matter or she was hiding something because she pointedly changed the subject as we began to eat and related in detail her plans to organize a yoga center in her apartment in Jerusalem.

Her disaffection unsettled me, the more so since it appeared to have sprung from nowhere. There'd never been a hint of the slightest uncertainty on her part. How did such things happen? I was bewildered and found myself regarding her as if she'd been struck by some mysterious mental illness.

When we said good-bye she seemed relieved at the parting.

The next morning Andrew informed me curtly that he'd organized a regimen for me:

1) I was to remain in silence and talk only to him.

2) I was to cook one meal a day.

3) I was to do two hours of meditation every morning.

4) I was to spend the rest of my time with the home group. In silence.

I agreed to do whatever he commanded.

But it was hard. In silence, the sharpness, the glisten and glitter of sensation got dull, instead of the reverse, as you might think. The person you thought you were seemed to die. (It didn't of course, otherwise you'd be enlightened rather than bored and somewhat depressed.) So what was left? Space. Dead space. I felt druggedly sleepy most of the time.

During all the retreats I'd gone to, it had never been difficult for me to keep silent. There had been relief in cutting down your contact with others and dropping the burden of being 'someone.' But I would often end up feeling as if I wasn't wholly animate, as if only my skin and muscles jittered with life but that deeper, along my nerves, particles of dissolution were settling. It was scary.

Andrew told me the feeling of deadness was fear. He said the deadness was his life before he met Poonja. "Reality is like a black sea overlaid by a dark blue filter," he said. "The filter is the sense of limitation, of pain, of fear etc. The black sea is the void (real reality)." He gave me a wry smile. "I still can't believe the extent of your resistance."

"I don't understand it either," I said, and added in a challenging tone, "Maybe I'm incapable of being free."

Andrew frowned. But he seemed pleased with me nonetheless. "Your first day of silence has been really fruitful," he assured me.

I went to practice yoga in the room Dvora and Bud shared and noticed a book on the floor under the window titled *Up from Eden* by Ken Wilbur. I opened it and found the author saying that we were not isolated beings, as we seemed to experience ourselves, but an integral part of the ALL. Our sense of separateness was an illusion that required all our energy to maintain. For a moment I was profoundly stilled, as if I'd never heard of this idea although I'd heard it a thousand times before.

Andrew regarded me as an intellectual mesmerized by 'concepts' that cut me off from my true Self. My mind was my enemy, he claimed. I didn't disagree. But when, after my yoga practice, I mentioned to him that I'd glanced at *Up from Eden* and he told me not to read further in the book because it was intellectually stimulating, I felt instantly mutinous, became terribly agitated while cooking lunch, and bitterly resentful at the responsibility he'd thrust upon on me to prepare a full meal every day.

Late at night Manny Rivers turned up from Totnes. He spent a long time in a corner with Andrew apologizing for some misdemeanor or other—I couldn't hear exactly what he said—and then he produced a bottle of champagne and boxes of English biscuits and chocolates and a brick of halvah as offerings to his guru.

I woke up the next morning with a sense of doom and went for a fast walk. After about an hour I stopped and ordered a portion of pickled herring from a street vendor and stood in the cold eating it. When I was through I realized suddenly I was totally happy. For no reason. I ran all the way home to tell Andrew about this strange phenomenon!

But as I came through the door, before I could say a word, Andrew told me he'd just talked to Manny. "He can help you more than I can," he said. "Manny is ready right now to have a session with you." At that moment Manny appeared and I followed him to my room. I lay down as directed on my mattress on the floor and he sat beside me.

He started by asking lots of questions about my past. While I was answering he put his hand on my solar plexus where I'd indicated I felt the psychic pain and asked me to breathe deeply and gently. When I was finished talking he said, "To accept Andrew as he now is, seems to mean to you that you'll lose your past relationship to him. You think you'll lose his love. How does that make you feel?"

I burst into tears. "I've been cast aside," I cried, all at once back at the beginning again with Andrew. "I feel like garbage," I sobbed. Then, after a couple of minutes I added what was the echo of a thought I'd expressed to Andrew yesterday, "Maybe I feel I don't deserve to be free?"

"You have a 'holding pattern,'" Manny said, "and it consists of a fixed idea that you must bear your suffering passively in the vain hope that ultimately someone will notice it and help you. You're afraid that to speak out in anger is to annihilate the last hope for love."

Manny was saying the obvious. I'd heard it all before. The fact was, the fear of losing Andrew's love was no fantasy. It was real. Although he encouraged you to speak your mind fearlessly, when you did, if there was even the slightest hint of defiance or anger in it, you were made to feel like a pariah. It was the same double bind my mother's contradictory messages conveyed to me when I was an adolescent: be fearless in the world and at the same time walk on the tippiest-toe because of possible repercussions. It used to paralyze me.

Later that week Andrew and Alka and I were invited to a meal at the apartment of a group of devotees. We were served a perfectly prepared beautifully presented vegetarian dinner. I sat observing the circle of shining adoring faces and was forced once more to recognize the enormity of Andrew's power over these people. I could swear that most, if put to the test, would lay down their lives for him! And I found myself considering again Andrew's invitation to them to give up everything and capitulate to him without compromise, in other words, to fall utterly madly in love with him. Then, their equilibrium, their peace of mind, even their sanity at stake, perpetually on guard lest they displease their guru-lover, they had to contain themselves until the day came when the ego was struck dead by enlightenment and they would emerge from their imprisoning chrysalis of ignorance into the void of perfect knowledge.

Did I believe this was possible? I hoped it was possible. I didn't disbelieve it.

Every follower of every guru has some kind of fantasy of what enlightenment will be like. This fantasy is usually based on how the guru appears to her or him. According to tradition the guru is the embodiment of the enlightened state. The guru is enlightenment. He is the example, the guide, and the reference point for every aspect of your behavior. That is why his authority over you is absolute. You carefully scrutinize his words, his gestures, his facial expressions for hints of the cosmic wisdom that is his and his alone. There is nothing he does that is not pregnant with meaning for you. He is the perfection you so vainly seek.

In the case of my fantasy of enlightenment, I took Andrew as a magic mirror in which I saw enlightenment reflected as supreme confidence. I saw flesh that had an ethereal inexplicable glow. And I imagined myself feeling like that and looking like that, and everything I'd ever wanted in the world—respect for my work, a great love, fame, fortune—fizzled away beside it. It seemed to me that Andrew's state transcended the best the world had to offer. He seemed totally at ease with himself, fully present at all times. He didn't worry about anything. He didn't want anything, he was the flow of life itself, at the heart of creation, not outside it, not separated from it, as all of us felt we were. I was convinced that he was that impossible phenomenon, that impossible dream—a completely happy human being.

The interesting thing was, I never imagined myself doing anything in particular in the enlightened state because doing anything seemed silly and beside the point. It wasn't a question of doing. It was a question of being. If I were listening to music, I would become the music. If I watched a bird in flight I would become the bird. There would be no separation between me and my experience.

And I imagined myself being full of a tremendous sweetness and richness and accepting everything that came along. It wouldn't matter what I did.

I didn't think of Andrew's character flaws. I didn't think of his cruelty, his insensitivity to another's pain, his arrogance, his anger. My fantasy of enlightenment screened all that out.

However there were moments when I was compelled to face Andrew's failings, and at those times my doubts about the possibility of enlightenment would rise to the surface like the debris of a shipwreck from the ocean floor, and I would be left floating helplessly in a rough sea with no land in sight.

One night after satsang Andrew invited me to join him alone for a drink at the American hotel. To be chosen by him in this fashion was thrilling. It was the aspiration of every disciple. I wondered why I'd been favored that night.

We both ordered steins of beer and then he asked what had been going on inside me for the last few days.

"My mind is willing," I said, "but my nervous system resists." I wasn't sure this was a completely honest answer.

"Eventually it won't," Andrew said reassuringly.

"But the ability to live in the present without reference to the past or the future must come through some deep inner change I've not even begun to experience," I said.

"You will," Andrew said with the utmost certainty, "you will."

I took his word for it.

In the living-room at home I sat listening to the others talking about the fact that people were being swept away by Andrew, that things had accelerated. Bud said it was like being pushed by a high-speed express. Then Andrew said something incredible. "Tonight, during satsang," he said, "my personal desires died." We all stared at him in wonder at this extraordinary confession. "You know, it's interesting," he went on, "Poonjaji said he'd seen eyes like mine only twice before, Ramana's and his own." Then, after a long pregnant pause, he laughed and clapped his hands. "Okay so it's going to happen. Something big. Let's go for it!"

My heart was pounding. Was Andrew the incarnation of the Buddha as some had suggested? Of Jesus Christ? Of Mohammed? What did it all mean?

I went to sleep in a state of excitement. How ridiculous and small-minded it had been for me to mourn the loss of a son when a master of freedom was to be gained!

Andrew accompanied me to the airport train. He balanced my suitcase on his head and ran ahead of me up the stairs to the tracks like a young gazelle. Then, when the train arrived, he hugged me and said good-bye so lovingly that I wondered—had I somehow passed muster at last?

11

O NE MONTH AFTER LEAVING AMSTERDAM I WAS sitting in an El Al plane on its descent into Ben Gurion airport. I gazed down at the dun-colored land I remembered from previous voyages here and was suffused by a feeling of love for this ancient biblical place. It had a resonance of history that to me was as alluring as if it were the landscape of a fairy-tale.

Orit had invited Andrew to come to Jerusalem to present his teaching, and he, in turn, as a great favor to them, had asked six of his British disciples to join him. Considering Orit's extreme state of doubt, I was surprised at her invitation, but didn't find out until three years later, that she had invited Andrew because she wanted to be absolutely sure about him, absolutely sure that she no longer trusted him!

Andrew, looking marvelous, in full bloom, embraced me warmly when I arrived at Orit's apartment. Andrew, Alka and I were going to live here, the disciples were to occupy a rented place next door.

Orit's apartment, though run-down, consisted of three bedrooms, two bathrooms, a kitchen, and an enormous living-room—the latter to be used as the satsang 'hall'—with a glassed-in balcony leading off it at the far end. Although I could have slept in the third bedroom, Andrew, overriding my objections, insisted that I share a room with Orit.

From now on he would prevent me, whenever possible, from having a room of my own. He seemed to think a room of one's own allowed an autonomy that was antagonistic to surrender.

At dusk I went shopping for food outside the Damascus Gate with an Israeli doctor, a friend of Orit's, and felt the same tingle of exhilaration I'd felt the first time I'd been there. The atmosphere still seemed charged and a little dangerous. The doctor obliged me by stopping on the way home to visit the Wailing Wall and we watched people praying for a few minutes. I was startled to hear a woman actually crying out aloud to God in a cracking heart-rending voice.

That night about twenty Israelis arrived. I found them challenging, curious, and tremendously intense. By the time I left a month later, more than a hundred people were crowding into Orit's living room and we had to borrow chairs and pillows from Orit's neighbors for the glassed-in veranda.

The next day, while having lunch at home with the others, Andrew informed me bluntly that since I was so full of opinions and nothing but opinions, I was absolutely forbidden to express an opinion about anything or anyone except myself for the duration of my stay here.

I felt squelched. I felt insulted, but not quite as insulted by being told to shut up as I once had been. I was getting used to it.

Andrew had honed to a fine point this ability to inflict what I can only call insult as transforming—stripping you down in public. I'd seen him do it countless times, not only to myself, but to everyone. In the fraction of a second you'd turn into a two-year old infant, terrified of your rage against the all-powerful parent essential to your survival. Andrew said these impulses on his part came from the *other* and that he, personally, wasn't responsible! The disciples continued to rationalize these impulses by calling them 'skillful means,' not to be fully understood by them but meant solely for their spiritual growth.

There'd been times after such insults, when, to escape from the awful tension of holding back my anger, I used to imagine myself leaping up from my pillow in the satsang hall and screaming out in front of everyone that I was through, I was leaving, and then stamping out, slamming the door behind me. I liked to invoke this scene of retaliation. It filled me with a perverse vitality; it filled me with a kind of joy.

I wandered about Jerusalem looking for a place to celebrate my birthday on June ninth. It was to be brunch with Andrew, Alka, and Orit. I felt I had to locate the finest possible restaurant in town, and arrange everything perfectly beforehand. I'd learned by now that if Andrew was involved in an outing anything less than your optimum best would signify lack of respect for him. But I hesitated to ask where he preferred to go or what he preferred to eat. I had the intuition that I had to guess and guess right. Even though it was my birthday and not his!

I checked out a few places, including the American Colony Hotel and decided, finally, on the King David Hotel dining-room.

A sizzling, dry Jerusalem morning. The moment I entered the kitchen, Andrew, Alka, Orit and the six English disciples, who'd found rooms next door, sang "Happy Birthday." To my extreme embarrassment, I was presented with flowers, chocolate, and candy. I knew this show was not for me. Not one of these people with the exception of Orit was more than a passing acquaintance. They all knew about my doubts and reservations in regard to Andrew and I felt some of them didn't even like me. No, this show was for Andrew, and only for Andrew.

The meal at the King David Hotel was very ordinary and very expensive, but served with a quality of graciousness not common in more pedestrian Israeli restaurants. We sat in air-conditioned splendor beside a window that looked down on an olympic-sized swimming pool and a lush English garden originally planted by the British when they were occupiers here. Abba Eban, terribly overweight, was eating at a nearby table, and his presence added a note of glamour to the occasion.

I sat at the table feeling out of it. I glanced over at Andrew. He was quiet too. His eyes were shocking—unblinking, and piercing. They frightened me.

In the evening, at satsang, a round-faced young Israeli woman with long blond braids was enlightened. Her face turned beet-red and she cried helplessly, like a baby. I watched her feeling jealous, wretchedly aware, as I was almost all the time now, of how ponderously I moved on this spiritual path. A rogue elephant lagging more and more behind the herd.

Joshua called late that night from New York with greetings. For some reason I'd been feeling as if I'd disappeared, and this birthday call had the effect of confirming my existence on the planet.

On the first day off I went to Tel-Aviv to visit a rather conventional young couple—cousins of a friend—I had met recently in New York. They surprised me by asking if they could come to a satsang in Jerusalem. I had told them about Andrew and they were curious.

Lying in a pullout bed in the living room of their apartment, I brooded over the stubbornness in me that refused to trust Andrew completely. There was always something happening that seemed to corroborate my misgivings. Last night for example, a woman who had come to satsang for the first time was sitting before Andrew in perfect lotus position with her hands opened upwards on her folded knees, thumbs and forefingers touching, eyes closed, in the classic Indian meditation posture.

"Why are you sitting like that?" Andrew had asked sharply.

The woman opened her eyes. She looked at Andrew, nonplussed. "I sit this way when I meditate," she said.

"Well, don't sit that way here!" he snapped at her.

The woman looked at Andrew unbelievingly, then down at the floor in front of her, blushing.

Andrew claimed that he had to be ruthless to break through a person's resistance. But this woman had not appeared to be resistent. She may have been ignorant of what he considered appropriate. But resistent?

Was it possible that Andrew was changing? Was his new power making him more intolerant? Self-indulgent? More arrogant? Perhaps I'd become so alienated from my former life that I was afraid I no longer had anything to go back to, and without Andrew— what was left? I looked blankly into the hot, steamy, street darkness.

The next afternoon I walked to the seashore and sat for a long time in an open-air cafe gazing out at the waves. Nostalgia drifted through me—a mist of sadness and regret. No matter if the memory was unhappy, even poisonous, I observed how it was held in the body lovingly, lingeringly, as smoke in the lungs, as a whiff of yesterday, of the familiar, of the I, of me.

But if I had been in touch with the person Andrew said I really was, if I had been in contact with the Other, the Self, the real me unshadowed by the past, wouldn't the noise of chattering, of traffic, of breaking waves, of memory, wouldn't all that have moved back, have become hardly a whisper, and sitting in that cafe, wouldn't time have stopped and the eternal present with its impersonal tenderness closed in around me? Wouldn't I have felt safe?

My hosts drove back to Jerusalem with me to see Andrew. At satsang he was astounding, bringing forth and making tangible what was great and radiant in his own experience of freedom. "When I sit down here in front of you," he said, "I fall into WHAT IS and that creates a magnetic vacuum into which the UNKNOWN rushes."

I looked at the couple from Tel-Aviv to see how they were reacting. They were sitting right in front of Andrew. Their faces were neutral. I wondered if they were bored. At the moment they were leaning back resting their hands behind them on the floor. They'd been wriggling almost constantly. Obviously they weren't used to sitting on the floor—it was painful for everyone at first— and kept re-adjusting their legs.

Andrew ended the session with a powerful exhortation to "Want IT! … Scream your desire from the roof-tops! … You have to want IT altogether, completely, without a single but!"

Immediately after satsang Andrew remarked in a rather ferocious tone, "I hope your friends don't ever come back again. They couldn't sit still for a moment."

Once more I considered him grossly unfair.

A dark-haired rather wild-eyed woman who came regularly to satsang had invited me to tea at the Intercontinental Hotel. People were always asking me out, intrigued by the idea of the mother of a guru. They were looking to fulfill some mental image, I felt. I felt it had nothing to do with me.

We sat at a table in front of a vast wall of windows that faced down onto the old walled city. It was approaching sunset and the air itself seemed tinged with a soft powdery pink. Below, the Blue Mosque, the original site of Solomon's temple, dominated the low beige structures surrounding it. Old Jerusalem looked just as you would imagine it to look, small, primitive, desert-hued and hugged to the earth.

At satsang a few evenings later, the very same woman who had taken me to the Intercontinental Hotel accused Andrew of shutting her out. She sounded hurt and angry. I had no idea what she meant, or what event, if any, had provoked this allegation.

"I'm not your teacher," Andrew responded icily. "You'd better look for another one elsewhere!"

The room became as still as death.

I froze, at once identified with the woman and terrorized at her rejection. During the interchange that followed I stared at the wall opposite me, unable to look at her.

"I don't owe you anything," Andrew said. "I don't owe anyone in the world anything. There's only one exception, my guru, to whom I owe everything!"

The woman got up and left without another word.

Andrew looked around the room slowly. "A person identifies with the suffering of another only if he identifies with his own suffering," he said. I felt as if he were addressing me, as if once again, he'd read my mind.

But what had the poor woman done to deserve such a sting-ing dismissal? My insides quaked with pity for her.

I awoke feeling a familiar premonitory flash of catastrophe. There was no memory of anything specific, just panic erupting from a source where some archaic menacing thought was lodged, out of sight, but operating at full capacity. I didn't want to go into it and climbed out of bed right away. If you looked back, according to Andrew, if you investigated, searched for tracks, hints, vague turnings, idiot associations, you'd be lured back along the road to hell. Andrew's advice in regard to hurtful memory was "Forget it! It's not you. It's only your conditioning."

Nevertheless a dull sense of suffocation remained.

At breakfast Andrew said, "You must not wait for enlight-enment but at the same time enlightenment must be choiceless."

What in God's name was he talking about now? My sense of suffocation deepened.

On a day off Andrew and the group went to stay overnight at a beach near Tel-Aviv. Orit and I remained at home, and in the evening, decided to go to the movies. Afterwards we walked home. It was a long way and we talked. Orit confessed that her doubts about Andrew were stronger than ever.

"I don't get it," I said. "Knowing what you know, how can you so deeply doubt Andrew? You've been one of his most ardent prose-lytizers." I was exasperated with her in spite of my own uncertainties.

"I feel cut off from him," Orit murmured almost inaudibly.

"But why?" I asked.

At first she didn't answer.

"Why?" I persisted, and leaned closer to her to hear her reply.

She sighed and related the following incident. The other day she'd been in someone's car with Andrew and an Israeli medical student, an old friend of hers. The student had said to Andrew, "My father thinks I follow you like a blind dog."

Andrew had laughed. But when the student had gotten out of the car Andrew had said, "He thinks he's not following me like a blind dog, but he is." And Andrew had laughed again.

I listened to our footsteps clacking loudly in the empty street. After walking a block in silence Orit went on to tell me something else. The student had had a Zen master in Japan for years and years and although Andrew had never directly advised the student to leave his master, he'd said, "If you want to be an enlightened man, you cannot have two masters, you can only have one."

"So what's wrong with that?" I asked Orit. "It's true."

I turned. Orit's profile, silvered by moonlight, moved slowly along beside me. She shrugged her shoulders. We didn't talk any more the rest of the way home.

Ensconced in a lounge chair in the living-room with the Jerusalem Post on my lap, I was staring at Andrew who was sitting in a rocking-chair on the veranda. Alka and Orit were still at the breakfast table in the alcove behind me. Andrew was sitting very still, his head turned to the right, his back to me, holding a mug of coffee balanced on one arm of his chair. The side of his face I could see looked severe and fixed. He seemed to be frowning. It made me nervous to see him like that. Was he annoyed about something? Angry? Was his coffee cold? Did he have a headache? Was he aggravated with someone? Fed up? I swallowed. With me? I looked up above him at the blazing sky. He'd been goading me more than usual the last couple of days to hurry up, hurry up! The others weren't dragging their feet. The others were getting IT. What was the matter with me?! All at once he spoke. "No one says thank-you in Jerusalem," he said in a resentful tone.

I was squinting at a tiny plane glittering in the distance.

"No one says thank-you," Andrew repeated.

Neither do I, I thought. Suddenly the stinginess of my soul disgusted me. With Andrew I was rich, I thought. The world was poor and shabby.

I got up and went to my room to find a pad and a pen and

came back and sat down again. Andrew hadn't moved.

I began to write quickly. The first word that leapt from my pen in unmistakable letters was Master. I'd addressed him as Master!

It must have been a mechanical act. The word had written itself! I ripped the page from the pad and gaped at it. Master. An old-fashioned word. Primitive. Naive. Restful somehow. Sweet. True? Possible? Horrible? Who knew?

Master. I relaxed. And under the salutation, I watched the words forming: "I belong to you body and soul forever. Luna." I folded the note and got up and placed it on the arm of the rocking chair next to the coffee mug and returned to the living room and sat down.

Andrew picked up the note and read it. Then he looked around and nodding, gave me a slow smile.

I got up from my chair and went to the room I shared with Orit and lay down on my bed and inspected the ceiling. I noticed for the first time that paint was peeling away in thick grey curls at all four corners. At the center, around the light fixture it had peeled away altogether leaving a ring of white plaster. I turned on my stomach, dug my face into the pillow and wept.

That night, during satsang, I had the remarkable sensation of my body being pulled downwards into the earth and my head expanding into the sky, and there was a quivering instant when I thought I was about to experience something wholly unknown.

Was I, I marveled, on the razor's edge of surrender?

At the next satsang a plump, extraordinarily pale-skinned British disciple, Lynn, sat with tears of what appeared to be ecstacy, streaming down her cheeks, and I realized woefully that my uncomfortable wary normal state was back in place again. Nothing had changed. People were still diving to the bottom and I was still loitering at the brink.

I accompanied two of the British women next door on a visit to Mea Shearim, the City of a Thousand Gates, home to ultra-orthodox Jews. It lay under the sweltering midday heat, a quiet peaceful place, a city within a city, re-created from a recollection of the past—narrow winding cobbled streets, old trees spreading pools of shade, low stone dwellings, people covered from neck to toe, fiercely modest, clothed for another climate in another country (Poland) and antagonistic to the greater city outside. What amazed me was their tenacity in clinging with such fanatical exactness to what had been, and maintaining it utterly intact in a new land.

It occurred to me that attachment to tradition was nothing more than an unwillingness to change. And wasn't my attachment to the old me really the same? I asked myself.

One morning when the air was pure, the light delicate, the sky an unblemished transparent blue, I went alone to visit the Garden of Gethsemane, the olive grove where Jesus had been betrayed by a kiss. Now pines and cypresses and eucalyptus trees grew around an ancient domed Russian orthodox church. Along one side, planted in orderly rows, lay a dusty sparse flower garden enclosed by a wire fence. I sat down on a bench and breathed in the dry spicy smell. A small metal plaque next to the bench revealed the legend: "Father, I can't understand you, but I trust you." Jesus' words. I was deeply affected by them. A number of people here had already suggested that perhaps Andrew was Jesus, the messiah, making another appearance in Jerusalem. I'd laughed at them.

Someone on the path in front of me bent and picked up a dead flower and pocketed it gingerly as if it were precious. I felt my scalp prickle. But what if…? Anything could be true, couldn't it? Couldn't it? Gooseflesh rose on my arms and legs. Anything was possible wasn't it? There might be some secret thread, some universal connecting principle that was using Andrew.

At the dinner table my head was buzzing again. Andrew told me I was beautiful.

Andrew, Alka and I (the latter two as 'wife' and 'mother') were invited to dinner by a Russian man who told us his wife was afraid of demons. I was fascinated. She sat at the table, a pale-skinned, thin girl, with a flowered red babushka tied under her angular chin. She held a tiny baby clutched to her chest—it had been born with a malfunctioning heart—and listened to our spiritually oriented conversation with an air of impatience, almost of contempt. I wanted to ask her about her demons but didn't dare. From the little she said in her few words of English, it was clear that she regarded this talk of enlightenment, surrender, the self, being, the unknown, as inexcusably superficial, an affront in the face of her child's affliction. From time to time she lay the baby on her lap and looked down at it with what seemed like stricken amazement. I heard later that the baby was taken to New York for medical treatment and that it died.

I was leaving for New York myself the next day, and Andrew had consented to have dinner with me alone, a favor that had become a sort of tradition on the eve of my departure. Someone suggested a fashionable Arab restaurant that had 'atmosphere.'

We were seated by a man in a tuxedo at a table covered with a clean linen cloth. Romantic desert scenes decorated the walls. A candle in an ornate brass holder was lit and gleamed softly between us. We ordered cous-cous with carrot and onion gravy.

Andrew seemed withdrawn. I sat opposite him wondering nervously what he was thinking. Up until now we had hardly exchanged a word, and when the food came, unforgivably insipid and tasteless in view of the price, we ate in silence.

Afterwards, at an outdoor cafe, over tiny cups of black Turkish coffee, Andrew appeared to relax. He smiled at me over the gold rim of his coffee cup. "Now we're having a good time," he said.

The relief I felt was instant, heady joy. I smiled back, my whole being opening to him—my son, my sun, whom I felt to be the most precious being in the universe.

On the way home I suggested that it might be a good idea for me to go and see Jackie, a Canadian psychotherapist friend from

Montreal. She was a remarkable, nearly blind woman I'd introduced to Andrew, who had become his enthusiastic disciple. "She might help me to understand my fear of you and my resistance to surrender," I said. "It won't do any harm and who knows, it might really help."

"Sure, why not?" he said.

"I'll go to Montreal in September and start the therapy," I said.

"Great," he said. He gave me a sweet encouraging smile.

In the morning, as the taxi that was to take me to the airport approached, I hugged him tightly. "No matter what," I said, "I love you, I love you."

"I love you too Luna. I love you too," were his parting words.

12

CANADA

I SPENT THE REST OF THE SUMMER OF 1987 AT MY SIS-
ter-in-law's farm in St. Venant, Quebec, and then, in
September, I moved to my brother's apartment in Montreal,
and began psychotherapy with Jackie. We arranged for two-hour
sessions five days a week for a month! I was in a hurry. I paid fifty
dollars for each session. When Andrew heard that I was paying for
these sessions, reasonable as Jackie's price was, he was furious
with her for charging a fellow disciple money for therapy.
However, even if Jackie had offered her services free of charge, I
wouldn't have accepted all those hours of therapy without paying
for them. Andrew, however, never forgave Jackie, and it played a
role in their future relations.

One day, about midway through the month, I had an experience that in retrospect, I regard as a turning point. I had just left
Jackie's home and was walking towards the subway when suddenly I found myself caught up in a feeling of rapture. I stopped at a
tea-room opposite the apartment building my father used to live
in—he died there—and ordered a café au lait in a 'bol.' Then,
dawdling over my drink, I sat gazing out the restaurant window at
my father's building. The windows of his apartment were around
the corner, hidden from view. But I was seeing him again in my
mind's eye, still straight as an arrow at eighty-four, very gaunt, his
face pared down to an unfamiliar delicacy.

A few months before he unexpectedly died—he had shown no prior signs of illness—and he'd asked me in a somewhat querulous, hoarse voice how I could spend so many hours with my friends talking, talking, talking. "What do you talk about?" he asked.

I was on my way to an appointment and I hesitated at the doorway. I looked around at him. "Life, people, ourselves," I answered unspecifically, guiltily.

"I could never talk much," he said and he pointed to his throat. "Something closes in here."

I had smiled and had closed the door with the sense of fleeing from a plea that somehow I should save him from a lifelong feeling of estrangement from his own existence.

The hot, sweet, milky coffee didn't turn bitter in my mouth. The memory did not bring on pity or compassion, or even sadness. It was simply a memory, no more. It did not interfere with the feeling that there was something newly born in me, newly soft, newly light, surging outward with each beat of my heart.

Was this the result of the therapy?

When I got home my brother told me Andrew had called. I was astounded at myself because I didn't want to speak to Andrew. I didn't return the call.

Two days later Andrew telephoned again when I was out, and again I didn't call him back.

At the time I didn't know why I was so unwilling to talk to him. I just knew that I didn't want to, that's all. But I realize now that it indicated an awareness, a barely conscious awareness perhaps, that I had, to an infinitesimal degree, through some aspect of the psychotherapy, moved out from under his absolute authority.

The third time Andrew called I was home. He was furious and suspicious and launched immediately into a savage attack on Jackie, psychotherapy in general, and me. I didn't defend myself. When he hung up abruptly I was left somewhat spooked but not overwhelmed. However, at my next appointment with Jackie, I told her I thought Andrew was right. Psychotherapy strengthened your ego and therefore weakened your ability to surrender.

It was at this juncture that Andrew's attitude towards psychotherapy changed. Whenever the subject came up again it was invariably referred to with an air of mistrust and hostility.

I planned to go to England again at the beginning of December. I hoped a lethal rift hadn't taken place between Andrew and myself, but I suspected that when we next met, I would find that he had shoved me further than ever away from him. Nevertheless I continued my sessions with Jackie and refused to think of the consequences.

13

TOTNES, ENGLAND

I WAS GREETED IN THE BEENLEIGH HOUSE (WHICH had been retained since last year by local disciples) with huge warmth—hugged and kissed and made much of by Bud, Dvora, Alka and Andrew, who, his dark eyes incandescent, looked more beautiful than ever to me. A festive dinner had been prepared which included, in my honor, a bottle of wine.

I suspected an element of artifice in this welcome—too much affection, too extravagantly expressed—and it made me feel wary and uncomfortable.

After dinner the bomb was dropped. Andrew told me I was not going to live in the house with him any more. "It will be better for you if our relationship is more formal for a while," he explained.

I wasn't surprised. But—I couldn't help myself—I was devastated. So this was the result of my not answering his phone calls in Montreal as I should have done! I was suddenly struck by the notion that he no longer viewed me as intimately linked to him, that he saw me now as alien, split away, severed, anonymous—the way soldiers regard the enemy during a war. The pain of it blasted through every nucleus of every cell in my body.

And I wasn't going to utter a word in my defense because at a deeper level, no matter that I had my reservations, I continued to be persuaded that no matter what he did, whether I found fault

141

with it or not, whether I understood it or not—I was convinced that he acted solely from love for me and for everyone else. At the deepest level, of course, I feared, as I always did, that any opposition might result in my losing him.

I was taken by car to a huge old stone farmhouse. About twenty disciples lived there. I hardly knew most of them but once more I was greeted with much embracing and kissing. People were now talking unabashedly, almost wildly, about Andrew as though he were a god.

My room was on the third floor. Andrew had arranged that I share it with Lynn, one of the English disciples who had been invited to Jerusalem. The house was unheated and it was freezing up there.

Late in the evening a fire was lit in the living room and the group watched a film about Jesus on video. I recognized, with a sense of tearful reverence, that there was nothing that Jesus said that Andrew had not said at one time or another.

I took a hot water bottle to bed. The house was cold, cold, cold, a damp, hard, bone-eating cold, that filled every nook and cranny like a palpable inimical presence. Only the kitchen retained a spectral trace of heat from the daily cooking.

Satsang no longer took place in the Beenleigh living room but in the barn next door to it. The walls had been whitewashed during the period we were in Israel and the barn looked clean and attractive, with straw mats and colored strips of carpeting covering the floor. Andrew's upholstered chair—the one he'd used on his last stay here—had been brought from the Beenleigh house and set down at one end of the barn.

I dropped my scarf on a pillow in front of his chair in order to keep my place, and left to say hello to the folks next door.

I went through the back entrance. Andrew, who was in the kitchen, noticed me immediately. He came out and said, "You have to leave. Except at satsang, I don't want to see you!"

I turned on my heel and left, grinding my teeth in ignominy. When I got back to the barn, it was filled to the overflowing. There were a lot of new faces. Someone told me that one hundred and twenty people were present. Andrew's message seemed to have spread like wildfire.

I sat down on my pillow. Soon a silence settled. I looked around and saw eyes closed and grave expressions on people's faces. I closed my own eyes.

About twenty minutes later Andrew appeared. He took his chair and examined the room very slowly and unselfconsciously.

"Are there any questions?" he asked at last.

There were a number of questions, all from people I didn't recognize. Andrew's answers were measured, unhesitating and clear. He seemed completely poised in his position as spiritual teacher; not an iota remained of the anxious boy he'd once been. In spite of my recent humiliation at his hands, tears of appreciation for what he had become pricked my eyes, and I realized, with a sense of wonder, that everything was turning out just as Poonja had predicted.

I woke up haunted by an acute awareness of my unworthiness and stayed in bed until eleven o'clock, positive that it was the only safe place in the whole world.

There was no satsang at night. Instead, we all went to an Indian-jazz concert given in the great hall of an ancient, but still beautiful and functioning, university. I loved the music. During intermission, I glimpsed Andrew from afar and couldn't keep some rankling thoughts from surging into my consciousness. After all, I had carried him inside my body, under my heart, for nine months; I had fed him, worried about him, tried to protect him from evil. I had esteemed him when others didn't, listened to him when others wouldn't. I had respected him, cherished him. And now I must not even approach him!

In the morning, Mel, an Australian disciple, drove me to Dartmouth. I took a leisurely stroll around the old town that was famous for training naval officers, and then went and sat in front of the fire in a hotel pub. It was a low-ceilinged room with dark wood walls and lamps shaded in pink silk. It was warm and snug and felt safe. I drank a pot of coffee and stared into the flames, my mind a blank.

I got home to find that Manny and his wife Spirit had arrived for lunch. When Manny and I were alone for a few minutes, I told him about my therapy with Jackie in Montreal. "Psychotherapy seems to strengthen the ego no matter what," I told Manny.

Manny nodded. But I was sure that he thought his particular therapy directed people away from the ego and towards spiritual awakening.

"I'm back at square one with Andrew," I said.

Manny said nothing.

"Even though I sort of suspected that when I got here he'd kick me out of his house, when it happened, I was devastated," I said.

After looking calmly at me for half a minute Manny grinned and said, "That man wants to kill me, too."

I saw Rebecca after breakfast. She was transformed—soft melting eyes, gentle smile. She had become beautiful. The Rebecca of Dharamsala had disappeared.

In the evening at satsang, Andrew, in a sarcastic tone of voice, compared his slow-moving mother to the swiftly born-again Rebecca. "Fear is fear, and authority, authority, no matter if it's between strangers or mothers and sons," he said. I wasn't sure what he meant by that. But it had an ugly sound.

Later, at home, during a birthday celebration for Sarah—a stocky, bright-eyed Israeli girl who had abandoned her third year of physiotherapy training in Jerusalem to join Andrew—I sat eating chocolate cake and listening to the others picking over every word Andrew had said that evening as if they were picking over a packet of emeralds, examining each one for its relative weight and color and brilliance.

The next morning I got up and rushed through getting dressed in order to meet the wife of a colleague of Manny's for lunch. She picked me up in her car. We stopped along the road and got out and stood on the rocky seashore for a few minutes watching the rolling and crashing expanse of grey water. Sea-gulls stood in the sand near us facing straight into the cold snapping wind. Their feathers ruffled as they rocked on their slender legs. I pointed to them. "Why do you think they stand that way?" I asked.

"How do you mean?"

"Facing into the worst of the wind?"

She shrugged. "They do hold their own, don't they? There must be a lesson in that."

We had lunch in Dartmouth at the same pub I'd visited two days ago and sat at the same table in front of the same crackling fire. She ordered grilled sole for both of us, and began to tell me about herself. She was an orphan and, as a child, had lived in a number of foster homes. Now she was married to a well-to-do homeopathic doctor and had two sons. She'd been enlightened by Andrew. It had not been a struggle for her. I looked deep into her large pretty wide-awake blue eyes with envy and admiration.

Why, why, couldn't I give up the battle?

I was drifting… just drifting. I found myself thinking about Andrew all the time. He was a king. No, a god. God? Andrew was no longer Andrew. Andrew was what? I was the mother of Andrew who was what? I was no longer the mother of Andrew who was no longer Andrew but was what? I was drifting through time and all the world's endeavors seemed trivial and useless.

One morning in our kitchen Mel, talking about the way people were beginning to follow Andrew everywhere he went in the world, said, "Let's face it. We're in this with Andrew forever. This is for life."

This was for life? This kind of existence was going to be mine for the rest of my life? I don't know why it should have, but the possibility startled me. It was as though I'd never thought of it point blank before.

I was getting a cold and my throat felt so raw that I had to keep swallowing during satsang to prevent a fit of coughing. At some point I heard Andrew saying, "What you think you are is merely an idea, your idea. It's just another thought. If you could see the truth of this, you'd have nothing to worry about."

True, true! If you could just realize that what you were was simply an idea, a thought in your head, if you could just realize that, you'd be free of yourself, free of the past. You'd be free. Everything he said was true.

I passed a sleepless night, my throat tickling incessantly. In order not to cough and disturb Lynn, I had to sit up in bed. Three blankets and a quilt were wrapped about me, a hot water bottle rested on my feet, but I remained trembling, chilled to the bone, feeling nauseated, and missing Andrew.

In the evening, I wrote him a note, adding it to the huge pile beside his satsang chair. Sometimes he read these notes to us. Sometimes he even read us long letters. He would pick up the pile, rifle through it, and strictly through his recognition of people's handwriting, select a few to read, either aloud or to himself. The entire sangha was deeply impressed by his ability to remember everyone's script, and assumed it was a manifestation of his enlightenment. Often he appeared to be expecting a written comment or question from a particular individual.

I had written that I missed him.

When he entered and sat down, he bent to the side to retrieve his messages and immediately picked out mine. He read it in silence and then let his gaze wander slowly around the barn, checking out who was there, as he always did, and finally, when his eyes came to rest on me, he said, "But I'm here." He paused. "I don't feel you love me Luna, despite what you say." He tapped my note. "I don't believe you. There are people here who really love me."

Although I felt he had just slapped my face, I answered emphatically, "But I do love you!"

"What you feel may be admiration, but not love," he said. He gazed at me with raised brows evidently expecting me to say more. When I didn't, he put my note down with an air of finality and picked up another envelope.

He had said the same thing to me in Amsterdam in front of the household, but never before in front of the whole sangha! Did I really not love him? What did he mean? Did he mean he was the Absolute and I didn't love the Absolute? What the hell did he mean? Terrified, I honestly tried to examine my heart. It was beating violently.

On the way home an American psychologist who was Andrew's favorite of the moment, quoted what Andrew had said during satsang at great length. Then he went on to explain various turns of Andrew's thought and to interpret Andrew's meanings for us as though he had become Andrew's intermediary.

He was sitting directly ahead of me in the car. I stared at the back of his neck. His frizzy hair grew thickly over his neck and down to his collar. He hadn't been friendly towards me and usually looked away whenever our glances met.

It had been Dvora's suggestion that she and I meet for lunch at the same pub in Dartmouth. Andrew had probably asked her to check out how I was doing.

I arrived overwhelmed by insecurity and doubt. We ordered sandwiches and tea and I started to cry. Without asking why—it must have been obvious to Dvora why—she said it would take all my strength to overcome the belief in my ego.

Strength? I hadn't thought strength was involved. I hadn't thought you had to exert strength. Exerting strength was effort, and Andrew taught that there was no need to make an effort, that when enlightenment came, it would be effortless. This was a cornerstone of his (and Poonja's) teaching.

"I thought you suddenly saw through the illusion of the ego and that it just sort of melted away," I mumbled through my tears.

"No," Dvora said, tossing her shiny dark curls, "you must use all your power to overcome the negativity of the ego."

I sat back, wiping my eyes with the table napkin and trying to grapple with this paradox.

"You must choose," Dvora said firmly as if she actually knew what she was talking about.

I stared at her. Choose to relinquish the ego? Choose with what? Who chooses if not the ego? Force it to go away? How? I felt pervaded by incomprehension and a sense of contradiction.

I blew my nose. A horrible spite against Dvora surged up in my chest. Who the hell did she think she was? She was just a kid, an arrogant Israeli kid!

I looked down at the table. A melted cheese sandwich lay on a white blue-rimmed plate. I pushed it away.

At satsang, after giving me a long look, Andrew rifled through his letters. I sensed that he was looking for a note I hadn't written.

My cold was worse. I could scarcely speak above a whisper. Before satsang, I wrote Andrew the note he'd been expecting yesterday. I told him I had finally chosen him over all my old beliefs. He found the note right away, read it, and smiled over at me. "Do you feel better?" he asked. "Do you feel at home now?"

I whispered yes to both his questions.

In the kitchen at home, I told Mel what a relief it was to have chosen Andrew at last.

He gave me a hard look. "I don't believe you," he said.

I was stunned.

"I don't feel it," he added, slapping his belly. "Here!"

What did he know? He certainly didn't know me! He was another arrogant bastard kid! Had Andrew's attitude sanctioned his speaking to me like that? I turned and went up to my room and climbed into bed with my clothes on and lay staring into nothing in a dazed, shaken state.

As I was about to go into the Willow (a vegetarian restaurant in Totnes) Andrew came through the door accompanied by Alka and Bud. I smiled shyly and uncomfortably at my godman-son with whom I was not allowed to fraternize. He smiled back. The rest of the day I went about transformed, once more bathed in love for him. At satsang he asked if I'd left a note.

"No," I said.

His eyes scrutinized me. He had expected a note today. Why hadn't I known that? It was as if I was not encoded like the others to foresee what was expected of me.

After satsang Manny and his wife disappeared into the Beenleigh house. I was to sleep at their home tonight and instead of waiting for them in the satsang hall, I dared to follow them across the way into the house itself. I had a hunch it would be okay, I don't know why.

At the living-room entrance I hesitated.

"You can enter," Andrew said.

There he was, smiling his welcome.

Later, Manny, Spirit and I, wrapped in blankets, talked for a long time in front of their open fire. We spoke only of Andrew, of what a marvel he was!

I slept in my sleeping bag on the floor in front of the fire, completely warm for the first time since I'd arrived in England.

Andrew called in the morning to say he was coming for lunch. He said it was an opportunity to speak to me alone. I was unbearably excited at the prospect. When he came, Manny and Spirit left us in the living room and went to prepare food in the kitchen.

We sat down opposite each other in front of the fire. For some minutes we were silent. I kept glancing at him, uneasily aware of two eyes inspecting me curiously and persistently. The look in the eyes was coldly detached, almost sullen. As each moment ticked by I became more and more apprehensive. What was wrong now? Last night I'd gotten the impression that I'd been allowed, although infinitesimally, back into the fold.

"You know Luna," Andrew began, "there's always been a hard edge to your personality.

My body tensed. "What do you mean?"

"I don't know, there's something tough about you. Hard," he repeated.

I'd never thought of myself that way. But maybe it was true.

"You demanded love from us," he went on.

"Us? From whom? What do you mean?" I was shocked at this accusation from out of the blue.

"You demanded that your sons love you but you didn't trust them. We were pushed into a corner and it produced a lot of rage."

Why was he saying this? Was that how I'd seemed to him? I didn't believe it. Demanded love? What did he mean? That I needed my sons' love to feel like someone? It wasn't true. I knew it wasn't true. And saying I didn't trust him! I had trusted him. Perhaps more than was good for either one of us.

The truth was, I had hated the power I had over my children by virtue, simply, of being a parent. I was aware of it from the beginning. It was a phenomenon of nature. I never enjoyed it. I hated it. I did what I could. I gave them as good an education as was possible and I presented them with liberal, tolerant values in the hope that someday they would become truly independent human beings.

To have Andrew, at this point in our lives, when he had me more or less under his heel, make accusations such as these seemed to be overplaying his advantage. I felt he was saying I'd never been perfect and he'd never forgive me. It was not the act of a mature man; it was the act of a spoiled, mean-spirited child.

"I have a favor to ask," he said.

"A favor?"

"I need to use your apartment in New York for a week next month."

"Of course."

"Alone," he said.

"Alone? Don't worry, I won't bother you. You can have the bedroom," I said, "I'll sleep in the living room."

He looked away.

"I'll just come home to change my clothes, I won't bother you," I repeated, and when he looked back at me, I added, "I have nowhere else to stay."

He turned towards the kitchen. "Let's go in and eat."

After lunch, while I was putting on my coat, he said, "This may be against my better judgement but I'm inviting you to stay at my house tonight."

I couldn't believe it. Was he still honoring our custom of my spending my last evening with him? I was leaving tomorrow for New York.

Or was it something else?

I didn't know what to think.

When I arrived at Beenleigh with my luggage, I found Manny and Spirit and Bud and Alka in the living-room. There was something tentative in their greetings. Andrew immediately took me aside. "You made a big mistake this afternoon," he said.

"What do you mean?"

"When I asked if I could use your apartment without you there, you didn't say yes right away. That's because you still don't know who I am. If you did, you would have said yes without making excuses!"

I began to apologize.

"I won't be burdened by your excuses!" he retorted sharply.

"Don't be so disappointed in me," I pleaded. My voice quavered at the edge of tears.

"One pays for one's acts, you know." He shook his head from side to side. "It's not possible for us to be friends yet. Not for a long long time."

Silence. Profound silence.

I turned and went upstairs to my room. I couldn't face the others. I was sure they'd spent the afternoon discussing me. I sat down on the bed. I had a stomach ache. A tempest raged in my brain. I hadn't the slightest idea, no one had informed me, that when the guru requested something—no matter what—you said yes posthaste, that the slightest hesitation was regarded as a betrayal of trust in him.

I had committed a crime without knowing it.

A few minutes later a voice called my name from below. I went to the landing. Andrew was standing at the foot of the stairs. I've reconsidered," he said. "Why don't you stay for another week?"

"Why?"

"It might make a difference."

"What difference?" I didn't know what he was getting at. Had they been conferring about me again? I was exhausted. My whole body was as tight as a drum. "No," I said.

"Why not?"

"No, no, it's not possible," I said. I went back to my room and climbed into bed.

On the way to the bus station Bud grilled me. I was sure he wanted some juicy morsel about Andrew's insubordinate mother to present to Andrew when he returned home.

At one point he said, "In spite of your doubts, why don't you decide not to resist and go the full distance with Andrew on his terms? Give it a whirl? Think of it as an adventure? And see where it takes you?"

These words sounded to me like Andrew's. I thought for a few moments.

"Apparently I can't," I said. "I've tried hard enough, heaven knows."

"Why can't you?"

"I don't know. I just can't. I suppose it's not in my nature."

We didn't speak again the rest of the way.

On the bus to London I slept fitfully. Every time I woke up I began to cry.

At Victoria station I checked my suitcase. An English disciple had invited me to stay the night but I was told not to arrive before five or six o'clock. I still had three hours to kill and didn't know where to go. I decided to visit the Portrait Gallery. I'd never been there before.

It was much smaller than I'd expected. I moved as slowly as I could through the rooms so time would pass, and forced myself to read every word of every tag under the portraits: how this king had been assassinated by his brother, how this one had poisoned his mother, how this queen had had her sister beheaded, how this king had been a crusader and had waded in the blood of thousands. I forced myself to scrutinize for as long as possible the faces of these ancient monarchs, all these power-mad schemers and murderers who had lived and died and lived and died and lived and died....

I left the gallery as tormented as when I'd arrived. How long could this go on? I felt I would never be able to rest again as long as I lived.

It was hot out in the streets, and I was overdressed. I pushed through the rush-hour mobs into the underground and took a train to Streatham Hills. When I got off, I walked, taut, sweating, ten long blocks before I asked and was told I was going in the wrong direction. I turned around. I told myself that this was the worst day of my life.

The disciple welcomed me warmly. I took off my sweaters and drank a cup of tea, and lay down on the bed assigned to me and waited for her (a homeopath) to finish a session with a patient. When she came, I blurted out the story about Andrew and my apartment—how ungenerous I'd been, how withholding, how begrudging, miserly, unworthy, undeserving of him I was, etc. etc. She was a soft-hearted girl and she seemed to listen with genuine compassion for my suffering, but when she left the room I was ashamed that I'd talked so much.

I began to feel a little saner during dinner with her visiting German ex-husband, a black-bearded man who appeared unaccountably hostile and domineering. The disciple later told me he had spent most of the day in meditation!

"His attitude doesn't say much for meditation, does it?" I said, and I smiled for the first time in twenty-four hours.

After dinner she sat in my room chatting for a while. She was leaving for Calcutta on Sunday to teach a course in homeopathy and showed me pictures of herself in the Calcutta slums. I was intrigued by what she had to say about her previous teaching trips there.

We went to bed early. I covered myself with my hostess's soft quilt and curled up on my side and buried my face in a down pillow and felt out of danger at last. The storm was over. A sense of peace began to creep over me and every muscle in my body began to relax.

Before I left Totnes I'd written to Andrew begging him to "pray for me or whatever gurus do to aid their errant disciples." Was my sudden serenity Andrew's answer to the appeal in my note?

I got up to write him another note. "Andrew," I wrote, "I don't miss you now because you are in my brain, in my soul. You have saved me. You are the savior. This is a miracle. Thank you for my not having to go home again still inside my prison cell."

Looking back now, what was I saying? I hardly knew what I was saying. It was gibberish.

The homeopath came to Victoria station with me to get my sleeping bag. She'd said she had to buy one for India and I'd offered her mine.

At five p.m. I was on a British Airways plane taking off for New York.

I was not to see Andrew again until February, in Rome.

My two sons, Josh
(*left*) & Andrew (*right*),
at our beach house
in Westhampton Beach,
Long Island, circa 1961.

Andrew & me,
Montreal, 1966.

Left:
Andrew & me in the
Laurentian mountains,
near Montreal, 1968.

Right:
Larry Cohen,
Andrew &
Josh's father,
in 1955,
just prior to
Andrew's
birth.

Above: Andrew & me in Switzerland, January 1971.

Left:
Andrew &
me at a
friend's
birthday
party,
New York
City, 1981.

Above: Andrew & me in New Delhi, December, 1985.

Below: Andrew & Alka on Mount Arunachala,
Ramana Maharshi's "holy mountain," December, 1985.

Above: Me, Andrew & Alka in Pondicherry, December, 1985.

Below: Poonja & Andrew in Hardwar, 1986.

Right:
Poonja
& me in a
temple garden
in Hardwar,
July, 1986,
the morning
after Poonja
told me he had
"been waiting
for Andrew
all my life."

Three aspects of our quarters at Rishikesh: (*left*) the roof of the temple, with stairs leading to our rooms; (*above*) the Ganges River from the roof; (*right*) me sitting at the foot of the ghat where we swam.

Above:
Poonja invites
Andrew to sit
beside him
on Guru's Day,
indicating his
acceptance of
Andrew as a
"fellow guru,"
Hardwar,
July 21, 1986.

Right:
Poonja &
Andrew in
Central Park,
New York City,
circa 1987.

Above: Two members of our group leaving Dharamsala by bus
for Kashmir; Orit and Andrew see them off, August, 1986.

Below: Group shot inside the temple in Hardwar, July, 1986.
Seated in front, the Belgian woman and her daughter.

Above: Josh & Andrew on the beach at Gloucester, Mass., during Josh's visit to Boston, September 1988.

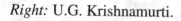

Right: U.G. Krishnamurti.

Above: Julie & me on the deck of our house,
the morning after separating from Andrew,
Mill Valley, California, July, 1989.

Below left: Jerry, Leslie & Paul. *Below right:* Isabel.

MOKSHA
Foundation

Moksha Foundation was founded by spiritual teacher Andrew Cohen and has been guided and inspired by his work. This work addresses the core questions of human life, perennial questions in which we seek answers as to how we as humans can come together in a fundamentally sane, trusting and responsible manner. Moksha Foundation's work is dedicated to the libera

Moksha Foundation promotes dialogues between spiritual retreats. Moksha Press publishes a large catalogue of audio *Enlightenment?.* The International Center for FACE will be centers and activities in London, Amsterdam, Tel Aviv, Cologn

Moksha Foundation   P.O. Box 2360   Lenox, MA 01240 US,

Above: The Massachusetts headquarters for Friends of A

...he human spirit from ignorance, conflict and corruption.
...worldwide, and each year organizes large international
...deotapes, books and the semiannual journal, *What Is*
...for all of Moksha Foundation's activities, including its
...ey, Toronto and Boston.

800-376-3210   or 413-637-3322   Fax: 413-637-3366

...Cohen Everywhere (FACE), and the Moksha Foundation.

TEACHINGS OF LIBERATION

You are invited to join
Andrew Cohen in a
revolutionary investigation
into the meaning and
significance of spiritual
experience in human life.

ANDREW COHEN

Friday, Nov. 8   7:30 PM
N. Y. Theosophical Society
242 East 53rd Street
Admission $5

Saturday, Nov. 9   7:30 PM
Doral Tuscany Hotel
120 East 39th Street
Admission $15

ONE DAY RETREAT
**Sunday, Nov. 10
9:00 AM - 6:00 PM**
Doral Tuscany Hotel
120 East 39th Street
Cost: $60
(Please register by Oct. 27)

"Seek to cultivate a condition where you are no longer frightened by the complexity of life, but indeed are thrilled by the challenge of trying to truly understand it."

For more information call: **(212) 978-4275**

Above: A flyer advertising Andrew's sessions in New York City, 1996.

14

I ARRIVED IN ROME ON A GLOOMY RAINY FEBRUARY day and went to stay with Donna Moylan, an American friend who'd been living there for many years. Donna, a painter, shared her antique Roman apartment with her son, aged fourteen. Her work, metaphysical, mysterious, probing, fascinated me. At that time she was working on huge engulfing canvases some of which covered entire walls.

I was given a room that looked out over the red tile roofs of old Rome. I could even see the rotunda of the cathedral in the Vatican. But, reminding me unpleasantly of England, my room was unheated, and consequently freezing.

Andrew lived somewhere not too far away. Unless invited, I was forbidden to visit him. Since I was never invited, I never found out exactly where he lived.

The satsang meeting place was a ten minute walk.

In the morning Andrew arrived at Donna's with Rebecca in tow. Considering our last bitter encounter, I was amazed that he had decided to visit me.

After a few awkward minutes of forced conversation, Andrew agreed reluctantly—I had to ask him three times—to have a cup of coffee with me alone. Rebecca left and we went down to

169

the tiny piazza next to Donna's apartment building and sat at an outside cafe in the weak winter sunlight and ordered two cappuccini. Andrew watched the busy street traffic while I talked about my stay in New York, and when our eyes occasionally met, he gave me a brief mechanical smile. He didn't seem interested in anything I had to say and I soon faltered into nervous silence. It was clear that he wanted nothing intimate to transpire between us. We parted without touching and I mounted the six long flights of stone stairs to Donna's apartment, feeling miserable.

The first satsang in Italy took place in the huge salon of an upper-class Roman apartment. We sat on grass mats and pillows and small rugs garnered I knew not from where. I found a place near Andrew's chair where I was able to lean back against the wall.

He started out by saying that certain people in the world, meaning the chosen ones like all of us here, search for peace, whereas the deluded others search for excitement.

Then he talked about the path, how most people don't follow the path to the end, but stop somewhere in the middle of it. "It's wanting the end of the path that counts," he said, "it's wanting freedom, not the road to freedom." He paused and looked around at the upturned, expectant faces. "You have to know who you are," he continued. "People say they want to know who they are, but another part of them, the conditioned part, doesn't want to know anything about who they are. You must make up your mind if you really want to know who you are."

This idea of making up your mind, this concept that it was possible to decide, still puzzled me. What decided? What part of the brain could escape being conditioned?

To a person who asked what his message was, Andrew answered cryptically, "I don't build people up. I destroy them." To another person who wanted to know whether the path had been difficult for him, whether it had required a lot of courage, Andrew answered, "Not really. At first the path seemed very hard, it's true, but then, suddenly, it was very easy." He gave the questioner a radiant smile and added, "If you're a noble searcher after truth—what is there to be afraid of?"

What indeed!

I listened, very affected, and as usual, close to tears. Andrew looked superb. His clothes were smarter. Everything matched. He had always liked clothes, but had seemed indifferent to his appearance during the last few years. Now Rome's stylishness must have stimulated his interest again. He sat before us resplendent in his new Italian trousers and sweater, King Andrew, monarch of us all.

It was a long, slow, peaceful satsang. I felt far away from Luna. I almost forgot her. I was nobody, doing nothing. And when it occurred to me that Andrew was my son, it was of no consequence. A remote fact. The Andrew who sat so gloriously before me was simply a nameless being. That was all.

But the next day a fit of loneliness took hold of me and I telephoned Andrew just to hear his voice. He suggested that I invite Alka out to dinner. He had never stopped trying to get Alka and me together. He was determined that we have a closer relationship. But my discomfort in her presence had endured.

Nonetheless I called a little later to invite her out for dinner before satsang. She accepted. Still feeling lonesome, I asked Alka if I could speak to Andrew again. When she told me he didn't want to talk to me, I flared up all at once and couldn't help crying out, "Why can't he just get up and come to the goddamn phone?!"

He didn't.

Over dinner Alka told me that my outburst was a big mistake. "You are showing the leftovers of your past relationship to him," she said in a severe voice.

God, how could I keep from wanting him to be my son? The night before there'd been an interval when I thought I'd reached a point of perfect detachment from him. But obviously it hadn't lasted. It would never last. I knew it in my bones. Because in the marrow of my bones, Andrew, my child Andrew, would abide until I died. And nothing would ever change that.

But over that pasta dinner and good inexpensive wine, in that homey old family-run trattoria, I found myself agreeing with Alka. I nodded my head anxiously and regretted that once again I'd fallen into Andrew's disfavor, and I reached into the pocket of my jacket and pulled out a tissue wrapped gift I'd prepared for her—a gold and ebony antique locket my mother had once given me. She examined it carefully, kissed me her thanks and put it in her handbag. A few days later she informed me that the link connecting the locket to a little ebony bow that served as a pin, wasn't real gold. I apologized and said I hadn't known about that. I hadn't.

Tonight Andrew gave the Italians a mantra. "Non deve capire niente." (It's not necessary to understand anything.) It was received as though the words had magic powers and Andrew was a magician. You could read it plainly in the wonder-stricken faces of his listeners.

Afterwards Andrew talked about romantic love. "Romance may be thrilling," he said, "but it's nothing compared to the thrill of the *other.* In the name of peace and tranquility," he counselled, "you must sacrifice romance."

Because of my difficulty hearing (an old ailment that had involved three ear operations and now required me to wear a hearing aid) I asked Rebecca, whose home group occupied the satsang apartment, to reserve a permanent place for me near enough to Andrew so that I could hear him comfortably. She agreed to do it. But when I arrived for the evening satsang Rebecca informed me that orders had come down from Andrew that there was to be no preferential treatment towards anyone, that no one could reserve a place to sit in advance.

"Surely Andrew didn't mean me," I said. "He knows about my hearing problem."

Rebecca regarded me with a pitying expression. "He said

everyone," she answered, "so that includes you."

"But I won't be able to hear him," I said.

"I can't help it," she said, frowning. She shrugged her shoulders and was about to turn away when I, like a fool, continued to remonstrate with this twenty-two year old, immovable disciplinarian, implying that she had misinterpreted Andrew's directive, that she was improperly exerting her authority, that it couldn't possibly be true.

She was adamant.

A grim idea came into my head: the order to refuse people the right to reserve a seat in the satsang hall was directed specifically at me!

Later that night, in bed, I lay staring into the freezing dark, rigid with anger and fear. Andrew was coercing me into acquiescing that I was nothing to him, and apparently he'd made up his mind that it had to be smashed into my consciousness with a crow-bar!

I was surprised when Rebecca called in the morning to apologize. She was brief and cool. I told her she had made me suffer horribly, that her tone had been mean, that I hadn't been able to sleep all night, that I still felt miserable. Rebecca repeated in the same tone as before that she was sorry and hung up.

I found out afterwards that Andrew had asked her to call and apologize to me. She must have told him what had happened and how I had reacted. I imagined that he felt a little guilty.

I was wrong. In the evening, in front of everyone, Andrew turned to me and said, "You over-reacted to Rebecca. Her simple apology should have been enough!" He gave me a long withering look.

Why, I thought, clenching my teeth, had he accepted her version of the situation carte blanche? Why hadn't he asked for my account before publicly announcing his verdict?

Donna, who had attended the satsang, tried to help me later on at home. She said, "He's doing it all for you. He knows what really happened. He'll take care of Rebecca. Just forget it. It's only emotion."

But I couldn't.

I woke up exhausted after nine hours of heavy dead sleep. I went down to the kitchen to get some coffee and found Donna's adolescent son there. He didn't look at me. He hates me, I thought. I wanted to ask, "Why do you hate me?" But I didn't. I went back up to my room without the coffee and lay down and gazed blindly out the window at the glaring white sky and listened to the din of battle inside me.

After twenty minutes I got up and wrote Andrew a letter. I told him he was right and I was wrong.

At satsang he read the letter silently and then looked over at me and said, "You've finally dipped the nail of your small toe in the water." There was contempt in his voice.

I spent the night at another friend's home. Once, on an extended stay in Rome, she'd made some clothes for me. She was a wonderful dressmaker and had become a dear friend. Lying on a mattress on the floor of her tiny living room I once again heard the noise of battle inside me and I closed my eyes. I started to sweat. What was I to do? I couldn't go on like this.

Suddenly I imagined holding tightly to Andrew's hand. I could actually physically feel the flesh of his fingers warm and alive in mine. I hung onto this hallucination until I fell asleep.

The next morning I telephoned Andrew to tell him about last night's experience, but immediately started to cry and found myself, instead, giving my side of the telephone conversation with Rebecca.

"You should apologize to Rebecca for berating her on the phone," he said, and added, "I was the one who told Rebecca there were to be no special privileges about seat reservations and I told her this rule applied to you in particular even though you had trouble hearing!"

So it was true!

"Even if you couldn't hear," he went on, "you could have just sat quietly."

Then he began a fresh attack. I had recently given him via Rebecca, seven hundred dollars as a donation. He hadn't thanked me, as he usually did, or even given any indication that he'd received it. Now he said, "And I have something else to tell you. You're weird with money. It's because you don't know how to give freely. You're preoccupied with money in a funny way, measuring it out and congratulating yourself when you think you're being generous."

All the blocked misery and gall in me erupted and I completely lost control. "You," I shouted, "treat me as if I were a moral moron. You treat me as if I don't know how to behave decently with anyone!"

Suddenly Alka's voice came over the wire, cold and calm. "This conversation with Andrew must end," she said. "Just saying thank-you to Rebecca after her apology would have been enough!"

I was beside myself. I felt crazy.

"Okay! Okay! I'll apologize," I cried, desperate all at once with fear.

"Your pattern is to apologize and then cry," Alka said, and she hung up.

After a few seconds, shuddering from head to toe, I called Rebecca. She wasn't home.

I decided to give her three hundred dollars more for the 'cause' and make it an even thousand.

I spent the night on the floor of my dressmaker friend's apartment again and awoke at three a.m. in a state of frantic gloom.

I got up and wrote Andrew a letter. I tore it up.

The next night Andrew quoted Nisargadata, a modern Indian sage who had said, "Desire is a projection of attachment and must be given up."

I knew how much Andrew wanted me to give up my maternal attachment to him. But I couldn't do it. It was an animal fact. It had nothing to do with civilization. In spite of my qualms about his behavior, in spite of my continuously over-excited nerves, my mood swings, my paranoia, in spite of feeling debased and demeaned by him—I couldn't do it.

I placed a letter next to Andrew's satsang chair. It told him he was right about everything. It told him I was a small-minded, cheap, petty little creature. Andrew read it right away, nodded at me, and said, "Good. Your letter is completely honest."

If this hadn't been so sad it would have been funny.

I managed to come up with two hundred dollars more to give Rebecca for Andrew. That made one thousand two hundred. It was a lot for me. But somewhere deep inside, wiggling, like the proverbial worm in the apple, the thought abided that no matter how much I gave Andrew it would make no difference. Even if I gave him everything and had to go out and work, cleaning houses like the others, it would make no difference.

The next day I had lunch with a very thin, pale-skinned German girl, a ballet dancer who was a recent disciple. We met in the garden restaurant above the Spanish steps, and over a carafe of red wine, the German girl talked about how she'd gotten the impression that everyone in the sangha lived in constant fear of Andrew.

"He is wonderful," she said, "but I, too, am too afraid of him. I am always feeling afraid of what he will say to me in front of the people. I am not afraid to dance in front of people, maybe make a mistake, maybe fall down, but I am afraid to speak one word to Andrew."

I had a ready answer as I always did. "It's Andrew's way of teaching," I told her, "if fear comes, it comes. Ignore it. It may come for the rest of your life, so what?"

The German girl was listening with an expression of gravity to my every word.

What was I saying? Why was I saying it? To shore up her doubts? Or was this the suspension of disbelief, the necessary illusion they talk about in the theater? God knows! I'd felt a spurt of fear myself as I was saying it.

On one of my happy days I found myself telling Andrew on the phone that I loved living this carefree vagabond life with him and that I already had quite a few good friends in the sangha. He retorted that the sangha was nice to me only because of him!

The fact was, I did have lots of friends amongst the sangha—people I genuinely liked. Many of them suffered from secret doubts and sensed, from Andrew's public insinuations about my opposition to him, that they could talk to me. They usually expressed surprise that I was able to listen without seeming in the least judgmental. I never felt judgmental. The opposite was true. I identified with them. However, I usually managed to assuage their misgivings with a rhetoric that seemed to pop up intact from some jack-in-the-box in my troubled mind, where, when the lid lifted, a grotesque little figure on a spring had answers to every question and every uncertainty for other people, but not for myself.

Fear, fear, fear. Not only had I never experienced such incessant fear before in my life, but up to the time of his enlightenment I'd never feared Andrew. On the contrary, until his evolution into—what—God?—I'd been confident of his love and sympathy just as he appeared to be confident of mine. And now it wasn't clear whether I was petrified of being cast aside by Andrew or by God!

The next morning I felt so morbidly apprehensive that I telephoned Andrew once more. This time he answered the phone. "I've never felt afraid like this," I said, and then, almost in a whisper, as if to lessen the impact of words I knew he didn't want to hear, "I'm scared to death."

"Why?" he shot back.

I was silent. I didn't want to tell him again that I was terrified of his disapproval, of losing him forever etc. etc.

"Go and talk to people in the sangha," he said.

"I want to see you," I begged.

"I don't feel it's right yet for us to meet." His tone was so resolute that I knew it was useless to insist.

While Andrew took a few days off I went to Naples with two young Canadians, a brother and sister. Both had been wandering across Europe and Asia, working at odd jobs. The brother sang and played guitar in metro terminals and street corners. The sister, like many of Andrew's female disciples, washed dishes, baby-sat, or cleaned houses. They were both college educated as were almost all of Andrew's followers.

To save money we shared one room at a pensione overlooking the Bay of Naples. The two young people were thrilled with the view. They slept in two bunk beds, one above the other, and I had the luxury of sleeping in a double bed all by myself.

The first morning I woke up in a state of unusual dread—great drowning waves of nauseating sensation. The brother opened his eyes and smiled at me. "Hi," he said. He looked out the window. "Is that mountain across the bay Vesuvius?"

"Yes," I said.

"Have you ever seen a real active volcano?" he asked.

"Yes," I answered.

"Where?"

"Years ago. Popocatepetl. In Mexico." I was beginning to feel better. "I've seen quite a few volcanoes," I said, and an odd thought strayed through my mind. "We forget that we live on just a thin crust of the earth," I said. "We live in constant insecurity. And we really hate it."

After an interval the brother turned to look at me. "That's true," he said. He seemed impressed with my profundity.

While the other two washed and dressed, I lay with my eyes closed, trying to relax some more. When they were through I forced myself to get up. I looked out at Vesuvius, quiescent for the moment, gleaming blackly in the sun. Beyond the rocking boats in the marina, the water danced and glittered.

Some taste for life returned.

Back in Rome, at the first satsang, Andrew said, "Luna, you can't sit there in a corner hiding forever and never speaking to me."

I was sunk in heaviness and apathy. I could hardly open

my eyes, and when I finally did, I couldn't open my mouth to answer. After satsang, in a bar across the street, an English disciple advised me to speak up more during satsang about what I was experiencing, positive or negative, that Andrew was probably waiting for me to make some personal statement in public and to welcome me back 'in.'

I did manage to speak the following evening. I told Andrew I had extended my airline ticket and would remain in Rome until the end of his stay. He seemed pleased.

But I persisted in feeling far too nervous and tongue-tied in front of the group to take off my clothes in public and tell the whole truth. I flinched when anyone else did it. They'd say the most ghastly things about themselves, that they were disgusting monsters of pride, or selfishness, or had succumbed to lust after swearing off sex for a designated period, and they would often break down and sob helplessly while the rest of us watched and waited for more revelations. Andrew seemed to regard this ritual as a necessary humbling act, a sort of final station of the cross that preceded enlightenment.

But I couldn't help feeling that I needed to keep up some kind of appearance as Andrew's mother, that as his mother I should bend just so low and no lower. And in spite of the fact that he hadn't hesitated to shame me in front of his followers, I couldn't bring myself to do the same to him, that is, tell what he said he wanted me to tell, the whole truth, which would of necessity include all my criticism of him.

I often wished I were invisible.

At dawn the following day I woke up exhausted by frightful dreams I couldn't recall, but it turned out to be my happiest day in Rome. Everything that happened seemed out of the far-away distant past, when long, long ago I'd had a day during which I was simply cheerful and content.

I went by myself to see the restored ceiling of the Sistine Chapel. Sunshine flooded the old streets. The delicate cobalt sky and ocher-tinted buildings seemed to combine to shed that unique light of Rome so loved by painters. I turned into the Via Della Conciliazone and walked briskly towards Vatican city. The grandiose boulevard, built in Mussolini's time and lined with white marble lamp-posts, had the consequential air of leading you to a New Jerusalem.

The chapel itself was crowded with tourists. I found myself enjoying the noise and bustle. I sat on a bench and gazed up at the rejuvenated ceiling. Some of the colors seemed too bright, as though robbing Michelangelo's vision of subtlety. Yet to me the hands of God and Adam reaching for each other, although I'd seen it reproduced a thousand times, still prevailed as one of the most tender and evocative images imaginable.

Afterwards I had red wine and pasta with basil and tomato sauce at an outdoor cafe and sat looking at the passing crowd completely at peace.

At satsang I told Andrew I'd had a light-hearted happy day. "It's because I trust you more," I said. At that moment I really believed it.

"It's the only reason," Andrew agreed, nodding.

He went on to speak to Manny Rivers about some difficulty between them. He didn't make clear what it was, but after satsang I saw Manny sitting next to Rebecca, clutching her hand, his head on her shoulder, crying like a baby. The sight shocked me. Manny? Leaning on Rebecca!? She sat with downcast eyes looking like the cat who'd swallowed the canary.

Manny had been Andrew's best friend since Andrew's enlightenment. Now he seemed as much Andrews's slave as myself. I wondered whether it was possible for a guru to have a friend? Or a mother? Or, for that matter, a wife? I had no idea what went on between Andrew and Alka now. But, in the eyes of the sangha, if he was the King, she was the Queen. If he was the perfect man she was the perfect woman. Everyone assumed she was enlightened too and regarded her with reverence.

I spent the next day, Sunday, with my dress-maker friend. We went for a walk amongst the Roman ruins while she gave me a run-down on the related history. At one point she told me about Caligula's bizarre sexual inclinations, making me shudder and laugh. I had come to this friend as to a mother, for warmth, comfort, and good food. And she'd given all three unstintingly. But it was a strain being with someone so locked into the outside world.

Andrew started satsang that evening by suddenly turning to me and saying, simply, "What?"

And without thinking, like an automaton, I heard myself intoning, "Andrew, I see the fire in you that Poonjaji talked about. I'm sorry it's taken me such a long time."

Andrew's face lit up. He seemed very gratified. Then he said, and it sounded somewhat like an apology, "This pressing quality in me that forces you, comes from the UNKNOWN; it is choiceless, just there, operating, for some reason."

When satsang ended I leaned close to Manny, who was sitting beside me, and said, rather melodramatically, "Manny, he's finally done it, he's killed me."

"What? Done what?"

"He's killed me," I repeated.

Manny, who was usually so quick, looked back at me blankly. He had his own problems.

For the first time in weeks I felt optimistic again. I had the unclouded perception that Andrew's hardness and harsh demands were attributes of his purity, a purity outraged by the vulgar doubts of people like me. His righteous anger was God's anger. I wrote him a note.

During satsang I sat right in front of him, looking straight into his eyes—so soft and deep and beguiling. His beauty stupefied me.

He looked back at me holding my note. "I'm satisfied with what is happening to you," he said.

I was ecstatic.

First thing in the morning I went to visit Sergio, an old Italian friend who lived on the outskirts of Rome in the Castello di Lunghezza. He had taken the job as the castle's caretaker because, he told me, it gave him the freedom to write poetry. I'd lost touch with him the last years and had run into him quite by accident while queuing up for a bus in the Piazza di Largo Argentina.

In and around the castle, an ancient crumbling structure, you could actually experience a powerful pressure from the past. Age piled upon age, beginning with the Etruscans. You got the impression that ghosts inhabited the cobweb-veiled, echoing rooms.

I told Sergio, somewhat self-consciously—we had once shared a sense of absurdity about the imbecility of mankind—the latest news about myself and Andrew. After listening with an impassive expression, he took a gulp of wine, lit a cigarette, and burst out with such a blast of ridicule and contempt that I was shocked. He said my involvement with Andrew and his philosophy sounded like some kind of crazy addiction, no different from an addiction to heroin. "It's a disease," he declared. "You're ruining your life Luna, an intelligent woman like you—!"

I didn't say anything in reply. But I felt our friendship was over.

When I left I glanced back at the castle. Only one tiny window amongst the hundreds in that vast, decaying edifice glowed with light—Sergio's bedroom. It was eerie.

At satsang that night Andrew asked me why I hadn't written to him for two days. He seemed annoyed. I shrugged my shoulders. To tell the truth, I didn't know why I hadn't written. He started talking about his fears. About being totally alone. About his enormous responsibilities. He looked straight at me and said, "See Luna? See what's happening to your son?"

I had no idea what he was hinting at. And I was bewildered by the fact that, of all things, he was reminding me that he was my son. Was he asking his mother to comfort him in some way? I telephoned when I got home.

"I'd like to see you," I said.

"I'll see," he answered.

"I've changed," I said. "I've really changed," and, after the tiniest hesitation, "I'm yours!"

"I believe you."

"My greatest fear has been that you will never love me again."

"That's a reasonable fear." There was a quiver of something different in his tone. It was not as abrupt and harsh and unyielding as before. "Now that you've put something down, you must pick something up," he went on, and I heard the reappearance of a certain hardness in his voice. "It's the burden of love," he said.

Again, I had no idea what he meant.

"Good-bye," he said, and he hung up.

I'd been dreaming that Andrew was my lover. I was lying in his arms, facing him, gazing into his eyes. They were fixed on the wall behind me while he absent-mindedly stroked my back. It was a dream I used to have about my father, whose attention I struggled for unsuccessfully most of my life.

Andrew told me to come and sit in the front row again. He said I looked too relaxed leaning against the wall. Then he spent most of satsang relating his experiences with Poonjaji—his meeting with the sage, his instant attraction, his awe at Poonja's respect for him, his growing love, his adoration, and finally, his realization that this perfect being, Poonjaji, was and would remain the most important person to him for the rest of his life.

He talked with his usual charming ingenuousness; his sincerity shone like the sun. I gazed at him, rapt. He belonged to a FORCE beyond us all. But towards the end of his talk, something curious began to happen. I found that I was getting peculiar schizoid here-he-is, here-he-isn't impressions. One moment he was the enchanting Andrew before me (Dr. Jekyll), and in the next, his face contorting, he became a cruel and unknown remorseless creature (Mr. Hyde). I sat watching my mind do these acrobatics and suddenly realized that all my trust had fled in the face of this double vision. I realized I still held inside my head a clearly etched image of what I thought a 'master' should be and Andrew didn't measure up.

It turned out that he and I, purely by coincidence, had reservations for our return to the States on the same plane! It would make a stop in Boston, Andrew's destination, before continuing on to New York, mine. He was on his way to Amherst, Massachusetts, where preparations had been made for him to teach. I was to join him there later.

"So," Andrew said to me, "you will have me to yourself for eight hours!"

At the airport he stood surrounded by a throng of adoring disciples jostling excitedly for a place next to him. They all wanted to take photos with their Master and he obliged them all, smiling cheerfully.

I bought cappuccini for everyone and stood apart watching what was going on. It was embarrassing to see these supposedly serious seekers behaving like a bunch of rock-star fans.

Andrew contrived to sleep or pretended to sleep throughout our entire journey together and we exchanged no more than a few banal words. I was sure this was by design. As for me, I watched two movies back-to-back.

At the airport in Boston I parted from him sadly. No matter what had happened the last few days, I felt I was I was saying good-bye to a remote stranger, more strange, more remote, than ever before.

15

I SPENT THE FOLLOWING TWO MONTHS IN NEW YORK. Andrew had asked me not to come to Amherst until May second, so that American disciples who had not seen him for some time would have more of his attention.

Two Americans, Alice and Fred Stanton—young friends of mine who'd met Andrew several times before his enlightenment, and had come to Amsterdam to investigate his teaching—were eagerly awaiting his return. Also requiring his attention, he told me, were quite a number of newcomers.

Alice and I had met years ago as beginners in a Tai Chi class. She had seemed a good-natured easy-going person, and we had gotten into the habit of giving each other self-deprecating grins after making fools of ourselves in some particularly vain attempt to imitate the Chinese teacher. Alice wanted to be a writer, she told me, but had landed in law school instead, to please her family. She reminded me a lot of myself when I was her age and that endeared her to me enormously. We grew to be intimate friends. Eventually she did become a writer.

I never got to know her husband as well as I knew her. His was a far more reticent personality. But what I intuited about him, I loved. He was also a writer, a tall slender, sensitive, witty man.

They were living in Maine now, approximately a three hour ride from Amherst. Soon after I arrived in New York, I heard from Andrew that they had come to his first two satsangs, but after the second one, had never returned. According to a report I got from them, the first night Andrew had complimented Alice on how quietly she was able to sit. He said nothing to Fred. On the second night he abruptly turned to Alice, and, in a brutal manner, without any preamble, said, "Alice, you've never done anything wholeheartedly in your life. Now maybe this is going to cause you pain, maybe it will even cause you torture. Look, I'm not interested in torturing anyone, believe me, but I want you to go home and not come back until you're willing to make a commitment to the best of your ability to do whatever I think is necessary for you to do." He laughed. "Wait a minute," he added, "I'm going to make it harder. Don't come back until you're absolutely willing to do whatever I tell you to do." Then he turned to Fred, and added rudely, "And the same thing goes for you!"

The two of them were absolutely crushed and bewildered. They told me they'd taken Andrew's words literally and, after ten anguished days of discussion, had decided that they could never in good conscience accede to unconditional surrender to Andrew's will.

"It was hell," Alice said. "For three months afterwards we doubted everything, specially ourselves."

Fred added bitterly, "We'd been with him for only that one week in Amsterdam, and he was demanding our total, unquestioning submission!"

Andrew always disowned responsibility in this affair. At first, he insisted that he'd never said what they claimed he said. Then he maintained that he'd forgotten the whole thing because there'd been nothing unusual about it to remember. When I timidly related in detail their view of the event, he turned to Bud Rivers, who was nearly always at his side, and said, "I didn't use those words, did I Bud? Did I really say that?"

"No, of course not," Bud agreed mildly.

"But even if I did say what they profess I said, why did they run away? Why didn't they stay and talk to me about it? Why don't they come back? They're fools! No, no, the answer is, they have no guts!"

And as far as he was concerned, that was that.

But I couldn't accept it. It rankled and rankled. Andrew seemed to have no idea how threatening and abusive he appeared to other people. Nevertheless, I was afraid, as usual, to be openly critical, afraid of being disowned myself.

16

I ARRIVED IN AMHERST IN A STATION WAGON BOR-
rowed from my son Joshua. Both Joshua and his wife, Pat,
had left for China. Pat, who taught English to foreigners, had
signed a year's contract to make English-teaching videos for
Chinese television. In order to join her, Joshua, fluent in Chinese,
had organized a deal with his business partner in New York to
carry on for a year without him. He intended to go to the university in Nanking and study Chinese history.

A small college town greeted me, quiet and tree-laden. Old
America. Emily Dickinson had lived here all her life. I drove out of
the town into the country, where a house had been rented for myself
and a few others. It had been built in the eighteenth century and
looked incredibly neglected. I was happy, nonetheless, to get my
own little room, shabby and broken-down as it was. Half the floor-
boards had been torn up and the window was cracked.

Andrew had been gracious enough—I was surprised at
this—to telephone me in New York to ask me if I would be comfortable with the people who were to be my house-mates. I said I
was sure I'd be quite comfortable.

Lynn, the disciple I'd shared a room with in Totnes, and
who'd been with us in Jerusalem, had already arrived, along with
some others, including a pretty blond young Englishwoman I'd
never met before and her two-year-old daughter.

I noticed that whenever Lynn addressed me, her tone was extremely patronizing. She had a certain snotty English way of speaking and it seemed to me that it grew particularly snotty when she spoke to me. At first I paid no attention, but then I was told by another disciple, a Chilean guitarist, that Lynn had objected strenuously to my being part of the group in this house, which, incidentally, had been organized by Andrew. The guitarist said that when his Dutch girlfriend, also a disciple, had told Lynn she thought I was a very nice person, Lynn had retorted, "You haven't lived with her!"

I tried to remember in what way I had offended Lynn. I could think of nothing. We hardly knew one another. For the hundredth time I wondered uneasily to what degree Andrew's public attacks had given people license to behave so disrespectfully towards me.

The satsang hall was the huge living room of a rather grand house surrounded on three sides by great spaces of grass and flowers, and backed by woodland. It was a fifteen minute drive from the town of Amherst. I heard Andrew had rooms on the second story, a bedroom he shared with Alka, and a small study. This was by far the most luxurious dwelling he had occupied as a guru.

On my first evening, at the beginning of satsang, as Andrew slowly inspected the room, his eyes met mine and halted. "How are things going?" he asked.

"Okay," I said.

This was Andrew's way of saying 'hello' to his mom.

"You know why you're all here?" he asked, still staring straight at me. No one spoke. I didn't move a hair. "You all came here for one thing," he said, "and that's to be blown away!" His eyes roamed on. "There is no right time," he continued. "You're never ready. There's no preparation. The time is now!"

Stirred by a whiff of something beyond the beyond, I felt goose-bumps rise on my arms and legs.

I was informed that Andrew wanted me to stay behind after everyone had gone. When he came out to see me, he asked if I knew the birth date of his dead father. He said he'd forgotten it and needed the information to fill out a form for Alka's green card. He didn't come into the satsang room but spoke from the doorway of what I was to discover was the kitchen, as if he wanted only this much contact with me and no more. However, all day I'd had an intense longing for contact with him, and I found myself running and hugging him. Maybe I surprised him into it, but he gave me a hug back. He invited me into the kitchen. I told him the date of his father's birth. After a short silence he said, "I've been thinking that it would be a good idea for you to write to Alice and Fred Stanton and tell them you think they were stupid to have run away after a few sharp words from me."

I looked away at the sparklingly clean, white, modern kitchen. The burst of love that had driven me to run and take him in my arms began to seep away. He was insisting I agree that he was right no matter what.

"Their feelings were hurt," I said.

"They're fools," he said, as he had the last time we discussed the Stantons and abruptly, he ushered me out.

Albert, a tall, bespectacled, stuttering Dutchman who lived in my house, had become my pal. He was still in his twenties, very smart, straightforward, and not defensive about Andrew. One day, we went for a walk together. It was a beautiful New England spring morning. The air was perfumed and the grass freshly green. We had a long chat about how we were feeling. Both of us admitted that being with Andrew involved a lot of suffering.

"The most unbearable feeling is the tension of not knowing who you are and where you're going," Albert said.

"The most unbearable feeling to me," I said, "is enduring the surrender of my ego." We both meant the same thing.

I can't remember who instigated the meeting, but I do remember having breakfast with Bud Rivers the following week at a local diner. For some reason I recall that we both ordered the specialty of the house—blueberry pancakes with real maple syrup. It was the first time we'd talked one-to-one in a long time. Bud had once had a good sense of humor but now he appeared subdued and humorless, very different from the amiable open-faced, unsure, babyish fellow I'd gotten to know in Rishikesh. Bud was now Andrew's right hand man. In fact, Andrew had stated at some satsang or other that apart from Poonja, there were only two people in the world he completely trusted—his wife and Bud!

I was aware that I had to be careful about what I said because every word was going to be repeated to Andrew. But at some point I slipped. I told Bud I really missed my piano lessons in New York. Bud must have related this piece of information to Andrew straightaway. That night Andrew cautioned me sharply. "Piano lessons, Luna? You have a greedy mind. You should know your priorities!"

Without it being spelled out, commitments or interests of any kind outside your household were regarded with suspicion. I was sure I was under constant scrutiny in this matter.

Ramesh, an Indian devotee of Poonja's who lived in New York, had become a friend of mine. I heard that he had come to Amherst and was staying as a guest in Andrew's house. But I was stunned when Andrew telephoned and invited me to join them on an outing to Shelburne Falls, so stunned, in fact, that Andrew had to repeat his invitation three times before I could grasp what he was saying. I couldn't believe it. Andrew was summoning me to a *social* occasion where he, Andrew, would be present.

Others had been invited on this outing as well. We all sat on huge boulders and talked and watched the falls come down in a myriad of graceful, fragile sheets that looked unreal and not like any waterfall I'd ever seen before.

Andrew's eyes appeared more hollowed and dark than ever. His face was thinner. When we were alone for a few moments I said, "You look different."

"Older," he said.

"And wiser?" I smiled.

He blinked. Instantly, I realized I'd implied that his enlightenment had not been complete before. "I didn't mean it," I hastened to say, "honest, it's just a cliché."

Apparently he hadn't minded for he was very loving towards me all afternoon and slapped me on the back several times, saying, "So you've joined the club at last." And he gave me so many affectionate glances that I allowed myself to believe my most extravagant dream—that one day I would be re-united with him in a new and thrilling way.

My group went house hunting since the ancient one we were presently living in had turned out to be too rundown. We found our new home in the town of Amherst—a huge, sprawling, filthy, fraternity house that took all of us five whole days to clean. During those five days I recognized, scrubbing away with the rest, the basic need to be included. One of the great charms of group living was that you never needed to feel lonely. There was a strong gratifying sense of belonging. We all scrubbed equally. In the sangha houses, during the normal course of things, all the housework was divided equally and maintenance jobs were circulated so that no one was stuck with toilet cleaning, for example, more than one week at a time.

On the second day, hot and exhausted, I lay down in one of the rooms on a mattress to relax for half an hour, and fell asleep. I dreamt that Andrew was conducting some kind of sex therapy class or some class where sex was the key to enlightenment. In the dream Andrew was my lover who had just cast me aside.

The new house was finally in order. I'd wrangled the only single room, a sweltering little cube in the attic. The idea of getting dressed and undressed in the presence of much younger women made me feel uncomfortable, but I hesitated to discuss it since everyone here believed in the total exposure of everything. I knew they wouldn't be able to understand. At the same time I knew I was considered covetous about my privacy.

At satsang that week Andrew told a young man he was a coward and a 'wimp.' His angry voice and hostile words stung me even though I knew they were considered impersonal and a goad to change.

On June 9, my birthday, Andrew accepted my invitation to lunch at a Chinese restaurant. Unfortunately Alka had to be included. Still, I was overjoyed at the notion of having Andrew almost to myself for a couple of hours.

His presence beside me at the table lifted me to such a blithe, carefree state, that throughout lunch I felt my insides glowing. He insisted on paying the bill, and afterwards, took me to a coffee house for dessert.

Back home I was confounded and astonished to find my housemates waiting with presents and congratulations. After satsang, I was even more confounded and astonished to discover that a gigantic surprise party had been organized.

Lots and lots of people came bearing gifts. It was embarrassing. Most of them were relative strangers. Just as in Israel, I knew this party was really for Andrew. Making a fuss over his mother was making a fuss over him. Anyway, I suspected that he'd engineered the whole thing, though I couldn't imagine why. I was absolutely shocked when he himself arrived, accompanied by Bud Rivers. I hadn't expected him. He didn't usually appear at people's birthdays. He hung about outside on the empty veranda with Bud, looking uncomfortable, the object of many longing glances from the doorway. No one dared approach without being asked.

I came out and sat beside him on a decaying plastic sofa. In this context I couldn't help but feel that I was in the company of visiting royalty and I was terribly nervous. Apart from exchanging a few stilted remarks, we said nothing to each other. Nevertheless, I was madly elated that he had come. It showed *something*. But what? That he still honored me as his mother? That he still respected me? Who knew?

At satsang the following evening Andrew said that when he was with his guru, he never wanted anything more. Just to be with his teacher was completion for him. "The day after I met Poonjaji," Andrew said, "I knew he held me in the palm of his hand." At this point, a woman from Australia said she felt wonderful with Andrew but something important seemed to be missing. "What is missing," Andrew responded sternly, "is your complete surrender." She burst into loud shuddering sobs.

After satsang Albert and I went to a club in Northhampton to hear a wonderful old jazz violinist, Papa Joe Creach. During a break between sets Albert told me that he'd sometimes seen Andrew's hands trembling when he took his seat to begin satsang. I found this touching, and somehow reassuring, to know that Andrew was still vulnerable. I bought a T-shirt for him with Papa's name printed on it.

The next evening Andrew said that small gifts like the T-shirt and a package of pistachio nuts I'd given him the week before, showed, more than the big money donations, the evolution of my new relationship to him.

But, as if to counter what Albert had told me about seeing his hands trembling, Andrew went on to describe at great length the consummate self-confidence and the sense of perfect safety his enlightened state had brought him.

Near the end of satsang an Italian man, who'd come from Rome with his girlfriend to see Andrew, burst into voluminous tears. He explained in Italian that although he didn't understand a word of English, his heart had been deeply roused by Andrew's 'vibrations.'

Andrew smiled serenely.

We were all very impressed.

Alice Stanton telephoned, I can't remember why; perhaps to seal the date for a trip I'd promised to make to Maine during the next break. I didn't know what to say. Andrew had continued to refer to her and Fred very disparagingly and each time there was an unmistakable insinuation that I was being subversive by not writing a letter to tell them that I thought they were stupid to have left him.

Ashamed of myself, and acting against every impulse I could still call my own, very late, after satsang, I sat on my bed and wrote them the following letter:

July 11, 1988
Dear Alice and Fred,

I am writing this letter because I feel uneasy about what may lie between us as a result of what happened between you and Andrew. I feel our phone conversations have been guarded and one thing you said, Alice, disturbed me. When I suggested that we talk about you and Andrew in person and not by telephone, you said, "There's no reason to talk about it at all." But it's impossible not to talk about it, and besides, I cannot avoid talking about what has become the center of my existence.

I love you both very much and I'm sorry about what happened. You well know what I've endured and you always encouraged me to do it Andrew's way. When, at last, I could, my basic struggle and resistance ended. My path is now one-pointed. I have surrendered. I don't really understand why you found Andrew's words so unendurable, but I do understand your fear, the same fear as mine was, and to some extent, still is—the fear of total annihilation of the ego.

I want to be able to talk openly with no holds barred. To be courageous together. If it is possible, please answer this letter, and then let's get together. In any case, I'd like to know how you feel. Whether we meet now or later, my heart is always open to you.

Love,
Luna

This letter had been wrenched from me—I felt its resonance in the pit of my stomach for days. Although I'd actually written it and had already mailed it, in my heart of hearts I could not concede that Andrew was right. I felt he was not only being unfair; he was being spiteful.

Judy, a housewife who claimed the honor of being the first British follower to be enlightened by Andrew, arrived a few days later, accompanied by her husband and her two young sons. A week later, Sarah, the Israeli girl I'd met in Totnes, arrived. At the time, she was in a 'relationship' with my friend, Albert, and they were to share a room. I'd heard that there'd been some objections to Sarah's joining our group, especially on the part of Lynn, the very same Lynn who had, a month before, objected to me.

Although Sarah and I had lived in the same house in Totnes, I knew little about her. But I had already made it my business to be one of her arch-defenders against the likes of Lynn and later on, Judy.

Lynn found an ally in Judy. They started openly criticizing Sarah, both to her face and behind her back. They disparaged her loudness, her boisterousness, her taste in clothes, and her relationship with Albert. There was an inappropriate sadistic flavor to these attacks on Sarah, and I gradually became aware, since no one voiced any protest against the mean comments of the two women, that Sarah had become the house scapegoat.

To solve interpersonal problems in the satsang houses, a tradition of house meetings had developed. A meeting could be called by anyone for any reason. I hated them because I was afraid of the aggression I saw in the others and naturally, feared becoming an object of that aggression myself.

At the first house meeting called in our new home, Lynn, in a tone of disgust, asked Sarah how often she had sex with Albert. I listened aghast as poor Sarah, intimidated into telling the truth, and as if she were confessing to a heinous sin, admitted apologetically that sex with Albert was a nightly affair.

I scrutinized Sarah, stocky, freckled, not pretty, but somehow appealing, immature, guilt-ridden, emotional, Jewish—as if for the first time. Why, I wondered, was she going along with them? She was sobbing. Her lover and my pal, Albert, sat stone-faced, looking straight ahead, seemingly scared to death and absolutely mute. Then I scrutinized Lynn, pallid, blond, over-weight, waspy, with her slow, cold, contemptuous manner of speaking her very British English, carrying on a Nazi-like inter-rogation of Sarah, aided and abetted by Judy, a less-deliberate, less-assured, blond WASP, but equally Nazi-like in her question-ing. Their prurience and cruelty shocked me. But *I* was intimidat-ed by them, too, and along with Judy's husband, and the Chilean-Dutch couple, and the mother of the two-and-a-half year old daughter, and of course, Albert, I, too, remained silent.

In the morning, Sarah burst into my room in tears and threw herself down on my bed. "I don't know what to do," she cried.

"Lynn and Judy are acting like fascists," I responded. "Something has to be done about it!"

Sarah lifted her flushed face and stared at me.

"For God's sake, why didn't you defend yourself?" I asked.

Sarah sat up and wiped her eyes with her fingers. "I don't know why," she answered.

"You don't know? You don't know?" I exploded.

"I couldn't help it. I don't know why." Sarah started to cry again.

"We have to do something about it." I repeated.

"What can we do?" Sarah blubbered.

I looked at her dark frizzy head bent over her shaking

hands. Her cowardice repelled me. But I'd been a coward too. I remembered my horrible silence of the night before. The spooky sensation of watching her being bullied by Lynn and Judy passed through me again. I felt I had to do something, anything. I had to be brave, perhaps call another meeting, speak up, face them head-on, tell Andrew about it, ask for advice. Something!

About five o'clock in the afternoon I had coffee in town with Albert and we discussed the situation. He apologized for his silence the night before and encouraged me to call another house meeting right away. "Don't be afraid of them," he said, Andrew would want you to do it." Since there would be no satsang in the evening, I decided I would ask for a house meeting as soon as I returned home.

But, as I went up the two flights of stairs to the veranda and saw the entire group sitting there, the anger in me escalated, and when I reached the last step, it suddenly exploded. I looked at Lynn and said, "Everyone here is scared silly of you. Are you at all aware of that?" I turned to Judy. "And you too!" I said. "They're damn scared of you too!" I looked back at Lynn. "You both act like a couple of Gestapo agents. You know that? I want to call a meeting now!"

They all gaped back at me stupefied. After a very pregnant silence, somebody said softly, "We'd better go in and have dinner first."

We went in slowly, one by one, and ate our meal without a word being said.

My heart was pounding. I was breathless. My hands were trembling. But later, in the living-room, when I began to speak, it took no more than a few seconds for my voice to steady.

"You two," I said, addressing Lynn and Judy, "you two are making a scapegoat out of Sarah. A scapegoat. You know what I mean? I've heard you out on the veranda night after night making fun of her. I've heard you talking about her with contempt and revulsion in your voices. Who the hell do you think you are? What makes you so morally superior?"

I looked around at eight, stiff, motionless faces. Then Lynn and Judy turned and stared at each other. Sarah glanced quickly at Albert, and then down at a large man's ring set with a blue agate stone she wore on the middle finger of her left hand—a gift from him. Suddenly she averted her eyes from that, too, and wound up gazing at me with what appeared to be a mixture of surprise and fear.

"And your curiosity about Sarah's sex life, asking her all those questions—what business is it of yours?" I paused, trying to control the anger that was accelerating again. "It's none of your business, is it?" No one answered. "Is it?" I reiterated. Again no one responded.

After a long interval Lynn remarked coolly, "Luna, you don't seem to understand something. You don't understand that we really care about Sarah."

Judy ran her fingers through her hair. "Yes, we care about Sarah a lot," she echoed. "You're dreaming all this up Luna."

"We're critical because we love her," Lynn said. And then she added, "You're just raving."

"Yes," Judy said, "You don't know what you're talking about. You must be out of your mind. We love Sarah and it was out of love that we discussed her on the veranda, and that we talked to her and tried to help her at the last house meeting, it was solely out of love."

Love—? I thought. What a cover for plain unscrupulous meanness! Or was it sexual envy? Or the irresistible urge to dominate a natural victim?

"Oh, I'm in my right mind, all right, all right," I broke in, "so don't give me this crap about love!"

Once again, silence.

Then Sarah spoke, hesitant, her freckled face awash with tears, and, I couldn't believe my ears, she was agreeing with them! She sat looking from Lynn to Judy with reddened, squinting little eyes, back and forth, back and forth. "You're both right," I heard her saying. "It's true, you're right. I don't know why I didn't see it before. I am ashamed of myself. Ashamed! I'll move out of Albert's room right away. I'll go to another house. I'll do anything you say."

I looked at Albert. His eyes skittered about the room, refusing to meet mine.

I looked at Judy and at Lynn. Both were staring tensely at the floor.

"See?" I cried, "There's collusion going on to avoid confronting you because, dammit, we're all afraid of you! We all want to appease you!"

No one spoke. Everyone was staring at the floor. Why didn't the Chilean fellow speak? Or his Dutch girlfriend? Or Judy's husband? Or the English mother? Or, for God's sake, Albert, damn him!

I couldn't believe that no one was going to come to my aid. I was alone. The rats had deserted the sinking ship.

Unexpectedly, Lynn began to cry.

Then Judy said, haltingly, "Luna, don't you trust me?" I looked at her speechless with amazement. Why in the world should I trust her?

Not another word was said.

After a time, one by one, we all wandered off to bed.

As I was falling asleep I was aware of feeling grateful to Andrew for my courage. The decision to speak up had come from my being able to own up to my cowardice, and for his sake, and his sake alone, to face it.

Judy came up to my room first thing in the morning and said, "Tell me the truth, Luna, what have you got against me?"

I was dumbfounded. She had understood nothing, and had turned last night's meeting into a personal vendetta against herself.

Later, Sarah came up. I didn't want to see her. I didn't want to speak to her ever again. She apologized to me for giving in to 'them.'

"You're a Judas," I said. And then, because I was so furious with her, I said something asinine that I was ashamed of as soon as I said it. I said, "You're like some of those Jews under Hitler who crawled on their bellies before their torturers."

I went out for the afternoon. When I got back I was told Andrew had telephoned to tell Judy and Lynn to 'cool it.' Obviously, someone had been quick to inform him about what happened last night.

At satsang I sat near him and felt invaded by his density, his smoothness, his super-humanness. That person was my son! That was my kid! Once more, the paradox shimmered in my brain.

Toward the end of the session he addressed me. "You're feeling amazed at everything, aren't you?" he said.

I nodded, eyes brimming. He'd read my mind again. I realized I was feeling closer and closer to him. I ached to have a conversation with him, eat a meal with him, go for a walk with him.

"You've gone from resistance to acceptance!" he said.

The next morning I woke up soft and excited. Everything outside me seemed insubstantial and inside, at my center, burned a singular bright reality, Andrew.

At satsang he said, "To an unawakened mind, devotion is separation; to an awakened one, bliss." He seemed to me strangely volcanic, his eyes smokier, his sentences less explanatory. He seemed to be saying: "Get it now or never! Drop everything and fly!"

I came home feeling intensely alive and realized once again that only at Andrew's side did my life catch fire.

He decided to go away for the week-end and I took a trip to Boston and talked about him for two days with one of his disciples, a social worker, who listened eagerly to my rantings even though I knew she had many reservations. I encouraged her to sell her home and give up all for Andrew. When I got to bed I was exhausted and high as a kite.

The next afternoon my hostess drove me to Harvard Square and suggested I walk around there for a couple of hours until she finished working with a client nearby.

On my way to The Coffee Connection, a nearby cafe, I was suddenly dizzy, inundated with bliss. A gnarled old lady smiled at me and stopped and said, "You look very contented."

"I am," I said.

"May it be for always," she said.

Awhile back, in Totnes, Andrew had exiled Dvora for a few months. I didn't know what form her recalcitrance had taken or where she had gone. He often asked people to leave for a while if they were particularly resistant to some aspect of his teaching. They were always terribly distressed at this request.

Now Dvora was back, sitting in the front row, her eyes fastened on Andrew as if in a trance. He concluded the satsang by saying, "Other teachers say you are imperfect and must strive for perfection, I say you are already perfect and must only realize it."

Dvora bowed her head and burst into loud heart-rending sobs and she remained where she was, weeping unabashedly during the entire time it took the room to clear. I was almost the last to go. At the exit I glanced over my shoulder and saw Bud Rivers motioning her towards the door to the kitchen. I knew in my guts that she was going to be invited back to live in Andrew's house and work for him as she had before, and I was filled with envy. In the morning I woke up feeling desperately lonely. I looked at my watch. It was still very early but I got up and called Andrew. He answered the phone. I said I wanted to see him.

"Why?" he asked, laughing.

"Just to talk," I said

"About what?" he asked.

"Things," I said.

"What things?" He chuckled. Then he said, "You might be invited to lunch here some day soon."

"But I want to see you alone. Can't I see you alone?"

"Why?" he asked.

"I just want to, that's all."

I was going through difficult days, days of tremendous mood swings, up and down, up and down days. Manny Rivers mentioned to me that he was spending most of his evenings after satsang in Andrew's house. More stabs of jealousy. Then he told me that Alka's sister was getting married and there would be a big wedding party in Bombay.

I hadn't been invited! Considering that I'd never met my daughter-in-law's parents, I felt insulted at being unceremoniously excluded from the celebrations. My mind lurched miserably at these happenings.

One evening I was called up to Andrew's study to discuss the uproar about Sarah. I'd been anxious to talk to him about it.

The study was a lovely little den containing a desk, a T.V., a couple of chairs and a narrow bed with a bright colorful cover. On the desk was a framed photo of a young girl who had once been an inspired devotee, and who had died in a car accident.

I went over my side of the story briefly. He sat listening with a certain chill detachment. Even my reference to Gestapo behavior brought no response. I began to have the sensation that the bottom was falling out of everything.

"I can't stand living with Lynn and Judy," I said finally. "I can't stand living with people like that. I want to move to another house."

"You're copping out," he said.

Copping out? Copping out? I felt myself grow hot. What did he mean? He hadn't heard a word I'd said. "What can you do if someone goes right on being aggressive after having been confronted about it time and time again?" I asked in a tight voice. "Tell me, what can you do?

Didn't he appreciate what I had done? I thought I'd stood up to unfairness, stupidity, low motives, unconsciousness. I thought I'd challenged a certain kind of evil. How could he say I was copping out?

"You face it over and over," he answered in the same chilly tone, "and gradually your fear of the other's aggression will disappear."

I wanted to say, "But the aggression won't disappear!" But I didn't.

I suspected that no matter what I said, there was no way that I could ever change Andrew's mind about anything. I always ended up feeling like a damned fool.

Andrew had a high regard for the potential of communal living, and viewed the satsang houses as experiments in a new kind of life-style, radical and love-dominated, machines that expedited the process of enlightenment. And he could not be, and never was, to my knowledge, shaken from this position regardless of what evidence to the contrary was presented to him. He himself, it should not be forgotten, had never lived in one!

Andrew went away for the following week-end and I returned to New York. I re-read the diary he had kept of the two and a half weeks with Poonja during which time he was enlightened. I'd made a copy of it, with his consent, some time ago, when we were still ostensibly 'close.' I also re-read all the letters he'd sent me from India.

When I was through all my doubts had vanished into the air like puffs of smoke. It was impossible for me to hold on to my wavering uncertainty in the face of the truth that had come rushing at me from the pages I'd read. I experienced again, as if for the first time, the shock of recognition at *who or what* Andrew was now— a mysteriously altered being, a transcendent soul, light-years away from my pathetic puny attempts to understand him.

I wanted to thank him. I decided to go out immediately and buy him something beautiful. Shopping for him had a special thrill; you were seeking a gift for a god. Money was no object. All the better if you bought what you couldn't afford. Then, perhaps, he'd notice you and consecrate you with a smile. And that was what you desired above all other things—to be acknowledged and approved of by God.

In Macy's I found a long-sleeved white cotton pique eyelet

shirt. It had been reduced to half its price. I paid seventy-five dollars for it nonetheless; I gave Andrew only the best. I would never have considered spending the same amount of money on a similar article for myself. However it wasn't too difficult for me to give Andrew the money and gifts I gave him because it cost me so little to live in his community. As I've mentioned, whatever extra I had usually went to him. And the same was true for most of his followers. After taking care of the essentials they gave what was left to support their master in style.

My first night back from New York I had an astounding visual experience. Fifteen minutes before the end of satsang the light in the room seemed to darken and I blinked. It was as if a heavy raincloud had entered the room and was drifting over us. I blinked again, and again. The light suddenly cleared and things seemed normal once more. Then the room grayed again, and in spite of blinking repeatedly, the room remained overcast, the light leaden, as if a storm were about to break. I was aware all at once that the rows of people sitting in front of me on the floor were no longer three-dimensional but had flattened out and appeared, row behind row, like two-dimensional planes at right angles to the flat plane of the floor, like the cardboard cut-outs you find in turn-of-the-century valentine cards. One row was very sharply delineated from the next, and at the far end, facing me, also flattened, his eyes darting devilishly from side to side, sat Andrew.

My own eyes had now become fixed, unable to blink. My heart pounded with terror. But abruptly, after what seemed like a timeless instant, I learned I could blink again. And then the world returned to what it had been.

Such experiences were becoming increasingly loaded with hope. I interpreted them as manifestations of the divine.

The next evening, when Andrew came into the satsang room wearing my beautiful white eyelet shirt, I felt almost hysterical with delight. I nudged people around me saying, "That's my shirt. I bought it for him in New York."

He started out by stating that not only the conscious, but that the unconscious must surrender to him as well! Surrender the unconscious? Wow! Was that possible? Andrew was demanding more and more and more and more.

We were about to move to Boston. House groups were forming and re-forming. People were being accepted, rejected, preferred or damned—depending upon whether the more powerful ones, the self-appointed choosers, exerted their influence to have someone selected or not. I felt queasy about it all.

People wanted to get into the houses they considered advanced, that is, where the tenants appeared to be close to Andrew. The entire process was cruel and threatening and many were utterly humiliated.

Why did Andrew allow this to go on, I wondered? Did he know what was happening? Did he know and approve? It was a mystery to me. The old Andrew would have been outraged at these unseemly power games.

One night I sat in the second row and stared at him intently. How remote he seemed! I found it hard to believe that he would ever allow me into his life again as his mother. The more remote he seemed to me, the more I craved to be with him, the more I was willing to do anything to appease him, the more groveling I became.

Nonetheless, deep, deep in my heart I knew how great the rift between us really was, and I simply couldn't face that fact because it threatened to tear me apart.

I closed my eyes. When I opened them I noticed that Jackie, the legally-blind psychotherapist from Montreal and her sister Constance, had arrived. Constance was an elegant, intelligent woman who appeared to be imprisoned in a staid middle-class life that was starving her soul. She told Andrew that years ago she'd had a powerful mystical experience that had resulted in a nervous break-down and for a short period, confinement in a mental institution. She talked quickly and intensely. We all listened to her with great interest.

When Constance was through, Andrew abruptly turned to Jackie. "Funny thing about you Jackie," he said, as though continuing a conversation they'd just left off, "unlike other people, you're not only confident, you're far too confident. You can plough through anything with that confidence." His tone was unnecessarily insulting, I thought. "That confidence is a wall protecting your ego," he said.

Jackie, sitting right in front of him because of her poor vision, took this calmly, nodding, as though she agreed with him. I was pretty sure that Andrew held it against her that, during her therapy with me, I had ignored his phone calls. As I've said before, it seemed to me he'd been speaking against psychotherapy ever since. After satsang I accompanied Jackie and Constance to their motel. I talked incessantly about Andrew, about how strongly his diary had affected me on my last trip to New York, how before that trip my doubts had roused again, but now my faith in Andrew was restored and burned in my heart more vividly than ever. When I got back home I was so high on talking I couldn't sleep.

Such was the see-saw of my erratic emotional life. I was always in some intense excitable state or other, whether positive or negative.

17

D URING THE THREE WEEK INTERVAL IN NEW
York, before the move to Boston, I spent two days in
Maine with Alice and Fred Stanton. Their despair over
Andrew still distressed and unsettled me. I didn't inform Andrew I
was going. I felt that he'd try to stop me because—how can I say
it?—because he knew the truth. I suspected he knew, despite my
seeming submission to his will, that I identified with the Stantons
and continued to hold his mistreatment of them against *him*. And
because he also knew how close Alice and I had been, I surmised
that he feared her influence on me.

At my request they re-told the tale of their last visit to
Andrew. They remembered every word he'd said to them, every
single word, as, naturally, they were likely to, because the experience had been traumatic only to them. In any case, I believed their
story absolutely, as I had from the beginning.

There were two sides to Andrew, and they didn't fit.

A long time afterwards, Fred's final comment on Andrew was,
"Andrew creates addicts. It's like giving people heroin." This was the
same image my friend Sergio had employed when I visited him in
Rome. And then Fred had offered an interesting idea. "When you're
in one of those tight abusive authoritarian relationships," he said, "the
slightest sign of non-hostility on the part of the guru allows the victim
to reward himself by a release of energy in ecstacy." I thought this
explained a lot of my sudden bursts of unaccountable happinesses.

Alice's opinion of Andrew's source of power boiled down
to one sentence. "I realize now that what one feels in Andrew's
presence, the bottommost feeling, is self-hatred!"

18

Boston, Massachusetts

I ARRIVED IN BOSTON AND WAS TOLD THERE WOULD be no satsang for two days. Andrew, to my vast surprise, called to say hello and I was delighted at this sign that things were improving for me. During the course of our conversation I remarked, "It's a drag coming here when there won't be satsang for two days."

There was a queer silence at the other end. Then Andrew said good-bye and hung up. A minute later he called back. "What did you mean about it being a drag?" he demanded to know. He sounded furious.

I was completely taken aback, and began to stutter. "I—I only meant it was a—a drag your not having satsang for two nights. I could have—uh—spent another night in New York."

"Another night in New York? Another night in New York?" His voice was heavy with sarcasm. "Look Luna, let's face it, you don't belong here. You are a selfish and self-centered woman." Suddenly he was shouting. "You were selfish and self-centered in the fraternity house in Amherst too, no different from the others you complained about. Why is it, tell me, why is it you are the only one who doesn't listen to me? Why? Who doesn't show respect?" He paused, and then added ominously, "You walk a thin red line with me Luna. I'm really pissed this time."

He hung up.

Five minutes later, he called again. "Listen," he said—", But before he could saying anything further I broke in, whimpering, "I wish you wouldn't hang up on me like that."

This seemed to provoke him into an even more savage stream of vituperation, attacking my character, my intentions, my fatal weaknesses, etc. etc. And then he hung up again.

All at once, trembling, I thought I knew what it was all about. He must be raging at the fact that I was still attracted to something in New York, something in my old life. For a few moments I seethed at the extremity of his wrath, then suddenly, I was terrified. I went up to my room and lay down. What exactly was the crime I had committed? I asked myself. I was aware of a desperate need to examine the situation calmly. But my mind became a blank.

At night, in bed, I tried again to look at the situation. I tried to become one with my fear.

I was sharing a small bedroom on the second floor of a jerry-built, cheaply furnished three-bedroom house with Sarah and a timid, middle-aged, rather endearing English woman. We all slept quite comfortably on mattresses on the floor. Next to us, a tiny room was occupied by a New Zealand girl and her two year-old baby who was still being breast-fed. In the third bedroom there were two men, one, a thin, very reserved, very shy Frenchman, the other, a droll English working-class fellow, miserable at the moment, because his wife, the sister of the New Zealand girl, had left him. She had announced her decision to separate from him in front of the entire sangha without having said a word about it to him in advance.

Almost every couple, married or not, had separated. Andrew was forcing people, by hinting, or openly suggesting it at satsang, that they had to give up their primary attachments which he viewed as serious obstacles to freedom. The implication was that once they saw the 'light,' they could re-attach to whomever they wished. At moments I wondered whether in the end, the only couple that would remain intact would be Andrew and Alka—the King and Queen of Sanghaland!

I'd been obsessed with Andrew all day. One moment I wanted to call him up and say, "Master, I bow to you, you know everything, you must be right!" The next, I felt a dupe, and saw myself the victim of his implacable demands, his unreasonable expectations, his irrationality. I questioned whether Andrew was harder on me than anyone else *because* I was his mother? I questioned that a lot.

Satsang took place at the Montessori school in a spacious hall. It became a custom to line up at the back entrance long before satsang time in order to get a good seat. In the worst possible weather we'd line up, and wait even an hour or more, getting soaked in the rain or freezing in the cold, and then stampede in when the door was opened, blindly pushing people aside to get a place as near up front to our guru as possible.

Inside the entrance there was a donation box, something I'd not seen before.

Once, at the beginning of our stay in Amherst, Andrew had mentioned resentfully to me that he was hard up for money and no one seemed to be thinking about how he was going to pay his expenses. To help him, I purposely repeated this to a couple of followers, knowing the news would travel like wildfire. The next day a few thousand dollars was collected and made available to him.

By now Andrew had some wealthy disciples who, in the future, would see to it that he had everything he desired and more. As I'd noticed time and again, people considered themselves honored to have him accept their gifts.

So did I. So did I.

At the first evening session in Boston, I placed an outlandishly priced sweater I'd purchased at Barney's in New York on a little table beside his overstuffed white lounge chair—the very same chair, donated by one of the disciples, that he'd used in Amherst. On three sides of the chair the floor was littered with wrapped bouquets of flowers. The first time I'd seen the flower gifts (an Indian custom) was in Amsterdam. Now they were arriving in the most extraordinary profusion. I knew that the next night I would see Andrew sitting in his chair backed by banks of these flowers.

During satsang, I was afraid, as I had been before, to look at Andrew, positive he would be able read my unstable mind and send me away forever. I felt that the situation between us had grown very dangerous and that any day soon, over the phone or at satsang itself, I would hear the dreaded words of excommunication.

About three a.m, when everyone was asleep, I lay across my bed on my stomach, and in a state of frenzy began to write Andrew a letter. I heard my pen stabbing at the paper, sounding loud in the drowsing silence. I heard myself panting like a terrified animal. I had never known myself like this before, so totally crazed with fear.

Suddenly something burst from heaven to save me. A way out. Suddenly, with a sharp pang of shame, I was looking at myself through his eyes. I saw the enemy I must seem. I saw my stubbornness. I saw my perpetual resistance that took more and more subtle shapes. I saw my stiff-necked refusal of that which so many had received with passionate gratefulness—the god in him! I was admitting it now. Since his enlightenment I'd been trying to fool him. I'd been trying to fool myself. My entire relationship with him had been superficial! And he knew it! How he must have suffered at my hands. I touched my cheeks. They were burning. Why hadn't I seen it before. I'd been blind. Blind!

This admission swept through me like a cool healing wave. Now I had the key to all the trouble. I looked around at my sleeping room-mates in a delirium of relief, the same feeling, I'd been told, that often precedes the decision to commit suicide. I wanted to shout my good news. When he said I was 'thick,' he didn't say it to insult me. He said it to wake me up. Everything he said to me had a divine purpose. But I'd let him down. I'd betrayed him. Again and again. It was even a betrayal of him that I'd been so 'thick.'

And lying there in that pre-dawn hush, in that pregnant stillness, I experienced sorrow and remorse in a way I had never experienced it before. I put my face down on the bed, and allowed the yawning sadness to engulf me.

I re-wrote the letter of last night four times. Even though Andrew had been inhumanly patient I had to be very careful what I said. At any moment he might reach his limit. Observing myself through his eyes had come as a revelation. A salvation. A stairway to paradise. I wrote, holding back nothing. My whole heart was in it.

But I was still locked in sadness. A measureless sadness. Deeper than tears.

At satsang Andrew looked unbearably beautiful. I continued to be afraid to look directly at him. I didn't deserve to sit within a thousand feet of him.

A middle-aged man stood up. Although he was quite famous and had a painting hanging in the Metropolitan Museum of Art in New York city, he said he was ready to renounce painting, as Andrew had counselled. He said he understood now that his art was nothing but an extension of his ego.

No one questioned the wisdom of Andrew's suggestion nor the painter's decision to do his bidding. All of us, including the painter's wife, sat smiling at the painter, happy for the painter, perhaps envious of the painter, completely in tune with Andrew's conviction that everything had to be sacrificed for the sake of enlightenment.

The next evening, surrounded by mounds of multi-hued sweet-smelling flowers, Andrew sat cross-legged in his soft white chair—a pale somber god. A man in the front row prostrated himself face down, spreadeagled in front of Andrew. He was sobbing. Andrew gazed down at the man with a tender expression for a long time and then he said softly, "You'd better sit up."

Although I'd gone to the back of the hall, as far away from Andrew as I could get, feeling too unworthy to come near him, I continued to find it difficult from even there to look straight at him for more than a moment. I was sure that even at this distance I'd see contempt in his eyes. It was what I deserved to see.

The next morning over coffee, I said to someone, "I used to think my personality deserved respect. Now I see it's garbage."

I left the following letter with Andrew.

September 19, 1988
Master:

I spent the day mostly alone with a strong impression that we were still connected by a sort of umbilical cord, as if you were part of my body, inside my chest, a dark churning thrilling presence. I had the feeling I was look- ing inside at your face that was at the very core of me.

The remorse for past blindness throws an immense shadow. Nevertheless I am bearing it and experiencing some kind of crazy relief.

Luna

Leslie, a young disciple who'd been a close friend of Joshua's at Bard College, told me that Joshua was definitely com- ing to Boston over the week-end to see his brother in action. We had agreed that she, rather than I, should invite Joshua to come for a week-end so that the invitation would be neutral and not a request from his mother. Joshua's wife, Pat, was not coming. I knew Pat was leery of authoritarian spiritual masters and I was not surprised that Joshua was arriving alone. In spite of the fact that he'd always shown an interest in Andrew's goings-on, Joshua had never shown the slightest inclination to visit and see with his own eyes what was actually happening. When I'd queried him about it he'd always said he was too busy.

Over the years Joshua and Andrew had had an arm's length relationship. I never knew what Joshua thought of Andrew. He did- n't say. But I suspected that Andrew, in spite of expressing contempt for Joshua's life style, and in spite of the fact that he considered

Joshua's interests shallow, he still wanted Joshua's respect.

Andrew actually did try at times to get closer to Joshua but Joshua resisted for some reason. When I asked him *recently* why, he answered that although Andrew had never *explicitly* demanded it, Joshua had gotten the impression from Andrew's inferences and behavior that he was trying to exact something from Joshua that he, Joshua, couldn't give. "He could never accept me as I was," Joshua said. "He wanted me to be more responsive, more attentive, and I just couldn't. And he took it as rejection."

"Do you think you've changed?."

"I think I'm more responsive to people." Joshua paused. "I really did want to be closer to him. But it seemed impossible. It wasn't clear why then. It was so subtle. I didn't realize he was a controlling person. I didn't see then that deep down he was very judgmental. I didn't know what it was. All I knew was that he had a fixed idea of how I should respond to him and if I didn't respond in the right way, he felt rejected. It was as simple as that."

Joshua arrived late Friday night. He and Leslie were invited by Andrew to a picnic on the beach at Gloucester the next afternoon. I went for a walk in Harvard Square. Hundreds of students had gathered to hear a Rock and Roll band. The sound was thunderous and seemed to fill my entire body, but not enough to prevent me from feeling painful twinges of envy in my belly. Andrew had invited Leslie, not me. Andrew had invited Joshua's friend, not his mother.

I set my jaw. I would trust him unconditionally regardless.

I saw Joshua at satsang for the first time. He came and sat next to me and seemed to listen to what was going on with intense interest. Twice, Andrew turned to us and gave us long loving looks. It was an evening full of Andrew's softness and humor. When Joshua and I left, we ran into Andrew about to get into his car, a brand new Toyota station wagon contributed by a disciple. Bud Rivers was at the wheel.

Andrew embraced Joshua and I stepped back. Then he came over and embraced me as well and said, turning to get into the car, "I'm very happy Luna, at the understanding you're beginning to have."

I was beside myself with joy.

Joshua and Leslie and I went off to the Sheraton Commander hotel to talk. We talked almost continuously about Andrew. I found out that Joshua had understood far more than I expected he would. But the next day he became somewhat restless and unresponsive as if he had a need to remove himself from the onslaught of our aggressive enthusiasm.

Monday Joshua went home and Jackie and Constance arrived from Montreal. They were disappointed to hear that Andrew had taken two days off to go to Cape Cod. The three of us spent a lot of time together. It dawned on me that I was feeling happy, my heart full of love for Andrew. I sensed him close, a soft throb in my solar plexus. Whatever I did, whatever I felt, filled me, brimmed over in me; it was more than enough. Even little ordinary things, like brushing my teeth or washing my face—were full. I experienced no lurking menace, my mind delivered no mixed messages. I felt as if I were living life in its pure sweet state.

Jackie told me that now she had total trust in Andrew and wanted nothing anymore. Constance said she'd been facing all her fears, waking up at night, trembling. A noble cleansing was taking place in the three of us.

During her third satsang, Andrew told Jackie that in spite of her near blindness she should not expect anyone to save a seat for her close to him. (I'd been arranging for her to have a seat in the first row every night.) "I can't allow anyone special privileges," he said, "including my mother." Then he turned in my direction. "Luna, the one thing that's keeping you from total surrender," he paused, "is your apartment in New York where you can still hide from me." I felt a flash of fear. He addressed the others: "It's one of those incredible places, cheap and attractive. A real find." He laughed and turning back to me, said, "You must have nothing in front and nothing behind you."

Was that what I did in my apartment? *Hid* from him? What was he getting at? I was afraid again.

Then he smiled at Jackie. "Jackie," he said, "don't you realize your home is here, with me, and not there with your family and your clients in Canada?"

Jackie's expression didn't change. She probably couldn't see his smile but she could certainly hear his pointed invitation! She was being prodded—as were we all—to trust him absolutely.

Later, Jackie told me she agreed with what Andrew had said about her over-confidence during her last visit, she agreed it was central to her ego.

When I got home I wrote to Andrew:

September 30, 1988
Master:
You are unerring. I bow to you… I will do as you say.
My days in New York are over….

Luna

As I folded the note I knew that I was signing away my old life forever. The following evening Andrew read my note aloud, prefacing it by saying, "This is a long overdue note from a mother to a son."

From a mother to a son? It was certainly not from a mother to a son. It was from a humbled disciple to her avowed master. But it had a tremendous effect. People cried. I had made Andrew happy at last!

When I think of it now, I realize how manipulative Andrew was. When it served him, I was not merely a disciple, but his mother. At other times, I was not his mother, but merely a disciple. That night when he read his 'mother's' note, he should have

217

realized that this mother of his was behaving as no normal sensible mother on earth would allow herself to behave. This mother was a kind of aberration.

In the morning I had breakfast in a cafe with the rich disciple who'd bought Andrew his station wagon. She looked and dressed as if she were hard up for cash. But I'd heard she was a millionaire. Our breakfast was very jolly. I felt close, close to Andrew, calm on the surface, but underneath, a sweet tumult.

I slept over in the home of a disciple where Jackie and Constance were staying. Constance started to rave incoherently. She seemed out of her mind with a dread she couldn't describe. I remembered she'd told Andrew on a former trip that she'd had a mind-expanding experience years ago and had ended up in a psychiatric ward. I was afraid that the same thing was happening to her again.

The evening before, after satsang, Andrew had advised her to go back to Montreal as soon as possible, but to make sure not to drive alone.

"I'll leave tomorrow morning," Constance had said.

But once home, she changed her mind and said she'd stay for another week. A few minutes later she reiterated that she was leaving in the morning. We were all appalled at what was happening to Constance and didn't know what to do.

During the night I was awakened by her creeping quietly into my bed. What was she doing? She was seeking some kind of comfort, I supposed, but I hardly knew Constance and felt overwhelmed and frightened by her need. Hating myself for my cowardice, I lay motionless, pretending to be asleep. After a few minutes she got up, tucked the blanket around me, and slipped out as silently as she'd come.

Constance raved all day. It was terrifying. We didn't know how to help her. She seemed to be in a state of chronic panic. But about what? we asked ourselves. We couldn't find out. She herself

didn't know. Even Jackie, usually so quick to find solutions to people's emotional predicaments, didn't seem to know what steps to take.

At satsang, a few minutes before Andrew arrived and everyone was seated, as usual, in silence, Constance, who'd been sitting bent over, with her head down on the floor, began to crawl slowly on all fours toward Andrew's chair. I watched, numb with horror. When Constance reached the chair she grabbed onto the seat and she drew herself up with small, weak, grasping movements as if she were an invalid, and then she sat down, and in a rasping unfamiliar voice, said, "See? I have the power! But I don't want it!" Her back ramrod straight, her body shaking, holding onto the chair arms, she stared rigidly ahead. No one moved. I felt glued to my chair. After an unbearably long interval Rebecca got up and led Constance, meek and unprotesting, back to her place on the floor.

Andrew arrived shortly after, and called Constance back to the room behind the meeting hall where he conducted his interviews. He returned in a few minutes and asked Jackie and the woman they were staying with to join him.

They took Constance home.

When Andrew emerged again, he sat down and looked around and said, "Enlightenment and madness are very close." Then he laughed, and added, spookily, "It could happen to any one of you."

I recalled something he had said a few months ago in Amherst. It had struck me oddly at the time. He'd said "All madness is aggression. For some reason I don't feel compassion for insanity. I feel it means *no* to me." An original point, I'd thought at the time, but heartless.

It was raining out. I felt haunted by the incident with Constance. Her husband had come to get her and she was back in Montreal by now, under a psychiatrist's care, thoroughly sedated.

At satsang Andrew said, "Enlightenment exists when it makes no difference whether anything is present or absent."

Simple.

Once more, I felt far away from him. Even so, I invited Tom Broome, a cold-mannered English aristocrat, a man I disliked, but a man who seemed on intimate terms with Andrew, out to lunch the next day for the sole purpose of currying favor. I sensed he didn't like me and I wanted to change his mind. Perhaps he was one of those people influencing Andrew against me. At the end of our lunch I was sure I hadn't changed his mind at all.

I'd been told he was one of Andrew's major financial supporters.

Everyone contributed to Andrew's upkeep. Even the foreigners who went out to clean houses in order to survive were more than happy to give whatever extra they had. Andrew needed a considerable amount of money. The rent for his home—a luxurious townhouse—the rent for the meeting hall, the maintenance of a car, the outlay for his household—Alka, Bud Rivers, Dvora—the cost of travel, publicity, all these expenses had to be met.

In the middle of October I drove to New York with Julie — late forties, attractive, intelligent, affluent—a woman I'd gotten to know well enough for us to exchange meaningful looks when Andrew said something of particular interest. She'd been brought into the fold by her boyfriend, George, an ex-follower of Da Free John (a.k.a Franklin Albert Jones, a popular American guru born in Jamaica, Long Island).

Julie, George, and I had begun, of all things, to take tap dancing lessons together with a private teacher in Brookline. Because the tap dancing was a happy physical activity, and the music accompanying it old-time buoyant jazz, it was a perfect escape from our fretful brooding minds. I don't think Andrew ever found out about these dancing lessons. Since they had been my idea, he would surely have attacked them as another one of my contemptible 'little activities.'

During satsang, the night Julie and I returned from New York, in response to George's complaint about his everpresent stifling ego, Andrew lifted a glass of water from the small table next to his chair and said, "I'm going to drink your ego, watch!" and he finished off the glass of water in one long swallow and replaced the glass on the table. It was an unexpected swashbuckling gesture, and so original, that the silence that followed crackled with confused titters. I didn't know what to make of it. I looked over at Julie. She was sitting next to George, her eyes glued to Andrew. George's face was a dark apoplectic red. He looked as if he might have a stroke. He kept swallowing and swallowing. Even from where I was sitting against the wall quite a few yards to their left, I could see his throat convulsing. He seemed to be in some strange overwhelmed state. Was it surrender? A shiver went up my spine.

Afterwards I joined a line of people back of the stage who were waiting to see Andrew.

I found him seated beside a table on which rested a large white bowl of freshly cut fruit. I sat down opposite him and he offered me the bowl. I shook my head. He looked implausibly delicate and sensitive. His eyes were on fire.

"Remember you said a while back that I was hitting deeper and deeper layers of ambivalence? I asked.

"Yes," he said, smiling. "But that's in the past now."

Whatever reserve had developed in me the last few days melted away instantly. I burst into tears, elated at what he had discerned in me even though I couldn't see it clearly myself.

"You have to admit," he said in a rueful tone, "that your spiritual path has been like a thick rope that thinned, and thickened over and over again."

In the glow of confidence that followed this last encounter with Andrew I invited Alka to have lunch with me at a Japanese restaurant in Harvard Square. When she sat down she handed me an invitation to her sister's wedding in Bombay. The envelope had been opened. I couldn't make out the date on the stamp. I was sure it had been sent quite some time ago since I'd heard about the wedding from Manny for the first time last July. Three months ago! The wedding was to be held on Saturday, the twelfth of November at

The Imperial Hall, Hotel Searock Sheraton in Bombay. Today was October the sixteenth. When we parted I started walking very fast, almost running. If I moved quickly enough, I thought, perhaps I could keep ahead of the sense of having been violated that was churning up from my stomach and was filling me with a kind of nausea. I knew it wasn't Alka. She wouldn't have dared. It was Andrew. Now he considered it his right not only to open my mail, but to keep it from me if he so desired. What next?

After satsang, suddenly fearful, I went to the back room to see Andrew again. He was very loving and gracious and my fear evaporated. I invited him out for his birthday next week. He consented. We talked about the wedding invitation from Bombay. I said nothing of my anger yesterday. Instead I said, "Whatever you want me to do will be okay with me." He explained that normally, that is, if I hadn't separated myself from him for so long, it would have been wonderful for us to go together to India. Alka's parents would love to meet me. Poonjaji would be at the wedding and he was very fond of me etc. etc. But somehow, he concluded, it didn't feel right to him to have this sudden coming together after such a long time apart.

I agreed. There was a pause. Then I said, "I'm free now of my life in New York, so there's no longer any need to give up the apartment, is there? It might be useful to all of us in the future."

"Now that you're free, keep it," he said.

So we were united again.

"You've really learned how to dress," I said. "Your clothes are fantastic."

He laughed. "They're my working clothes. They're for my job." A long minute passed.

"You look more beautiful than ever," I said.

"Have I really changed?" he asked.

I hesitated. I was remembering what had happened when I'd responded to the same query from him in Shelburne Falls and had said that he'd grown wiser.

"The beauty you see is in *your* eyes," he said.

"I don't know Andrew. God, I don't understand at all what this force is that's passing through you!"

"Believe it or not," he said, "I don't either."

The endearing English lady who slept beside me went back to England. A few days later her place was taken by another Englishwoman, a raving maniac, who insisted on prostrating endlessly before Andrew. She had to be stopped again and again. She used to spend her days in the basement of our house making collages of photographs of Andrew's face. Eventually she became such an embarrassment that he sent her away.

One morning, gazing out the window at the sky from my bed, I felt a dark sensation begin to slither along my nerves. My first thought was that it was loneliness. No, what it was was despair, an ancient despair that I was experiencing as a kind of inner deadness. Now that I had nothing to despair of—out of habit I told myself, exasperated—I continued to feel this despair.

In the afternoon of the same day, Joshua and Pat arrived. I didn't know why Pat had consented to come. Joshua seemed uneasy. Perhaps he anticipated being fatefully torn between his wife's skepticism and his brother's certainty.

Andrew had suggested to me a number of times that I write another letter to Poonja. I decided to write the following:

October 20, 1988
Dearest Master:
I am writing to tell you that my surrender has taken a leap into the unknown. There occurred one magical moment a while back, when, deep into the night, while writing a letter to Andrew, I suddenly saw myself through his eyes. All at once I was overcome with shame and sorrow at the pain I've caused him because of my endless,

persistent resistance. It all happened in one second, but in that second, I understood his anger, his disappointment in me, and I felt tremendous gratitude for his long patience and love. For the first time in my life, I totally distrusted this mind of mine that had delivered such vast messages of distrust, of insensitivity, of ignorance, of paralysis. And my heart fell open. Andrew became my absolute master.

For this miracle I have once again to thank you on my knees.

I love you very much and hope this letter finds you in glowing health.

Luna

At satsang I left the letter beside Andrew's chair for his approval.

Eight o'clock in the morning Andrew telephoned to inform me rather nastily that Poonjaji would not be interested in my letter. I couldn't understand what his objection was, but he sounded so irate I was afraid to ask. I immediately wrote him a note apologizing for being an 'insensitive slob.'

Later in the day I called Alka to inquire what Andrew's preference in food for his birthday tomorrow might be.

"It's a mistake to ask him," Alka said curtly.

Although I thought I knew the answer I asked "Why?"

"You, and you alone have to accept the responsibility for the choice!" she said.

So my intuition had been correct when I'd decided not to ask what Andrew preferred to eat for the celebration of *my* birthday in Jerusalem. Once again, I realized how important it was to guess, and guess right!

The next day Dvora, who had become a vehicle through whom Andrew frequently conveyed his displeasure with me—I hated when he did this—telephoned to say that Andrew thought I'd been altogether too casual about his birthday. "You should have made the arrangements for his birthday much more in advance. He thinks you're selfish," Dvora said. "He thinks you can't give."

I let myself experience only a single stroke of anxious irritation and then sat down to write Andrew a note, but decided that I had to say something at satsang tonight instead. Writing was too easy. I had to speak out in front of everyone.

During the afternoon Joshua drove me to Joyce Chen, a Chinese restaurant, and ordered a meal in Chinese for his brother's birthday. He was very helpful and sweet, and surprisingly, not at all resentful, even though Andrew hadn't invited him to join his party. I thought Joshua was beginning to bend, beginning to come under Andrew's spell.

On the way back I asked him what he thought of Andrew. "He's clear," he said. I later heard that when Bud Rivers asked him about his reactions, Joshua had answered, "The leaves are turning." There was a poetic turn to Joshua's mind that he usually kept hidden.

At satsang I apologized to Andrew for my insensitivity in regard to his birthday lunch. I still felt his expectations in that regard had been extreme. But I felt I had to apologize anyway.

"It's not insensitivity," Andrew said, "it's a mixture of fear, selfishness, laziness, half-heartedness, and not taking responsibility for your impulses."

Embarrassed during the ensuing silence, I tilted my head almost imperceptibly to the left, enough so that I could see where Joshua and Pat were sitting. I wondered what Joshua thought of Andrew's sharp rejoinder to what must have sounded to him like a servile apology. His face revealed nothing. But from Pat's expression I drew the conclusion that she had maintained her old suspicions about controlling charismatic teachers. Pat had not uttered a single word of praise or criticism about Andrew since she'd arrived and I felt a certain tension between her and Joshua. Perhaps she feared, and with reason, that in spite of the fact that she and Joshua seemed to have a harmonious marriage, she might nevertheless lose Joshua to his brother.

When satsang ended, sensing danger, I felt compelled to go

back to see Andrew and apologize again. I'm sorry," I told him, "I'm really sorry."

"You've always had a problem with giving," he said, repeating more or less what Dvora had told me, "You should give fully or not at all."

"That's true," I said. "I'm ashamed of myself."

He looked gratified. "Good," he said.

Before the others arrived at Joyce Chen, I decorated the table with flowers and then placed a birthday card containing five one hundred dollar bills on Andrew's plate. It was all I could afford at the moment but I wished I could have given him more. Inside the card I'd written, "I can never repay you for this beautiful inner and outer life."

Andrew arrived with Alka, Bud and Dvora. He opened the card on his plate and thanked me very sweetly with a kiss on my cheek. I was jubilant. When the food came, Alka or Dvora immediately served Andrew first. He seemed to take this treatment for granted. I don't know why, after all the reverence for him I'd witnessed, I should be disturbed by his nonchalant acceptance of privilege. But I was. I could not shake the devils that seemed set on poisoning my love for him.

After the meal, Andrew invited me to go with his group to the circus. The tickets had already been purchased.

It didn't matter that the circus was boring. I was in heaven. From time to time Andrew leaned on me in the old familiar manner, with his elbow on my shoulder, and although he claimed to have left us all behind and there was no room any longer for a personal connection to him, that gesture seemed personal to me, and moved me personally, as his mother, to the core.

When I left to go to the bathroom, I returned to find Dvora sitting where I'd been sitting before—next to Andrew. I stood, waiting for her to move, but she didn't, so I asked her to. It was with undisguised reluctance that she pushed aside and gave me back my place.

We all felt the same way about Andrew.

Joshua called this morning to say good-bye and asked how the lunch had gone. I said, fine. He said he'd return sometime in December. Then he added, "Pat feels uncomfortable because of Andrew's attitude."

"What do you mean?"

"You know, the way he is."

"Why don't you come up alone in December?" I asked.

"I can't," he said. "Pat thinks if I come up alone, she'll never see me again."

What I'd imagined was true.

At the time I thought Pat was holding Joshua back from the freedom Andrew offered, but I didn't think she could hold him back forever. Not from his brother's divinity. Not once he'd seen it. And I believed he *had* seen it.

At satsang a young girl, about twenty years old, told him she was experiencing joy.

"You mean happiness," Andrew said.

"No," the girl said, "happiness comes and goes. Joy doesn't." Andrew's smile of acknowledgment was dazzling.

The next day Andrew was leaving for Alka's sister's wedding in Bombay. I felt uncomfortable about staying behind. It was not so much that I wanted to go. as that I wanted to feel welcome to go. To tell the truth, I was afraid of intimacy with him right now. I felt I wasn't ready for it yet.

I wrote another letter to Poonja:

October 29, 1988

Dearest Master:

I am writing to tell you what you already undoubtedly know: your beloved son and my beloved son is a fantastically successful fisher of men and women. Every day some new soul gets caught in his net. Although he is ruthless in his love, and demands everything, people keep coming to him. And he is able (with few exceptions) to break down every barrier that separates a human creature from God.

No son ever showed his father more fierce dedication. More humbly. More purely. He is love itself.

For this I thank you on my knees and hope this letter finds you in glowing health.

Luna

Andrew approved of this letter before he left and I sent it off.

After one month, at the beginning of December, Andrew returned. At the first satsang he was very odd, talking in riddles, his words hesitant and his meanings obscure. I surmised that something must have happened in India. I knew he'd seen Poonja. He looked thinner and more intense.

He told us that on the way back to Boston he'd stopped in England for a week and had found that lots and lots of new people were interested in him. "Things are changing," he said. "Many new people are coming."

But he seemed askew.

The next night Andrew was odder than ever. He talked again about the many people who had come to see him in England, of profound changes going on, of surrendering to these changes. "Can't you see what's happening?" he asked us. He seemed nervous and excited.

The 'changes,' I thought, must be related to what had transpired in India between himself and Poonja. He said he could no longer think about the future. I pondered over what he meant by that. Everything he was saying sounded so mysterious.

He talked about dropping positive attachments. He said he was sitting on the toilet in Lucknow one day, mulling over the

memory of some wonderful incident with Poonjaji, when he suddenly realized he had to let it go, throw it away, and, before us all,
by way of demonstration, he ripped off his watch and flung it to the
floor. It was a strangely savage gesture. It made me ponder about
what had really happened with Poonja.

As for me, I was further than ever from dropping *my* positive attachment to *him*. I'd lost control again and couldn't halt the
rising mists of nostalgia, of the melancholy recognition that I no
longer appeared to matter to him. Not a quarter as much as Alka
did. Not nearly as much as Manny did. Or Bud Rivers did. Not even
as much as Dvora did.

One morning I woke up completely lost in the past. Sad.
Sad. Sad. Perhaps, I thought, nature really meant us to be half-con-
scious ego-centered boors and that it was an unnatural, even a perverse impulse, to want to do anything about it.

Then Andrew called out of the blue to say it was stupid of
me to have told Joshua during his last visit that Joshua had done
some terrible things to him, Andrew, in the past. He said that his
past was beside the point, that he'd dropped his past entirely and
therefore it was no longer an issue.

Before hanging up, Andrew accused me of being afraid of
Joshua and I was left speculating—was I afraid of Joshua? I didn't
think I was afraid of Joshua. I was afraid of Andrew.

I couldn't imagine what had prompted the call because once
in a while, at satsang, Andrew himself had related horror tales of his
childhood with Joshua. For example, Andrew had told the sangha
that Joshua, five-and-a-half years older and therefore substantially
bigger and stronger than he was, used to beat him on the arms in
such a way that it left no tell-tale marks. "Like a Nazi torturer," he
would say, grinning. He seemed to enjoy saying that.

Andrew had a knack for telling stories, specially funny
ones, and he was able to imitate any dialect. Joshua and I used to
think he might become a stand-up comedian.

Andrew insisted his sessions with a number of psychoanalysts had never helped him one iota; this was another source for his humor. He told his sangha, with a certain relish, that he had started analysis at three years old and had never stopped until his twenties. This inevitably got a big laugh. But in spite of the drollery there was something sour and unforgiving in his attitude—as if his parents had been obtusely blind to his needs or had had questionable motives in bringing him to a psychoanalyst.

Because he'd been so down on me lately, I was surprised when he called a few days later and asked me to edit a book Manny Rivers had put together about him. "Not just edit," he said, "you'll have to re-write it. It's going to be a lot of work." I didn't enjoy the prospect, but I was delighted at having been asked. So the bad times were over for now.

When I went to our first editing meeting, I saw Andrew's very comfortable three-storeyed townhouse for the first time and was impressed by its luxurious space and large windows. I can't remember who let me in but I recall being told to wait in the foyer. I noticed that the floor was beautifully waxed and buffed and that sunshine flooded the room ahead, a dining-room.

I saw Andrew coming down from the floor above dressed in jeans and a grey hooded sweatshirt. It struck me immediately that his bearing was regal—more confident and more powerful than ever. And when he came over to greet me in a calm unhurried gait, I was suddenly flustered and experienced a wash of awe so overpowering that I lowered my gaze. It seemed to me that my son had become the sovereign of a powerful foreign country to which I, a poor immigrant, had not as yet been granted entry, but had been left outside peering through the gate.

When I was ushered into the living room my heart fell at the sight of Bud and Rebecca and Manny, already seated at a round dining table with open notebooks in front of them. So this was to be a group editing job.

Manny's book was a wandering, aimless tale that included Andrew's diary and Andrew's letters to and from Poonja, all embedded within a clumsily written narrative, telling how Manny met Andrew and directed him to Poonja, how at first it was thought that Manny would become the enlightened one, but it turned out to be Andrew, etc. etc.

Andrew said there would be frequent meetings, as he intended to control the whole operation. I was delirious with joy at the opportunity to spend so much time with him. But on the way home, for the first time in my life, I knew what it was to fear happiness. To trust in it was to trust that my heart wouldn't be broken. To trust it was to trust Andrew.

I ran into Manny that evening and teased him a bit about the book we were going to work on together. "The life of a writer is hell," I said, in the tone of one struggling colleague to another. It was meant as a joke. Later Manny told someone who then told me that Manny thought I'd been condescending to him. I couldn't figure out how he had given that interpretation to what I'd said, but I was instantly panicked. I called Manny and apologized, terrified he'd tattle to Andrew.

That night Andrew remarked at satsang that there were four things he'd asked me to give up and I hadn't as yet acted on any of them. He didn't say what they were, leaving me in a state of anxious suspense. The next evening I asked Andrew what the four things were that he'd asked me to give up. He didn't answer the question. Instead, he said, in a sarcastic voice, "You're not *really* part of the group involved in the book, are you Luna?"

Had Manny said something about me? My heart was pounding in my throat.

"Don't you feel it?" he asked.

I could hardly articulate the words. "I've thought about it," I said.

Actually I'd been against the idea of five people editing a book because it created incredible disagreement and conflict and confusion. I'd expressed this opinion to the editing group, but no one had agreed with me.

Andrew stared at me for a few seconds. Then he said, shaking his head from side to side, as if at a hopelessly mutinous undisciplined child, "My dear, I've been frustrated with you for a long long time. More than frustrated."

Later, when I went back to see him he added, "Apparently what satisfies you is a lot less than what satisfies me!" What did he mean by that? I racked my brains. What had Manny told him? "Something has to change," he continued. "Dvora says you're like an old fighter who gets used to being knocked out, and six months later comes back in full strength, ready to fight again." He paused. "You, my dear, have to be completely *knocked out*."

I went to sleep in a nightmare mood. Nevertheless, some lingering fragment of grit buoyed me up. This time I refused to cry.

The next morning I went out into, to me, the incongruous sunshine for a walk. It was windy and chilly. The streets were filled with bits of flying debris. I decided to visit a couple from Santa Cruz I'd met recently. I wanted to talk about Andrew. I wanted to be comforted. And they had seemed an unusually kindly couple.

They tried to help me. One of them said, "Whenever I've been made to feel raw by Andrew I feel I've been blessed." The other added, "We've all asked to be brought here, haven't we? Haven't our prayers been answered?"

My despair lifted.

But at an editing meeting the following day whatever transcendence I had achieved the day before was shot away. I made another faux pas. Feeling nervy, chattering too much, wanting to make up for whatever bad feelings Manny might still be harboring towards me, I turned to him and thanked him profusely for writing Andrew's book. I thanked him twice.

Andrew was instantly outraged. "The book is basically my diary and my letters," he said, "and you keep thanking Manny—?!"

My head started spinning. As usual, I had no idea what I was doing. I felt pretty crazy and had nothing to say in my defence. Apparently I could no longer control what I might do or say in the next moment. I might say anything.

All at once Andrew got the idea that he must have the long letter addressed to myself and Joshua that he'd written from India right after his enlightenment. He thought it should be included in its entirety in the book. It was in my filing cabinet in New York.

"Joshua can get it and fax it here," Andrew suggested.

"The cabinet's locked," I said.

"Where's the key?"

"In a sewing basket in my closet."

"Tell him where it is. No problem."

"But I don't want someone fooling around with my papers."

"Even Joshua-?"

"Anyone."

"Why? What do you have to hide?"

I gaped at him. What indeed?

"What do you have in there anyway?"

"My work. My novels. My plays."

Andrew leaned back and regarded me quizzically. There was a long silence. His dark eyes seemed to become a transparent amber color and a little glare in them lit up. In his fixed gaze there was something obstinate, something implacable, that made me think of the gaze of a flesh-eating animal.

"Your work," he said. "You don't really want to inflict all that neurosis on the poor suffering world do you?" he said slowly. "Think of what it would be like if you threw it all away. Think of it!" He paused. "You'd be lighter. Freer. Maybe you'd even be able to fly." He laughed. "And you'd have a lot more room in your filing cabinet."

When I could speak my voice was barely audible. "I'll call Joshua," I said.

I telephoned when I got home. Joshua didn't seem surprised at what was being asked of him, and agreed to take care of the matter right away. It was a very unexpected response. Normally nothing could drag him away from his desk during the day. He always insisted he was too busy.

As promised, the letter was retrieved and faxed the same day.

When Andrew wanted something, he wanted it at once, and he got it.

After satsang, beside myself, I got my diary and wrote:

Master:
    Now I have nowhere to stand.
    Thank-you.
    You have done everything possible for me. Thank-you.
    I understood nothing.
    I wanted to be comfortable.
    I wanted safety.
    You offered the fire.
    I stayed inside the cage.
    I remained inside the cage of
    My neurosis, my arrogance.
    Repeat. Repeat. Repeat.

    It is not a melodrama.
    It is ignorance. Foolishness.
    Hence, not tragedy.
    Just waste.

    I understand now that freedom
    Is freedom.
    Not free from.
    You have invited me to become

A part of nature.
And I cling to my artificial panacea
Of ego. A hard nugget
Made of stone.

There is no reason to believe me.
But my heart feels open to you.
Bleeding at your feet.
Let it bleed.
Whatever is—is.

To bleed like this is your blessing.
Thank you.
I have asked for it
And not taken responsibility.

I see my smallness, my pettiness
As from a distance.
Yet it is me.
What to do?
I am horrified.
What to do?
To have refused you in any way
Is a sin against God.
Forgive me master.
I know I ask a lot of you.
You whom I have burdened so.
Yet I ask again—for forgiveness.

There is nowhere to go. Nothing to do.
Only lay at your feet. Close to your fire.
I want nothing else.

The day before Christmas we had another editing session. When I arrived, everyone was already there seated around the table. Andrew turned to me. "We're not going to work today," he said. "I want to talk to you."

I sat down opposite him, instantly terrified. He launched into a long tirade: I kept myself separate, I was not one of 'them'; I was selfish, living my own life, absorbed in my own 'little activities'; I had 'special relationships' with people and did not show enough loyalty to my house group; he knew I was miserable and it made him uncomfortable; I had never done what he asked me to do, etc., etc. Then he said he had read the letter faxed by Joshua and was shocked all over again, really shocked, at my ingratitude! In the letter he'd told me that I was the first person he was coming to see after his enlightenment. He realized anew how much he'd given me, how much respect he'd given me, how much love..."

He was livid. Everyone was watching me with a mixture of disgust and pity.

He went on and on and on.

At last he stopped.

Then after a curious silence during which the others sat motionless as though they had died, he said, "I want you to go out now to a restaurant, there's an Italian coffee place around the corner, and write me a letter about how you honestly feel and what you intend to do. Then come back."

I wasn't sure what he wanted, but I couldn't ask. I was supposed to know. Sunk in shame and confusion, I got up and slunk out. I went to the Italian coffee shop and ordered a cappuccino. I felt blank and mute. The words that were finally forced onto paper had nothing to do with me. But I had to produce something! They were invented for HIM, to satisfy HIM. I can't recall one of them. I felt him pushing me inexorably into this false voice. I couldn't retreat. I had to advance, masquerading under the disguise of a fervent slave. My pen raced across the page with a life of its own, following through to the bitter end this path of submission, of abject renunciation of everything I felt myself to be. I glanced up. There was a mirror beside my chair. I looked curiously at my strange pinched face.

I walked back to Andrew's townhouse dragging my leaden legs. He greeted me expressionlessly, and led me into the living-room where he sat on the sofa with Bud on one side and Rebecca on the other. Apparently Manny had left. Andrew indicated that I should sit opposite him. There was no chair opposite him so I knelt on the floor. He read my letter in silence, slowly, then looked down at me, and said, "You didn't write anything about what you intend to do."

What *did* I intend to do? I peered up at him paralyzed. Three deadpan faces examined me. Inquisitors all. Then, from a riverbed of pure primal dread, the words came, squeezed from my throat, not from me.

"I'll burn all my work and get rid of my apartment."

Without a moment of hesitation, Andrew said, "Okay, then go and do it!"

Terror. Terror. "Now—?"

He didn't answer.

"I promised to treat my house to a Christmas dinner in a restaurant tonight," I said.

"Good." He waited.

"I'll go tomorrow," I said.

I got up. I was dizzy. I saw myself through their eyes: a pathetic old woman, a deluded dog of a woman, brought to heel at last.

Andrew followed me to the stairway. I started down without a word. When I reached bottom and had put on my coat, he called out, "Come back up for a moment."

I went up, a nerveless robot. Bud and Rebecca had joined him. Their eyes were brimming with pity.

"Take Sarah with you to New York," Andrew said.

"Sarah?"

"If you want to. Isn't she a friend of yours?"

"No, I want to go alone."

Did he think Sarah, of all people, could be a comfort to me? Sarah? Why Sarah? Had she been talking to him about me? Insinuating things? We did share the same room. We did talk to one another. But Sarah? I glanced at him quickly. Did he know me anymore? Had he ever known me?

I turned and went down the stairs again.

At home I called Joshua and asked him if he wanted my apartment. He was amazed, but he didn't try to talk me out of it. He said he'd probably keep it for guests because the price was so reasonable. He was leaving for L.A. and he'd speak to me when he got back.

I telephoned Andrew and told him Joshua would probably take the apartment. For some reason Andrew sounded angry. "You're on your own," he said. "You have to act from your own understanding. Don't do anything for me!"

My misery seemed to make him sick.

Christmas dinner took place in an Indian restaurant. Everyone was very gay. They toasted Andrew with champagne and laughter.

I took a train to New York. I couldn't read and stared out the window. When I arrived home I went straight to bed without eating, too weary for the task ahead.

I woke up at six, intensely alert, aware of what I had to do without delay. It was still dark out. I pushed the bed-covers aside, put on my robe, and unlocked the filing cabinet. Two drawers were packed with my manuscripts and notebooks. Except for one play, none of it had been published. If I threw it all out, it was gone forever. I grabbed an armful of files, opened the front door, walked to the incinerator, and pulled back the metal door. It fell shut with a bang that sounded like thunder in the empty carpetless corridor. I went back. Behind my tongue, at my throat, there was a throbbing cavernous feeling as if the muscles there had opened wide to receive some enormous object. In the next moment my throat closed like a vise. A second later I ran to the toilet to vomit. Nothing came up.

The rest of me felt inert. I was aware of observing myself guardedly, out of the corner of my eye, not wanting to see too clearly what I was doing. I watched a remote alien being move to and fro, to and fro, from filing cabinet to incinerator, from filing cabinet to incinerator, from filing cabinet to incinerator…

It took about five trips to annihilate a total life's work. When it was over I didn't know what I was feeling. I didn't know if I were dead or alive.

I called Andrew and told him the job was done. I thanked him.

His response seemed to come from behind a wall of ice. "Yes," he said, "show me how much you thank me. Show me!" And he hung up.

He was still angry!

I went to Saks Fifth Avenue and bought him a pair of leather gloves for seventy-nine dollars. I hesitated because the gloves were made of the finest softest baby kid. It occurred to me that he might not want to wear a baby animal skin. But I bought the gloves anyway—removed the folder inside one glove that said it was *baby kid*—and had them gift wrapped.

Then I took the train back to Boston, and on the way, wrote Andrew a note:

Master:
I burned the work. I will drop the apartment. I humbly thank-you.
I should have been sensitive to the truth—you are the truth.
I am a fool. I am frightened of my foolishness. I want nothing in this world but to be with you.

Luna

I visited Julie and George in the afternoon, and told them where I had been and what I had done. I told the story matter-of-factly, without even the slightest hint of tears. But during the telling I suspected with a sinking heart that nothing had changed. All the drastic action had altered nothing. Andrew had said over and over that we were all free but didn't know it. And now, even after all the radical measures I'd taken in an attempt to reverse things and bring myself closer to freedom, I continued to cling to the past. I still wanted Andrew back as my son—my sweet, sensitive, responsive Andrew of old. I wanted my son.

Yet later, when I opened the door to my house, I was suddenly exploding with joy. I ran upstairs and lay down on my bed and closed my eyes. I was brilliantly conscious, as never before, of what Andrew was offering me—the grandest adventure of all time!

At satsang, I told him, "This afternoon I went from hell to heaven."

"It takes only a millisecond," he said gravely.

A big party was organized for New Year's Eve. I knew there'd be loud music and dancing and I didn't feel like going, but I did, afraid of being criticized if I didn't.

Andrew didn't come.

At some point I was standing next to Bud at the refreshment table filling my plate with cold pasta salad and cheese and bread. Rebecca was on my other side. I had the impression that Bud was staring at me. I turned to him and said, jokingly, "Bud, you always look at me in the strangest way."

Rebecca piped up. "Like a spy," she said, and she laughed.

Out of nowhere I thought of the title of one of Anais Nin's books, *A Spy in the House of Love*. "You're a spy in the house of love," I said, laughing.

Bud winced.

I felt a flash of terror. "It's a joke, it's only a joke," I said. "I'm sorry." I was aghast at the idea that he might tell Andrew. "I'm sorry!" I repeated. He looked down at his plate. He looked up. "You frighten me," I said. He walked away. I watched him sit down in a chair, apart from the others, and begin to eat. For the next hour, I couldn't keep my eyes from drifting back to where he sat, sometimes alone, sometimes engaged in conversation. His expression was genial. I was obsessed by the necessity to reverse the situation between us at all costs because I knew that Bud told Andrew *everything*. I worried about how he had interpreted what I'd said. But he never once looked in my direction.

Before I could think of a way to approach him, I was astounded to see him coming over to me. He said he wanted to talk. We went out into the foyer and stood next to the front door, where there was less noise. The blood was thudding in my ears.

"I'm really angry with you," he said.

"Why?"

"You talk at me, not to me."

"Do I? That's terrible. I don't mean to. Honest."

"And you have that knowing tone."

"I'm really sorry."

Tears of panic filled my eyes. He walked away. I was sure he hated me and would tell Andrew what had happened from the worst possible perspective. The party had become a bad dream. I was going to be thrown out.

In spite of the suffering, I refused to close my heart. I went to bed feeling I loved Andrew more than ever. But at satsang, once again, I hardly dared to look at him, afraid to attract his attention. He sat, backed by tiers of gorgeous flowers, looking like the King of Paradise. He didn't say anything. But I was still certain Bud had informed on me. I left the following note:

January 1, 1989

Master:

You said, in a millisecond, one can see the truth. Also, one can slip and fall.

I slipped and fell. And went from heaven to hell.

241

One fraction of a second of loss of awareness, and an old facet of my insensitivity and arrogance sprang forward. I apologized to Bud. Now I am apologizing to you.

But apologies are not enough. Only change counts.

Master, I am a mountain of ignorance and false knowing. But I've never loved you as I love you now. My stomach aches with shame but my heart stays open.

Luna

When I saw Bud after satsang, I apologized to him again. He surprised me by smiling back, and I experienced the usual blast of relief to my nervous system after such scary episodes.

I started writing frequent letters to Andrew...

January 3, 1989

Master:

I don't know what has really happened. I only know there seems to be a current of excitement running along my nerves all the time, and an interior sense of blueness and spaciousness, like the sky. At the same time—a quiet. Nothing matters. Memory of what has been is vague. No strong sense of time. No me. No conclusions. Thank you.

Luna

January 11

Beloved Master:

On the edge. On the edge. Everything must go. One after another. The obstructions (attachments) have to go. No choice, therefore, no objections.

I feel broken and allowing the brokenness. What will come, will come.

Thank you. Thank you.

Luna

After this last letter Andrew told me what he had said once before, that he was very satisfied with what was happening to me. He regarded me with soft warm eyes and added, "I believe you're serious this time."

I told him Joshua was definitely going to take my apartment. "You don't have to give it up now," he said. "I trust you."

January 14, 1989

Dearest Master:

How lovely it was—to feel so natural with you. So full of love. So simple. I realize how much I took for granted and I am ashamed. What is given is a fantastic gift, a jewel beyond price. I thank you and thank you and thank you.

Luna

At satsang—apparently he'd given it some thought—Andrew turned to me and said, "How do you know you won't become blind again? There can be pride in such an assumption. Humility lies in not knowing."

I heard him and agreed. Whatever he said now, I heard. It was the word of God. It was the truth. A great flowering love for him had engulfed me like a tidal wave. I felt finally capable of giving him everything I possessed.

January 20, 1989

Beloved:

Just as a leaf turns toward the sun, am I turned towards you. I am aware of choosing this and not choosing this. These days everything seems to have a double edge. Paradoxes everywhere, revealing the truth. I feel a constant rumbling at the center of my solar plexus, and with this, go small faint trills of excitement, and a push, as if from the outside, to free myself of every attachment, every impure connection.

You are the power of this inner motion.

Thank you. Thank you. Thank you.

Luna

January 21, 1989

Beloved:

Woke up this morning in my usual panic and realized again that the panic was the fear of death. I used to think it was fear of actual death, but I suddenly knew it was the fear of psychological death, the loss of all attachments...

The deepening understanding comes only from you, my beloved one, and it is thrilling! Wow!

Luna

Andrew's book had been completed without my editing. I was given the manuscript to read. I thought it was beautiful. I thought I'd never read anything like it.

Everybody was very excited.

Andrew telephoned and asked me to write a short biography for the book. I wrote it that very evening and read it to him on the phone. When I was through, he said, "Luna, you'd be better off if you could forget everything you knew about me." I didn't know what he was referring to. Then he said, "Don't mention the fact that I got an inheritance from grandma and used it to go to India."

"But it's little personal touches like that, that make a bio interesting," I said.

"No," he said, "I don't want anything personal in it. Just the bare facts."

Where he got the money to go on his first trip to India was certainly a bare fact. But he didn't seem to want anything about himself in the bio that preceded his meeting with Poonja except the date of his birth, places of residence, etc. It was as if he didn't want anything human or uncertain or vulnerable to remain of him for public consumption. No matter how hard I tried, I couldn't keep the thought that Andrew was being manipulative and misleading from sneaking into my consciousness.

February 9, 1989

Darling Master:

This note is to acknowledge that what you said on the telephone yesterday is true—as always. Yes, it would be best for me if I could forget completely who you were. Whether this is totally possible or not—I don't know. But I do accept what you say, and by now, understand the beautiful meaning of 'emptiness means endless'.

Luna

This last business of 'emptiness means endless' although it seems comical now, had been the source of some disagreement.

In his diary Andrew had used the phrase 'emptiness means endless.' I thought he'd made a grammatical mistake and that he'd meant emptiness means endlessness, and had suggested the correction at one of our first editing sessions. He said I was right about the actual grammar, but it was more poetic and truer somehow, to say emptiness means endless, rather than emptiness means endlessness and had turned to the rest of the editing team and said, "Don't you agree I'm right? Don't you feel it's the right way to express what I had to express?" Without a moment's hesitation, they had all nodded their smiling vigorous assent. I'd been, as usual, odd man out, and was therefore not only wrong, but made to feel pig-headed and insensitive, as well.

We were going to Mill Valley, California. As usual, a group had been designated to go house hunting there for Andrew in advance of his arrival. These house-hunting delegates invariably suffered the torments of hell before making a decision. It was felt that nothing but an absolutely perfect house would do for the guru and the spur to energetic, even frantic, searching was, as usual, fear of Andrew's disapproval.

Julie, Leslie, her seven-year-old son, Paul, a psychotherapist named Jerry, myself, Isabel, a Polish-American woman, and Isabel's dog, Marushka, an English Corgi, were going to live together. A lot of people had wanted Isabel as a house-mate because she was much favored by Andrew, but they refused to consider her if she insisted on including her dog. She told us she'd been attacked viciously because of her 'attachment' to Marushka.

By this time Julie had separated from George. Since, as I mentioned before, almost all the couples who had come to Andrew had separated, even those with young children, Leslie and Jerry, who were in love, feared that Andrew might object to their occupying the same house. It had been made clear that certain attachments, what Andrew called 'special relationships,' romantic or otherwise, were to be avoided for the sake of enlightenment. There was to be no escape route. Followers were to have nowhere to turn except to their guru.

Around the middle of February there was a break and I went to New York. As I left my apartment to take the train back to Boston, I grabbed, without looking, a book amongst those that belonged to Andrew in my book-case. It was titled, *The Mystique of Enlightenment —The Unrational Ideas of a Man Called U.G.* U.G. was U.G. Krishnamurti, an Indian gentleman who happened to be born in the same area of south India as was the famous J. Krishnamurti—Andhra Pradesh—where Krishnamurti is a fairly common name. They were not in any way related, but, oddly enough, both had worked for the Theosophical Society and had met each other there. In actual fact, J. Krishnamurti was U.G.'s favorite target in many of his attacks on gurus and their false promises and their lust for power.

I read the book all the way to Boston, some of it aloud to Julie, who was as fascinated as I was by my random choice. Julie was on the train with me because Andrew had asked her to stop driving. A close disciple had told him she was afraid to get into a car with Julie who, normally so compliant and obliging, became, in the driver's seat, "controlling and aggressive."

In Boston the book went the rounds of our house. Everyone was equally captivated. No one saw any conflict between U.G.'s ideas, and those of Andrew. Instead they saw yet one more confirmation of Andrew as a godman.

Right after my return Andrew suggested that I write another letter to Poonja. I guessed that he wanted his master to see more of what his 'son' had wrought with his rebellious mother. The letter was paean of praise and thankfulness. I left it in the satsang hall for Andrew to look at.

That same evening Andrew called me at home. I could tell right away, by the slight echo, that he was speaking over his speaker-phone, and that therefore there were probably others near him, listening.

He told me not to send the letter. "It's not humble enough," he said.

"In what way?" I asked.

"Addressing Poonjaji as *dear dear*—" His voice got hard. "And don't ever, you hear, ever, address me as *Darling Master* again either!" I received this criticism like a knife slash. My mind worked like lightning. I understood instantly that certain endearments were looked upon by Andrew as sins of familiarity and therefore disrespect!

"I understand what you mean," I said meekly.

"It's about time," he snapped, and hung up.

I did see his point but I hated it.

That night I had a dream in which someone said to Andrew, referring to me contemptuously, "Are you still bothering with *her*?"

The next day on the trolley-car I thought I would faint. U.G. had said in his book that extreme changes in perception were biological; they occurred in every cell, every nerve. Was that what was happening to me? I felt close to danger all the time now.

A friend invited me to a jazz concert in the Regatta Bar of the Charles Hotel. Halfway through the concert Andrew appeared, accompanied by Bud, Alka, and some others. I was sitting against a wall surrounded by people so he didn't see me. I longed to go over and say hello but I knew I had no right to approach him, and became suddenly terribly sad. I hid behind my companion. After a few minutes, I got up and left, alone. The deserted streets around the hotel appeared to me like yawning canyons, unbearably lonely and desolate, as I waited for a cab.

My last letter to Andrew in Boston follows:

March 25, 1989

Dear Master:

A very edgy, beautiful, frightening time. Lots of physical sensations. Mostly of impending collapse—like on the trolley the other day, I thought I might faint. Flashes of insubstantiality. . .Terrible, worse than ever morning terrors. Inundations of blinding love.

The mother-son relationship with you seems very distant—almost like a mirage. I have only a dim memory of sweetness. What does seem real, is a sense of impersonal forces—you and me—whatever they are.

To actually fall, drowning, into this river of truth, is my heart's desire. No matter what.

With deepest respect and love,

Luna

We were all moving out in a few days. In a month, we'd meet again in California.

19

THE ONE AND ONLY LETTER I WROTE TO ANDREW from New York:

April 5, 1989

Andrew:

Don't know where I am. On the edge. Drifting in nowhere. Nervous. Helpless. Loving. Loving. Loving. Crazy. Head bursting. Whatever is, is. Strangely calm behind all the noise. You are there. You are everywhere. Distant and close, close, inside. I glimpse you and I glimpse the mystery. No words. Nothing even seen. Something other than the five senses is involved. I can only say I love and honor you above all others.

Luna

Just as I was about to leave for California, Leslie called from Northampton and told me that she and a few other western Massachusetts disciples had lunched with Andrew in Boston. She said she had shown him pictures of the house we'd rented for our group in Mill Valley.

"It's a weird house," Andrew said, and he added, derisively, *"Why would Jerry want to live with a bunch of old ladies?"*

Old ladies—!

Since I was the oldest lady, he was certainly pointing his finger at me. The implication seemed to be that because of my sex (female) and age (over the hill) I would be of no particular interest to the likes of Jerry.

As to the rest of the old ladies, Julie was nearly fifty and Isabel, a few years older. On the other hand, Jerry and Leslie were hardly callow youth. They were both close to forty.

And Andrew had reiterated on countless occasions that *age was as illusory as gender, skin color, or the shape of your nose!*

When I put down the telephone receiver, I felt as if I'd received a blow to the head. Bizarre as it seems—maybe laughable to some—that perfunctory remark to Leslie was the catalyst that would alter the chemistry of my relationship to Andrew forever. I felt clobbered by something I hadn't wanted to acknowledge before—the fact that my once sensitive, understanding, woman-loving (I'd thought) tender-hearted son had so changed.

I sat down next to the phone feeling a rush of nausea. How had this come about? Had I been negligent about something? Had there been signs in the past that I missed? I'd always been adamant with both my sons about the necessity to treat a woman as the equal she is. With my hand still resting on the receiver, I sat without moving, stunned, sick with disappointment, and wondering whether the transformation in Andrew was the inevitable outcome of absolute male power.

During the next few days I asked myself that question over and over again, vibrating with an indignation I could no longer master. Why was it, I reflected, not for the first time, that gurus of every stripe—except perhaps for the female of the species—at the moment of their alleged enlightenment, became enlightened in every respect but that of the true identity and worth of women?

Well, I was a woman. I was also a person. And I was the guru's mother. Andrew was putting me down as a woman, as a person, and as his mother. Slowly, unalterably, some pivotal organ inside my body began to recoil into a state of uncontrollable rebellion.

20

J ULIE AND AN OLD FRIEND OF HERS, JOHN, PICKED me up at the airport in San Francisco. The plan was to spend three days at John's house in Carmel and then go up to Mill Valley, a suburb of San Francisco, where Julie and Leslie had signed a lease, starting May first, for a house at 34 Florence Ave. Andrew was to come west from Boston a week or two later.

The first words out of Julie's mouth were, "Guess what? We're invited to lunch to meet U.G.!"

"U.G.?" I'd almost forgotten about U.G.

On the way to Carmel she told me the story. She'd gone to Pilgrim's Way Book Store in Carmel Village to try to find a copy of U.G.'s book, *The Mystique of Enlightenment,* for John, and to her astonishment, she'd seen another book of U.G.'s teachings displayed in the bookstore window titled *Mind Is a Myth.* She'd gone into the store, gotten the book, opened it, and inside had found a card on which the following message was typed: "If you are interested in meeting U.G., he will be in Seaside and Mill Valley for a few days." It was signed, Dr. Narayana Moorty, Professor of Philosophy, Monterey Community College. There was also a telephone number with a Seaside exchange.

Julie had bought two copies of the book and had gone back to John's place and telephoned Professor Moorty. In the course of a

251

long conversation Andrew was mentioned. Julie told Professor Moorty that Andrew was a guru in the lineage of Ramana Maharshi, and Professor Moorty interrupted her to say—and this had surprised Julie—that Ramana Maharshi had no official disciples and no official lineage! Professor Moorty then invited Julie over to give her some of U.G.'s audio and video tapes and John had taken her there in his car to get them since Andrew's injunction against Julie's driving was still in effect. Professor Moorty promised Julie that he would call her as soon as U.G. arrived and true to his word, a week later he telephoned and invited her and John for Sunday brunch on April twenty-eighth to meet U.G. Julie told the professor about me, and he said I was invited too.

When we were alone in our room in John's enormous and luxurious mountain dwelling, I told Julie about Andrew's disturbing remark ("Why would Jerry want to live with a bunch of old ladies?") and was suddenly seething again at the humiliating rejection and contempt contained in Andrew's words. The magnitude of my outrage shocked me. "It's so mean-spirited!" I cried. "It's so insulting!"

I immediately apologized. "I don't want to turn you against him," I said, alarmed at my loss of control. "I could never forgive myself for that."

"Don't worry about it," Julie said, and gave me a reassuring smile.

But in the next moment I burst out, "He won't stop vilifying me! If it's not one thing, it's another. I can't stand it any more!" Once more I halted abruptly.

"Go on," Julie said.

I shook my head as though shaking off a headache. "I'm sorry, I shouldn't be doing this."

However I was helpless in my rage, and exploded again a couple of minutes later. "With a bunch of old ladies! Is that all we are to him? A bunch of old ladies?" After a moment, calmer, I added sadly, "Is that all I am to him now? He never used to be like that. He used to be a gentle sensitive fellow. I thought he respected me.

I even thought he admired me. And I loved him so much."

But I couldn't stop. I talked and talked. I talked on our long walks in the mountains and in our room late into the night. In the end Julie astonished me by admitting she'd been having secret doubts about Andrew herself for a long time!

"It was his fanatical behavior in relation to his book," she said. (She'd worked on the book for a while in Boston.) "There was a lot of ego in it. I remember especially his bullying demands to have the book cover re-done over and over. It was re-designed so many times, it almost drove the poor guy who did it crazy."

John drove us to our brunch in Seaside, but he refused to stay. Something in the prospect frightened him—perhaps the possibility of some kind of personal exposure. In any case he offered to pick us up a couple of hours later.

We went up a few steps to a modest little bungalow and were welcomed at the door by Professor Moorty, a short jovial Indian man with a shock of white hair. About ten other people had already arrived. Julie gave Professor Moorty a bread she had baked in the morning and we went and sat down on a sofa in the living-room. We were told that U.G. had gone on an errand and would be back shortly.

A few minutes later he arrived, an unusually handsome man, somewhat androgenous looking, slender, of middle height, with beautiful, wavy, longish, grey hair. He appeared much younger than his then seventy-one years. He was wearing a beige turtle neck sweater and a pair of beige cotton trousers. I had an instant impression of simplicity and unpretentiousness. He took a seat opposite us, crossed his legs, and waited for people to ask questions.

A lot of people asked questions that U.G. seemed more than willing to answer. But very soon my mind began to go fuzzy and I was unable to really listen to what was being said. Nevertheless the same iconoclasm I'd encountered in U.G.'s book penetrated the miasma of my gloom enough to make me aware once more of being attracted to it. I suddenly found myself swamped in a sensation of solitude and estrangement. When finally the questions had ceased and there was an extended silence, I roused myself to ask, "What about love? Where does love fit in?"

"Love is a four letter word," U.G. shot back. I looked at him, dumbstruck. It was such a renegade opinion! I didn't quite understand what he was getting at, but for me, right then, it had a ring of the awful truth. "It's wanting something from someone," he continued, "and if they don't deliver, your love turns either to hate or to indifference." And then, with an air of impatience, he said the session was over.

I felt my question had irritated him.

We went back to the kitchen to get our food and I sat alone, eating, while Julie went and talked to U.G. I was puzzling over his retort to my question. Obviously, to him, love was a dirty word! I found this curious coming from a 'spiritual' man. But how spiritual was he? Looking back now, I realize that *The Mystique of Enlightenment* criticized everything 'spiritual' and postulated nothing. Why hadn't I realized that? It was unbelievable that I hadn't instantly seen crevasses of disparity between his thinking and Andrew's thinking. But I hadn't. Reading *The Mystique of Enlightenment* then had given me, more than anything else, a kind of visceral sensation. I'd had an immediate feeling of being freed somehow, not from Andrew, not from anything I could have pointed to, just freed—God only knew from what. At the time I hadn't perceived the need to examine my reaction—which proves that if you are not prepared to encounter something new because it threatens the security of the status quo, you don't, no matter what.

Julie came back to tell me that New York was U.G.'s favorite city and that he loved Times Square! I had a strong urge to get out of Professor Moorty's house as soon as possible. It was like an attack of claustrophobia. I said that I wanted to leave. But Julie wanted to stay. I felt I couldn't insist, and anyway we had to wait for John.

Eventually, he came as he'd promised. When I saw him through the window waiting in his car across the street, I sprang up from the sofa and motioned to Julie. We took our leave of U.G. He told us he was leaving in the morning for Mill Valley and gave us his telephone number there.

We left and went to buy a foam mattress for me to use in the house in Mill Valley which had been rented for one year devoid of any furniture or cooking utensils.

John drove Julie and me north to our new home. It was a huge place situated on a hill. Wandering in from the nearby woods, a few deer, looking lovely and magical, could often be seen in the back garden nibbling on the grass. All the rooms in the house were spacious, and the bathrooms elegantly appointed. A veranda over-looked beautiful Mount Tamalpais. The rent was expensive—twenty-four hundred dollars a month—and we needed to find additional house-mates to help us pay it. There were no cheap residences in Mill Valley. It was said to be the most expensive suburb in the country. The people who'd been scouting around for months for a perfect abode for Andrew had rented an equally expensive house in Larkspur, a few miles from Mill Valley. Andrew's veranda over-looked the Golden Gate Bridge.

By the time Julie and I arrived, Leslie, Leslie's son Paul, Jerry, Isabel, and Isabel's dog, Marushka, were already ensconced in the house. There was one other person, Donald, a disciple in his early twenties, who'd been given a temporary place to sleep while exploring the area for a house for his own group. Julie and I related our experience with U.G. to everyone and everyone, except Donald, wanted to meet him too. They had all, except for Donald, read *The Mystique of Enlightenment.* We sensed that Donald was afraid to show interest in any teacher other than Andrew, for fear of reprisals.

The next morning was spent going to the Salvation Army and various thrift shops to buy dishes and pots and silverware and bedding, etc. etc. We couldn't afford any real furniture and the house remained so cavernous and barren that our voices never ceased to echo in the emptiness. We sat on meditation pillows and ate off a plywood board set on four fruit crates. Nevertheless we were all cheerful and were looking forward to a year together with our beloved Andrew.

In the afternoon, at the request of everyone except Donald, I called U.G. at his new residence in Mill Valley. He answered the phone himself. I asked if the five of us could come and visit. He said we certainly could, and suggested the following day, May third, at five p.m.

It happened that U.G.'s place was only a few minutes away by car. He was staying in the home of his friend, Terry Newland. We went around the back of a very small wooden house and up a stairway to a porch and knocked on the door. Terry, a large, pleas-ant-featured man, opened the door and ushered us in. Whenever U.G. came to Mill Valley, Terry told us later, he gave his home over to U.G. and went to stay with friends.

We entered a tiny room with a low ceiling. The curtains were drawn. U.G. was sitting in the gloom at one end of a sofa next to the windows. He greeted us courteously. We took seats opposite him and waited in an uncomfortable silence for someone to say something. U.G., who didn't seem in the least uncomfortable, played with a loose thread on one of the knees of his trousers.

I can't remember who it was that started to tell U.G. about Andrew, that we'd been Andrew's disciples for some time, that we'd come here to Mill Valley to spend another year with him, and that I was Andrew's mother.

U.G. received this information without comment.

Then Julie asked U.G., "Is it necessary to surrender to a guru?"

"Well, what can a guru give you?" U.G. responded. "When you surrender to a guru, all that happens is that you give up your self-reliance."

Guiltily, in secret, I had thought these exact words myself! Many times.

"And if you sometimes fall down in life, so what if you fall?" U.G. continued. "You'll get up again and go on." He paused. "What can a guru give you?" he repeated.

Then Isabel said—and I didn't know if she was joking—"You know U.G., I sometimes think my dog is my real guru."

"With a dog, it's easy," U.G. replied. "It's a one way dialogue. No back-talk."

We all laughed.

"The trouble is," U.G. said, "You people are always looking to the outside for help."

We gaped at him. It was true.

"It will never come," he said. "No one can give you anything. The looking outside, itself, is the barrier. The seeking, itself, is the obstacle."

"So what you are saying," I said, "is that listening to you or anyone else, for that matter, will never bring about a change in us?"

"No," U.G. agreed. "And the fact is, you are not even listening. You are not listening at all. Listening is not in your interest. You are interpreting."

Someone asked if there was a way to live that he could recommend.

U.G. said, "That's a ridiculous question! With extraordinary intelligence in every cell of the body, the body is already living and living well. The body knows how to feed itself, reproduce itself, and heal itself. It doesn't need the interference of thought. Thought can only create problems but it cannot help us to solve the problems."

I found this answer tantalizing.

There was more talk.

After twenty minutes U.G. said, gently, "Well, don't you think it's enough?"

We took this to mean we should go, and got up.

"May we see you again?" I asked.

"Call me," U.G. said.

We murmured our thanks and Terry Newland followed us out and down the stairs. When we reached the front of the house we paused to say good-bye to him.

"You didn't have to go," Terry said. "You could have stayed."

"Really?" I said.

"Yeah," Terry said, "he doesn't mean it when he says it's enough. You could've stayed."

"He's so plain and straightforward, does he consider himself a guru?" Jerry asked.

"No, of course not," Terry said. "He usually tells people not to come back."

"What is he then?" I asked.

Terry shrugged. "Beats me," he said. "I've known him for years and I still don't know." He smiled and went back upstairs.

We remained where we were and stood there looking around at one another. Something had happened, something, a force, a powerful invisible current had moved through all of us without our knowing it. We were no longer the same. It was suddenly, unbelievably, astoundingly evident, to each of us, that during the last twenty minutes we had cut loose, we had discarded Andrew as our teacher! I don't know how we knew. We just knew. We started hugging one another and laughing. Everyone talked at once. We were terribly excited.

"We're free," I declared loudly, "we're free!" A savage exhilaration filled me.

"It's a miracle," Julie cried.

"A miracle," Leslie echoed.

Jerry was grinning idiotically. "Tell me what happened. I don't know what happened," he said.

Isabel was beaming.

"No one will believe this," Jerry said.

Leslie was looking at him, nodding. "We'll never be able to explain it."

"Let's go and celebrate," I shouted.

"Where?" Julie asked.

"A bar," I said. "Let's drink to our freedom."

When we reached Jerry's car, he turned to Julie. "Do you want to drive?" he asked, chuckling.

She gave him a brilliant smile and, without a word, leapt into the driver's seat.

We drove to the bar, breathless, giggling, overwrought, bursting with an irrepressible, convulsive hilarity.

I ordered a scotch on the rocks. The others had fruit drinks or soda. Everyone, including Leslie's son, raised glasses high and sang out, "To freedom!"

We were enthralled with ourselves.

When we got home, we told Donald only that we'd been blown away by U.G.

All the next day we talked and talked and talked. There was no end to our need to communicate and get accustomed to our new status as ex-disciples of Andrew. We had to pinch ourselves to believe what had so unexpectedly happened to us.

Julie, who had given Andrew five thousand dollars towards publishing his book, had recently been asked to double her contribution. Late in the afternoon she called Boston to speak to the devotee who had asked her for the additional money. "I've lost faith in Andrew as my guru," Julie said, "and I refuse to send another cent for the book. I can't allow myself to be pushed around anymore. I'm tired of being a victim." We all congratulated her with hugs and kisses.

Afterwards Julie and I went for a walk. When we returned Leslie told us Andrew had just called from Boston. She was very jittery. "I lied to him," she said. "He asked if everything in the house was okay, and I said yes."

"It's more than okay," I said smiling. "It's terrific."

"I was afraid to tell him the truth," Leslie said.

"You don't have to tell him anything," I said.

"He said our house was acting as if it were separate from the sangha."

"He's reading our minds," Julie said, sounding scared herself.

I looked at Julie. "Don't be silly," I said.

Leslie went on. "He is shocked and amazed at us. He wants half the house to move out. It's a non-evolutionary house, he said." (Andrew had an idea that his teaching was evolutionary, that his disciples were in a process of evolving spiritually.)

"Non-evolutionary—?" I laughed.

We all laughed, even Leslie. These sweeping demands from Andrew were ludicrous to us in view of our sudden, dramatically changed relationship to him.

"And Luna, you and Julie are not allowed to stay in the same house any more," Leslie said, "because, quote, 'Julie can't live without Luna'."

"That's ridiculous," I said.

"He told me I was wishy-washy," Leslie went on. "He's probably right," she added ruefully.

"What's wrong with wishy-washy?" Julie said.

During dinner, Donald complained that he felt shut out by us. He wanted to know what was going on.

Earlier, I had warned the others not to reveal to Donald our altered situation in regard to Andrew just yet. "He'll rush away to tell the whole sangha before we have a chance to sort things out and speak to Andrew ourselves." But I was overruled. They seemed to think there existed, a priori, a moral obligation to tell Donald the truth whether we were ready to reveal it or not. Therefore, when Donald made his demand to know what was going on, he was told, and in full detail, and, as predicted, went off right after dinner, to a bonfire party at a campsite where some new arrivals had pitched their tents. And, of course, he told everybody.

In the morning Julie called U.G. to thank him and to tell him all five of us had left Andrew.

"No you haven't," he said gently, "you've just replaced one teacher with another teacher. Take it easy. Give it some time."

"May I call again next week?" Julie asked.

"Next week will be fine," he said.

After that we stayed around the house, talking and considering our new circumstances from every angle. We wanted to avoid meeting sangha people and having to defend ourselves. We still felt too raw. And we felt sure that the sangha would be feeling anxious, even infuriated, at this mass defection (Andrew's word). Especially my defection. After all, I was the mother of God and I was forsaking Him. In the normally besotted state of the sangha I was positive they would interpret this as a dreadful betrayal.

Some of us decided to write letters to Andrew. We read them to each other. The following is my letter:

May 5, 1989

Dear Andrew:

This is to notify you immediately that something crucial has happened.

I saw U.G.—and as a result—when I left him twenty minutes later—I was suddenly aware that I was free of the fear and bondage I've felt (off and on) in regard to you, as my teacher. I felt free—as if some enormous weight had lifted. It was a choiceless event, and I felt amazed, and at peace. It is up to me now. I want no teacher.

There is a lot to say—but I feel, perhaps wrongly—that you don't want to hear it. I didn't call because I didn't want to engage in an angry—I thought you might be very

261

angry with me—conversation (as in the past) on the telephone.

There is no end to my gratefulness. I have learned so so much from you.

I am terribly sorry and sad that we may never see one another again. I would love to see you. But perhaps you don't want to see me. Well, as you have often said— "That's the way it is. So be it."

I will always love you.

You will always, somehow, somewhere, be my son.

I hope you are happy for me and my freedom.

Luna

I mailed my letter to Andrew from the post-office in town and then we all went to a movie. And after we returned home, Andrew's aristocratic English cohort, Tom Broome, whose snide personality I could never abide, arrived with a five thousand dollar check from Andrew for Julie. It had been her initial investment in publishing Andrew's book now titled *My Master is My Self.*

"Andrew is behaving like a spoiled brat," Leslie said.

"I bet he had a temper tantrum about us," I said. I was delighted Julie had gotten back her money. "Great," I said, "just great." I hugged her. I was in a state of euphoria, drunk on my new sensation of freedom.

The following morning I rang Andrew. Strangely enough, when I lifted the receiver, I discovered that our telephone had suffered some mechanical failure and had stopped operating.

After breakfast Julie and Leslie and I left to go to an art fair in town. As we approached the central square, we saw some of the sangha at The Depot, an outdoor cafe. Our presence was noted instantly. Judy, the English housewife with whom I lived in Amherst and had learned to dislike intensely, got up and came over. "We'd like to talk to you," she said. Leslie hung back but Julie and

I began to follow Judy to a cafe table. I didn't know what Julie was thinking, but I felt that before I departed I had to say something to these people, and say it clearly and uncompromisingly.

Judy began to question me aggressively.

"I don't need a teacher anymore. That's all there is to it," I answered quietly.

She looked back at me blankly. I had to repeat the statement a number of times before the expression on her face changed. "But Andrew isn't just a teacher," she said. "He's started a new way of life for us. Our life is beside him! Don't you understand? Our life is with him forever!"

I told her about my encounter with U.G. and repeated, "I understand now that I don't need a teacher anymore."

The other person who was sitting at the same table, a Dutch woman, offered the information that she'd read a book on U.G. in Amsterdam and saw no contradiction between U.G. and Andrew. Both women looked tense and angry. Everyone else from the sangha was staring at our table.

"Have you spoken to Andrew?" Judy asked accusingly.

"No," I said.

"Why haven't you?"

"I needed time."

"But how could you not have called Andrew straightaway?"

"Everything happened so quickly. I needed time."

"He'll be terribly hurt!" Her face was a grimace of contempt and disapproval. She looked as if she hated me. There was fear in her eyes. "How can you do that to Andrew?" she wailed.

A tall dark-haired man came over and sat down. He leaned across Julie and put his face as close to mine as he could get it.

"I don't care about Julie," he snapped, "but I'm certainly very worried about you."

I looked into a black maniacal stare. I'd met him in Totnes and had considered him strange from the beginning, crazy maybe.

He was a taut, taciturn Englishman, and his eccentrically extreme reserve had suggested something eerie and dangerous. He certainly didn't give a damn about me.

I got up to leave.

Julie and I walked around looking for a public phone for me to call Andrew, but there were only open street phones. Nor was there a hotel to be found that might have a phone booth in the lobby.

We went back to the house. The telephone there was in service again, so I put a call through to Boston. Andrew wasn't home. I left a message on his answering machine to call back.

We were all restless. Isabel and Julie and I decided to go for a hike in the mountains. Leslie, who had by now been reduced to a state of panic by her decision to leave Andrew, wanted to be alone. Jerry went down to talk to the people at the campsite. I didn't inquire why he was going, but I suspected that, like Leslie, he was regretting his decision too.

When we got back from our walk, we found Leslie in tears. She had just spoken to Andrew. Apparently he'd not gotten my message for some reason but had already heard rumors about us. Leslie said she had revealed everything. "Everything," she repeated, "including the fact that Jerry and I are "in a relationship." She wiped her eyes. "I couldn't help it," she said, wagging her head from side to side. "Then he called me a wimp and a coward and said the only reason Jerry and I liked each other was because we were both wimps and cowards." Fresh tears started to wind down her cheeks. "He told me to telephone again in two days."

The sight of Leslie's tear-swollen face infuriated me and sent me into a delirium of impatience to have the talk with Andrew. Leslie stood looking at me expectantly as though waiting for some direction. Her inflamed blue eyes expressed such naivete and misery and gullibility, that at that moment the tolerance I'd managed to sustain up until now for the suffering Andrew inflicted upon people who trusted him came to a precipitous end. I suddenly saw him as some sort of medieval inquisitor—his face bleak, tense, and cruel. When the phone rang again a few minutes later, and Leslie answered and said it was Andrew wanting to talk to me, I was ready.

I went downstairs to the telephone in Isabel's room and closed the door. But as I picked up the receiver, my heart began to hammer; the old fear gripped me.

"Hello," I said.

"Hello." His voice was neutral.

"The first thing I want you to know," I said, "is that I don't think I need a teacher anymore." I'd blurted it out. I closed my eyes frowning. Had my voice trembled? I couldn't tell.

"You don't?"

"No," I said, "I definitely don't want a teacher anymore."

"How come?" The voice was quiet, neutral.

"I don't know how it happened," I said, "but I met U.G. and everything changed."

"U.G." he said.

"Remember U.G.?" Silence. "There was a book about him in my bookcase. Your book."

"My book?"

"Did you ever read it?"

"I can't remember."

"But he was only a trigger," I said. "That's all he was—a trigger. And then—" I paused.

"And then—go on."

It seemed he was using his speaker-phone. I thought I heard the echo. I was sure someone else was listening.

"And, well, what he said was like a miracle. And I don't know, I realized I didn't need a teacher anymore."

An ominous silence followed. Finally he said in a terrible bitter voice, very slowly, he said, "Luna, just wait until you crash!"

It was a curse.

My heart stopped hammering. All at once I was incredibly calm. In the next moment I'd turned to ice.

"If you dare to threaten me one more time, I'll hang up," I said quietly and, after another silence, "I will never allow you to threaten me ever again, you hear? Never!"

I waited.

"Go on," he said finally, neutrally.

"I realize now that I've always been uncomfortable in the sangha and the reason is that it's fascist. It has a fascist mind-set. It's run by fear."

Silence.

"Everyone lives in terror. Of you. The people nearest you are all spies. For you. They're also sycophants, telling you only what you want to hear, because they're afraid to tell you the truth. So you get no feedback. There is nothing at all to modify your behavior. Nothing."

I took a long breath and waited for him to hang up. But he didn't.

He said, "The sangha is dirty, and marred by a lot of things, Luna, but it's perfect. Perfect," he repeated. His voice had grown sonorous with conviction.

"The people who have power act like Gestapo agents," I said, and when he didn't respond, I added, "believe me when I say the people around you are an insult to you." This last particle of flattery came from my still blurred vision. I still wanted to be able to love him. "That English guy," I continued, "the lord or earl or something is a petty tyrant, so are the others, Rebecca, and—"

"What about Bud? he broke in. "You can't say that about Bud."

"Bud is a zombie. He doesn't exist any more. He's become no more than your shadow."

Andrew did not speak again. I can't remember what else I said, but I know I covered everything. I didn't leave anything out.

And when I was through, I said, "I realize this may be the last time we talk to one another. I won't call you again. If you want to get in touch, you'll have to call me."

I hesitated.

"Go on," Andrew said.

"I love you," I said, "and will always love you, but as your mother. And if you ever wish to see me, I will meet you anytime, anywhere, as long as you come alone."

Once more I paused.

"Go on," he said.

"Well, that's it," I said. "I have nothing else to say." I waited. But there was no response at the other end of the line. "Good-bye," I said. Again, I waited, and then hung up.

The monstrous dream was over.

I went to the door and opened it. Julie and Isabel and Jerry and Leslie were standing on the other side. They clapped their hands.

"We heard everything," Leslie cried.

"You were great," Jerry said.

"You sounded terrific," Isabel said.

Julie gave me a hug. They were all smiling, excited.

"If I'd known you were listening, I wouldn't have been able to do it," I said. I felt extraordinarily alive. I felt as if I'd taken part in some decisive moral conquest. A bloody battle had been won.

They couldn't stop expressing admiration for my courage to speak to Andrew as I had.

"It's not courage," I said. "It's just that I'm straight about it all now."

When we'd quieted down a bit, Jerry went in to call Andrew. We heard him ask for a leave of absence. "I'm not ready to commit myself to leaving forever," he said. He sounded scared and apologetic. Julie and I exchanged looks. Afterwards he told us ruefully, "I sounded just like Andrew said. I sounded like a wimp."

We all had a peaceful dinner together.

Our temporary visitor, Donald, who'd rushed to the campsite to tell the sangha about our treachery and who had therefore been instrumental in bringing things to a head, had already moved out.

In the morning Jerry left on a trip to Mendocino. He said he wanted to be alone for a while.

Leslie called Andrew and cried a lot on the phone. He said, "Either my mother is totally right and I am totally wrong, or I am totally right and my mother is totally wrong."

"Can't your mother be right about anything?" Leslie asked in a pathetic placating voice.

"No!" Andrew exploded.

Then Julie called Andrew. She'd heard that he had called her a pig and she complained about it to him.

"Well," he said, "aren't you a pig? You offered to pay for half the cost of the publication of the book and then you backed out."

He stayed on the phone with her for over an hour. She told me he couldn't stop talking about me. "He ranted on and on," she said, "I was actually bored. He kept repeating how ungrateful you were, how everyone had tried to help you, had given so much of themselves to you—Dvora, Bud and others."

"It's amazing," I said, "he doesn't understand a thing. He doesn't know what's going on."

Everything in him must have been geared to shoring up his position. How could he possibly allow himself to see or understand what was going on with us right then? But I wondered, was he experiencing some fear? No, he couldn't allow himself the luxury. It would menace his seamless conviction about himself as a realized guru, and probably threaten to blow him to smithereens.

Just before dinner I went to the beach with Isabel. Sitting on a rock, staring at the cold grey sea, there arose in my consciousness the phrase, *everything is perfect.* I'd heard Andrew use it at times to describe his mental state. And at that moment, on that beach, for me, everything was perfect. All the turmoil had vanished. What was, was. Perfect. It was a moment of intense happiness. I marveled that when I'd reached the breaking point of my endurance, when the flimsiest hope had died, when there was no longer the slightest chance to snatch at any possibility whatsoever—with the unexpected trigger of U.G.'s uncommon common sense—it had happened—an abrupt startling sanity had arrived just in time to save me. And I remembered saying the day before, "It's not courage. It's just that I'm straight about it all now." It really was as elementary as that.

Julie, Isabel and I had dinner with George at a Spanish restaurant. He could not swallow what had happened to us. He kept repeating how fantastic it was to be with Andrew, how rare a being Andrew was, a truly enlightened man, etc. etc. At one point, when Isabel disputed something he said, he leaned over toward her, and was so menacing in his demeanor, that she abruptly got up and left the restaurant.

Isabel was the only one of us who had managed to maintain a constant composure. She had refused to telephone Andrew or write to him. "I'm through with him," she said, "I owe him nothing." And that was that. But the others felt they still owed him a certain respect.

Respect was Andrew's obsession.

At three-thirty a.m. I woke up with a terrible start, my entire body resonating with dread. I looked over at Julie, with whom I was sharing a room. Her lamp was on. "I can't sleep, she said. "My mind is driving me crazy." Her face seemed set in some kind of permanent grimace.

"Me too," I said. "I've just had a nightmare about betraying Andrew. Mother betrays son. Melodrama! Greek tragedy!" I tried to smile at her through the receding wave of horror.

But Julie didn't smile. She didn't seem to have heard me. "There are no touchstones any more," she said.

"That's true." The horror edged forward a bit.

"Anything is possible now. Maybe the blue sky is really green?"

"What are you talking about?"

Julie's gaze was strange, hard and inscrutable. "Maybe you're angry at Andrew because he ran off with Alka," she said.

"He didn't run off with Alka,"

"Maybe your relationship with him was too intense."

The horror was spreading inside my chest. I got up.

"Maybe a lot of things," Julie continued. Maybe Andrew is right about everything."

I began pacing across the room. "He's a devil," I said tensely.

"Yes, he is demonic, but maybe he's right!"

Julie's frenzied doubt leapt across the space between us like an electric current. She stared at me with dilated eyes. I suddenly felt crazy too. I was a loathsome person. I'd committed an abominable crime. I was a murderer. . .

Julie, her voice shrill, her expression demented, continued to rant, articulating her apprehension, her uncertainty, her misgivings. I ceased my pacing. "Stop it," I screamed.

We gazed at one another in the ringing silence.

"This is nuts," I said.

I went to get my walkman, inserted a tape by U.G. and pulled on the ear-phones. But the walkman wouldn't start. I threw it aside and climbed into bed and pulled up the sheet. The horror had invaded every cell of my body. It seemed to be radiating from all around me, from Julie's lamp, from the unadorned white walls, from the vast uncurtained windows filled with sinister blackness. I closed my eyes and lay unmoving. Julie extinguished her light.

What or who was this uncertain, unreliable, uncontrollable, capricious, conditioned mind? Was it me? All there was to me? What would remain if it blinked out?

After a short while, my body relaxed and I fell asleep

I woke up about an hour later. Julie had turned her light back on. I woke up a few more times before daybreak. Each time I looked over at Julie, and each time her eyes were wide open fixed on the ceiling.

Sarah telephoned late in the morning. I told her I didn't want to speak to her. She said I owed it to her as an old friend to see her for ten minutes. She wasn't an old friend and I knew she would come and spout the party line. "I don't want to talk about the present situation," I warned her. She said okay, so, I don't know why, I said okay, too.

She came, and immediately started doing what she'd promised not to do in her guilt-provoking pushy way. I stood up. "Get out," I ordered, and when she didn't move I repeated in a louder voice, "Just get out!" and I left the room.

She then waylaid Leslie. They went for a walk together. When Leslie returned, she was back in Andrew's fold! She sat down at once, to write him a letter of apology, and then took off for the camp grounds to tell the sangha the good news. I was appalled.

I had to get away from this madhouse. Isabel offered to go on a two day trip to Mendocino.

We drove north, along the sea route, a glorious, winding, mountainous road. The ocean was sparkling and frothy. Occasionally we saw sea lions capering close to shore. Isabel took out a tiny hashish pipe. "Do you mind if I smoke?" she asked.

I was astonished. "No," I said.

She filled the pipe with one hand, her other on the wheel, demonstrating an expertise that suggested a long-standing habit. She had seemed so much more detached and self-governing than the rest of us, but I realized she was more fragile than I'd thought.

"I smoke pot. Other people drink," she said by way of explanation. She offered me a puff. At first I refused. But then I accepted. It didn't change anything for me. I'd been feeling calm and the ride had been pleasant.

We spent the night in a sleazy motel because we hadn't much money between us. Right after dinner I telephoned Mill Valley. Julie answered. She sounded stronger, but still wobbly. There was no news.

We went back to our tiny motel room and stretched out on our beds. I gazed, for a time, at the water-stained, insect-spotted ceiling. A large cobweb was stretched across the corner near the door. I turned towards Isabel. She lay forbiddingly silent, with her arm covering her eyes. I saw a blue vein protruding from the pale-skinned back of her forearm, I observed her taut wrist and her clenched fist, and I felt she was hiding terrible tension behind that arm and that she didn't want to be intruded upon. But I was desperate to talk, struck again with the same horrible sensation as had come over me last night with Julie.

There was the sound of a fly colliding in flight with a window-pane and then buzzing plaintively. My throat began to close. I took a wheezing lungful of air. I was overcome with the idea that I didn't deserve to live another moment. I was a traitor, a double-crosser, a Judas, a renegade. Petrified, I lay as if any movement might strike me dead, as if the next tic of time would be a mortal blow. I had betrayed the fruit of my womb, my own flesh and blood!

The room had become unendurably cold. Suddenly I was shuddering. I was freezing. Something pulled me to my feet, something dragged me to the sink in the bath-room and held my wrists under hot water. I looked up into the mirror and saw what I usually saw—the usual face. It was a million miles away from me. It was not my face. It wasn't anybody's face. I turned away and stumbled back to the room. Isabel hadn't moved a muscle. She was probably asleep by now. I started to get undressed. As I lay my T-shirt on the bureau, I noticed a small black speck moving near the collar. I looked closer. It was a tick. We had been warned about Lyme disease. I was sure the tick had already bitten me. But this information arrived from a great numbing distance and I didn't look for the bite. I picked up the tick with a match-holder and tossed it out the door. Then I got into bed and closed the light.

All at once the panic receded and a calm refreshing wave of confidence swirled through me. I lay in sudden peace! What kind of energy inside my head was playing these games with me? What interpretation of events was authentic? What thoughts were real?

We returned to Mill Valley in the evening to be told by Julie that someone had telephoned to say Andrew wanted Leslie to call him, and that when Leslie did, Andrew threw her out of the sangha for six months. Julie said Leslie had promptly gone to the camping grounds for solace. Julie herself had received a biting denunciation about her decision to leave Andrew in the form of a letter from a close disciple. And last but not least, Andrew, still in Boston, had telephoned the woman devotee who was responsible for organizing sangha housing in Mill Valley, and had commanded her to gather the sangha together and announce to one and all that he had had a conversation with his mother and that no one, no one, had ever dared to speak to him as she had! She was diabolical! She had betrayed him! She was a traitor! Everyone should be informed.

There was something low and vicious in this situation. Andrew had not only cursed me on the phone, now he was rousing his mob against me. I couldn't believe it. I couldn't believe this was happening to me. I wanted to get on a plane and flee instantly, but my housemates implored me to stay on a bit more. So I did. I guess we all needed each other for moral support.

I began to feel uncomfortable about leaving the house. I knew the sangha regarded me as a pariah, and I felt in jeopardy. I thought of the people who'd been around Rajneesh, and around Jim Jones. It was grotesque, I suppose, to compare Andrew's group with those others, or, for that matter, to compare Andrew to those other gurus. But was it? I asked myself. Was it really? The phenomenon was the same—absolute master and unquestioning devotees. It was only a matter of degree. Anything was possible. There were even moments when I had the fantasy that some disciple might want to throw a grenade over the fence that surrounded our house.

A couple of days later, at five o'clock in the afternoon we went to see U.G. again. He was sitting, as he was last time, on a corner of the sofa next to the curtained windows. A lamp had been lit as before, but the room remained dim, bathed in the same twilight. When we were seated a young woman entered carrying an enormous basket of fruit. She placed it on the coffee table and introduced herself to U.G.

"I don't eat fruit," he said, not ungraciously.

Nonplussed, she sat down smiling uneasily, and looking around at the rest of us.

I waited for a minute or two and then I said, "I came to say thank you."

"Don't thank me," he said. "I didn't do anything."

"Something happened," I said.

"If you'd really gotten my message you wouldn't be here. You'd never come back," he said, and he smiled.

I sat there looking back at him. I was confused. "No matter what you say, I feel grateful," I insisted.

He shrugged his shoulders, then darted a mischievous glance at me. "But tell me, how can you do this to your son? You can't do this to your son, can you?"

He was testing my conviction. "Well—I've done it!" I said and laughed.

I saw U.G. a number of times after this, in New York, and California, and Switzerland, and was always very appreciative that with him there was no need for cover-ups. Everything was open. There were no constraints, no rules, not even rules of conduct apart from simple decency, and no one and nothing to respect, no way to be, nothing to do. What was, was. That was all he seemed to want us to acknowledge. What was—was! Accept it! That seemed to be his message, and it was my impression, in spite of everything he said to the contrary, and even though he declared it couldn't be done, that he had some sort of irresistible urge to pluck, with his words, the cataract of illusion from our eyes.

Yet he insisted and insisted that there was no way to accomplish this surgery because whatever you did to free yourself from the illusory identity you call yourself, i.e.your conditioning—was the self. How could he make us understand this simple thing? And the illusory self didn't want to end, he would repeat over and over again, so that we would know it once and for all.

So there was no way.

"All my life," he said, "I've searched and wanted to be an enlightened man, and I discovered that there is no such thing as enlightenment at all.... I don't give a hoot for a sixth-century B.C. Buddha, let alone all the other claimants we have in our midst. They are a bunch of exploiters, thriving on the gullibility of the people. There is no power outside of man. Man has created God out of fear. So the problem is fear and not God...."

"I discovered for myself and by myself that there is no self to realize.... It comes as a shattering blow. It hits you like a thunderbolt. You have invested everything in one basket, self-realization, and, in the end, suddenly you discover that there is no self to discover, no self to realize—and you say to yourself, 'What the hell have I been doing all my life?!' That blasts you."

I don't know how U.G. knows all this, but he seems to know it unequivocally. He seems to know it with the kind of certainty that gurus communicate to their disciples. And this quality of absolute certainty expressed by U.G. keeps people circling around him like flies droning around a honey pot. It is fed by the same old hope for freedom from suffering, even though U.G. states over and over again that they'll never find freedom through him, that they'd best go home and live their lives as best they can. "If you fall," he is in the habit of pointing out, "you'll get up again and go on, don't worry about it."

But some remain obdurate followers, insisting on endowing U.G. with powers he emphatically denies. Some have remained followers for years, even decades. U.G. allows it. He refers to them as his 'friends' and allows them to visit him more or less whenever they wish to. I don't know why. He himself, the quintessential anti-guru, must know that they nevertheless persist in regarding him as a guru, perhaps, paradoxically enough, as the guru above all other gurus, just because he denies being a guru—and he lets them come.

The fact is that people create gurus out of their need for certainty in the atmosphere of eternal uncertainty which is our world, and will use the appropriate person nearest to hand as a vessel for their needs and fantasies.

But why does U.G. bother to talk to people at all, I wonder? I've wondered about this for a long time and have not been able to come up with a satisfactory answer. When asked this question directly, he answers, "Even if I wanted to hide away somewhere, they would find me."

Maybe he flies around the world year in and year out answering people's questions because he has never found anything else he wants to do. Who knows?

This time, remembering Terry's admonition, we didn't leave when U.G. held up his palms and said, "That's enough." We just stayed on.

I was definitely uncomfortable lingering any longer in Mill Valley. A few people who had parted from Andrew some time ago telephoned to find out what had happened and to give their support. But the sense of intimidation from without our garden gate frightened me. I had the feeling that waves of hatred and fear were penetrating the very walls of the house where I remained, in a sense, a prisoner, and that it was directed mainly at me. On May thirteenth I decided to leave and called to make a reservation on the Northwest Airlines red eye to New York.

My housemates tried again to convince me to stay, but I was adamant. I was leaving.

They came to the airport with me and we hugged and kissed one another, and planned to meet again very soon. It was a beautiful intimate moment for all of us. We felt bound together by a critical life-altering experience.

Flying through the night, I mused over what had happened. I saw as never before that the mind built the entire persona around fear. We were fear. The I was fear. But without the I, what was I?

Unanswerable question.

But I knew something important in my life had come to an end. I was no longer a seeker. Not that I had found anything. According to U.G. answers were never found because there were no answers. Sometimes the questions simply burned away.

In the morning, not at all tired, peculiarly alive with energy, I wrote and sent my final separation letter to Andrew:

May 16, 1989

Dear Andrew:

I, too, surmised that this would be called a Greek tragedy. But it is totally unreal and produced by the mind. The fact is, you are my son, and I am your mother—and I love you and will love you until the day I die.

My seeing through the need for a teacher has produced the edge, the turmoil, the insight—everything you would wish for me. I am going through some incredible process—dealing with the Fear behind all the fears.

U.G. just happened. An accident. Luck maybe. It was a trigger—no more.

I've never felt more alive, more aware, more scared (at times), and more tranquil (at times)...

There is the whole web of thought. And there is this soft centered awareness. As I see it now—surrender is surrender to the soft yielding center where all is accepted as it is without judgement.

There is no betrayal. Just a great big bang of a misunderstanding.

Luna

I feel obliged, for the sake of clarity, to make a comment about this letter after six years of separation from Andrew. It represented the way I felt at that moment, and although I had turned a sharp corner away from Andrew, I was not nearly as confident and sure of things as I thought I was. All I definitely knew was that I was through with Andrew as my teacher. But that was about it.

21

CANADA

I WENT UP TO MY SISTER-IN-LAW'S FARM IN EASTERN Quebec to rest. On my first walk alone I hesitated at the entrance to the woods nearby, afraid to go in because I'd heard that bears had recently been seen in the vicinity and I was afraid I might surprise one wandering about behind those stands of wide-spreading somber evergreens. I sat down on a rock and gazed into the dense green thickets ahead. Thoughts, or the fragments of thoughts, images of the last three years began to flicker in my mind.

"I love you as my son," I'd said.

"Your son is dead," he'd said.

Suddenly it struck me anew that I would never see Andrew again. I felt myself losing control and spiralling down, down, into a sensation of such violent sadness that I stood up abruptly and began blindly moving forward into the woods, stumbling over fallen logs, pushing between bristly clumps of bush that caught at my clothes and my skin, and crashing into the low-lying branches in my way. Impervious, I had forgotten where I was.

I couldn't get my mind off Andrew.

I was remembering that there was a time when I'd seen him as an irresistible object of love, an unquestioned object of love, a forever thing. Until death do us part.

He was my child.

The next day, on a similar walk, I was able once more to accept the truth that my link to him had been irrevocably broken, shattered chip by chip by the hammer of his insistence during the last three years, that not only did a link to him no longer exist, but for me to dare to entertain the idea that it still did, was tantamount to sin.

I was not his mother. He was not my son.

It was preposterous how Andrew not only turned everything ordinary and normal and taken for granted upside down, but that he turned it into something villainous.

The next morning I woke up at the farm after a thundering night-mare. I went outside and sat on the veranda with a cup of coffee. A gentle sun warmed me. Ranges of feathery grass and spans of glossy buttercups stretched before me. All was softness and birdsong and peace, peace, peace—except that my bad dream kept stubbornly passing, frame by frame, before my mind's eye. The pain of loss was back. Would I have to live like this for the rest of my life?

When I returned to Montreal a week later Joshua telephoned from New York to inform me that Andrew had called to find out what I'd told Joshua and how he felt about it.

"Is she bitter?" Andrew had asked.

"No," Joshua answered, "she's okay. In fact she's in a better state of mind now than when she first got involved with you in India."

"You think so," Andrew answered sarcastically.

"Yeah. I've been thinking about it. She should never have been your disciple in the first place. She's your mother for Pete's sake."

"I don't agree," Andrew said, and had gone on to give Joshua a picture of me as a hateful witch, and a satanic perpetrator of evil deeds. Joshua told me he thought Andrew had gone crazy on this issue.

Andrew concluded his harangue by demanding that Joshua be sure to keep in touch. Joshua promised he would.

So he still wanted contact with me. At the very least, I

thought, he wanted the contact with Joshua to continue.

I felt deeply harmed by Andrew. Everything I'd had to give him as a mother and as a human being had gone down the drain in the face of the lure of power.

Back in New York, on the twenty-first of July, I received a telephone call from California telling strange tales about Andrew's doings:

Because of some infraction, Sarah was asked to do two thousand prostrations a day for a month—perhaps longer—I can't remember. It took her ten hours a day. She had to save up enough money to quit her housecleaning jobs to comply with Andrew's order. She complied.

An attractive Italian adherent was asked to shave her head after admitting she was too preoccupied with her appearance.

Another woman disciple, one who had given Andrew considerable sums of money, was led into satsang blindfolded. My informer had no idea why.

A young man who owned a new twenty-seven thousand dollar Saab was accused by Andrew of identifying his ego with his car and it was suggested that he junk it. Soon after, I was told, Andrew and the young man went to have the car washed and then drove it to a crusher. The workmen there were horrified at what they were asked to do, thought the two mad, and at first refused to commit the grotesque deed. But eventually they gave way. I was also told, although I couldn't believe it to be true, that Andrew had demanded that the owner of the car press the button that started the crusher. Andrew's explanation for the workmen's antagonism was that for them, destroying the car was an experience of death!

On July thirty-first Joshua told me Andrew had called him, very angry, because he, Joshua, hadn't telephoned as he had promised to. This conversation ended with Andrew's shouting into the phone that he'd never telephone Joshua again.

Joshua, it seemed, had felt badgered, and was made uneasy by Andrew's rancor and self-dramatizations and emotional appeals for support. He probably felt torn between Andrew and me.

A few days after the October earthquake in San Francisco Andrew telephoned Joshua once more and exclaimed, "Everyone here has been called except me! How could you not call to see how I was?"

"You're north of San Francisco," Joshua said. "I knew the damage was south of you."

"That's no excuse. How could you know that?"

"I saw the news."

"Really!"

"I knew."

"But we're in the middle of a family crisis. How could you not call?" He was yelling again.

"Calm down," Joshua said. "Don't get so excited."

Andrew hung up.

It was the last time they spoke.

22

New York

EVER SINCE I BROKE AWAY FROM ANDREW I FEEL as if I've been liberated from a lot of the life-long constraint of internalized authority.

I still miss Andrew, the son I once knew. I will probably always miss him. But Andrew, the guru, has become a stranger.

Joshua returned my apartment to me without a word, saying that he and Pat had guessed from the beginning that my decision to give it up was made under stress and was temporary.

Implausibly, Joshua's wife actually found my three novels in her book-case—packed in a box. I had absolutely no memory of ever placing all three in the one single box, nor of giving them to her. She hadn't either. If there are miracles, this certainly was one!

The last six years have been spent mostly thinking about, then writing and then re-writing the present book. The minute I began to glimpse the dynamics of the phenomenon that had entrapped me I felt compelled to write my story. I couldn't rest until it had been told.

Right after I left California, I was telephoned by Steven Hassan, an ex-Moonie who had become an exit counselor. He told

283

me he had been hired by Rebecca's family to wean her away from Andrew. At the time she was at home, having been expelled by Andrew for some intransigence or other, probably for the arrogance to which she was prone.

Steven said she had arrived home shaven-headed and so discombobulated that her family had seized the opportunity to introduce her to him. Unfortunately, the moment she met him she telephoned Andrew, who told her to return to the fold immediately.

Steven Hassan had written a book, *Combatting Cult Mind Control,* and wanted to speak to me about my experience with Andrew. We met in the green room of the broadcasting station where Sally Jessy Raphael, a talk show hostess, was about to interview him.

After the show Steven and I went to lunch. At one point I asked him what he knew about the guru's mind-set, whether the guru ever felt uneasy, whether he ever doubted, etc.

"Of course he does," Steven answered.

"But Andrew's confidence seems unassailable," I said.

"It isn't," Steven said. "Underneath, the son you knew is still there. Look, it's like this." He placed his palms together and held them parallel to the table surface. "On top is the guru but right below is the son you once knew. He is still there and he always will be."

"It's hard for me to believe," I said.

"Believe it," Steven said. "You have to figure out a way to get through that guru on top to the vulnerable person you knew and loved."

"I'll never be able to do that," I said. "Never." Then an idea came to me. "But Steve, what if Poonja spoke to him? What if Poonja told him about the terrible fear he creates, about his cruelty..." I lapsed into silence. "No," I said, "Poonja won't do anything."

"Why?"

"I don't know. He won't listen to me. He adores Andrew. And Andrew is crazy about him. They're like lovers having an eternal passionate affair. You should see their letters." I opened my handbag and got out Andrew's book. On its shiny black cover there was emblazoned in huge violet characters: *My Master Is Myself.* I handed it to Steven. "Even the title," I said, "just look at the title."

He took the book and stared down at the book cover. Then, as he flipped slowly through the pages, he stopped to read aloud some of the passages from the letters.

November 2, 1986—from Poonja—"You have occupied my whole mind day and night, I do not know what Romance is being enacted by both Lovers to each other."

November 17, 1986—from Poonja—"I have to uncover more sacred secrets to you, when and where I can't say... and I must hand over my robe to you."

September 25, 1987—from Andrew—"YOU ARE MYSELF FOREVER MASTER. YOUR FACE IS MY OWN and I bow before you in silent awe OF YOUR ENDLESS GRACE and INFINITE LOVE. YOU are LOVING ME ALWAYS. YOU NEVER LEAVE ME. YOU NEVER LEAVE ME MY LOVE MY LOVE MASTER TEACHER."

April 13, 1988—from Andrew—"MASTER I LOVE YOU SO!... My each breath is only YOU and YOU and YOU !"

February 1, 1989—from Poonja—"What is going on around is a miracle.... Whenever I move I feel I speak through your mouth and live in your body."

Steven handed the book back to me frowning and shaking his head.

"Steve," I asked, "what would happen if Poonja disagreed with Andrew about something important and really castigated him?"

The ex-Moonie replied without the slightest hesitation, "Then inevitably Andrew will set himself above his teacher."

"Oh that won't ever happen," I said.

I simply couldn't imagine it.

But a lot of people who felt Andrew was too harsh and aggressive went to complain to Poonja and some even stayed on as

disciples. After a time I was amazed to hear that Poonja had started to drift away from Andrew. He began to criticize Andrew behind
his back.

Ultimately, after repeated rejections and reproaches by
Poonja, Andrew separated from his teacher. By way of explanation,
as Hassan had predicted, in Andrew's *Autobiography of an
Awakening,* Andrew actually states: "I had obviously surpassed my
own teacher." And even in his latest book, *An Unconditional
Relationship to Life,* we find Andrew still complaining about
Poonja's "glaring inconsistencies and outrageous hypocrisy." So
this is how he dealt with Poonja's rejection. He rejected Poonja!

The two 'enlightened' ones who used to salute one another
in letters as "dear myself"—finally and irreversibly repudiated one
other!

A lot of what Poonja said about Andrew was true; that he
couldn't tolerate being criticized, that his disciples were afraid of
him, and that Andrew's notion of communal sangha life was for
sheep. I had had similar objections. But the fact was, Poonja could-
n't stand being criticized either. And he had shown himself to be a
hypocrite. For example, I heard that he told a former student of
Andrew's, now called Gangaji, and presently operating successful-
ly as a guru out of Hawaii, that he had been waiting for her, too, all
of his life, and as he'd said, after teaching Andrew, he was ready to
die! (She subsequently became Poonja's replacement for Andrew.)

When I met Poonja for the first time in India, he was a man
in his seventies who, after many years as a guru, had surprisingly
few disciples. I think he was hungry for fame and, when he met
Andrew, he must have seen a golden opportunity to broadcast his
name in America by inflaming this young person's impressionable
mind with ideas of 'starting a revolution amongst the young.' Then,
when Andrew turned out to be unsuitable, it took him no time at all
to find a replacement from amongst Andrew's disaffected follow-

ing. And his strategy worked. He is now regarded in America as one of India's foremost gurus!

According to *Autobiography of an Awakening,* when Andrew heard rumors of Poonja's condemnation of him he tried to get Poonja to tell him what was wrong, but Poonja would never confront him honestly. He would tell people Andrew was "off" and at the same time continue to be friendly and supportive to him in letters and phone calls. Apparently, so I was told, Poonja hated 'confrontations.'

In his book Andrew defends himself as an absolutely wronged man. Wronged by his spiritual father and wronged by his flesh-and-blood mother. And he challenges the powerful modern gurus who, according to him, have failed because they are less than perfect—"marred with some degree of confusion, hypocrisy, and in more cases than not, even deceit." His major accusation against his brother gurus is that they have sex with their followers. To my knowledge Andrew has not yet engaged in these activities. His game is power, not sex, and for the moment he is not tempted to use his power for obtaining sexual favors from his followers.

He presents himself as a perfect man, endowed as no other, a selfless being of pure intention who dares to know the truth. In a letter to Poonja he cries out, "If my insistence that people should cease to deceive themselves causes them to turn against me, what should I do? What can I do?. . .Why are you blaming me if some get hurt? This is unavoidable, the condition of humanity being what it is. You yourself have explained this to me in detail many times."

I'm not sure what it was exactly, that turned Poonja against Andrew. Possibly he'd taken offence at something Andrew had done or said. It could have been anything. It probably started when some of Andrew's disciples came to Poonja with loud complaints about Andrew's arrogance and cruelty, and he chose to believe them.

He certainly didn't believe me. Before there existed even the faintest intimation of a break between Andrew and Poonja I had sent Poonja the following letter.

Feb. 1/1990

Dear Poonjaji:

I can keep silent no longer. I am concerned about my son. He is, in part, miraculously clear and wise, as you know, but on the other hand, he is exercising great power without anyone or anything to modify in any way what he does. He interferes enormously in people's lives—where they should live, how they should live, their marriages, sex relations, ad infinitum. No one is allowed to criticize him, but everyone is encouraged to criticize himself or herself, especially in public, before the entire sangha.

He calls people vulgar names in public like pig, for example, and displays a great deal of contempt and anger. His followers are dreadfully afraid of him. When they confess their fear, he says they don't trust him enough!

This reckless, uncontrolled behavior seems totally unlike you or your method of teaching. Something has been unleashed in him that is frightening. No matter what he has told you, this is the other side, the dark side, of the situation.

Since December 2, 1987, with few exceptions, I've seen him only at satsang. This was supposed to "help" me see him as my teacher. Nevertheless, I became, *like the others,* his slave. I could not afford to express my feelings honestly because, if I did, I feared that he might send me away forever. I lived in absolute terror, willing to do anything in order not to invoke his rage, in order to get any crumb of attention—a glance, a smile, and, at the very least, was pitifully grateful if he didn't attack me in front of others. The smallest misdemeanor was always treated as a major crime. I suffered endless humiliation at his hands.

When I left him he told people I was "crazy" and I know one woman who gave him up as a teacher because she disagreed. He called me a traitor, a betrayer, and telephoned from Boston to California to have it announced formally in front of everyone there. But he would not meet and talk with me. I offered to meet him anywhere at any time. He refused. When I spoke to him on the telephone—the final time I spoke to him—in California last May, I said everything I had been afraid to say for almost three years. I spoke calmly. The terrible fear was gone at last. He listened and then said, in hateful tones, "Just wait until you crash!" It was a curse from my son.

I know this is painful for you. It is no less painful for me. I hesitated to write for a long time, out of a sense of loyalty to him. But it is my duty to tell you this. I fear for Andrew's sanity. Please help him! With much love and respect,

Luna

When I received no answer, I wrote to Poonja again:

May 7/90

Dear Poonjaji:

I am at a loss to understand why you have not answered my last letter, and anxious to know what you think about the situation with Andrew. I've heard that others have come to see you in India who have had experiences similar to my own.

Your first words to me when we met were, pointing to Andrew, "He is my son!" I imagined at the time that you thought I might be offended. On the contrary I was pleased that a man such as yourself should take my child to your heart as your son. Therefore, since you regard Andrew as your son you must surely feel some responsibility for what has happened to him. He worships you as a god and believes every word you utter. He believes your grand plan for him. He believed you when you said he would start a revolution among the young. In his eyes your authority validates everything he does.

Surely you must have some intention to correct the damage and suffering he has inflicted, and continues to inflict, in your name, as your "son."

Please alleviate the concern of this distressed mother and write me what you are thinking and what you propose to do.

Sincerely and respectfully,

Luna

I discovered from a disciple, Phyllis, who visited me in New York from time to time, that Poonja had sent my first letter to Andrew with a notation in the margin saying, "Need I answer this?" Phyllis had seen the letter and the notation with her own eyes. I was sure Andrew had shown it to her so that she would report what she saw to me.

I felt betrayed by Poonja.

Neither of my letters was ever answered.

Much later, after Poonja and Andrew had become open enemies, Poonja did send apologies to me through the letters of two strangers. For a man who writes letters by the score, I was indignant that he hadn't sent an apology in his own hand.

According to Joel Kramer and Diana Alstad in *The Guru Papers,* the most significant conclusion a guru seems to draw from his experience is the belief that he or she has "arrived at a place where self-delusion is no longer possible," but "this is, in fact, the most treacherous form of self-delusion of all, and the foundation for all the others."

I believe that Andrew is trapped inside his self-delusion, and from that position he has nowhere to go, because if a guru admits fallibility, it is the end of him; his adherents will look elsewhere for a replacement. Whenever the realization of this comes home to me, as it does time and again, it makes me shiver with dread for Andrew.

From my perspective he is not enlightened—whatever that might be and whatever experience he might have had. Still, his sangha expect him to enlighten them, and he promises that he can positively do it if only they will surrender to him.

What can be said about this, finally? It just seems to me that he is as duped by his own propaganda as were all those other brother-gurus in the marketplace who promised deliverance from suffering—from Hitler to David Koresh.

One thing appears plain to me: once you think someone is going to save you, you become their property. You belong to them. Your autonomy is gone. You are a slave.

23

NEW YORK

IN THE AUTUMN OF 1991, ANDREW TELEPHONED from California still under the cloud of separating from his guru, H.W.L. Poonja. The phone rang one evening about seven o'clock, and, incredibly, there was his familiar voice sounding as if nothing had ever happened. I felt a great burst of gladness.

"I'm so pleased you called," I cried. "It's so good to hear your voice!"

"You never know what's going to happen next do you?" He sounded very contained, even a little amused. "I didn't know if I could get through to you," he said.

"If you speak in that friendly tone you can always get through to me," I said.

We talked in a desultory fashion for a couple of minutes and then something came up that had to do with our recent difficulties—I can't remember what it was— and I heard my voice getting edged, and his getting defensive. But I could tell he didn't want to fight.

He said he wanted to see me.

For a moment that made me terribly happy. I said, "Okay! Sure!"

He wanted me to fly immediately to California. I paused and said, "I can't possibly."

But even if I could have, I would not have jumped to do what he evidently expected me to do, as he expected everyone who believed in him to do.

"If you want to see me you'll have to make the trek east into my territory," I said.

He was surprisingly agreeable. "If I could just meet you I'm sure I could convince you that what I'm doing is the right thing," he said. "But I'm on my way to India in a few days and I don't have the time."

"Why are you so sure?"

"About what?"

"That you could convince me?"

"Well, for one thing I know now it was a mistake for you to become my disciple."

"I'm glad you realize that," I said.

"It was a mistake," he repeated.

"It certainly was."

I wondered what had happened to change his mind. Had his teacher said something? I suspected he was very upset about the split with his teacher.

"You know," he said, "the other day I telephoned Giorgina," a former girlfriend he'd met in Italy. They had broken up years before, but had remained in contact as friends.

"Giorgina—?"

"Yeah. I called her in Rome."

"How is she?" I asked.

"Pathetic," he said, and he laughed again.

I didn't want to argue about it, but I found this one-word comment insolent and condescending about a girl he had once loved deeply. One night at satsang in Rome, she had cried out, "It's too much, too much—"

"What's too much?" Andrew had asked.

"To find you so completely changed," she had answered in a breaking voice. "I can't get over the feeling that I am no longer, in any way, special to you anymore. I am like anyone else. Anyone."

Just like me, I'd thought. She's suffering just like me.
Having known Andrew intimately long before his enlightenment, she was suffering from the same sense of loss as I was, and felt spurned in exactly the same way.

All at once I decided that it was best, for the moment, to end the conversation. I was surprised at how breathless I had become.

"We can talk again. I have to get off now," I said. "I have a guest who's starving and I have to fix some food."

But he seemed bent on lingering on the phone. A few moments later I repeated, "I've got to go, Andrew, I really do. Anyway, it's enough for now, don't you think? Why don't you call again soon." I was feeling breathless.

He said he would call again soon and true to his word, he did, two or three days later. Again we began by talking about superficial matters, but in no time found ourselves arguing about the attitudes in his sangha, the hierarchy, the cruelty, his absolute power etc. etc. I saw not one iota of new awareness in him. He repeated the same old formulas of his beliefs. At one point he called me 'my dear,' a form of address I remembered he used to employ when he was provoked, and which I found patronizing. "Don't refer to me as 'my dear'," I said sharply. "It's insulting." He laughed but he remembered not to repeat the error.

Finally, after a long half hour of polite side-stepping dissension he said good-bye and asked me to please call him from Montreal where I was to be in a few days. I got the idea that he thought he might just be able to meet me before he went on to India.

Reluctantly I agreed to it. But the moment I hung up I knew I'd made a mistake.Although I longed to meet him, I knew in my bones that if we met under these circumstances we would part from each other more estranged than we already were. Feeling horribly tense and sad, I wrote him the following note:

Nov. 24, 1991

Dear Andrew:

In view of our phone conversations I have come to the conclusion that unless you reach the point of being able to question your position and your views, it is inappropriate for us to meet. It is unrealistic to think our past relationship can be ignored and we can start out from square one. It is precisely our past relationship that is the problem. So there's no point in calling.

Luna

Perhaps that note was a goodbye forever. I didn't know. Perhaps I should have seen Andrew after all. As a mother perhaps I still had some shred of power to sway my son. I just don't know. But the sense that I was doing the right thing by refusing to see him, even though it felt like a nail being driven into my heart, was over-powering. I knew that the impasse between us hadn't altered and I did not, above all, want to make things worse than they were.

In September, 1992 I heard that Andrew was in New York giving satsangs downtown. All of my friends predicted that he would call but I knew he wouldn't and he didn't.

Phyllis telephoned—she was the disciple who'd informed me that Poonja had sent my letter to Andrew. She said she'd just arrived from Massachusetts to attend the satsang with Andrew and asked if we could meet. I invited her over for breakfast.

She expressed regret over and over again during our four hours together that this enormous rift had opened between Andrew and me and she didn't seem to understand why we couldn't make peace between us. She was a sweet-natured, warm-hearted person and I was very fond of her. At one point, in reference to something I can't recall, I said, "It seems to me, that when all is said and done, the secret of a tranquil mind lies finally in the acceptance of life as it is."

She burst out hopefully, "Oh, that's what Andrew always says. You both say exactly the same things!"

"You don't have to be a guru to know stuff like that," I answered, laughing.

She told me Andrew had softened his style and didn't attack people publicly anymore. He'd met a Roshi (Zen master) in Bodh Gaya who had cautioned that not everyone is ready to hear the teaching in the same way at the same time. "He told Andrew people are in different psychological places and must be approached accordingly," she said.

"Sounds like Psychology 101", I said wryly, "but I suppose it was received by Andrew as a piece of esoteric truth because it came from a Roshi in Bodh Gaya." I paused. "So tell me," I continued, "what's the difference between Andrew and any ordinary unenlightened member of our species? Don't we all tend to lend our ears more willingly to those who speak from positions of authority?"

Phyllis looked nettled and unhappy at the trend our talk was taking and I immediately regretted what I'd said. It was useless anyway.

The next day George, Julie's ex-boyfriend, telephoned. Because George was a very angry man with a tendency towards violence, sometime after I'd left Mill Valley, Andrew had named him Mad Dog, and had told everyone in the sangha to address him in that fashion. I presumed he meant this as a 'teaching' although to me it was only another example of Andrew's cruelty.

Now, on the phone, George sounded ebullient. "Why don't you come to satsang to see your wonderful wonderful son?" he asked, as an opener.

He knew the details of my history with Andrew. "Are you crazy?" I said.

"It would be so very, very wonderful," he gushed.

Not knowing how else to respond, I laughed. "If Andrew wants to see me, he knows where he can get me," I said. I am certainly not going to a satsang to see him!"

"I can give you his phone number," he coaxed.

"No," I said.

A few days later I woke up depressed. After a short struggle I sat down and wrote Andrew a note. I couldn't help myself. I longed to see my child. Hadn't he admitted at last that he was fallible? Hadn't he acknowledged at least one mistake—that I shouldn't have been his disciple? Maybe there was reason to hope.

September 25, 1992

Dear Andrew:

I am really sorry that so far I haven't heard from you during your stay in New York. You made the gesture toward contact last time and for many reasons I won't go into now, I rejected it. But if you still feel open to meeting, please get in touch.

I am not telephoning although I was offered your number because I do not want to speak to anyone else at your end. I want this to be just between us.

Luna

Julie was going to have lunch with George at one o'clock. I spoke to her at nine a.m. I asked her to take my note for Andrew to George and have him give it to Andrew that evening.

"You're capitulating," Julie said.

That scared me. "No, no," I said, "it doesn't mean a thing. If I see him it'll make me feel better, that's all."

Excited now, morbidly so, I was reminded of how I used to feel as Andrew's disciple—jittery, erased, and filled with a single overpowering desire for his approval. I sat down to correct the note, amended it a number of times to get it just right—not too compromising—not too anxious—not too cool—and careful not to leave the faintest trace of sarcasm or censure. At a certain moment I found myself using the word reconciliation for our projected meeting. I punched it out instantly and sat transfixed, staring at my computer screen. Was I insane? How could there be a reconciliation? Even though Andrew had admitted to one mistake, talking to him on the phone had made it clear that he was still unconditionally defending his ideas about himself and what he was doing and what his sangha was doing. So what was the use? I had to face the truth, bitter as it was. There could be no kind of reconciliation. I had let myself go, lost control, reverted to some aboriginal maternal consciousness. Julie was right. It shamed me to think how little it had taken for me to collapse like a pricked balloon the moment I allowed myself the delusion that I might get back the child I'd lost. No, no, there'd been a memory lapse, a surge of self-pity. It was over.

When Julie called to tell me she was coming over for my note, I told her I had changed my mind.

"I'm so glad," Julie said, "so glad."

The day before, she said, in response to George's persistent petition that I call Andrew, she'd said, "Why doesn't Andrew call Luna? After all, she's the mother."

"No," George had replied, "she should call HIM, he's THE ENLIGHTENED ONE!"

She said that she'd told George nothing as yet about my wanting him to deliver my note. Now it was my turn to say, "I'm so glad, Julie, so glad!"

It had been a close shave.

Two days later Joshua telephoned to tell me that he had gone to Andrew's last session in New York. I was shocked. "You've capitulated!" I said, echoing Julie's warning to me.

"No I haven't! I heard from someone who'd gone to see him that he wasn't as hard as he used to be and I was curious. I didn't feel nervous or anything. If I had, I wouldn't have gone." Then he said, "I wanted to see if our relationship could be re-instated."

There was a silence. "Well, do you think there's a chance?" I asked.

"No."

"No—?"

"No."

"How did he look?" I asked.

"The same," he said.

"He looked well?"

"Yes."

But Joshua seemed irked at me. I was sorry I'd said he had capitulated. After all, a couple of days ago I had been on the verge of the real thing myself, whereas Joshua had just gone on a sort of fishing trip to gauge the possibilities. Besides, he'd never succumbed to Andrew's spell as I had. And last but not least, it was a matter of Joshua's life, it was a matter of Joshua's brother, and I had no right to tell him how to feel or what to do.

"He seems cooler now, more rational," Joshua said.

"He does?."

"Yeah, his answers to questions are really quick."

"What do you mean—quick?"

"Free from editorializing."

"They should be. He's always saying the same thing. He doesn't have to think up new answers any more."

"Anyway he doesn't attack people like he used to," Joshua said.

"In public," I said.

"Yeah, in private maybe it's the same old thing."

"Did he see you?" I asked.

"I'm not sure. I sat in the back."

"He saw you," I said. "He sees everything. Now let's see if he calls you."

When I got home I telephoned my artist friend, Donna Moylan, who had left Rome, and was now living in New York. She said that I had to understand that my position vis-à-vis Andrew was quite different from Joshua's. "You want to change Andrew," she said, "because he's your son. That's why you refused to see him last time. You wanted him to realize something. You wanted him to see that his past actions had consequences. You wanted him to see how much he had hurt you, how cruel he'd been etc. For his sake. But Joshua doesn't think that way. Joshua just wants to see what's going on and if there's a possibility for contact."

The next morning I rang up Joshua and made a date at our neighborhood Chinese restaurant for lunch.

As soon as we sat down I asked, "Did he call?"

"No. I didn't really expect him to." He shrugged. "Maybe he didn't see me. There must have been seventy people."

"He saw you." I said.

"Maybe he didn't recognize me because of my beard."

"He'd know you. You're his brother!"

I looked up. A girl was standing at the table waiting for our orders. We told her what we wanted.

"Was there anyone else there you recognized?" I asked.

"No. Only Alka. She was sitting in front of me."

"Alka! She didn't see you?"

"She didn't see me."

"You're sure?"

"I'm sure."

"What's she look like?"

"The same. A little heavier."

"Did you see any shaved heads?"

"A couple."

A good while after I left California I was told that some old timers, to demonstrate their zeal, had begun shaving their heads. And later on I heard that novices who felt ready to commit to Andrew were requested to show their purity of intention by taking a vow to be celibate and keep their heads shaven for one year.

"Well, Andrew has left New York by now," I said, "and he didn't call his brother. Does it hurt?"

"No." Joshua said. "That's over."

"Why didn't you stay after satsang to talk to him?"

"There was a big line. I didn't want to wait. I hung around a bit looking at some of his books they had on display. But I refused to wait in line. I decided that before I went."

"You would have found it humiliating?"

"You could say so. I wouldn't wait." Some Chinese crackers were brought and we started nibbling on them. "You know," Joshua said, "if all he did was what he did at this last satsang, answer people's questions in a helpful way, it would be really okay. He's good at it."

"Yeah," I said. "He would've made a great politician. He's got that charisma."

"He wouldn't have wanted to be a politician," Joshua said.

"No," I agreed. "It's too dirty." I gave Joshua a grim smile.

"Maybe he's stopped being so judgmental," Joshua said.

"Maybe," I said.

Then Joshua related something that surprised me. "Y'know," he began, "my therapist met him once a long time ago. I think he came to one of her sessions. She hardly talked to him at all, but she said afterwards that he was one of the most judgmental people she'd ever met."

I stared at him astonished. I'd never considered Andrew judgmental in the old days. "Did you think Andrew was judgmental?" I asked.

"Are you kidding? It was obvious."

The waitress placed a dish in front of Joshua. I watched him pour a little soy sauce.

My soup arrived and I picked up the white enamelled spoon. "How long did satsang last?" I asked.

"One hour and forty-five minutes."

I sipped my steaming soup thinking that years ago, before the enlightenment business, way before that, I must have gotten Andrew all wrong. Or at least half wrong. To me the son I loved had been tender-hearted, alert to the feelings of others, sweetly communicative, and touching in his vulnerability. I was unconscious of his being judgmental. Yet to Joshua it had been obvious. I suppose a mother's magnanimous prejudice is a veil so opaque, most of us mothers never see through it.

What else had I missed? Hidden ambition? Overweening pride? Sexism? And what about the drive towards patriarchal control? Where could that have come from? His father? His brother? From me, in the form of some masquerade? Was it inherent? Genetic? Chromosomal?

EPILOGUE

WE MET AGAIN NOVEMBER FIFTH, 1995. ANDREW had sent me his latest book, *An Unconditional Relationship to Life,* and inside, on the facing page, I found a short note asking if he might see me on his next trip to New York. I wrote back that I would be glad to meet him.

He arrived a couple of months later and telephoned. We made a date. He would call me on the appointed day, Sunday, at six-thirty, after leading a one-day retreat at the Doral Tuscany Hotel on East Thirty-Ninth Street.

"I'll be working until about six," he said. "I'll call you at six-thirty. You decide where to eat."

"Do you have any preferences?" I asked.

"You're the New Yorker," he said. "You pick a place."

"The dinner's on you," I warned.

"Sure." He laughed.

I knew he'd come alone although I was told that he almost never goes anywhere without an entourage. I worried what we would talk about.

He didn't call at six-thirty. He didn't call until seven-fifteen. I was angry by then. I was remembering what a hard time he used to give a disciple who wasn't absolutely prompt, how he would malign the person with a barrage of degrading contemptuous criticism — "you're not serious, everyone else here is serious but you're

303

not serious, you don't belong with me, you're not interested in what's going on here etc. etc."

"Hello," he said.

"Hi."

"I'm ready to go," he said.

"You're late."

"We ran over the time," he said.

"After six years this is no way to start a rapprochement with your mother," I said. My voice was sharp.

"I'll leave this second," he said. "Where shall we meet?"

I gave him the address of a restaurant a couple of blocks from where I lived.

On my way over it flashed through my mind that he was always surrounded by assistants, and it would have been nothing to ask one of them to call his mother to say he would be late. Then I realized that he must be accustomed to arriving anywhere and everywhere as late as it suited him. People wouldn't complain. On the contrary, they'd be ready to prostrate themselves at his feet in gratitude that he came at all.

Crossing Tenth avenue I glimpsed him sitting at the bar through the restaurant window. He was leaning one elbow on the bar gazing towards the entrance.

The moment I went through the door he got to his feet and came over and embraced me. It was a very light embrace. We barely touched. He looked the same, attractive, well turned out in a sleek collarless shirt and vest, his eyes soft and dark as ever.

"You look the same," I said, after we both sat down at the bar.

"So do you," he said, as if it surprised him a little.

The restaurant was almost empty. There was no one at the bar and only a few tables were occupied at the far end.

"Let's have a drink," I said.

The bartender came over. We both ordered red wine and then I turned to face him. "You know Andrew," I said, "in the past if anyone had come three quarters of an hour late to an appointment, you would have made mince-meat of them."

He seemed unfazed at my words. The drinks came and I took a sip of wine. He didn't say he was sorry. I was amazed. It would have been an opportunity for him to break the ice a little. But he didn't say he was sorry. Instead he asked, "Did you read my book?"

"Yes," I said, "I read it from cover to cover."

"Did you like it?"

I understood that this was a pivotal question and I hesitated for a moment, but in the next moment I knew I was going to supply him with an answer he wouldn't like. I was going to tell him the truth. "Not exactly," I said, smiling slightly. The faintest crease showed on his brow.

"But didn't you think the writing was good?"

"I didn't think it was clear," I said.

I thought I saw a flash of pain, or was it shock, on his face. But in the next second he was grinning. I marveled that he could dare to ask me what I thought about his book when he had once succeeded in getting me to throw my entire life's work down the incinerator! Was it possible that he had forgotten?

I saw his hand move towards his wine glass. He raised it slowly and drank.

I didn't tell him I had found all my work again. I had this instinct, that I'd had all along, of not wanting him to know anything personal about me, as if it might appear to him to be an invitation to some sort of intimacy, some sort of control. During the last six years various disciples had looked me up or had telephoned me, and I had always suspected that they'd been sent by him, to find out what I was thinking, what I was doing, what I was planning.

We sat for a time in a tense silence during which I had the thought that maybe he was competing with me. He was the *writer* now, self-published, it's true, but published nevertheless. And I had never had anything published except for a play a long time ago.

At last I heard him ask, "What have you been doing the last six years?"

"Writing," I said and I laughed. "Writing a book about you." I knew he knew.

"I hear Alka is the villain," he said, grinning again.

"Alka?" I said. "Oh no, Alka's not the villain. Alka is just an incidental character. You're the villain!" I said it lightly, as if it were some kind of joke.

Did he flinch? I wasn't sure. An expression of mocking amusement seemed affixed to his face. How come he'd heard that Alka was the villain? What else had he heard?

As we were about to sit down at our table he took my coat and with a certain special care folded it over the side of a chair. All his movements showed an elaborate considerateness towards me. He was very much the courteous gentleman, a quality I'd never especially noticed in him before, not that he'd been conspicuously ungentlemanly.

He asked me if I wanted another glass of wine. I said I did. He hailed the waiter, ordered the wine, and then waited for me to choose something from the menu. I pointed to the first item on the list of main dishes, some kind of chicken. I wasn't hungry. He ordered a vegetarian pasta.

He started to tell me about his accident. A year ago, on a September evening, he and Alka had been hit by a cab on their way to the New York Theosophical Society where he was going to give a talk. At the corner of Fifty-Third Street and Park Avenue, they stood waiting for a light to change. When it did, they stepped off the curb and were instantly hit by a speeding taxi. Andrew related in detail what happened next. What I remember most is that his right arm had been badly broken and his right calf ripped open, exposing the bone. He was lucky, he said, that there were no internal or spinal injuries. Alka had suffered a bad concussion and had a fracture in her upper jaw, but her brain wasn't damaged.

He asked me to feel his arm through his jacket. I did, but I didn't notice anything unusual. Then he pulled up his trouser leg to reveal a still raw-looking gash on his leg.

"Oh my!" I said.

The truth was that he was so untouchable where I really wanted to touch him, that I resented having to put my hand on his arm or to look at his naked leg with its shocking thick red scar. It seemed too intimate under the circumstances.

I didn't tell him I'd heard at the time of his accident that someone had asked him if he wanted his mother informed, and that he had said no. I hadn't been surprised. I had interpreted his behavior as an unwillingness to allow me to see him incapacitated or weakened in any way.

"Did you have any medical insurance?" I asked, for lack of anything else to say.

"No," he answered.

I made no comment. He'd be well taken care of. There was no question about that.

Our food arrived. He asked for another glass of wine. I'd forgotten what I ordered and did not expect to see something as substantial as half a roasted chicken and a mound of mashed potatoes on my plate. I took a forkful of potatoes and swallowed. "Where are you staying?" I asked.

"At a bed and breakfast on Seventy-First Street and West End," he said.

"I used to live on Seventy-First Street," I said, "that first year you were in India. It's an interesting neighborhood."

"Yeah." He looked at me. "I'd like to find some place in the Catskills for our main center. I miss New York."

"You'd move from California?"

"Yeah. Why not?"

"You used to hate New York."

We ate without speaking for a couple of minutes. Then I asked him if he had seen any good movies lately.

"Yeah I saw a great movie," he said.

"What was that?"

"Burnt by the Sun," he said.

"That was a wonderful movie," I agreed, "the best movie I've seen all year."

"Yeah," he said.

We were silent. I was eating but I don't remember tasting anything. I felt oddly anaesthetized, as if I were in some sort of glass bubble.

He asked, "How's Josh?"

"Josh? Oh, he's fine. Fine."

"He came to a satsang last year."

"I know," I said. "He thought maybe you didn't see him, but I said you saw him all right." I heard the edge in my voice.

"Yeah, I did see him," he said.

"He told me he waited around for a few minutes looking at your books and magazines on display, but no one came, so he left."

"I sent someone after him immediately, but he disappeared!"

"That's not the way I heard it."

"But it's true!" he insisted. He put down his fork. "Right after you left California I called him five times, Luna. Five times! He never, never, returned one call." His voice was growing heated.

"Well," I said, "he told me he didn't call because he'd always had to go through someone else to get to you, sometimes more than one person, and it always seemed to him that somebody or other was listening in on your speaker phone. That's not very pleasant, you know. I remember how I used to hate it, Anyway, it made him very uncomfortable."

"And after the earthquake," he went on, as if he hadn't heard me, "when he didn't call me after the earthquake, when he didn't care enough to call—"

"I know," I broke in, "you called him and you started screaming and hung up on him. Look, he found out right away that you weren't in a dangerous area. He found out that the earthquake was a hundred miles south of Marin county."

I had stopped eating. So had he. I took a sip from my glass of wine. After a long interval I pointed to his plate.

"How do you like your pasta?" I asked.

"Not great," he said tensely.

"I'm sorry. It's usually quite good here."

He leaned forward and stared at me. "Why, tell me why you didn't telephone me from California to tell me you wanted to leave?" he asked.

"I telephoned as soon as I could. I left a message."

"I heard about it from Judy," he said accusingly.

"Our house phone broke down," I said. "Besides, I needed time to get clear myself. It all happened so fast."

"You should have found a way to call immediately!" he said. He looked at me with an angry, outraged expression, and then he picked up his fork and speared some pasta and began to eat again.

I watched him for a few moments and then I said, "It amazes me Andrew, it really does, that you don't seem to realize how much you wounded me, you wounded me terribly." He didn't look up from his plate. "And unless you and I go through every issue between us," I went on, "there is no way that we can communicate."

He put down his fork and gave me a quick, piercing glance. "We may never be able to communicate," he said threateningly.

"That's true," I said calmly, "we may never be able to communicate."

He frowned and looked down at his plate again, and muttered as though to himself, bitterly, "No one can say I didn't try!"

I was sure he wouldn't let anything lead to an explosion. He was here to keep the peace. He was here to get his MOTHER back without saying he was sorry, without apologizing for anything. He thought he could do it!

But why was I here, I wondered? I didn't know why I was here. I had understood a long time ago that there was no possibility of my changing his mind about his life. He wasn't going to give it up. He believed in it.

I guessed I was here because he was my son and I wanted to take a look at him again after six years.

It was after another interminable silence that I said, "I hear Bud isn't with you any more."

"No," he said. He gave me an unhappy look. "It was hard, very hard." His tone was that of a person who had been victimized, but I knew that no one was ever given the opportunity to victimize Andrew. He was the victimizer.

"This is the best part of my life," I exclaimed suddenly.

"Really!" he retorted dryly.

"Since I left you, all that suffering — it turned me into a strong person."

He gave me a derisive smile.

"It's true. It was sink or swim, Andrew. I was lucky that I didn't end up in the loony bin. If you don't sink, you become a strong person. I'm much stronger than I was before." I turned to watch an elegantly dressed couple passing by on their way out. "Maybe I should thank you for torturing me," I said, turning back to him, and looking him in the eye.

"I didn't torture you," he replied, still smiling derisively.

I looked at him. "No, of course, you would call all that horror some kind of enlightened teaching. You think you can enlighten people by tormenting them."

"I never said I was enlightened."

"Didn't you?"

"But if people ask me about my experience, I can't deny what happened to me."

I drank some wine. "You don't have to say you're enlightened. Everything you do implies it!"

I forgot to mention that he had told me more than once that he was God. My blood started to rise and I didn't try to stop it. It

310

hit me that maybe the real reason I was here was because I was still furious with him, and I wanted him to know the depth and breadth of my fury.

"I should have known, I should have known—" He was shaking his head from side to side and regarding me with an expression that was almost hatred. "I'm only here because you're my mother!" he burst out.

"Really!" I snapped. "I happen to be a very interesting woman!"

"The unexpectedness of the remark seemed to force a laugh from him. I laughed too, grateful for a moment of comic relief.

But then, in the next moment, in a sudden shocking gesture he reached across the small table and took hold of my shoulders and drew me to him and held my head tight against his chest.

"I want you to listen to me," he said, his voice hissing, "just listen!"

I struggled madly against his vise-like grip until he finally released me. I shot a glance behind, and then another towards the yawning space in front of me, but the waiters and the few people left dining in the strangely deserted, fashionable restaurant seemed not to have noticed us.

He placed his elbows on the table and stared at me. At last, in a reasonable voice he said, "We think alike, you know. I think like you. We have a similar philosophical turn of mind."

"That's not true." I said. "I used to think it was true, but I was wrong."

He looked at me as though taken aback. "I want to explain," he went on, "I want to explain simply and clearly, what I'm trying to teach people." He waited, with that expression of astonishment still showing faintly on his face, then continued. "Underneath everything, deep down, at the bottom, where there's no thought and no emotion, most people feel that the world is all wrong, that nothing is right."

"And—?"

"I try to teach them the opposite, that basically, at the bottom, nothing is wrong." He paused. "It's a new way to approach life."

"How can you have an approach to life without thought or emotion?" I asked. I was thinking that without thought or emotion what functions is primordial consciousness, and in this primordial consciousness there are no notions of right and wrong and therefore no 'approaches' to life. There is, in fact, nothing there you can change.

"It's a new way to approach life," Andrew repeated.

What in the world was he talking about? What else is underneath, deep down, at the bottom, where there is no thought and no emotion but primordial consciousness? Did he imagine that somehow or other he could reach into the unreachable and change something?

I didn't want to continue this conversation. As ridiculous as his idea sounded, I knew I'd never be able to talk him out of it.

He must have been so discouraged by the look on my face that, shaking his head once more, he said exasperatedly, "You still don't get it!"

We had each ordered an espresso coffee. I asked him if he had any friends. "It must be impossible for a guru to have friends," I said.

"No," he said, "not at all."

"No? Who are your friends?"

He gave me a look that was both challenging and mocking. "I'm afraid to tell you," he said.

"You're afraid? That's a funny thing for you to say!"

"My two best friends are Tom Broome and Spirit."

"Tom Broome!" I stared at him speechless. Tom Broome was the man I had most despised in the entire sangha.

"He knows you hate his guts!" He chuckled.

"So he's your best friend," I said slowly, recalling what a cold, bullying snob Tom Broome had been.

"And Spirit?" I asked, "is she still with Manny?"

Andrew's mouth seemed stretched into a permanent, patronizing grin. "She divorced Manny and married Tom," he said. "They run the center in London."

The waiter brought us our coffee.

"Poor Manny," I said, dropping a sugar cube into my cup. "And imagine, I used to think he'd be your John the Baptist!" I looked up into his eyes and had the feeling that I was looking into the eyes of a foreign being, a creature who had nothing to do with me. The eyes stared back unblinkingly. They didn't know me.

Had they ever known me?

Suddenly, and with a blinding clarity, I understood we could probably never manage to have a real talk. In the end, there was nothing to say.

The impact of this thought was so strong that I turned to get my coat folded on the chair beside me. He sprang up at once to help me on with it.

We walked in a strained hush back to my apartment building. I sensed that now, as our meeting was about to end, he was dejected. Was it frustration? Feelings of rejection? Perhaps an unfamiliar confusion had taken hold of him. He wasn't accustomed to being flatly refused, as I had refused his every overture.

I was oblivious of the traffic on Twenty-Third Street, of people passing by, of the glaring lights of advertising slogans and store windows. I was only conscious of the increasing tension between us, of how strange I felt to myself, and of how unhappy he appeared. I felt sorry for him. I wanted to get away from him.

I broke the oppressive silence by asking, "Are you still with your wife?"

"It's gotten better lately," he answered rather obliquely. He walked me to my door and then we stood facing one another. "Andrew," I said, "there's one last thing I want to tell you."

"What is it?"

"You were wrong once, you were wrong about Poonja. You've admitted that you made a mistake about him."

He was quick to answer. "No, that was something else, it was different at the beginning, it was—"

"It makes no difference about the beginning," I cut in, "in the end you realized that you had misjudged the man. You'd made a mistake about him."

He didn't answer me. I peered at him in the shadowy light but his eyes were unreadable dark hollows in his face.

"If you can make one mistake, Andrew, you're quite capable of making another," I said. "Think about it."

There was no answer.

Then, after a pause, he said, "I'll be back here in the spring. Would you be willing to see me again?"

"Yes," I said.

"Well, good-bye," he said, and I thought I saw a smile flicker across his lips.

"Good-bye Andrew."

He turned to go. I watched him walk to the curb and hail a taxi. There was something stooped about his shoulders. I understood that not only did he want his mother back but that for him I was still the one who had to be vanquished so that he could feel totally unchallenged as the knower of the TRUTH. Although many others who had been close to him had disappeared for one reason or another, I was the biggest fish that got away.

I didn't wait for the taxi to stop. I went through the glass doors into my lobby. In the elevator I was suddenly aware of a crushing fatigue. My body felt insubstantial, as if it were filled with air, as if I were floating a few inches above the ground. I had almost no sense of my body. And later, as I pulled the bed quilt up to my chin and switched off the light next to me, I realized that my mind had gone blank. I'll never be able to tell anyone what happened tonight, I thought. I've already forgotten it all.

A few days later I began to remember again and I made

some notes, but it was two months before I could bring myself to write this final chapter.

In later recollections, that last evening with him was engraved sharply and clearly as the strangest and the saddest evening of my life.

He didn't call in the spring.

IN CONCLUSION...

ANDREW SAYS THAT ANYONE WHO LOVES AND surrenders to him is guaranteed enlightenment, meaning, according to *The Guru Papers,* that he "will be able to lead people to salvation... bliss, self-knowledge, immortality, peace, an end to sorrow, and ultimately being one with God." The latter notion, the feeling of oneness with everything, is the core idea of enlightenment. Andrew promises that this state can be permanent. He claims his own state of enlightenment to be permanent.

But there are those who say that enlightenment is just another illusion. They say there is no such thing as enlightenment, and that all the symptoms I manifested that are considered stepping stones to enlightenment, the buzzing in my head, the fainting feelings, the altered visual experiences, have other than mystical explanations. Again, according to *The Guru Papers,* "Many people, through various routes, have experienced what has become known as altered states of consciousness. By 'altered' what is meant is that the way experience is both taken in and framed is different from one's ordinary day-to-day experience. The two main routes of alteration (perhaps as old as humanity) are through substances (chemicals in plants and synthetics) and practices that loosen up the way the mind structures experience. Altered states can also occur through near death experiences, great stress, or spontaneously, without any known cause."

My own mind was probably 'altered' because of the acute stress I was experiencing and my desperate need to show some signs of 'improvement' to Andrew, that is, to be able to point to concrete evidence that my doubt had diminished—so that he wouldn't suddenly turn and hurl me out of his life forever!

Perhaps you could compare the guru and his disciples to a dysfunctional family. Recently I followed with great fascination the trial, on television, of the Menendez brothers, two young men who shot their parents to death. One of the psychiatrists or defense attorneys, I can't remember which, gave a list of the psychological factors prevalent in seriously dysfunctional families. I was struck by the similarity of those conditions and Andrew's abusive ways with his followers.

1) You are never sure what the rules are.

2) You are not sure what the transgression was that took love away.

3) If you stand up against your parent or parents you think you will be banished.

4) Everything is your fault.

5) One of your parents' biggest power plays is to keep you waiting.

6) All the above items produce a feeling of worthlessness.

7) The only way to avoid attack is to try to be as invisible as possible.

It is my understanding that if you become seriously attached to a guru, that means you have been searching for someone to give you a center of gravity; that means looking for someone who will take over the responsibility for your life. And when you think you've found the right person, to you, he or she appears, in a magical way, to be an all-knowing god, and, you, in comparison, perceive yourself as some poor fool of an ignoramus. Finally, whether you know it or not, to maintain this fiction you *both* need one another.

It seems to me that power is the key—a belief in the power of the guru to save, and a belief in your powerlessness to save yourself.

I've frequently been asked what sort of people are attracted to Andrew. All kinds of people are attracted. Most of them range between twenty-eight and forty-five years old. They come from every walk of life and every culture. At the time that I left, about seventy or eighty such people made up the core of Andrew's following. I've heard that by now, the core group has grown and that there are hundreds more on the fringes. Andrew travels all over the world these days delivering his message.

I suppose the reasons I submitted to Andrew were the same as everyone else's. I wanted an end to my own suffering. But what held me so long in spite of my private opposition to his behavior was my love for Andrew, my son, and the tormenting fear of losing him forever.

Impossible as it may appear, unattainable as it may seem, it is my opinion now that only acceptance, a deep inmost consent to life in all its contradiction and complexity, can dispel our suffering. And our search for meaning? Our questions? Perhaps then they will all vanish.

Is this really possible?

I don't know.

Most of the main characters in this book have left Andrew or have been booted out by him for one reason or another. Orit's comments on why she left seem to sum up the reasons of the people who 'defected.'

She told me, on a trip I took to Jerusalem three years after I had parted from Andrew, that she had already been apprehensive about him when she went to Holland.

"I couldn't face the doubts," she said, "so I went to see him again in Amsterdam and felt very divided again. I was sure he was a fake but I couldn't figure it out because he seemed to have this power. And afterwards I invited him to Israel to check him out in my own house, and you know what happened. I finally left him."

"Why did you think he was a fake?" I asked her.

"Some things shocked me," she said. "For one, at satsang he seemed to relish reading out loud all the flattering letters he received."

"What else?"

"Oh, he wanted more and more followers and he was too quick telling people they were enlightened."

"Go on."

"Well, it turned out they weren't enlightened. He was wrong. So he didn't have as much power as I thought." She paused. "He couldn't deliver the goods."

A child of your body is a child of your body and remains so until you die. So how could I bring myself to write a book that some might think savages my child?

I can only say that the intensity of my own experience made it a compulsion to expose the danger in the link between guru and disciple. It is a tie that at first seems so benign, so beautiful, so full of the promise of paradise, but it has the potential to end in an atrocious abuse of power, drastic disillusionment, even death.

Today is Andrew's birthday. He is forty-one years old. I have just typed the last word of this manuscript. It is like saying a last good-bye to my son. Everything that happened seems to me now strange and fictitious. The blistering realization is that I have lost a beloved son. And against all probability, I hope that someday Andrew may have the strength to cast off his emperor's clothes and come home.

THE GREENHAVEN PRESS
Literary Companion
TO AMERICAN AUTHORS

READINGS ON

THORNTON WILDER

David Bender, *Publisher*

Bruno Leone, *Executive Editor*

Brenda Stalcup, *Managing Editor*

Bonnie Szumski, *Series Editor*

Katie de Koster, *Book Editor*

Greenhaven Press, San Diego, CA

Every effort has been made to trace the owners of copy-
righted material. The articles in this volume may have
been edited for content, length, and/or reading level. The
titles have been changed to enhance the editorial purpose
of the Opposing Viewpoints® concept. Those interested in
locating the original source will find the complete citation
on the first page of each article.

Library of Congress Cataloging-in-Publication Data

Readings on Thornton Wilder / Katie de Koster, book editor.
    p.   cm. — (The Greenhaven Press literary
companion to American authors)
    Includes bibliographical references and index.
    ISBN 1-56510-815-9 (lib. : alk. paper). —
ISBN 1-56510-814-0 (pbk. : alk. paper)
    1. Wilder, Thornton, 1897–1975—Criticism and
interpretation. I. De Koster, Katie, 1948–   . II. Series.
PS3545.I345Z86   1998
818'.5209—dc21   98-9891
                                                   CIP

Cover photo: Archive Photos

Copyright ©1998 by Greenhaven Press, Inc.
PO Box 289009
San Diego, CA 92198-9009
Printed in the U.S.A.

> **EMILY:** *. . . Do any human beings realize life while they live it?—every, every minute?*
> **STAGE MANAGER:** *No. (Pause.) The saints and poets, maybe—they do some.*

—— Thornton Wilder, *Our Town*

CONTENTS

wrote about social groups. Wilder was concerned with individuals, yet he found universal patterns in human experience that could be illustrated in the lives of people of any place or time.

Chapter 3: Pulitzer #1: *The Bridge of San Luis Rey*

Chapter 4: Pulitzer #2: *Our Town*

Chapter 5: Pulitzer #3: *The Skin of Our Teeth*

Date Due Receipt

Items checked out   02/28/2019   at

San Rafael Public Library

Renew online at marinet.lib.ca.us

173
178
180
181

TITLE **Readings on Thornton**

BARCODE **31111024057190**

DUE DATE   **03-21-19**

FOREWORD

> *"'Tis the good reader that*
> *makes the good book."*
>
> Ralph Waldo Emerson

The story's bare facts are simple: The captain, an old and scarred seafarer, walks with a peg leg made of whale ivory. He relentlessly drives his crew to hunt the world's oceans for the great white whale that crippled him. After a long search, the ship encounters the whale and a fierce battle ensues. Finally the captain drives his harpoon into the whale, but the harpoon line catches the captain about the neck and drags him to his death.

A simple story, a straightforward plot—yet, since the 1851 publication of Herman Melville's *Moby-Dick*, readers and critics have found many meanings in the struggle between Captain Ahab and the whale. To some, the novel is a cautionary tale that depicts how Ahab's obsession with revenge leads to his insanity and death. Others believe that the whale represents the unknowable secrets of the universe and that Ahab is a tragic hero who dares to challenge fate by attempting to discover this knowledge. Perhaps Melville intended Ahab as a criticism of Americans' tendency to become involved in well-intentioned but irrational causes. Or did Melville model Ahab after himself, letting his fictional character express his anger at what he perceived as a cruel and distant god?

Although literary critics disagree over the meaning of *Moby-Dick*, readers do not need to choose one particular interpretation in order to gain an understanding of Melville's novel. Instead, by examining various analyses, they can gain numerous insights into the issues that lie under the surface of the basic plot. Studying the writings of literary critics can also aid readers in making their own assessments of *Moby-Dick* and other literary works and in developing analytical thinking skills.

The Greenhaven Literary Companion Series was created with these goals in mind. Designed for young adults, this unique anthology series provides an engaging and comprehensive introduction to literary analysis and criticism. The essays included in the Literary Companion Series are chosen for their accessibility to a young adult audience and are expertly edited in consideration of both the reading and comprehension levels of this audience. In addition, each essay is introduced by a concise summation that presents the contributing writer's main themes and insights. Every anthology in the Literary Companion Series contains a varied selection of critical essays that cover a wide time span and express diverse views. Wherever possible, primary sources are represented through excerpts from authors' notebooks, letters, and journals and through contemporary criticism.

Each title in the Literary Companion Series pays careful consideration to the historical context of the particular author or literary work. In-depth biographies and detailed chronologies reveal important aspects of authors' lives and emphasize the historical events and social milieu that influenced their writings. To facilitate further research, every anthology includes primary and secondary source bibliographies of articles and/or books selected for their suitability for young adults. These engaging features make the Greenhaven Literary Companion series ideal for introducing students to literary analysis in the classroom or as a library resource for young adults researching the world's great authors and literature.

Exceptional in its focus on young adults, the Greenhaven Literary Companion Series strives to present literary criticism in a compelling and accessible format. Every title in the series is intended to spark readers' interest in leading American and world authors, to help them broaden their understanding of literature, and to encourage them to formulate their own analyses of the literary works that they read. It is the editors' hope that young adult readers will find these anthologies to be true companions in their study of literature.

INTRODUCTION

One major biography of Thornton Wilder is called *The En-thusiast*, emphasizing that enthusiasm and an abiding be-lief in the ability of humankind to endure any calamity are hallmarks of Wilder's writing.

A popular teacher—he considered teaching his "real" vocation—Wilder loved finding novel ways to help his stu-dents learn. Enthusiasm and the ability to share knowledge and understanding by using seemingly simple examples were two of the characteristics that made him a favorite of his students. In teaching, as in writing and talking with friends, he drew on vast reserves of knowledge he eagerly gathered throughout his life. Theatrical director Tyrone Guthrie recalled a conversational style that matched the way he wrote:

> Wilder is learned but no pedant. I have never met anyone with so encyclopedic a knowledge of so wide a range of top-ics. Yet he carries this learning lightly and imparts it—the important with the trivial, the commonplace with the ex-ceedingly bizarre—in a style and with a gusto which is all his own.

A good teacher eventually leads people to think and fig-ure things out for themselves, while providing clues and guidance. Many of Wilder's works—and especially the three for which he won Pulitzer Prizes—explore and ulti-mately lead to an understanding of the common ground of humanity. He described his two Pulitzer-winning plays, *Our Town* and *The Skin of Our Teeth*, as viewing the same basic story from opposite ends of the telescope: The inti-mate, personal stories of the former echo the mythic sor-rows, troubles, and joys of everyday living of the Antrobus family—the long-lived Adam, Eve, and entourage—in the latter.

Looking back over Thornton Wilder's work shortly be-fore his death, the *New York Times* commented on the en-during popularity of his work:

Wilder's plays are now more than ever in rhythm with our changing habit of theatergoing. . . . He relates the moment to eternity, seeks the infinite in the immediate, finds the universe in each grain of wheat. His plays have not so much been "revived" over and over again, as they have almost continuously stayed alive among us.

THORNTON WILDER: A STUDY IN CONTRASTS

Edith J.R. Isaacs, editor of *Theatre Arts* magazine, remembers meeting Thornton Wilder in 1921 when Wilder was twenty-four years old. An aspiring playwright, he had just come from a postcollege year in Italy and France and was on his way to his first teaching job in New Jersey. Onboard the ship coming home he met theater reviewer Stark Young, who introduced him to Isaacs. After commenting on Wilder's having already "seen more of the world than many men ever see," Isaacs gives this picture of Wilder:

> It may have been something about the touch of many lands that gave him the double, but not at all divided, quality that is one of his distinguishing characteristics. Even in that first visit it was easy to see that although he was extremely serious, he was also very gay. Although very shy, he was unusually friendly; although he was surprisingly learned, he was never pedantic; he was as deliberate in his thinking as he was explosive in his speech, letting the words roll off his tongue one on top of the other but every one the right word aimed exactly at expressing the right idea. He was both temperate and enthusiastic, bold and unafraid but very modest, and above all he was one of the most amusing young men I had ever met.

This unassuming young man who went on to win three Pulitzer Prizes—unprecedentedly in two categories, fiction and drama—presented a series of contrasts in both his life and his work. An indifferent scholar, he was a voracious reader and an excellent teacher. He was a romantic at heart, but cast his works in classical form. His critical success was matched by popular acclaim; Bernard Grebanier, Brooklyn College professor emeritus of English, expressed the prevailing sense of surprise when he wrote: "Despite the three Pulitzer prizes awarded him Thornton Wilder may very well turn out to be one of the few enduring writers of our time."

AMOS AND ISABELLA WILDER

The contrasts in Thornton's life began with his parents, Amos and Isabella Wilder.

Amos Parker Wilder, son of a dentist who later founded a successful oilcloth manufacturing company, was raised in Augusta, Maine. He reported in the 1884 *Yale Class History* that during the after-school hours, "I was 'all over the place' . . . peddled things, carried water for elephants, worked in a grocery, and especially in a bookstore at odd hours." He was a bright and self-assured child, but when he entered the larger world of Yale University, his self-confidence suffered; "I was in terror of being dropped," he remembered later. Nonetheless, he was class orator in his first and second years, and Wilder biographer Linda Simon recounts some of his other academic and social successes:

> He was a member of Kappa Sigma Epsilon, Psi Upsilon, Skull and Bones; he sang in the class and university glee clubs, edited the *Courant* in his senior year, and acted as one of the class historians. His greatest disappointment—an embarrassment he was never to forget—came during his freshman year. He was selected for the staff of the *Record*, but was quickly dismissed for incompetency. "This was the severest humiliation I have ever known," he wrote later. In his small room on High Street he felt deeply dejected; but, characteristically, he summoned his strengths and rallied.

The humiliation may have spurred him to prove himself capable, for he later turned to the pen to make his living. After graduation, he taught school in Connecticut and Minnesota for a couple of years before taking a job as a reporter in Philadelphia. He then returned to New Haven for four years to earn a doctorate at Yale (his thesis was on municipal government) while editing the New Haven *Palladium*. He reveled in writing strongly opinionated editorials, one of which finally caused such controversy that he moved on to New York, where he worked for several papers. "Salaried journalism" did not have the job security he sought, though, so he bought a one-fourth interest in a Milwaukee, Wisconsin, newspaper, the *State Journal*, and became the paper's editor. Always one to keep busy, he also began giving a series of lectures on city government, sponsored by the University of Wisconsin.

In 1894 Amos married Isabella Thornton Niven, daughter of a Presbyterian minister from Dobbs Ferry, New York. The Wilders settled in Madison, Wisconsin, where their first son, Amos Niven, was born in 1895.

Isabella "was unlike her husband in temperament," notes Linda Simon:

> While Amos was outgoing, forceful, a fiery speaker, his wife was quiet and reserved. Though she had not been highly educated, she was artistic and refined. At Sunday school in her father's church, the teacher had found her "brilliant and highly cultivated." She had had aspirations of attending college or becoming a teacher, but her father, the Reverend Thornton Mac-Ness Niven, had definite restrictions for the education of his daughter. . . . Amos, too, showed a skepticism of Isabella's artistic inclinations. He was ever the patriarch and, for his wife and some of his children, a formidable force to confront.

Deterred from achieving her own ambitions (she had wanted to become a physician, but her father forbade it even after she had been accepted by Barnard College), Isabella Wilder did not abandon her aesthetic interests. Despite having four children in five years, Simon notes, "Neighbors would often see her taking her children on afternoon outings: her oldest son, Amos, was barely walking, steadying himself by holding on to the baby carriage with the three younger children inside, and Isabella herself would be pushing the carriage as she read a book of poetry."

THE MISSING TWIN

Those four children had nearly been five: On April 17, 1897, Isabella Wilder bore identical twins, but one son lived only a few hours. The surviving twin was named Thornton Niven, for Isabella's father. Born prematurely and weak, he had to be coddled for weeks to insure his survival. Perhaps this less-than-hale-and-hearty start predisposed his father to think of him as unable to care for himself; Amos Wilder more than once mourned that this "poor boy" would always be a burden.

Surviving his twin affected Thornton throughout his life. When he was twenty, he wrote his father, "I suppose that everyone feels that his nature cries out hourly for it knows not what, but I like to believe that mine raises an exceedingly great voice because I am a twin, and because by his death an outlet for my affection was closed." In later years, his older brother, Amos, wrote:

> Though Thornton and I were not twins, I have always felt that there was some sort of occult affinity in my makeup for his fabulations, like the telepathic understanding between Manuel and Esteban in *The Bridge of San Luis Rey*. . . . As himself a twin who lost a brother at birth, he was predisposed

to fascination with this relationship. Indeed one could hazard that he was haunted all his life by this missing alter ego. Thus he plays with the afterlife of this twin in the dual *persona* suggested by the title of his last novel, *Theophilus North,* "North," of course, representing an anagram for Thornton. In this was he was able to tease both himself and the reader as to the borderlands between autobiography and fable.

Observers also labeled as "his missing twin" Thornton's sister Isabel, who in later years handled his business and personal affairs and served as his intermediary with the public when he disappeared to write. These characterizations point up the closeness the children maintained throughout their lives, nurtured in part by their father's insistence that they write thoughtful letters to one another during their many separations.

Those first few years, though, brought few separations. From spring to fall the family (which now included Charlotte Elizabeth, born August 28, 1898, and Isabel, born January 13, 1900) lived in a rustic cottage on Lake Mendota, four miles from Madison. Thornton, now called Todger, was no longer frail, and "all the Wilders were lively; indolence was as alien as luxury," writes Thornton biographer Gilbert A. Harrison.

"Their intellectual growth was overseen by both parents," Simon notes, "with each contributing something in accordance with his or her personality. Amos preferred Scott, Dickens, and Shakespeare; Isabella, Yeats and Maeterlinck. Amos was concerned with imparting moral lessons; Isabella, a sense of beauty."

A LARGER ARENA

By the turn of the century, the outspoken Amos Parker Wilder, who now held a controlling interest in the *State Journal,* had become an important force in state politics. This had not led to financial security, though; a ratings war between newspapers and Wilder's crusade against corruption and alcohol (he refused to run liquor ads) cut sharply into the Wilders' income, making it ever harder to support his growing family. Yet beyond financial considerations, it was a desire to find a larger stage for his talents and a larger audience for his strong views that led Amos Wilder to seek a political appointment. A friend from Yale, William Howard Taft (who would later be elected president), was the secretary of war in President Theodore Roosevelt's cabinet. After

Amos was passed over for his first choice, as U.S. minister to Uruguay-Paraguay, he called on Taft to support his appointment as consul general at Hong Kong. He was confirmed in the post on March 7, 1906, and on May 7 the family landed in Hong Kong.

Thornton was enrolled in a strict, German-language school in Hong Kong. He remembered being carried about in a sedan chair and coming home for lunch with Wong, the "number one boy." But Isabella was unhappy in the colony, and on October 30 the rest of the Wilder clan left Amos behind and returned to the United States, settling in Berkeley, California. Here Thornton—with his mother's help—found the theater. His sister Isabel recalled Berkeley in her 1977 foreword to Thornton's play *The Alcestiad:*

> The magnificent Greek theater built into the hillside of a euca-lyptus grove was a new and lively part of the life of the university and the town. Several times a year the Classics Department mounted productions of plays by Sophocles, Aeschylus, and Euripides. Our mother joined the volunteer workers in the costume shop and stenciled furlongs of borders in the Greek key or laurel leaf patterns on gorgeously colored togas. She made a little blue one with shells around the hem for Thornton—and a green one for brother Amos—and sent them off to apply for roles as members of the Athenean mob. Thus Thornton discovered "total" theater and the Golden Age of Antiquity. His experience until then had been a performance of *As You Like It* seen from the top gallery of a Milwaukee theater.

> By now Thornton was ten; black-haired, blue-eyed, acquisitive and radiant. Even before this he had claimed his share of a writer's allotment of the twenty-six letters of the alphabet and had begun to tame them into a vocabulary that would allow him—in good time—to speak in his own way. He went to bed early and got up early to write, and the full range of his enlarging vocabulary was turned to inventing dialogue. He draped us and the neighbors' children in yards of begged or borrowed cheesecloth and coaxed us into declaiming his grandiloquent speeches.

In 1909, after Amos took the post of consul general in Shanghai, he made two trips to California to be with his family. (A third daughter, Janet, was born in 1910.) He was nearly a stranger to his children. When he returned to Shanghai, his frequent letters exhorted his offspring to follow his own stern precepts. He frowned upon the Greek theater ("As for Greek plays, you know Papa has only a limited admiration for 'art.' . . . *Character* is the thing in life to strive for"), and instructed the children to read aloud to one another *Pilgrim's Progress, The Vicar of Wakefield,* and *The Boy's Life of John Wesley.*

Although the family enjoyed Berkeley, money was tight. Consuls general were instructed to help U.S. firms establish overseas business. The positions paid a modest salary and required a fair amount of entertaining; it was assumed that the companies they helped would be generous in helping them cover their expenses. Amos Wilder, ever sternly righteous, would never accept such remuneration. (He also refused to help companies that sold alcohol, even when instructed to do so by the State Department; he offered instead his resignation, which was not accepted.) The money Amos sent to Berkeley ($1,500 of his $8,000 salary) did not go far to support his wife and five children, and after the birth of Janet, the strain led most of the family (the younger Amos remained in California) to reunite in China once again.

Charlotte and Thornton were sent to the China Inland Mission Boys and Girls School at Chefoo, in Shantung Province. They were there, 450 miles north of Shanghai, when Sun-Yat Sen led a revolution in central China and was proclaimed president of the new republic. The turmoil does not seem to have affected their schooling, although Thornton wrote to his mother that the revolutionary army had offered the school's servants twice their salary to enlist. "Result: boys work; result: Wilder washes dishes and cleans carrots, serves table and carries water for other people (boys) to wash in (not himself! Oh no!)."

Discipline at the school was strict and the academic requirements were tough, especially since his schooling in Berkeley had not prepared him with the competence that was expected in Greek, Latin, algebra, and geometry. He and Charlotte were allowed a few minutes together once a week. Gilbert Harrison reports that "uniformed in white pith helmets and white suits with knee-length pants, the boys were marched on Sundays through hot, dusty streets to attend Church of England services, seeing on all sides goiters, tumors, abscesses, stumps of lepers' arms and legs, the blind, the skeletal Chinese children. It was Thornton's first sight of omnipresent misery—untended, ignored, endured." That recognition of the endurance of the human race would form the basis of some of his most powerful works.

Once again, Mrs. Wilder was unhappy living with her husband in China; this time she took the two younger daughters, Isabel and Janet, to stay with her sister in Florence, Italy. Charlotte and Thornton stayed at Chefoo, their brother Amos was still in Berkeley, and their father was in Shanghai.

Thornton had persuaded the school authorities to let him substitute long-distance running for the required group sports of soccer and cricket. His father deplored his failure to be a sportsman—not realizing until some years later that his second son was severely nearsighted—but Thornton exulted in the long stretches of time alone: He knew that writers needed such time, and he used his running time for thinking.

Students were required to write their parents every Sunday, so Thornton had to write both to Shanghai and to Florence. His letters to his father rarely had trouble conforming to the school's standards (they were read by a teacher before they were sent), but his fanciful letters to his mother occasionally elicited the comment, "Too fantastic!"

A year later, Mrs. Wilder, Isabel, and Janet returned to the United States, while Thornton, Charlotte, and Mr. Wilder sailed for California from China. (Mr. Wilder had contracted a debilitating tropical disease, Asian sprue, that left him listless and unhappy. He had resigned his post, and would never regain the vigorous health he had enjoyed before.) Thornton joined Amos at the Thacher School in the Ojai valley in California, a school that normally attracted affluent students. The headmaster, Sherman Thacher, was another Yale buddy of Thornton's father's, and with his help the boys were able to get an education they could not otherwise easily afford. In *Thornton Wilder: An Intimate Portrait*, Richard Goldstone notes that Amos warned his old friend about his younger son:

> He had "nerves," was "silent, sensitive," and slept badly; he could swim, but beyond that had no interest in sports; his interests, rather, were directed toward "music, art, drama and literature"; he was "not a good mixer," but was sensitive and self-conscious, though "radiantly happy when with those who like and understand him." Amos added, in relaying these unfortunate characteristics to Headmaster Thacher, that "he may develope 'moods'."

It was about this time that their father demanded a pledge of temperance from Thornton and Charlotte; he made them sign a promise never to drink alcohol. In Thornton's case, that promise did not take; by his college years, he was regularly enjoying social drinking. (Years later, Richard Goldstone asked him, "One of your most celebrated colleagues said recently that all a writer really needs is a place to work, tobacco, some food, and good whisky. Could you explain to the non-drinkers among us how liquor helps things along?" Wilder replied, "My springboard has always been long walks. I drink a great deal, but I do not associate it with writing.")

In his foreword to *The Angel That Troubled the Water and Other Plays,* Thornton remembered himself at sixteen:

> It is a discouraging business to be an author at sixteen years of age. Such an author is all aspiration and no fulfillment. He is drunk on an imaginary kinship with the writers he most admires, and yet his poor overblotted notebooks show nothing to prove to others, or to himself, that the claim is justified. The shortest walk in the country is sufficient to start in his mind the theme, the plan, and the title, especially the title, of a long book; and the shortest hour when he has returned to his desk is sufficient to deflate his ambition. . . .
>
> Authors of fifteen and sixteen years of age spend their time drawing up title pages and adjusting the tables of contents of works they have neither the perseverance nor the ability to execute. They compass easily all the parts of a book that are inessential. They compose dignified prefaces, discover happy quotations from the Latin and French, and turn graceful dedications.

That short attention span might have hampered a lesser writer, but Thornton kept writing a series of "three-minute plays for three persons." He went on to compose at least forty of these short works, finding in them "a literary form that satisfied my passion for compression" and avoided "the needless repetition, the complacency in most writing."

COLLEGE

After a year at Thacher, Thornton transferred to Berkeley High School, which Charlotte was attending, for two years, planning to attend his father's alma mater, Yale, when he graduated. But Amos Wilder feared Yale was too worldly for his spiritually inadequate son. Instead he enrolled Thornton in Ohio's Oberlin College, an evangelical college founded by two Congregational ministers, which Thornton's brother also attended. After two years, Amos was allowed to transfer to Yale, and Thornton wrote a friend that "I have [my father's] promise in writing for one year only." In the end, he spent two years at Oberlin, transferring to Yale under protest.

Although Amos had hoped Oberlin would mold his son into his own image, the Ohio campus held other interests for

Thornton. Among its many appeals, the school offered an excellent music department, an outlet for his passion for theater, and the "salons" of Mrs. Martin, the wife of one of the professors. Martin invited a circle of students to meet on Sunday afternoons. These salons were, writes Richard Goldstone, "of considerable importance to the young man's development of poise and self-assurance; there he could talk about theater, about new writers—George Moore was one of his enthusiasms—and he was respectfully listened to." He joined the editorial board of the *Literary Magazine* and was made archivist of the CYMOC club, a group of students that met monthly for intellectual discourse. (The members swore not to reveal what the initials CYMOC stood for.)

Besides the respect of his peers, Thornton was encouraged by Professor Charles H.A. Wager, the chairman of the English Department. Wager, whom Wilder described as "the greatest class lecturer I have ever heard," invited the young author home, "and encouraged him to read aloud the stories and plays which, a year or so before, he could show only to his mother," according to Goldstone.

So by the time Amos decided to transfer his younger son to Yale in New Haven (where the family was now established), Thornton was "completely devoted to Oberlin and deeply resented my father's moving me to the East." His father insisted, for several reasons: to bring the family together, to save money, and to earn a Yale diploma, which would be most valuable in finding a job in teaching, the profession he had decided on for Thornton.

During the summers, Amos required his sons to work at physical labor; he usually found a farm where they would be required to do chores in return for a small wage. Thornton also had one other break in his college career, from September 18 to December 31, 1918, when he joined the Coast Artillery Corps. He had long wanted to serve in the war being fought in Europe, World War I, but his nearsightedness had made him ineligible until just before the war ended. He resumed his studies in January 1919 and received his diploma in June 1920, listing his profession in the yearbook as journalist.

NOT EXACTLY THE GRAND TOUR

Thornton wanted to make his living as a writer; Amos thought that absurd. Richard Goldstone describes the father's worries:

Now fifty-six years old, his earning potential limited by age and dwindling opportunities, Amos, the head of a household consisting of four females and an elder son about to enter the ministry, saw in Thornton the only bulwark—and an insubstantial one at that—against poverty and disgrace should he, Amos, be stricken and incapacitated. Not for a moment did Amos entertain the thought that Thornton could, through writing, maintain even himself ("Carving olive pits!" "Carving olive pits!"). Viewing his second son as basically ineffectual, somewhat indolent, and not overly intelligent, Amos reached the conclusion that Thornton could eke out a living in the only way open to failures and incompetents: as a schoolmaster. Having arrived at that decision through his own inexorable logic, Amos communicated it to Thornton who, faced with the vision of his mother and sisters facing starvation, bowed to Necessity and accepted his Lot.

But first there would be a brief respite. Thornton would be allowed to spend a year as a resident visitor at the American Academy in Rome. He could learn Italian and brush up on his Latin—both useful for a teacher—while performing some healthy physical labor swinging a pickax at the school's archeological digs. Why Italy? His mother had discovered that the exchange rate for dollars was at that time very favorable. After due consideration, Gilbert Harrison reports, Amos told his son:

My dear boy, . . . I am going to give you $900, in installments. If the money situation over there is as your mother says it is, that will sustain you very well for a year. . . . So make the most of your advantages in Rome. When you return, I hope you will be prepared to teach Latin in some school somewhere, and as far as money is concerned, let me not hear another word out of you for the rest of our lives.

Although the more immediate product of Thornton's Italian journey was his first novel, *The Cabala*, part of the influence of this year abroad later found its way into Wilder's *Our Town*. In a preface for that play, he wrote:

For a while in Rome I lived among archeologists, and ever since I find myself occasionally looking at the things about me as an archeologist will look at them a thousand years hence. Rockefeller Center will be reconstructed in imagination from the ruins of its foundations. How high was it? A thesis will be written on the bronze plates found in New York's detritus heaps—"Tradesmen's Entrance," "Night Bell."

In Rome I was led through a study of the plumbing on the Palatine Hill. A friend of mine could ascribe a date, "within ten years," to every fragment of cement made in the Roman Republic and early Empire.

An archeologist's eyes combine the view of the telescope with the view of the microscope. He reconstructs the very distant with the help of the very small.

It was something of this method that I brought to a New Hampshire village.

LEARNING FRENCH

At the end of eight months, money running short, Thornton prepared to leave Italy. He had been hinting to his father that it would be a good idea for him to go to Paris (which was becoming a mecca to expatriate Americans, especially expatriate American writers), "to learn French." As one of the two positions Amos was contemplating for his son was as a teacher of French, he agreed to finance a few weeks in France but warned Thornton to return promptly, ready to teach the language at Lawrenceville, a New Jersey prep school. Lawrenceville agreed to hire Thornton for $1,500 per year on the recommendations of his Yale professors, and Thornton wrote to his mother (then in England): "Well, well, I am as excited as a decapitated goose." He enjoyed Paris, but returned early to New York to take French lessons at the Berlitz School.

MADE TO BE A TEACHER

Unexpectedly, Thornton enjoyed his new job, which included housemaster duties for the thirty-two boys who lived at Davis House. Nights after ten, weekends, and vacations were devoted to writing; the rest of his hours were devoted to his students. Gilbert Harrison writes that he was a popular teacher:

> The boys were entertained by his rapid walk and talk and grateful for his cheerful tolerance of their nonsense. He was *different.* "Mr. Wilder seemed to find us endlessly intriguing and disturbing," one of the boys, Marshall Sprague, recalled, "though we knew that his interest was that of a spectator at the zoo watching the monkeys, charming and repulsive by turns, happy to be noticed, especially when he erupted like a volcano at some misconduct of ours and threw blackboard erasers and chalk at us." They retaliated by dropping a trunk down the stairs from the third floor, so that it would knock the door off his room and end up inside. . . .
>
> He tried without conspicuous results to introduce French into everyday conversation. For the enlightenment of one lad who was having trouble with irregular verbs, in this instance the present tense of venir, he leapt over the back of a couch, flapping his arms and shouting "On wings of gauze they come!

they come! ILS VIENNENT!" . . . First-year boys were directed in scenes from a popular Broadway show, *Nelly Kelley,* taught to sing "Don't Send Me Roses When It's Shoes That I Need" and how to form a chorus line. Halfway through the study period, Mr. Wilder visited all rooms to observe work habits, decisively solving such problems as a snake crawling between sheets. At bed-check, he rushed to a window and shouted, "No, madam! You can't come in. This is a boy's room!" Yes, Mr. Wilder was *different.*

Thornton supplemented his salary with other small jobs: preparing a publisher's catalog and tutoring during the school year, more tutoring during summer breaks, and finally publication of a portion of the book he was working on, then called *Memoirs,* in a small New Orleans magazine, *Double Dealer.* He finally had enough money to send some to his family and offer, "Tell me when you need more."

THE PARENTAL INFLUENCE

Amos Wilder, who would die in 1935, no longer controlled his son's life. While biographers and critics uniformly agree that Isabella Wilder nurtured, supported, and encouraged her son's gifts, they disagree on the influence of Thornton's father.

At least one biographer, Richard Goldstone, believes Amos Wilder's influence on his second son was harmful. He notes that Isabella was unlike most American women, who stayed with their husbands in diplomatic postings and sent the children to boarding school:

> There is no avoiding what is more than a possibility that, in 1906, she effected the separation of her children from her husband because she had already observed that his influence was unwholesome and psychologically damaging. Not only did Amos's stern Calvinism hang like a cloud over the young children, but he imposed on them his iron will, his lofty standards of conduct, achievement, and principle, and his sense of himself—law-giver and dispenser of absolute justice. . . .

> Maintaining a fatherless household [in Berkeley] was to be a struggle—financial and physical—for Isabella. . . . But whatever the physical handicaps she encountered in making do with the meager allowance remitted by her husband, Isabella was enabled to remedy—if remedy she could—the psychologically crippling influence that her husband exerted upon their children.

Those who feel Amos was a hindrance rather than a brace to his talented son find support in such outbursts as Thornton's defense of himself and his oldest sister in this letter to his father, written when he was twenty-one:

Sometimes I get so annoyed by your desperation over a chance cigarette or a frivolous word that I have a good mind to give you a real jolt, such jolts as other fathers get from their sons, the real griefs of Old Eli [Yale]. I am too good for you, that's all, and you make a luxury of martyrdom to yourself out of my slightest defection. Likewise Charlotte's friends consider her an amazing, rare personality, such as New England is only able to cast up once in an age, but you wear us all out with your instigations to Napoleonship and fame [and] look upon the first YMCA secretary or Settlement House directress as more interesting than Charlotte. Do try to console and comfort your declining years with the incredible news that you have produced at least two children that are the amazement and delight and amused despair of their circles (the more finely grained the spectator the greater the appreciation). Let others produce obscure devoted women and faithful Assistant Pastors; you have fathered two wild fowl flying in the storm of the 20th century.

Thornton's brother offers a different perspective on biographers' speculations in *Thornton Wilder and His Public:*

It is inevitable that I should give special attention to the role of our father in my brother's development. . . . This parent of Maine background had certain of the robust and granitic traits and that "interfering spirit of righteousness" associated with the Calvinist heritage, a type widely derided today. My brother had his troubles with him. . . . But the paradox in this case was that this same overshadowing father was also the one who imbued my brother with his deepest insights into American grass-roots values and their hidden operations.

Although Thornton thought of his father as "a sort of Don Quixote" without any sense of the aesthetic, writes Gilbert Harrison,

Still, Thornton took from him a desire to shape and improve lives, a facility with language, a histrionic virtuousity, moral energy, nostalgia for small towns and respect for anonymous multitudes. . . .

However hard-pressed, he had always found the money a child needed. He had sent his son to farms not as punishment but to provide lessons in the value of the dollar and in health building. His strictures were not motivated by selfish concerns, certainly not by dislike. Whatever the frustrations of his married life, he held that "the drama of the home is a great mystery," a mystery Thornton would celebrate in his plays, and that nowhere else do all manner of men "grow tender and have longings to be good: hugging their children and walking about in the dark hours safeguarding their dependents." Moreover, Papa's conviction that literature would not pay was commonplace for his generation.

ROMAN MEMOIRS

At the end of the spring 1924 term, Thornton requested a two-year leave of absence from Lawrenceville, intending to finish his *Memoirs* and try to find a publisher. He spent that summer at the MacDowell Colony in Peterborough, New Hampshire, the first of several stays at the prestigious artists colony, where he was encouraged by the benefactor of the colony, Mrs. Edward Mac-Dowell, and managed to finish five of the portraits for *Memoirs*. At the end of that year, he submitted part of the manuscript to New York publishers Albert and Charles Boni. The Bonis were mildly encouraging and Wilder completed more sections; they finally offered him a contract in November 1925. By then Wilder had returned to school, attending Princeton to earn a master of arts degree in Romance languages. If the book—now called *The Cabala*—did not sell well, he counted on the M.A. to help him find better-paying work.

The book appeared in April 1926, and was hailed by the *New York Times* as "the debut of a new American stylist" and a "magnificent literary event." Other critics agreed, and sales were respectable. But when Thornton discovered that his contract said that no payment was due him until February 15, 1927, he realized he could not live on his earnings as an author just yet. He accepted a job as chaperone to Europe for a young man; he could travel and be paid for it, earning enough to last until Christmas. However, the young man, twenty-year-old Andy Townson, proved an uncongenial companion; by the time he left for home at the beginning of December 1926, Thornton was impatient to get back to work on his next book, *The Bridge of San Luis Rey*. He wrote his publisher and asked for $150 against his royalties so he could resume work on the book in Europe, now that he no longer had the Townson subsidy to cover his living expenses. He considered rooming with Ernest Hemingway to save money, but "his wife is about to divorce him and his new wife is about to arrive from America; so I think I better not try." He wrote, went to the Riviera for Christmas, dropped in on Sylvia Beach at her famous Paris bookstore Shakespeare and Company, and wrote his mother that he was homesick. At the end of January 1927 he sailed for home.

THE BRIDGE OF SAN LUIS REY

Occasional tutoring jobs to meet expenses continued to eat away at his writing time; when Lawrenceville invited him to return as master of Davis House, he agreed to come for one school year, 1927–1928. Perhaps the anticipation of a secure position helped; within two weeks of accepting the position, he finally finished the manuscript he had been working on, *The Bridge of San Luis Rey.* Ironically, when the book came out that fall, Thornton was recuperating from surgery for appendicitis and anxious to return to Lawrenceville; "otherwise, what will become of my SALARY."

The book was a smash hit. By December, it had earned him $20,000 in royalties—quite a sum for a man who was eager to return to a $4,000-a-year position as a schoolteacher. The excitement—especially after the book was awarded the 1928 Pulitzer Prize for fiction—made teaching school difficult. But it did bring a measure of celebrity that had him hobnobbing with the famous: Gene Tunney, world heavyweight boxing champion, invited him to dinner (the two men, who got on well, would later go on a walking tour in Europe together). Broadway producer Jed Harris asked for the right of first refusal on Thornton's next play. And Scott and Zelda Fitzgerald invited him to spend a weekend with them at the house they had rented in Delaware.

SUCCESS

Thornton could do what he wanted now, without worrying overmuch about money. His mother had long wanted the family to have a house of their own; he purchased property in Hamden, Connecticut, in March 1929 and spent a substantial part of his new earnings on "The House *The Bridge* Built." With Thornton's help, his father, who was physically ailing, retired from working and spent much of the next few years in sanitoriums or on health farms. Besides supporting his parents, he also provided for Isabel (and, after the mid-1930s, for Charlotte); only Amos and Janet—the oldest and youngest siblings—were making their own way. Isabel began to take over the day-to-day work Thornton's celebrity necessitated; she dealt with his mail, acted as literary agent, served as hostess, dealt with the myriad details that did not interest Thornton. He never married, and this convenient arrangement continued until he died. Isabel often traveled with Thornton; besides running interference in practical matters, she was a congenial sounding board for his new ideas.

He was working on *The Woman of Andros* when the stock market collapsed at the end of October 1929, marking what would become known as the Great Depression. When the book was finally published, it did not seem appropriate or "socially relevant" during a period of widespread hardship; critics were especially hard on its foreign setting, and a vitriolic attack by proletarian writer Michael Gold in the *New Republic,* entitled "Wilder: Prophet of the Genteel Christ," lambasted him for not having written a novel about the working class. His next book, *Heaven's My Destination,* was a sympathetic and funny picture of middle America.

CHICAGO

Thornton still loved teaching, and had happily accepted a position at the University of Chicago for the appealing sum of $666.66 per month. He later said that his years in Chicago, 1930–1936, were the happiest of his life. He became a member of a group of men and women who were bright without being intellectual, fun loving and informal. The longtime loner ecstatically told his friend Alexander Woollcott, the *New Yorker*'s theater critic, "They love me humanly and I love them inhumanly."

Despite his new affluence, Wilder did not spend money easily on himself. "Things don't speak to me," he noted with dismay when people showered him with presents. Two suits would suffice for summer, and when he gained weight, Isabel could let them out so he could get another five years' wear out of them. He provided for his family, contributed to a wide variety of charities, and took pleasure in treating his friends generously.

In 1934 Gertrude Stein came from France to give a series of lectures on English literature; she had not returned to her native country for over three decades. Wilder invited Stein and her companion, Alice B. Toklas, to stay in his apartment while they were in Chicago. She and Wilder struck up a friendship that lasted until her death in 1946; during the years to come she would often importune him to collaborate with her on her next book. He always graciously avoided the requests, but tirelessly championed her writing and wrote introductions for three of her books.

BACK TO THE THEATER

In 1939 *The Bridge of San Luis Rey* was one of the first ten Pocket Books—twenty-five-cent paperbacks—published in the United States. But regardless of the enduring popularity of the novel, Malcolm Goldstein, author of *The Art of Thornton Wilder,* chronicles his subject's return to his early love, the theater:

> After the publication of *Heaven's My Destination* Wilder made up his mind to write no more fiction. The decision did not come as a result of the poor showing of the novel, he later insisted, but from a growing dissatisfaction with narrative technique: he had become uncomfortably conscious of his "editorial presence." By this he meant the prodding and emphasizing of theme from an all-seeing, all-knowing position. . . . He turned to the form which at least seemed to prohibit a sense of the author's presence. In drama the author does not hover over the personalities of the characters, cannot point directly to those of their traits which express the meaning of the play, and is, in fact, expected to make his revelations through action and dialogue alone. Gertrude Stein had taught him that "you should talk to yourself in your own private language and be willing to sink or swim on the hope that your private language has nevertheless sufficient correspondence with that of persons of some reading and experience." From 1937 to 1943 in accordance with this principle he wrote and brought to Broadway *Our Town, The Merchant of Yonkers,* and *The Skin of Our Teeth.*

Two of those three plays won him Pulitzer Prizes for drama; Wilder saw them as basically the same story, seen through opposite ends of a telescope. The third, *The Merchant of Yonkers,* was a disappointment at the time. But when he rewrote it as *The Matchmaker* in 1954, it achieved immense popularity, as did the musical version, *Hello, Dolly!*

World War II had begun in 1939, and soon after the Japanese bombed Pearl Harbor in December 1941 Wilder chose to join the military; he was commissioned a captain in the air force. He had a few weeks before he had to report, so when Alfred Hitchcock asked for his help on the script for *The Shadow of a Doubt,* he traveled to Hollywood for intensive sessions with the great director. Hitchcock was so impressed with his work that he rode the train with him back to Washington, discussing the screenplay all the way. Wilder's own play *The Skin of Our Teeth* opened just before he was to go overseas; its message of the enduring strength of the human race was aimed at a wartime audience.

After the war, Wilder went back to work: teaching and lecturing, writing, even acting occasionally. He was especially popular as the Stage Manager in *Our Town,* and he also enjoyed playing Mr. Antrobus in *The Skin of Our Teeth.* In collaborating with Sol Lesser on the movie production of

Our Town, he agreed to give Emily a reprieve:

> In the first place, I think Emily should live. I've always
> thought so. In a movie you see people so *close to* that a dif-
> ferent relation is established. In the theatre they are halfway
> abstractions in an allegory; in the movie they are very con-
> crete. So, insofar as the play is a generalized allegory, she
> dies—we die—they die; insofar as it's a concrete happening
> it's not important that she die; it's even disproportionately
> cruel that she die.

> Let her live. The idea will have been imparted anyway.

His teaching assignments now were no longer the refuge
of the inept or unsuccessful. Harvard awarded him the
Charles Eliot Norton Professorship of Poetry; he lectured on
Thoreau, Poe, Whitman, Dickinson, and Melville. Other
honors followed, including the 1952 gold medal for fiction
from the American Academy of Arts and Letters, the 1963
U.S. Presidential Medal of Freedom (the first year the award
was given for distinguished civilian service in peacetime),
and the 1968 National Book Award for *The Eighth Day.* He
continued to write: *Theophilus North* was published in 1973.
But he did not live to see the publication of the play he had
been working on since before the Second World War, *The Alcestiad;* it was published posthumously in 1977.

On December 22, 1975, in its Transitions column,
Newsweek magazine offered an obituary for Wilder, who had
died on December 7; "Exit the Stage Manager" was written
by Bill Roeder in the style of *Our Town.* It ended this way:

> He was getting up in years at the age of 78. Still, it was a jolt
> for us folks in Grover's Corners—and I'll bet for a whole lot
> of other people, too—when Thornton Wilder slipped away
> with a heart attack during his afternoon nap the other day.
> God rest him. H'm—11 o'clock in Grover's Corners. You get a
> good rest, too. Good night.

CHAPTER 1

A Personal Perspective on Wilder

An Interview with the Author

Richard H. Goldstone

In the late 1950s the *Paris Review* published a series
of interviews with such prominent authors as
William Faulkner, Georges Simenon, Truman
Capote, and Thornton Wilder. Wilder was inter-
viewed by Richard H. Goldstone, who would later
write *Thornton Wilder: An Intimate Portrait* and
coedit *Thornton Wilder: An Annotated Bibliography
of Works by and about Thornton Wilder*. In the interview, Goldstone and Wilder discuss a wide variety of
topics, including the author's need for daily contact
with nonartists, the difference between novels and
plays, and the social functions of drama.

*It is unlikely that more than a few of his countless friends
have seen Wilder in repose. Only then does one realize that he
wears a mask. The mask is no figure of speech. It is his eye-
glasses. As do most glasses, they partially conceal his eyes.
They also distort his eyes so that they appear larger: friendly,
benevolent, alive with curiosity and interest. Deliberately or
not, he rarely removes his glasses in the presence of others.
When he does remove them, unmasks himself, so to speak, the
sight of his eyes is a shock. Unobscured, the eyes—cold light
blue—reveal an intense severity and an almost forbidding
intelligence. They do not call out a cheerful* "Kinder!
Kinder!"; *rather, they specify:* "I am listening to what you are
saying. Be serious. Be precise."

*Seeing Wilder unmasked is a sobering and tonic experi-
ence. For his eyes dissipate the atmosphere of indiscriminate
amiability and humbug that collects around celebrated and
gifted men; the eyes remind you that you are confronted by
one of the toughest and most complicated minds in contemporary America.*

An apartment overlooking the Hudson River in New York City. During the conversations, which took place on the evening of December 14, 1956, and the following afternoon, Mr. Wilder could watch the river lights or the river barges as he meditated his replies. . . .

INTERVIEWER: Although military service is a proud tradition among contemporary American writers, I wonder if you would care to comment on the circumstance that you volunteered in 1942, despite the fact that you were a veteran of the First World War. That is to say, do you believe that a seasoned and mature artist is justified in abandoning what he is particularly fitted to do for patriotic motives?

WILDER: I guess everyone speaks for himself in such things. I felt very strongly about it. I was already a rather old man, was fit only for staff work, but I certainly did it with conviction. I have always felt that both enlistments were valuable for a number of reasons.

One of the dangers of the American artist is that he finds himself almost exclusively thrown in with persons more or less in the arts. He lives among them, eats among them, quarrels with them, marries them. I have long felt that portraits of the non-artist in American literature reflect a pattern, because the artist . . . portrays the man in the street as he remembers him from childhood, or as he copies him out of other books. So one of the benefits of military service, *one* of them, is being thrown into daily contact with non-artists, something a young American writer should consciously seek—his acquaintance should include also those who have read only *Treasure Island* and have forgotten that. Since 1800 many central figures in narratives have been, like their authors, artists or quasi-artists. Can you name three heroes in earlier literature who partook of the artistic temperament?

INTERVIEWER: Did the young Thornton Wilder resemble George Brush, and in what ways?

WILDER: Very much so. I came from a very strict Calvinistic father, was brought up partly among the missionaries of China, and went to that splendid college at Oberlin at a time when the classrooms and student life carried a good deal of the pious didacticism which would now be called narrow Protestantism. And that book [*Heaven's My Destination*] is, as it were, an effort to come to terms with those influences.

The comic spirit is given to us in order that we may analyze, weigh, and clarify things in us which nettle us, or which we are outgrowing, or trying to reshape. That is a very autobiographical book.

INTERVIEWER: Why have you generally avoided contemporary settings in your work?

WILDER: I think you would find that the work is a gradual drawing near to the America I know. I began with the purely fantastic twentieth-century Rome (I did not frequent such circles there); then Peru, then Hellenistic Greece. I began, first with *Heaven's My Destination*, to approach the American scene. Already, in the one-act plays, I had become aware of how difficult it is to invest one's contemporary world with the same kind of imaginative life one has extended to those removed in time and place. But I always feel that the progression is there and visible; I can be seen collecting the practice, the experience and courage, to present my own times. . . .

A WRITER'S HISTORY

INTERVIEWER: I don't know exactly how to put the next question, because I realize you have a lot of theories about narration, about how a thing should be told—theories all related to the decline of the novel, and so on. But I wonder if you would say something about the problem of giving a "history" or a summary of your life in relation to your development as a writer.

WILDER: Let's try. The problem of telling you about my past life as a writer is like that of imaginative narration itself; it lies in the effort to employ the past tense in such a way that it does not rob those events of their character of having occurred in freedom. A great deal of writing and talking about the past is unacceptable. It freezes the historical in a determinism. Today's writer smugly passes his last judgment and confers on existing attitudes the lifeless aspect of plaster-cast statues in a museum. He recounts the past as though the characters knew what was going to happen next. . . .

INTERVIEWER: Did you have a happy childhood?

WILDER: I think I did, but I also think that that's a thing about which people tend to deceive themselves. Gertrude Stein once said, "Communists are people who fancied that they had an unhappy childhood." (I think she meant that the kind of person who can persuade himself that the world would be completely happy if everyone denied himself a vast number of free decisions, is the same kind of person who could persuade himself that in early life he had been thwarted and denied all free decision.) I think of myself as having been—right up to and through my college years—a sort of sleepwalker. I was not a dreamer, but a muser and a self-amuser. I have never been without a whole repertory of absorbing hobbies, curiosities, inquiries, interests. Hence, my head has always seemed to me to be like a brightly lighted room, full of the most delightful objects, or perhaps I should say, filled with tables on which are set up the most engrossing games. I have never been a collector, but the resource that I am describing must be much like that of a collector busying himself with his coins or minerals. Yet collectors are apt to be "avid" and competitive, while I have no ambition and no competitive sense. Gertrude also said, with her wonderful yes-saying laugh, "Oh, I wish I were a miser; being a miser must be so occupying." I have never been unoccupied. That's as near as I can get to a statement about the happiness or unhappiness of my childhood. Yet I am convinced that, except in a few extraordinary cases, one form or another of an unhappy childhood is essential to the formation of exceptional gifts. Perhaps I should have been a better man if I had had an unequivocally unhappy childhood.

INTERVIEWER: Can you see—or analyze, perhaps—tendencies in your early years which led you into writing?

WILDER: . . . The future author is one who discovers that language, the exploration and manipulation of the resources of language, will serve him in winning through to his way. This does not necessarily mean that he is highly articulate in persuading or cajoling or outsmarting his parents and companions, for this type of child is not usually of the "community" type—he is at one remove from the persons around him. (The future scientist is at eight removes.) Language for him is the instrument for digesting experience, for explaining himself to himself. Many great writers have been extraordinarily awkward in daily exchange, but the greatest give the impression that their style was nursed by the closest attention to colloquial speech. . . .

THE DRAMATIST'S PARADOX

INTERVIEWER: Well now, inasmuch as you have gone from story-telling to playwriting, would you say the same tendencies which produced the novelist produced the dramatist?

WILDER: I think so, but in stating them I find myself involved in a paradox. A dramatist is one who believes that the pure event, an action involving human beings, is more arresting than any comment that can be made upon it. On the stage it is always *now;* the personages are standing on that razor-edge, between the past and the future, which is the essential character of conscious being; the words are rising to their lips in immediate spontaneity. A novel is what *took place;* no self-effacement on the part of the narrator can hide the fact that we hear his voice recounting, recalling events that are past and over, and which he has selected— from uncountable others—to lay before us from his presiding intelligence. Even the most objective novels are cradled in the authors' emotions and the authors' assumptions about life and mind and the passions. Now the paradox lies not so much in the fact that you and I know that the dramatist equally has selected what he exhibits and what the characters will say—such an operation is inherent in any work of art—but that all the greatest dramatists, except the very greatest *one*, have precisely employed the stage to convey a moral or religious point of view concerning the action. The theater is supremely fitted to say: "Behold! These things are." Yet most dramatists employ it to say: "This moral truth can be learned from beholding this action."

The Greek tragic poets wrote for edification, admonition, and even for our political education. The comic tradition in the theater carries the intention of exposing folly and curbing excess. Only in Shakespeare are we free of hearing axes ground.

INTERVIEWER: How do you get around this difficulty?

WILDER: By what may be an impertinence on my part. By believing that the moralizing intention resided in the authors as a convention of their times—usually, a social convention so deeply buried in the author's mode of thinking that it seemed to him to be inseparable from creation. I reverse a popular judgment: we say that [George Bernard] Shaw wrote diverting plays to sugar-coat the pill of a social message. Of these other dramatists, I say they injected a didactic intention in order to justify to themselves and to their audiences the exhibition of pure experience.

INTERVIEWER: Is your implication, then, that drama should be art for art's sake?

WILDER: Experience for experience's sake—rather than

for moral improvement's sake. When we say that [Dutch painter Jan] Vermeer's *Girl Making Lace* is a work of art for art's sake, we are not saying anything contemptuous about it. I regard the theater as the greatest of all art forms, the most immediate way in which a human being can share with another the sense of what it is to be a human being. This supremacy of the theater derives from the fact that it is always "now" on the stage. It is enough that generations have been riveted by the sight of Clytemnestra luring Agamemnon to the fatal bath, and Oedipus searching out the truth which will ruin him; those circumambient tags about "Don't get prideful" and "Don't call anybody happy until he's dead" are incidental concomitants.

INTERVIEWER: Is it your contention that there is no place in the theater for didactic intentions?

WILDER: The theater is so vast and fascinating a realm that there is room in it for preachers and moralists and pamphleteers. As to the highest function of the theater, I rest my case with Shakespeare—*Twelfth Night* as well as *Macbeth.*

INTERVIEWER: If you will forgive me, I'm afraid I've lost track of something we were talking about a while back—we were talking about the tendencies in your childhood which went into the formation of a dramatist.

WILDER: The point I've been leading up to is that a dramatist is one who from his earliest years has found that sheer gazing at the shocks and countershocks among people is quite sufficiently engrossing without having to encase it in comment. It's a form of tact. It's a lack of presumption. That's why so many earnest people have been so exasperated by Shakespeare: they cannot isolate the passages wherein we hear him speaking in his own voice. Somewhere Shaw says that one page of Bunyan,[1] "who plants his standard on the forefront of—I-forget-what—is worth a hundred by such shifting opalescent men."

DRAMA'S SOCIAL FUNCTIONS

INTERVIEWER: Are we to infer from what you say that the drama ought to have no social function?

WILDER: Oh, yes—there are at least two. First, the presentation of *what is,* under the direction of those great hands, is important enough. We live in *what is,* but we find a thousand

---

1. seventeenth-century English preacher John Bunyan, author of *The Pilgrim's Progress*

ways not to face it. Great theater strengthens our faculty to face it.

Secondly, to be present at any work of man-made order and harmony and intellectual power—Vermeer's *Lace Maker* or a Haydn quartet or *Twelfth Night*—is to be confirmed and strengthened in our potentialities as man.

INTERVIEWER: I wonder if you don't hammer your point pretty hard because actually you have a considerable element of the didactic in you.

WILDER: Yes, of course. I've spent a large part of my life trying to sit on it, to keep it down. The pages and pages I've had to tear up! I think the struggle with it may have brought a certain kind of objectivity into my work. I've become accustomed to readers' taking widely different views of the intentions in my books and plays. A good example is George Brush, whom we were talking about before. George, the hero of a novel of mine which I wrote when I was nearly forty, is an earnest, humorless, moralizing, preachifying, interfering product of Bible-belt evangelism. I received many letters from writers of the George Brush mentality angrily denouncing me for making fun of sacred things, and a letter from the Mother Superior of a convent in Ohio saying that she regarded the book as an allegory of the stages in the spiritual life.

Many thank me for the "comfort" they found in the last act of *Our Town;* others tell me that it is a desolating picture of our limitation to "realize" life—almost too sad to endure.

Many assured me that *The Bridge of San Luis Rey* was a satisfying demonstration that all the accidents of life were overseen and harmonized in providence; and a society of atheists in New York wrote me that it was the most artful exposure of shallow optimisms since *Candide*[2] and asked me to address them.

A very intelligent woman to whom I offered the dedication of *The Skin of Our Teeth* refused it, saying that the play was so defeatist. ("Man goes stumbling, bumbling down the ages.") *The Happy Journey to Trenton and Camden* received its first performance, an admirable one, at the University of Chicago. Edna St. Vincent Millay happened to be in the audience. At the close of the play she congratulated me at having so well pictured that "detestable bossy kind of mother."

2. tale of the adventures of a determinedly optimistic young man by eighteenth-century French philosopher Voltaire

Most writers firmly guide their readers to "what they should think" about the characters and events. If an author refrains from intruding his point of view, readers will be nettled, but will project into the text their own assumptions and turns of mind. If the work has vitality, it will, however slightly, alter those assumptions.

INTERVIEWER: So that you have *not* eliminated all didactic intentions from your work after all?

WILDER: I suspect that all writers have some didactic intention. That starts the motor. Or let us say: many of the things we eat are cooked over a gas stove, but there is no taste of gas in the food. . . .

ONLY ONE OR TWO IDEAS

INTERVIEWER: Someone has said—one of your dramatist colleagues, I believe, I can't remember which one—that a writer deals with only one or two ideas throughout his work. Would you say your work reflects those one or two ideas?

WILDER: Yes, I think so. I have become aware of it myself only recently. Those ideas seem to have prompted my work before I realized it. Now, at my age, I am amused by the circumstance that what is now conscious with me was for a long time latent. One of those ideas is this: an unresting preoccupation with the surprise of the gulf between each tiny occasion of the daily life and the vast stretches of time and place in which every individual plays his role. By that I mean the absurdity of any single person's claim to the importance of his saying, "I love!" "I suffer!" when one thinks of the background of the billions who have lived and died, who are living and dying, and presumably will live and die.

This was particularly developed in me by the almost accidental chance that, having graduated from Yale in 1920, I was sent abroad to study archaeology at the American Academy in Rome. We even took field trips in those days and in a small way took part in diggings. Once you have swung a pickax that will reveal the curve of a street four thousand years covered over which was once an active, much-traveled highway, you are never quite the same again. You look at Times Square [in New York City] as a place about which you imagine some day scholars saying, "There appears to have been some kind of public center here."

This preoccupation came out in my work before I realized it. Even *Our Town*, which I now see is filled with it, was not so consciously directed by me at the time. At first glance, the play appears to be practically a genre study of a village in New Hampshire. On second glance, it appears to be a meditation about the difficulty of, as the play says, "realizing life while you live it." But buried back in the text, from the very commencement of the play, is a constant repetition of the words "hundreds," "thousands," "millions." It's as though the audience—no one has ever mentioned this to me, though—is looking at that town at ever greater distances through a telescope.

I'd like to cite some examples of this. Soon after the play begins, the Stage Manager calls upon the professor from the geology department of the state university, who says how many million years old the ground is they're on. And the Stage Manager talks about putting some objects and reading matter into the cornerstone of a new bank and covering it with a preservative so that it can be read a thousand years from now. Or as minister presiding at the wedding, the Stage Manager muses to himself about all the marriages that have ever taken place—"millions of 'em, millions of 'em . . . Who set out to live two by two . . ." Finally, among the seated dead, one of the dead says, "My son was a sailor and used to sit on the porch. And he says the light from that star took millions of years to arrive." There is still more of this. So that when finally the heartbreak of Emily's unsuccessful return to life again occurs, it is against the background of the almost frightening range of these things.

Then *The Skin of Our Teeth*, which takes five thousand years to go by, is really a way of trying to make sense out of the *multiplicity* of the human race and its affections.

So that I see myself making an effort to find the dignity in the trivial of our daily life, against those preposterous stretches which seem to rob it of any such dignity; and the validity of each individual's emotion.

INTERVIEWER: I feel that there is another important theme running through your work which has to do with the nature of love. For example, there are a number of aphorisms in *The Bridge of San Luis Rey* which are often quoted and which relate to that theme. Do your views on the nature of love change in your later works?

WILDER: My ideas have not greatly changed; but those aphorisms in *The Bridge* represent only one side of them and are limited by their application to what is passing in that novel. In *The Ides of March*, my ideas are more illustrated than stated.

Love started out as a concomitant of reproduction; it is what makes new life and then shelters it. It is therefore an affirmation about existence and a belief in value. Tens of thousands of years have gone by; more complicated forms of society and of consciousness have arisen. Love acquired a wide variety of secondary expressions. It got mixed up with a power conflict between male and female; it got cut off from its primary intention and took its place among the refinements of psychic life, and in the cult of pleasure; it expanded beyond the relations of the couple and the family and reappeared as philanthropy; it attached itself to man's ideas about the order of the universe and was attributed to the gods and God.

I always see beneath it, nevertheless, the urge that strives toward justifying life, harmonizing it—the source of energy on which life must draw in order to better itself. In *The Ides of March* I illustrate its educative power (Caesar toward Cleopatra and toward his wife; the actress toward Marc Antony) and its power to "crystallize" idealization in the lover (Catullus's infatuation for the destructive "drowning" Clodia—he divines in her the great qualities she once possessed). This attitude has so much the character of self-evidence for me that I am unable to weigh or even "hear" any objections to it. I don't know whether I am uttering an accepted platitude or a bit of naïve nonsense.

A Brother's Perspective

Amos Niven Wilder

"Though Thornton and I were not twins, I have always felt that there was some sort of occult affinity in my makeup for his fabulation, like the telepathic understanding between Manuel and Esteban in *The Bridge of San Luis Rey*," wrote Amos Wilder. In the following excerpt from his book *Thornton Wilder and His Public*, Amos—Thornton's elder brother by eighteen months—derides the critics who believe Thornton's work must be unimportant because it is popular. Although his brother's work is both accessible and appealing, he says, it has been distilled by a keen and discerning mind from an immense repertoire of material ranging from international literature (in many languages) and intellectual discussions and correspondence with brilliant thinkers to Wilder's own humanist convictions.

There is a greater analogy between the instinctive life of the wider public and the talent of a great writer . . . than in the superficial verbiage and the changing criteria of the official judges.[1]

—Marcel Proust

For some time the critics by and large have not been able to fit the novels and plays of Thornton Wilder into their picture of modern writing and its agenda. They evidently have some qualms about this, since his work was so innovative and versatile and has had so profound a resonance in a wide public both at home and abroad. Yet there is a certain traditionalism in his outlook which undermines the modern premise. In his best-known plays and in much of his fiction he appears to speak for a grass-roots American experience which they may look on as banal, insipid, or moralistic. But what if his "notation of the heart" is, indeed, that of Mr. and

1. *A la recherche du temps perdu* (Pléiade edn., vol. III). Paris, 1957. pp. 893–894.

Mrs. Antrobus, that is, Everyman? And what if his inquisi-
tion goes beneath the sentiment of Grover's Corners or the
Philistinism of Coaltown, Illinois, to some deeper human
marrow?

It is a question of the anonymous millions in our streets
and countryside, and of finding a register and a language for
their potential. In 1957 Wilder spoke on "Culture in a
Democracy" to a German audience in Frankfurt at the
award of the Peace Prize of the German publishers.[2] He took
as his text a shocking passage from Walt Whitman: Is there
one of the great classics of the ancients or of Europe "that is
consistent with these United States . . . or whose underlying
basis is not a denial and insult to democracy?" He went on
to speak of the dangers but also of the "unknown factors"
and the "promise" of an enfranchised society of equals of the
kind which Whitman had envisaged. This kind of passionate
empathy for Grover's Corners or Main Street—both magnanimous and austere—is too often missing in our modern
classics and our critics of culture. The response to change
and its advocacy takes precedence over the deeper human
continuities.

CRITICAL SUSPICION OF POPULAR SUCCESS

Critics and critical schools in this country have understandably been suspicious of writers who have had large popular
success. They have been baffled by any conjunction of true
excellence with midbrow or lowbrow appeal as registered in
the categories of "best-seller" or "book-club" selection. In
the case of Wilder there has been a long history of embarrassment if not attack, and even of assignment to limbo. One
can recall disparagement of the first three novels as effete or
precious; [literary critic Richard] Blackmur's dissatisfaction
with *Heaven's My Destination* as aimed at the book clubs; the
critics' "snubbing" of *The Ides of March;* more recently, dismissal by Stanley Kauffmann and others of *The Eighth Day*
as a sermon or an exercise in old clichés.

As for the plays, while they are continually being staged at
the grass-roots level throughout the country, any more
ambitious revival is likely to meet the critical incomprehension which recently greeted *The Skin of Our Teeth* in its
Bicentennial presentation in New York.

2. *Kultur in einer Demokratie.* Frankfurt, 1957.

For awareness of this dilemma one can cite a review in the London *Times Literary Supplement* of Wilder's last novel, *Theophilus North.*

> In a literary career spanning half a century, Thornton Wilder has successfully resisted any kind of classification as novelist or playwright. We cannot pin him down, as we can Hemingway or Scott Fitzgerald, to background or subject matter (though both his first and his latest books are almost entirely autobiographical), and it is impossible to group him conveniently with any coterie of writers, whether prewar or postwar. Popularity and success—implicit in the huge sales (10,000 copies a week) of *The Bridge of San Luis Rey*—may have dented his reputation a little among those for whom starving in a garret is the sole criterion of artistic excellence. How, on the other hand, are we to account for the fact that in several European countries Mr. Wilder, along with Shakespeare and Joyce, is one of a mere handful of English-speaking writers known to the reading public?[3]

Yet many accomplished critics by now have their minds made up. Wilder, they agree, is indeed somewhat anomalous and hard to pigeonhole, but he falls outside the main line of advance of the novel or the drama. His work has been on the margin of those explorations and engagements so essential to our twentieth-century experience. Worst of all, he smacks of Middle America and even a disguised religiosity. Thus all across the board—subject matter, outlook, style—he does not fit the common premise or lend himself to the central debate.

In seeking to identify the reservations of the critics we can at least set aside some of the earlier imputations. Literary judges have long disallowed partisan Marxist charges made against him in the thirties, even if changing categories of social realism and relevance may still be invoked. *Our Town* is no longer banned in the USSR despite its alleged complaisance with the bourgeois family. *The Skin of Our Teeth* is similarly permitted there, though formerly excluded on the ground that wars and other calamities are not attributed in it to capitalist exploitation.

Critics have also now long dropped the charge of plagiarism against one of James Joyce's most revering excavators and glossators. Wilder happily conceded that, like some irreproachable predecessors, if he was a shoplifter he always preyed upon the best emporia. As Emerson remarks in his

3. July 12, 1974.

essay on Shakespeare, "Thought is the property of him who can entertain it and of him who can adequately place it."

THE BASIC PREMISE OF MODERN LETTERS

The reservations of the critics today have other grounds. Their disparagement, neglect, or bracketing of Wilder's work is not necessarily to be put down to the insensitivity of reviewers or to critical fashion and partisanship. The situation is much more interesting than that. As I have suggested, it comes down to the basic premise with regard to modern letters. One must beg the original question. Where, indeed, does the main engagement lie in our modern situation? Granted that "modernism" has had a great and necessary task of liberation to carry out in our epoch, what may have been left out in its view of that task and its engagement with our contemporary reality? . . .

The modern focus has understandably been one of revolt and emancipation, and Thornton Wilder has not been a stranger to it. But there should always be those who speak for the deeper ground which continues through change. Perhaps artists of this kind fall through the net of the existing tribunals. While the instinctive response of the wider public recognizes them, the official judges are at a loss.

When one moves the question to the American scene the issues become clearer. How do we define the "modern" here, and what is the relation of its proper iconoclasm to our older American heritage? It is a question of locating the deeper potential and the hidden springs of our many-layered society. One premise is that the clue and norm for us runs from the expatriates after World War I down through those writers who have extricated themselves not only from an earlier "genteel" tradition but from any rootage in what seem the blinkered pieties and conformisms of an older America.

It is true that many of our best writers have rightly been in revolt against Philistinism and inhumanity in our folkways. In aesthetic terms they have rightly sought a new language and new vehicles for a new sensibility. But, along with the critics, have they not also scanted the depths of our people and left a great deal of unfinished business? The fertility of the New World has always thrown up its own original and even plebeian celebrations, versions of its own native mythology. Here is one point at which Thornton Wilder comes in.

CRITICAL MYOPIA

Nothing is more revealing of critical myopia than assignment of Wilder to the category of "midcult." Granted that this is a step up from "masscult," it still connotes ingratiation of a Philistine public. But is the general public so obtuse and so negligible? This kind of classification makes things too easy for the critic. It is his task to distinguish between the wheat and the straw, and not only between the modern and the traditional. Just as there is a great deal of the new which is mainly imitative and of mediocre talent, so there is much of the seeming traditional which is highly creative in its own context and horizon. But the category of midcult sweeps both the saccharine and the profoundly disciplined into one common basket. One recalls how grudgingly many critics came to concede the merits of Robert Frost.

Even more shallow is the implied judgment on the wider public. There are in our population various kinds of literacy and illiteracy, various registers and acoustics for the arts and the imagination. No doubt there is much of the moronic, the sentimental, and the crass. These exhibit themselves also in many of our iconoclastic novelties. But the great continental public "out there," seemingly regressive and insensitive, is highly complex and unpredictable. No one dogma or program of the aesthetic should pretend to arbitrate for so rich and incalculable a gestation.

In any society, granted a wide mediocrity, if there is a valid pioneering elite of artists and intellectuals, there is also a diffused and unrecognized remnant which bears the heritage of the many and its costs and its promise. However scornful the elite may be of Main Street and suburbia, it should not cut itself off from the voices that witness through the shapeless and the inarticulate.

DISTILLING SIMPLICITY FROM A RICH BASE

In assigning Wilder to midcult, certain critics identify his work with cliché, banality, and indulgence. But this is to overlook certain highly rigorous aspects of his work. Such glossy or superficial writings as can properly be assigned to this category rest, for example, on no such extensive literacy as that of my brother, no such intimacy with the great models and their exacting demands. Whatever readability for a general public his books possess, this simplicity or wide appeal rests on an immense repertoire of aesthetic and intellectual tuition, which is, as it were, distilled in them. The ambiance of his thought, his mental climate or *habitus* was that of the masters, and there is no greater achievement of the "art of the difficult" than that of simplicity, if that is the word for it.

I can suggest the range of this American writer's acquaintance with the world of letters by offering a few examples. His familiarity with the Greek and Roman classics is evident in much of his writing. This goes back especially to the year he spent after his graduation from Yale at the American Academy in Rome. It was especially on classical epic and drama that he lectured during numerous summer terms at the University of Chicago. Classicists will appreciate the significance of the close friendship and animated conversation he carried on over a period with the great scholar Karl Reinhardt, discussions that bore not only on the Greek tragedians but also on such German poets as Hölderlin.

As for Romance languages his early stylistic "crush" on Mme. de Sévigné carried over, of course, to *The Bridge of San Luis Rey*, in which the letters of the Marquesa de Montemayor to her daughter echo the pattern. Thornton's M.A. degree at Princeton was in French under Professor Louis Cons, and his earliest teaching, at the Lawrenceville School, was in this department. Later, one of his longtime distractions, as a problem in literary detection, was the dating of the plays of the Spanish dramatist, Lope de Vega, a topic on which he wrote a paper for the Modern Language Association. He enjoyed his correspondence with the leading Spanish authority on this intricate topic, as he did his correspondence with Walter Lowrie about Kierkegaard, to whose work Lowrie had introduced him when they were both in Rome where the former was rector of the American church, St. Paul's.

Another picture-puzzle passion of Thornton's for years was his annotation of *Finnegans Wake*, the decoding of which inevitably required a large fund of linguistic and literary resource. In a quite different sector Thornton also followed with close attention the publication of the many volumes of the Yale Edition of *Horace Walpole's Correspondence*, edited by his friend and former schoolmate, Wilmarth Lewis. The latter has testified to the helpfulness of my brother's many letters about Walpole and the acuteness of his observations. They both had been introduced to the writers of this period by the great Chauncey Tinker at Yale.

I refer at a later point to Thornton's acquaintance with Goethe and other German writers and the opening this afforded him especially to circles of German students in his visits to that country. Other areas of literary initiation could be cited, not least the American classics on which he lectured at Harvard. Yet though he was in so many respects a polymath, in his own writing he availed himself of all such resources in his own sovereign way.

In categorizing his role as an American writer this broad literary culture should be kept in mind. It was this range of his literacy which explains the mutual cordiality and correspondence between him and Edmund Wilson. Both were "men of letters" in the European sense. With this kind of tuition Thornton's art, however accessible to a wide public, could never be popular in a disparaging sense. Nor should his academic associations be viewed as suspect since his humanism was as deep as it was wide.

PUTTING THE WORKS IN CONTEXT

Assessment of my brother's contribution in the long run will need to take account of more than his few novels and plays. Their resonance can be trivialized if seen out of context. In this case the author's life and work were interwoven, and one illuminates the other. There are writers best known for a few works who, nevertheless, constitute one kind of "presence" in their period, one kind of option or index or even synthesis in their times. Their writings can have a kind of divinatory impact related to the cultural scene, and this is related to their personal history and involvements. What Thornton Wilder represented in terms of cultural ripeness and mastery—as teacher, figure in world letters, correspondent, idea man and conversationalist—all this reflects itself in his formal writings, and vice versa. Just as in his plays, so in his quicksilver-like talk, whether at the Algonquin Hotel or in a PEN [International Association of Poets, Playwrights, Editors, Essayists, and Novelists] session abroad or a college common room or a bar, he brought worlds together and sparkled with searching insights.

Commentators have, indeed, been puzzled by the fact that he wrote so little and by those intervals in his career in which he did not seem to be productive. Even the wider public had heard of projects which he did not complete such as the Kafka-like play to be called *The Emporium* or the cycles of one-act plays devoted to the seven ages of man and to the seven deadly sins, both series evidencing his interest in modernizing the old "morality" genre typified by *Everyman.* It was suggested that he too easily allowed himself to be diverted by academic appointments or cultural missions, or even by war service.

It is true that he could joke about a proposed epitaph: "Here lies a man who tried to be obliging." Annals of his residence terms in Burton-Goodspeed Hall at the University of Chicago and in Harvard's Dunster House evoke the protracted meal times and midnight sorties with students, the fledgling manuscripts read, the many speaking appointments accepted, and the personal crises of youth for which he was so skillful and austere an analyst. There were wider calls he could not refuse: an unexpected additional course at Harvard; some Broadway production of a friend calling for a translation from the French, or requiring surgery; a plea from Alfred Hitchcock and Hollywood.

But this artist's role included all such gregariousness, involvement, pedagogy, and missions. His private fabulation carried over into all such public and oral occasions. His theater carried over into daily life. His formal works are related to this wider deportment as sage, mage, democrat, and soldier. He liked to act in his own plays. There was something of the histrionic in all he did. When he lectured he was all over the platform and down the aisles, gesturing, challenging, clowning, and taking the parts of the characters discussed. So it was also with his talk on more intimate occasions. His gusto and affections evoked scenarios "as good as a play."

LITERATURE IS A PART OF LIFE

With some authors, life is one thing and literature another. When this observation was made to Edmund Wilson he replied: "But isn't literature simply a part of life as much as conversation?" In the case of my brother, at least, this is highly pertinent. Like his conversation—understood either as his talk or in the old biblical sense of his deportment or way in the world—his novels and plays were gestures or overflow of his life. I cannot therefore deplore that he spent himself in so many other theaters at the expense of his writing.

In retrospect, what may well deserve attention in the cultural history of our period will be Wilder as a distinctive type and product of our American society. His formal works will only be part of the total image. No doubt other authors will be credited with greater achievement in their own kind. Other novelists and playwrights will be identified with crucial movements in the age. But at the level where American roots are linked with modern sophistication, and where American moralities are linked critically and imaginatively with old-world legacies, there have been fewer witnesses in our time. No doubt humanist scholars have sought to bridge these gaps. But what is more difficult, yet essential, is that these poles should be linked in art and poetry.

One test of this scope and role is afforded by international cultural encounters. On certain occasions when meetings were held abroad under such auspices as UNESCO [United Nations Educational, Scientific, and Cultural Organization] it was difficult to find American delegates who were not only scholars familiar with European literature past and present, but also and at the same time creative artists whose work was appreciated abroad. That Wilder could fill this double role and share in discussions in several languages meant a unique kind of American participation in Western culture. The same kind of total humanistic outreach was exhibited in the Goethe Festival at Aspen in 1949 when . . . my brother found himself called on to assist on the platform with the translation of the addresses of Albert Schweitzer on one day and of Ortega y Gasset on the next.

LARGE CHARITY AND UNCOMPROMISING SEVERITY

I have been illustrating my brother's extensive acquaintance with the world of letters as one answer to the charge of banality or indulgence in his writing. But rigor rather than indulgence appears also in the ethos of his work. If there is, indeed, a large charity in his portrayal of life and much gaiety, yet no one should miss the uncompromising severity that accompanies these. There was iron in his outlook, some combination perhaps of granite from Calvin and worldly wisdom from his cherished Goethe. We can recognize it not only in the austere Caesar of *The Ides of March* but also in the disabused acidity that runs through *The Skin of Our Teeth*. The unmasking of human motivation associated with modern thought was taken up by him into a more radical suspicion. But it did not leave him in the condition of so many who are tempted to cynicism, or who have nothing but pathos to fall back on with respect to their heroes or anti-heroes. This combination of generosity of spirit with austerity is far from sentimentality, but equally uncongenial to many moderns.

Even in the first year of his exposure to Europe and his ravishment by its high culture, when in Italy he was piecing together his most fastidious novel, *The Cabala* (at one time to be called *Romans*), he writes in a letter home: "A horror grows on me for the purely aesthetic; I am fierce for the strange, the strong, the remorseless; even the brutal and the coarse. The vivid and the significant; not the graceful.". . .

A MORE UNIVERSAL VISION

Thornton Wilder was no stranger to the anomie of our epoch. And just as he was intimate over long periods of immersion in the works of Kafka, Joyce, Proust, Broch, Stein, and other modern masters, so he was at home with the great pioneers and iconoclasts of modern thought and with the master texts and pamphlets of the time. Just as his earlier correspondence echoed his attention to Kierkegaard, Spengler, Lukács, and Valéry, so his later letters show him absorbed in the successive volumes of Lévi-Strauss. It should be clear from this review that he was no outsider to the cultural and aesthetic dislocations of our period or the great debates which have accompanied them. Whatever "Puritan" or "academic" or "classicist" liabilities may be charged against him and against his family background, these do not appear to have isolated him from the main currents of the age. Quite the converse, they may rather have endowed him with a deeper human orientation that could assimilate the new experience in a more universal vision.

CHAPTER 2

Major Themes in Thornton Wilder's Work

The Master of High Comedy

J.D. McClatchy

In this essay marking the one hundredth anniversary of the birth of Thornton Wilder, poet and critic J.D. McClatchy, editor of the *Yale Review*, deplores the "sophisticated" tendency to judge Wilder a sentimentalist and therefore no longer relevant. As a master of high comedy, rueful joy, and deep humanity, McClatchy maintains, Wilder should be ranked among such artists as Jane Austen and Ivan Turgenev.

A friend of mine, now a distinguished author and scholar, remembers that as a teen-ager in California she would wander in the stacks of the Berkeley Public Library. One day, with a random curiosity, she picked a novel off the shelf and turned to the opening paragraph. "The earth sighed as it turned in its course; the shadow of night crept gradually along the Mediterranean, and Asia was left in darkness. The great cliff that would one day be called Gibraltar held for a long time a gleam of red and orange . . . at the mouth of the Nile the water lay like a wet pavement." She was enthralled. She decided right there to become a writer, and hoped sometime, somehow to write sentences as ravishing as these. The novel was *The Woman of Andros,* by Thornton Wilder.

Others have had a similar experience with Wilder's books. Mine came later than my friend's, and therefore less dramatically, but the pleasure was as profound and as enduring. April 17, [1997,] marks the hundredth anniversary of Wilder's birth. The customary tributes are planned: a commemorative stamp is being issued, a Web site established, a Modern Library reader published. But the celebrations, I suspect, will be scattered and modest. Wilder's star, so bright on either side of World War II, has dimmed. For many readers nowadays, his name carries the faint whiff of the sachet, and his best work will seem sentimental and sententious to those who prefer their books braced with raw passions or caustic ironies.

THE WAY WE REMEMBER THE PAST

His best-known work remains *Our Town,* which was first performed in 1938 and has ever since been by far the most often produced American play. When Raymond Massey took it on tour to American G.I.'s in Europe in 1945, soon after the fighting had stopped, he reported that tears streamed down the faces of hardened soldiers. (They still stream down mine.) What undoubtedly touched those soldiers is the play's plangent nostalgia, the ache for home, for home's rootedness and security. But Wilder's portrait of the citizens of Grover's Corners, their lives and deaths, is not about the past so much as it is about the way we remember the past, what is illuminated and obscured by memory, gained and lost, the pathos of innocence, the sublimity of the ordinary, the acceptance of the dark ineluctable. And it is about what Wilder called "the eternal part" of us all. The religious reader will sense something more in that phrase. But Wilder himself would have called it the mind—an impulse, a characteristic, a power that sets us apart and onward.

To speak in such terms nowadays risks the sophisticate's smirk. Wilder stitched on homespun, and the result sometimes resembled the motto on a sampler. The instinct to generalize shouldn't be confused with softness. Wilder was no sentimentalist—a type, in his own definition, "whose desire that things be happy exceeds his desire and suppressed knowledge that things be truthful; he demands that he be lied to. He secretly knows that it is a lie; hence his emptiness, his elations and his heartlessness." Like [Oscar] Wilde or [Anton] Chekhov or [George Bernard] Shaw, he was essentially a moralist. Each of these playwrights could dramatize ideas and conduct, could make us think about our feelings. They sought, in their different ways, to clarify life by portraying its contradictions. Wilder took the given and raised it to the higher power of reflection. And he did it the hard way: by telling the truth.

A COMPLEX MAN

Wilder was a complex man. There are the plays and the novels, for which he was awarded three Pulitzer Prizes. But

there is a great deal more. He had a profound respect for tradition and thought that literature "more resembled a torch
race than a furious dispute among heirs." He was an erudite
scholar of James Joyce and Lope de Vega, and lectured at
both Harvard and the University of Chicago. He served in
both world wars. He played the piano well enough to tackle
the Beethoven sonatas, and wrote an opera libretto. He
wrote screenplays for George Cukor, Alfred Hitchcock and
Vittorio De Sica. He translated *A Doll's House* and *Waiting for
Godot*. His published journals shimmer. He had a dizzying-
ly wide circle of friendships and counted among his
acquaintances Gertrude Stein, Montgomery Clift, Coco
Chanel, Sigmund Freud, Henry Luce, Alexander Woollcott,
Laurence Olivier, Dorothy Parker, Jean-Paul Sartre, Tallulah
Bankhead, Gene Tunney, Max Beerbohm, Felix Frankfurter,
Ernest Hemingway and Sibyl Colefax.

He looked, Tyrone Guthrie said, like a piano tuner, owned
only one suit at a time and spoke in a fidgety, accelerating,
inexhaustible manner. He left all his domestic and business
affairs for a devoted sister (his de facto "wife") to handle. He
drank and smoked too much, was gregarious and self-
effacing. He loathed self-pity. His compassion was clear-
eyed and his generosities practical. He was endlessly obliging. Sylvia Beach said tartly that he reminded her of a man
taking everyone in the world on a Sunday school picnic and
trying to get them all on the bus at the same time. He especially liked helping old friends and talented beginners. He
encouraged, for instance, a young actor named Orson
Welles; and when the young Edward Albee was a fellow
guest at Yaddo and busy writing poems, he remembers
Wilder suggesting to him, "Why don't you try writing plays?"
He was never without a new enthusiasm; even into his 70's,
he was boning up on advances in microbiology, studying
Greek vase painting or the theories of Claude Levi-Strauss.

Wilder seems to have been a repressed homosexual, baffled by his own desires and ashamed of his furtive attempts
to act on them, and yet he made family life the arena of his
imagination and wrote about it with a rare and compassion-
ate understanding. Perhaps for this reason too, he cultivated
the company of older, intelligent women as confidantes,
hostesses, muses. He was a compulsive traveler and social-
izer, simultaneously to savor and to protect against a deep
loneliness. His identical twin had died at birth, and there

was a side to Wilder that was always restlessly searching to allay an unsatisfiable need. He had no "sturdy last resource against the occasional conviction 'I don't belong.'"

Myself, I prefer his novels to his plays. They haven't the accumulated glamour of those by [F. Scott] Fitzgerald and [Ernest] Hemingway and [William] Faulkner already in the pantheon. But the best of them remain remarkable accomplishments and deserve a wider audience. His first, *The Cabala* (1926), involves an Innocent Abroad, and is filled with worldly shrewdness and lapidary wit. It was an astonishing feat for a 29-year-old tyro, and won him instant acclaim. A year later he published *The Bridge of San Luis Rey.* With *The Woman of Andros* (1930) and *The Ides of March* (1948), Wilder upended the heavy social realism that dominated books of the day, and gave the exotic historical novel a genuine philosophical poise. But his two best novels have American settings. *Heaven's My Destination* (1935) is a picaresque comedy about the adventures of an itinerant textbook salesman, the earnest, self-righteous, Bible-thumping George Brush. *The Eighth Day* (1967) is a remarkable hybrid, part murder mystery, part family saga. Its hero, a mining engineer named John Ashley, is another of Wilder's unsettling anatomies of the fabled American innocence. Americans, he once said, are people who have outgrown their fathers. Like [Walt] Whitman's, Wilder's Americans are solitary, energetic, inventive, restless but disciplined, responsible but detached. They are one with the cold moonlight that falls equally on corpse and cradle, apple and ocean.

FINDING THE WONDROUS STRANGE IN THE ORDINARY

"I am not interested," he told an interviewer, "in the ephemeral—such subjects as the adulteries of dentists. I am interested in those things that repeat and repeat and repeat in the lives of the millions." He meant, of course, the mysteries and marvels of the heart. Wilder once described Tolstoy as "a great eye, above the roof, above the town, above the planet, from which nothing was hid." Wilder too looked on our life, steadily, never blinking at its pain and incongruities. But he was not a tortured artist or an embittered one. Instead, he was a master of high comedy. Into sorrows and convictions he mixed humor. In the ordinary he found what is wondrous strange. The tone of high comedy, he confided to his journal, is "lyrical, diaphanous and tender." If one added to those qualities a rueful joy and a deep humanity, then Wilder could be said to belong to a special group of artists—Jane Austen, Ivan Turgenev, Jean Renoir and Elizabeth Bishop are among them—whose work refreshes our intelligence. The older I get, and the more often I reread Wilder's novels, the brighter they seem, more subtle and courageous, filled with new surprises and earned wisdom.

Wilder's Tragic Themes

Robert W. Corrigan

Robert W. Corrigan has edited many anthologies on the theater, including *The Art of the Theatre* and *The Making of Theatre: From Drama to Performance;* his own essays on theater are gathered in his anthology *The Theatre in Search of a Fix.* Corrigan finds Wilder the most difficult of modern American dramatists to define. While all of Wilder's plays affirm life and cele- brate love, Corrigan believes his view of life is essential- ly tragic. Since he presents tragedy in an everyday con- text, which is often not dramatic, many critics have failed to comprehend his true beliefs. Yet, Corrigan acknowledges, Wilder manages to avoid despair with an "animal faith" that is stronger than logical argument.

Of all modern American dramatists, none is more difficult to pin down than Thornton Wilder. He is thought of, together with [Eugene] O'Neill, [Arthur] Miller, and [Tennessee] Williams, as one of our "Big Four," and yet his reputation is based on only three full-length plays and was made on one. And whereas reams of criticism have been written on the other three playwrights, only an occasional article on Wilder is published. This is all the more surprising since no one seems to agree about his work. For some he is the great American satirist; for others he is a soft-hearted sentimen- talist; and for still others he is our only "religious" dramatist. Furthermore, no American playwright is more respected by contemporary European dramatists than is Wilder; Brecht, Ionesco, Duerrenmatt, and Frisch have all acknowledged their debt to this "great and fanatical experimenter." Therefore, it is about time that we reevaluate his work.

DEISTIC PLATONISM, NOT CHRISTIANITY

From his earliest volumes of one-acts, *The Angel that Troubled the Waters* and *The Long Christmas Dinner*, to his

From "Thornton Wilder and the Tragic Sense of Life," by Robert W. Corrigan, *Educational Theatre Journal*, vol. 13, no. 3 (1961). Copyright © 1961 by the American Theatre Association, Inc. Reprinted by permission of the Johns Hopkins University Press.

last full-length play, *The Matchmaker,* Wilder has dealt bold-
ly and affirmatively with the themes of Life, Love, and Earth.
Each of his plays is a hymn in dramatic form affirming life.
But the important question is: What is the nature of this
affirmation? It is not, as some would have it, Christian. To
begin with, Wilder has no belief—at least as expressed in his
plays—in a religion that is revealed or historical. These are
basic premises of Christianity. To be sure Wilder is deistic,
but as almost all of his critics have pointed out, he is essentially a religious Platonist; and this position must ultimately
reject the historic dimension as meaningful. Francis
Fergusson ties these two ideas together when he writes:

> The plays are perfectly in accord with the Platonic kind of
> philosophy which they are designed to teach. The great Ideas
> are timeless, above the history of the race and the history of
> actual individuals. Any bit of individual or racial history will
> do, therefore, to "illustrate" them; but history and individual
> lives lack all real being; they are only shadows on the cave
> wall.

Mary McCarthy approaches this another way when she
writes of *The Skin of Our Teeth:*

> In other words, if George misses the five-fifteen, Chaos is
> come again. This is the moral of the piece. Man, says Mr.
> Wilder, from time to time gets puffed up with pride and pros-
> perity, he grows envious, covetous, lecherous, forgets his
> conjugal duties, goes whoring after women; portents of dis-
> aster appear, but he is too blind to see them; in the end, with
> the help of the little woman, who has never taken any stock
> in either pleasure or wisdom, he escapes by the skin of his
> teeth. *Sicut erat in principio* [as it was in the beginning]. . . .
>
> It is a curious view of life. It displays elements of Christian
> morality. Christ, however, was never so simple, but on the
> contrary allowed always for paradox (the woman taken in
> adultery, the story of Martha and Mary, "Consider the lilies of
> the field"). . . . No, it is not the Christian view, but a kind of
> bowdlerized version of it, such as might have been imparted
> to a class of taxpayer's children by a New England Sunday
> School teacher forty years ago.

Now, I happen to believe that both Fergusson and Miss
McCarthy (even in their admiration for Wilder) overstate
their arguments, because Wilder, except in his preface to
The Angel that Troubled the Waters, has never thought of
himself as a Christian or a religious playwright. He best
states his position when he writes: "*Our Town* is not offered
as a picture of life in a New Hampshire village; or specula-

tion about the conditions of life after death. . . . It is an attempt to find a value above all price for the smallest events of daily life." Wilder is talking about *Our Town*, but what he says applies to all of his work. In short, Wilder is a humanist, an affirming humanist, a "yeasayer to life" as Barnard Hewitt calls him.

LOVE AND DEATH

When we examine the nature of Wilder's humanistic affirmations, what do we discover? His plays celebrate human love, the worth and dignity of man, the values of the ordinary, and the eternity of human values. From the little boy in Wilder's first play who says: "I am not afraid of life. I will astonish it!" to Dolly Levi and her cohorts in adventure in *The Matchmaker,* Wilder has always been on the side of life and life is seen to be most directly affirmed through love. Love, then, is his most persistent theme and it has been for him an inexhaustible subject. Of its worth he is convinced, but it is interesting to note that Wilder has never been able to make any commitments as to the reasons for its worth. Wilder can deal with life and love directly and concretely; but when he moves to the edges of life, the focus becomes less sharp. Certainly, Wilder deals with death—he is not afraid of it, but death in his plays is terminal. When Mrs. Soames says in Act Three of *Our Town:* "My, wasn't life awful—and wonderful," Wilder is reminding us that beauty is recognizable because of change and life is meaningful because of death. But as both John Mason Brown and Winfield Townley Scott have pointed out, Wilder never deals adequately with Death's own meaning. And as for what's beyond death? The Stage Manager in *Our Town* tells us:

> You know as well as I do that the dead don't stay interested in us living people for very long. Gradually, gradually, they let go of the earth. . . . They get weaned away from the earth— that's the way I put it—weaned away. Yes, they stay here while the earth-part of 'em burns away, burns out, and all that time they slowly get indifferent to what's going on in Grover's Corners. They're waitin'! They're waitin' for something that they feel is comin'. Something important and great. Aren't they waitin' for the eternal part in them to come out clear?

But what is this eternal part, this Platonic essence, which in our imperfect awareness of living is only a shadow on the wall of the cave? What is death's meaning? The Stage Manager has just told us:

> Everybody knows that *something* is eternal. And it ain't names, and it ain't earth, and it ain't even the stars . . . everybody knows in their bones that *something* is eternal, and that something has to do with human beings. All the greatest people ever lived have been telling us that for five thousand years and yet you'd be surprised how people are always losing hold of it. There's something way down deep that's eternal about every human being.

So, we are right back where we started: Life is reality and eternity is the perfected essence of that reality to which we are too often blind and of which we can't stand too much.

A TRAGIC VIEW OF LIFE

It is this tendency, a tendency consistent with his Platonism, to reduce the dimension of eternity so that it can be encompassed by life itself, that has led me to believe, although he has written no tragedies, that Wilder has essentially a tragic rather than a Christian or even religious view of life. To be sure, Wilder has not created any Ahabs or Lears, but this is not because he lacks a tragic vision. He happens to believe, as did Maeterlinck, that there are times in each of our lives when we are conscious of moving into the boundary situations of the tragic realm, and that furthermore, life's tragedies can best be seen in the drama of the everyday, in life's smallest events. For this reason he does not dramatize great conflicts in order to capture the quintessence of tragedy. I think it is important to see the validity of this, although we must point out that while this approach is tragic it is not always dramatic. And this, I think, accounts for the fact that Wilder's plays are usually referred to as "hymns," "odes," "songs," and so on, and most critics feel that there isn't much conflict in their plots. It might be helpful to take a specific example to illustrate Wilder's position on this matter.

Over and over again in Wilder's work, the belief is stated directly and indirectly that "life is what you make of it." The fullest discussion of the idea is in his novel *The Ides of March*, where Caesar says: "Life has no meaning save that which we confer upon it." Later he says:

> Am I sure that there is no mind behind our existence and no mystery anywhere in the universe? I think I am. . . . How terrifying and glorious the role of man if, indeed, without guidance and without consolation he must create from his own vitals the meaning for his existence and the rules whereby he lives.

Many of us believe this idea when stated in its simpler form: "Life is what we make of it." But we are unaware that this is really an existential position and that Wilder is very close to Sartre's "Man is condemned to be free."

AVERTING DESPAIR THROUGH ANIMAL FAITH

In fact, upon reflection, we discover that in starting from "Life is what we make of it," Wilder is really in the mainstream of the modern drama beginning with Ibsen and Strindberg. And this is a dangerous position and usually in the drama has led to despair. The image of man in this drama is an image of collapse. Certainly, Kierkegaard saw this in [this] passage from *Fear and Trembling:*

> If there were no eternal consciousness in a man, if at the foundation of all there lay only a wildly seething power which writhing with obscure passions produced everything that is great and everything that is insignificant, if a bottomless void never satiated lay hidden beneath all—what then would life be but despair.

Most modern dramatists have answered with "that's all!" But Wilder hasn't, even though he holds a position that should lead this way. I think he averts despair—and also tragedy, even though his view of life is essentially tragic—with a kind of Santayana-like belief in life. In fact, Wilder's Platonism can make sense only if it is seen as coming through Santayana.[1] Wilder is, as probably most of us are, saved from despair and its paralyzing effects by what Santayana has called "animal faith." Many will admit that by the rules of logic life is little more than an irrational nightmare in which the only reality is that grotesque illusion which we happen to believe in at a given moment; but somehow our animal faith, which bids us believe in the external world, is much stronger than all the logical arguments which tend to make life seem absurd. As Joseph Wood Krutch put it: "Everybody acts as though he believed that the external world exists; nearly everybody acts as though he believed that his version of it is a dependable one; and the majority act as though they could also make valid value judgments about it." It is this belief, this animal faith, that permits Wilder to say "Life is what you make of it," and still come up in affirmation on this side of despair. All his plays might be described by that

---

1. George Santayana (1863–1952), poet and philosopher born in Madrid, Spain; wrote several volumes of verse, and philosophical works including *Scepticism and Animal Faith* (1923).

verse of Theodore Spencer's (and I think Wilder and Spencer have great affinities):

> Oh how to praise that No,
> When all longing would press
> After the lost Yes!
> Oh how redress
> That disaster of No?

But although Wilder can assert meaning to life, the meaning is almost in the assertion itself and this is not a very comfortable position to be in. One gets the feeling that Wilder has to keep saying it to make sure that it is true. The danger of this position is that it lacks the necessary polarity and tension for full meaning. This in itself keeps Wilder from being a religious dramatist. In all great religious drama—the works of Sophocles, Calderón, *Everyman,* and in more recent times the later plays of Hofmannsthal, Eliot, and even Fry—there is the backdrop of religious belief which gives meaning to and informs the hero's "life is what you make of it." There is the greater stage. The medieval theatre and the Spanish theatre of Calderón exhibit this, and this is what Hofmannsthal tried to achieve at the Salzburg festivals with his productions of *Everyman, The Great World Theatre,* and *The Tower.* In all of these plays the actors—man—are faced with a moral choice under the very eyes of God and his angels upstage. The scaffold of these multiple stage structures not only serves as a magic mirror for the visible world and its invisible order, but the invisible order is made visible. For in these plays the idea of man as a player on the world's stage becomes the very principle of the *mise-en-scène* [stage setting]. For God, the master, speaking from the top of the scaffold, actually orders the world to produce a play under his eyes, featuring man who is to act out his part on earth.

REDUCING THE SENSE OF DRAMATIC PLACE AND TIME

More important than the absence of a religious dimension to Wilder's work, however, are the many experiments he has made in theatrical technique to compensate for this lack of an ultimate perspective. It is a commonplace in talking about modern literature to comment on the loss of a community of values and the disappearance of public truths in our time. It is equally well known that writers tend to compensate for the lack of a community of belief with new tech-

FOUR FUNDAMENTAL CONDITIONS OF DRAMA

In "Some Thoughts on Playwrighting," Wilder explained some of his views on the theater. His elaborations on these points bring in references to painters, dancers, and novelists as well as dramatists.

Four fundamental conditions of the drama separate it from the other arts. Each of these conditions has its advantages and disadvantages, each requires a particular aptitude from the dramatist, and from each there are a number of instructive consequences to be derived. These conditions are:

1. The theater is an art which reposes upon the work of many collaborators;
2. It is addressed to the group-mind;
3. It is based upon a pretense and its very nature calls out a multiplication of pretenses;
4. Its action takes place in a perpetual present time.

Thornton Wilder, "Some Thoughts on Playwrighting," in Augusto Centeno, ed., *The Intent of the Artist.* New York: Russell & Russell, 1970.

niques of expression. The problem for the dramatist is how to make a highly individual standard of values appear to the audience to be a natural objective standard. Most of the modern dramatists have attempted to meet this problem by focusing on the psychology of their characters. In so doing they leave begged the question of value by confining the world of the play to the limits of an individual character's mind and then assessing value solely in terms of the consciousness of that mind. Thus, an incident in *Hedda Gabler* may not be important by any communicable standard of human significance, but if the universe is confined to her mind and Ibsen makes us look deeply enough into it, we can at least see it as important in that tiny context. In this way psychology makes possible such a drastic limitation of context that a private world can be the subject of a tragedy. Furthermore, by new techniques of presentation that private world and its values can be made, at least for the duration of the performance, convincing.

Wilder has not been interested in psychology and has never used psychological techniques to solve the "modernists'" problems in the theatre. This accounts, I think, for his great influence on the Continental avant-garde dramatists who are rebelling against our psychologically oriented theatre. Wilder sought to achieve the sense of an ultimate perspective by immaterializing the sense of dramatic place on stage. The bare stage of *Our Town* with its chairs, tables, and ladders, together with the Stage Manager's bald exposition, are all that he uses to create the town. The same is true of *The Skin of Our Teeth;* you never really know where the Antrobuses live, nor when. This is his second dominant technique; by destroying the illusion of time, Wilder achieves the effect of any time, all time, each time. But this is risky business, for without the backdrop of an ultimate perspective to inform a play's action, it can very easily become sentimental or satirical, or even pretentious. Wilder at his best keeps this from happening, but his only weapons are wit and irony. And a production which does not succeed in capturing these qualities (as, alas, most college and school productions do not) is bound to turn out bathetic and sentimental; when technique is used as a compensation for the ultimate perspective, the resultant work of art always lies precariously under a Damoclean sword.

A Tragic Sense of Destiny

It is important that we see the dangers in Wilder's methods, but that a tragic sense of life informs his plays is best illustrated by his sense of destiny. In Wilder's novel *The Woman of Andros*, Chrysis tells her guests a fable of the dead hero who receives Zeus's permission to return to earth to relive the least eventful day of his life, on the condition that he see it both as onlooker and participant.

> Suddenly the hero saw that the living too are dead and that we can only be said to be alive in those moments when our hearts are conscious of our treasure; for our hearts are not strong enough to love every moment.

He quickly asks to be released from this experience, and it is the opinion of Chrysis that

> All human beings—save a few mysterious exceptions who seemed to be in possession of some secret from the gods— merely endured the slow misery of existence, hiding as best they could their consternation that life had no wonderful surprises after all and that its most difficult burden was the incommunicability of love.

Eight years later Wilder incorporated this into the last scene of *Our Town*. When Emily comes back on her twelfth birthday, she discovers that "we don't have time to look at one another. I didn't realize. So all that was going on and we

never noticed. . . . Oh, earth you're too wonderful for anybody to realize you. Do any human beings ever realize life
while they live it?—every, every minute?" The answer, of
course, is no, and Emily must conclude with "That's all
human beings are! Just blind people."

What Wilder is saying here is that human beings cannot
stand to have a sense of destiny—the awareness that there is
a continuity in all our acts, the awareness that every present
moment comes from a past and is directed to a future. Only
at moments, usually of emotional crisis, do we have this
sense of destiny, this sense of awareness of the future. It is
this sense of destiny that is the great human reality and the
tragedy of life lies in our fragmentary and imperfect awareness of it. Wilder is aware, like Eliot, that "human kind cannot bear very much reality," but his plays fall short of
tragedy because he takes the Platonic escape, he moves into
a world that denies the reality and the nemesis of destiny.
Nor does he have the solution of an Eliot. For in denying,
finally, the reality of destiny he shuts out the possibility of
ever providing the means to perfect our fragmentary and
imperfect vision. He fails, to use Karl Jaspers' phrase, to go
"Beyond Tragedy." That Wilder lacks this dimension is not to
discredit him, however, for no other American dramatist
more fully affirms that miracle of life which so much modern drama would deny.

Morality in Wilder's Work

Malcolm Cowley

Malcolm Cowley, author of *Exile's Return: A Literary Odyssey of the 1920s*, has written widely about his contemporaries, the members of the so-called Lost Generation—American writers who first published in the decade or so after World War I. In this essay, Cowley finds fundamental differences between Thornton Wilder and the other writers of his time. While most of the members of the Lost Generation wrote about social groups, Cowley notes, Wilder was concerned with individuals. Yet at the same time Wilder found universal patterns in human experience that could be illustrated in the lives of people of any place or time.

There is a . . . fundamental difference between [Thornton Wilder's] work and that of his contemporaries. The others write novels about a social group—sometimes a small group, as in [F. Scott Fitzgerald's] *Tender Is the Night*, sometimes a very large one, as in [John Dos Passos's] *U.S.A.*—or they write about an individual in revolt against the group, as in [Ernest Hemingway's] *A Farewell to Arms*. The central relation with which they deal is between the many and the one. Very often—to borrow a pair of terms from David Riesman—their theme is the defeat of an inner-directed hero by an other-directed society. They feel that the society and its standards must be carefully portrayed, and these writers are all, to some extent, novelists of manners.—Wilder is a novelist of morals.

Manners and morals are terms that overlap, sometimes confusingly, but here I am using the two words in senses that are easier to distinguish. Manners would be the standards of conduct that prevail in a group, large or small, and hence they would change from group to group and year to year. Morals would be defined as the standards that determine the relations of individuals with other individuals, one with one—a child with each of its parents, a husband with his wife, a rich man with a poor man (not *the* rich with *the* poor)—and also the relations of any man with himself, his destiny, and his God. They are answers found by individuals to the old problems of faith, hope, charity or love, art, duty, submission to one's fate . . . and hence they are relatively universal; they can be illustrated from the lives of any individuals, in any place, at any time since the beginning of time.

THE GREAT UNSOCIAL AND ANTIHISTORICAL NOVELIST

The characters in Wilder's novels and plays are looking for such answers; his work is not often concerned with the behavior of groups. An outstanding exception might be *Our Town* (1938), in which the Stage Manager speaks with the voice of the community. But the community hasn't much to say about itself and will not admit to having local color; it might be any town, a fact that explains the success of the play in towns all over the country, and other countries. The events portrayed are coming of age, falling in love, getting married, and dying; in other words they are not truly events—except for the characters, who are not truly characters—but rather they serve as examples of a universal pattern in human lives; and they are not greatly affected, in the play, by the special manners of this one community. *The Cabala* (1926) also starts by dealing with a group, but very soon the young American narrator shifts his attention to its separate members, explaining that he is "the biographer of the individuals and not the historian of the group." The statement applies to the author himself, and in a simpler form: Wilder is not a historian. In Rome he had studied archaeology and had learned to look backward and forward through a long vista of years; that sort of vision is a special quality of all his work. But what he sees at the end of a vista is what the archaeologist often sees, that is, fragments of a finished pattern of life in many ways similar to our own. It is not what the historian tries to see: a living community in a process of continual and irreversible change.

The other novelists of his generation are all in some way historians. Their basic perception was of the changes in their own time, from peace to war, from stability to instability, from a fixed code of behavior to the feeling that "It's all right if you can get away with it." For them the Great War was a true event, in the sense that afterward nothing was the same. All of them were "haunted fatally by the sense of time," as [Thomas] Wolfe says of his autobiographical hero. His second novel was *Of Time and the River*. Hemingway's first book was *In Our Time* and he let it be understood, ". . . as in no other time." [William] Faulkner saw his time in the South as one of violent decay. When Dos Passos tried to put thirty years of American life into one big novel, he invented a device called the Newsreel, intended to convey the local color of each particular year. Fitzgerald put the same sort of material into the body of his stories; he wrote as if with an eye on the calendar. *The Great Gatsby* belongs definitely to the year 1923, when the Fitzgeralds were living in Great Neck, Long Island, and *Tender Is the Night* could have ended only in 1930; no other year on the Riviera had quite the same atmosphere of things going to pieces. Both books are historical novels about his own time, so accurately observed, so honestly felt, that the books are permanent.—Wilder would never attempt to draw such a picture of his time. He is the great unsocial and antihistorical novelist, the master of the anachronism.

THE VAST LANDSCAPE OF TIME

Like Dos Passos he gives us a newsreel, or rather two of them, to introduce the first two acts of *The Skin of Our Teeth* (1942). The contrast here is complete. Where Dos Passos recalls such episodes as the capture of the bobbed-hair bandit, the Florida real-estate boom, and the suppression of a revolt in Canton (to the refrain of "I'm Dancing with Tears in My Eyes"), Wilder presents another order of phenomena. Before the first act, when the lights go out, the name of the theater flashes on the screen and we hear the Announcer's voice:

> The management takes pleasure in bringing to you—the news of the world! (*Slide 2. The sun appearing above the horizon.*) Freeport, Long Island. The sun rose this morning at 6:32 a.m. This gratifying event was first reported by (*Slide 3*) Mrs. Dorothy Stetson of Freeport, Long Island, who promptly telephoned the Mayor. The Society for Affirming (*Slide 4*) the End of the World at once went into a special session and postponed the arrival of that event for *twenty-four hours* (*Slide 5*). All honor to Mrs. Stetson for her public spirit.

> New York City. (*Slide 6, of the front doors of the theater.*) The Plymouth Theater. During the daily cleaning of this theater a number of lost objects were collected, as usual (*Slide 7*), by Mesdames Simpson, Pateslewski, and Moriarity. Among these

objects found today was (*Slide 8*) a wedding ring, inscribed: To
Eve from Adam. Genesis 2:18. The ring will be restored to the
owner or owners, if their credentials are satisfactory.

Wilder's news of the world is first what happens every
day, and then what happened at the beginning. In all his
work—except for that hint of the Creation—I can think of
only one event that marks a change in human affairs: it is
the birth of Christ, as announced on the first and the last
page of *The Woman of Andros* (1930). Perhaps another event
is foreshadowed in a much later novel, *The Eighth Day*
(1967): it is the birth of new messiahs, something that might
resemble a Second Coming. That other Christian event, the
Fall, is nowhere mentioned and seems to play no part in
Wilder's theology. Everything else in his plays and novels—
even the collapse of a famous bridge—is merely an example
or illustration of man's universal destiny. Nothing is unique,
the author seems to be saying; the Ice Age will return, as will
the Deluge, as will Armageddon. After each disaster man
will start over again—helped by his books, if he has saved
them—and will struggle upward until halted by a new disaster. "Rome existed before Rome," the shade of Virgil says
at the end of *The Cabala*, "and when Rome will be a waste
there will be Romes after her." "There are no Golden Ages
and no Dark Ages," we read in *The Eighth Day*. "There is the
oceanlike monotony of the generations of men under the
alternations of fair and foul weather." The same book says,
"It is only in appearance that time is a river. It is rather a vast
landscape and it is the eye of the beholder that moves."

UNIVERSALLY SHARED EXPERIENCE AND ETERNAL RETURN

At this point I think we might glimpse a design that unites
what Wilder has written from beginning to end. He has published not quite a dozen books, each strikingly different from
all the others in place, in time, in social setting, and even
more in method, yet all the books illustrate the same feeling
of universally shared experience and eternal return.
*Everything that happened might happen anywhere and will
happen again.* That principle explains why he is able to
adopt different perspectives in different books, as though he
were looking sometimes through one end of a telescope,
sometimes through the other. In *The Ides of March* (1948) a
distant object is magnified and Rome in 45 B.C. is described
as if it were New York two thousand years later. In *Our Town*

he reverses the telescope and shows us Grover's Corners as if it had been preserved for two thousand years under a lava flow and then unearthed like Herculaneum. He has many other fashions of distorting time. *The Long Christmas Dinner* (1931) is a one-act play in which the dinner lasts for ninety years, with members of the family appearing from a bright door and going out through a dark door, to indicate birth and death. *The Skin of Our Teeth* epitomizes the story of mankind in three acts and four characters: Adam, Eve, Lilith, and Cain. They are living in Excelsior, New Jersey, when the glacial cap comes grinding down on them. In Atlantic City, just before the Deluge, they launch an ark full of animals two by two from the Million Dollar Pier.

Because Wilder denies the importance of time, his successive books have proved to be either timely or untimely in a spectacular fashion—and in both cases by accident. *The Bridge of San Luis Rey* (1927) exactly fitted the mood of the moment, and nobody knows exactly why. *The Woman of Andros* was published thirty years too late or too soon. *The Skin of Our Teeth* had a more complicated history. Produced on Broadway in 1942, it was a success largely because of Tallulah Bankhead's so-jolly part of Lilith, or Lily Sabina. Hardly anyone said that the play expressed the mood of the moment, or of any other moment. But when it was staged in Central Europe after World War II, it was not only a success but a historic one, for any cast of actors that played in it. The Germans and the Austrians seem to have felt that it was a topical drama written especially for them, to soften their defeat and give them strength to live.

The Skin of Our Teeth is derived in part from [James Joyce's] *Finnegans Wake*, as *The Woman of Andros* is based in part on Terence's[1] *Andria*, and as the plot of *The Bridge* was suggested by one of Mérimée's[2] shorter plays. We read in a note on *The Matchmaker* (1954), "This play is based upon a comedy by Johann Nestroy, *Einen Jux Will Er Sich Machen* (Vienna, 1842), which was in turn based upon an English original, *A Day Well Spent*, by John Oxenford." There are many other acknowledged derivations in Wilder's work, from authors of many times and countries, and together they reveal another aspect of his disregard for history. He feels that a true author is independent of time and

---

1. Roman playwright of the second century B.C. 2. French writer Prosper Mérimée, 1803–1870.

country, and he also feels, apparently, that there is no history of literature, but only a pattern consisting of books that continue to live because they contain permanent truths. Any new author is at liberty to restate those truths and to borrow plots or methods from older authors, so long as he transforms the borrowed material into something of his own. Not only was every great book written this morning, but it can be read tonight as on the first day. That principle, in two of Wilder's plays, becomes a metaphor that is a masterpiece of foreshortening. In a one-acter called *Pullman Car Hiawatha* and again in the third act of *The Skin of Our Teeth*, the great philosophers are presented as hours of the night. One of the characters explains: "Just like the hours and stars go by over our heads at night, in the same way the ideas and thoughts of the great men are in the air around us all the time and they're working on us, even when we don't know it." Spinoza is nine o'clock, Plato is ten, Aristotle is eleven, and Moses is midnight. Three thousand years of thought are reduced to four hours, which pass in less than two minutes on the stage.

This foreshortening of time becomes an opportunity for the novelist as well as for the playwright. When history is regarded as a recurrent pattern rather than as a process, it becomes possible to move a character from almost any point in time or space to almost any other. In *The Bridge* Mme. de Sévigné[3] reappears in Peru as the Marquesa de Montemayor. [John] Keats is presented in *The Cabala*, with his genius, his illness, his family problems; and he dies again in 1920 among a group of strange characters who might be resurrected from the *Memoirs* of the Duc de Saint-Simon,[4] or who also might be classical gods and goddesses in modern dress. Persons can be moved backward in time as well as forward. Edward Sheldon,[5] the crippled and blinded dramatist who lived for thirty years in retirement, dispensing wisdom to his friends, appears in *The Ides of March* as Lucius Manilius Turrinus, and one suspects that Cicero, in the same novel, is a preincarnation of Alexander Woollcott.[6] As for the hero of the novel, he is not a historical character but a model or paradigm of the man of decision, as such a man might exist in any age. Wilder has called him Julius Caesar, much as Paul

3. French writer, especially of letters, 1626–1696. 4. French philosopher and social scientist, founder of French socialism, 1760–1825. 5. American playwright, 1886–1946. 6. American journalist, writer, drama critic, 1887–1943.

Valéry called his man of intellect Leonardo da Vinci, and much as [Ralph Waldo] Emerson gave the title of "Plato" to his essay on man as philosopher.

EMERSONIAN TRANSCENDENTALISM

So Emerson's name comes up again, as it did in the case of e.e. cummings (though it wouldn't make sense to mention the name in connection with any other writer of the Lost Generation). Emerson was of course the prophet who gave no importance to groups or institutions and refused to think of history as a process. When he discussed Montaigne[7] or Shakespeare, it was not against the background of their times, but rather as "representative men" whom he might meet at any dinner of the Saturday Club. Wilder, in the brilliant series of lectures that he gave at Harvard in 1950–51, started with Emerson, [Henry David] Thoreau, and other classical American writers, notably [Herman] Melville and [Walt] Whitman. What he tried to deduce from their works was the character of the representative American, but what he actually presented was, I suspect, partly a reflection of his own character. Here are some of his statements:

> From the point of view of the European an American is nomad in relation to place, disattached in relation to time, lonely in relation to society, and insubmissive to circumstances, destiny, or God.

> Americans could count and enjoyed counting. They lived under a sense of boundlessness. . . . To this day, in American thinking, a crowd of ten thousand is not a homogeneous mass of that number, but is one and one and one . . . up to ten thousand.

> Since the American can find no confirmation of identity from the environment in which he lives, since he lives exposed to the awareness of vast distances and innumerable existences, since he derives from a belief in the future the courage that animates him, is he not bent on isolating and "fixing" a value on every existing thing in its relation to a totality, to the All, to the Everywhere, to the Always?

Those are perceptive statements, but I should question whether they apply to most Americans today, or to many American writers since the First World War. Their primary application is to all the big and little Emersonians, beginning with Thoreau (who is Wilder's favorite) and Whitman. In our own day they apply to Wilder himself more than to

7. French essayist, 1533–1592.

any other writer—more than to Cummings, even, whose later work revives the Emersonian tradition, but chiefly on its romantic, mystical, anarchistic side. Wilder is neoclassical, as I said. He goes back to Pope[8] and Addison[9] in his attitude toward the art of letters, but in other habits of thought he clearly goes back to the Transcendentalists. His work has more than a little of the moral distinction they tried to achieve, and like their work it deals with the relation of one to one, or of anyone to the All, the Everywhere, and the Always. Like theirs it looks toward the future with confidence, though not with the bland confidence that some of the Emersonians displayed. "Every human being who has existed can be felt by us as existing now," Wilder says in another of his Norton lectures, as if to explain his foreshortening of history. "All time is present for a single time. . . . Many problems which now seem insoluble will be solved when the world realizes that we are all bound together as the population of the only inhabited star."

8. Alexander Pope, 1688–1744, English poet. 9. Joseph Addison, 1672–1719, English essayist and poet.

Plays That Portray the Truth of Human Existence

Thornton Wilder

Asked to write a preface for a collection of three of his plays—*Our Town, The Skin of Our Teeth,* and *The Matchmaker*—Wilder took the opportunity to discuss his dissatisfactions with contemporary theater. The aristocracy had limited the theater, he explains, but it was the rise of the middle class that turned a vibrant art into an inconsequential diversion. The new middle class's desire for a "soothing" experience led to audience detachment. Wilder shows how his plays are an attempt to return the passion to the theater.

Toward the end of the 'twenties I began to lose pleasure in going to the theatre. I ceased to believe in the stories I saw presented there. When I did go it was to admire some secondary aspect of the play, the work of a great actor or director or designer. Yet at the same time the conviction was growing in me that the theatre was the greatest of all the arts. I felt that something had gone wrong with it in my time and that it was fulfilling only a small part of its potentialities. I was filled with admiration for presentations of classical works by Max Reinhardt and Louis Jouvet and the Old Vic, as I was by the best plays of my time, like *Desire Under the Elms* and *The Front Page;* but it was with a grudging admiration, for at heart *I didn't believe a word of them.* I was like a schoolmaster grading a paper; to each of these offerings I gave an A+, but the condition of mind of one grading a paper is not that of one being overwhelmed by an artistic creation. The response we make when we "believe" a work of the imagination is that of saying: "This is the way things are. I have always known it without being fully aware that I knew it.

Now in the presence of this play or novel or poem (or picture or piece of music) I know that I know it." It is this form of knowledge which Plato called "recollection." We have all murdered, in thought; and been murdered. We have all seen the ridiculous in estimable persons and in ourselves. We have all known terror as well as enchantment. Imaginative literature has nothing to say to those who do not recognize— who cannot be *reminded*—of such conditions. Of all the arts the theatre is best endowed to awaken this recollection with-. in us—to believe is to say "yes"; but in theatres of my time I did not feel myself prompted to any such grateful and self-forgetting acquiescence.

This dissatisfaction worried me. I was not ready to condemn myself as blasé and over-fastidious, for I knew that I was still capable of belief. I believed every word of *Ulysses* and of Proust and of *The Magic Mountain*, as I did of hundreds of plays when I read them. It was on the stage that imaginative narration became false. Finally, my dissatisfaction passed into resentment. I began to feel that the theatre was not only inadequate, it was evasive; it did not wish to draw upon its deeper potentialities. I found the word for it: it aimed to be *soothing*. The tragic had no heat; the comic had no bite; the social criticism failed to indict us with responsibility.

I began to search for the point where the theatre had run off the track, where it had chosen—and been permitted—to become a minor art and an inconsequential diversion.

The trouble began in the nineteenth century and was connected with the rise of the middle classes—they wanted their theatre soothing. There's nothing wrong with the middle classes in themselves. We know that now. The United States and Scandinavia and Germany are middle-class countries, so completely so that they have lost the very memory of their once despised and ludicrous inferiority (they had been inferior not only to the aristocracy but, in human dignity, to the peasantry). When a middle class is new, however, there is much that is wrong with it. When it is emerging under the shadow of an aristocracy, from the myth and prestige of those well-born Higher-ups, it is alternately insecure and aggressively complacent. It must find its justification and reassurance in making money and displaying it. To this day, members of the middle classes in England, France, and Italy feel themselves to be a little ridiculous and humiliated.

The prestige of aristocracies is based upon a dreary

untruth: that moral superiority and the qualifications for leadership are transmittable through the chromosomes, and the secondary lie, that the environment afforded by privilege and leisure tends to nurture the flowers of the spirit. An aristocracy, defending and fostering its lie, extracts from the arts only such elements as can further its interests, the aroma and not the sap, the grace and not the trenchancy.

Equally harmful to culture is the newly arrived middle class. In the English-speaking world the middle classes came into power early in the nineteenth century and gained control over the theatre. They were pious, law-abiding, and industrious. They were assured of eternal life in the next world and, in this, they were squarely seated on Property and the privileges that accompany it. They were attended by devoted servants who knew their place. They were benevolent within certain limits, but chose to ignore wide tracts of injustice and stupidity in the world about them; and they shrank from contemplating those elements within themselves that were ridiculous, shallow, and harmful. They distrusted the passions and tried to deny them. Their questions about the nature of life seemed to be sufficiently answered by the demonstration of financial status and by conformity to some clearly established rule of decorum. These were precarious positions; abysses yawned on either side. The air was loud with questions that must not be asked.

These middle-class audiences fashioned a theatre which could not disturb them. They thronged to melodrama (which deals with tragic possibilities in such a way that you know from the beginning that all will end happily) and to sentimental drama (which accords a total license to the supposition that the wish is father to the thought) and to comedies in which the characters were so represented that they always resembled someone else and not oneself. Between the plays that Sheridan wrote in his twenties and the first works of Wilde and Shaw there was no play of even moderate interest written in the English language. (Unless you happen to admire and except Shelley's *The Cenci.*) These audiences, however, also thronged to Shakespeare. How did they shield themselves against his probing? How did they smother the theatre—and with such effect that it smothers us still? The box-set was already there, the curtain, the proscenium, but not taken "seriously"—it was a convenience in view of the weather in northern countries. They took it seriously and emphasized and enhanced everything that thus removed, cut off, and boxed the action; they increasingly shut the play up into a museum showcase.

Let us examine why the box-set stage stifles the life in drama and why and how it militates against belief.

JUGGLING WITH TIME

Every action which has ever taken place—every thought, every emotion—has taken place only once, at one moment in time and place. "I love you," "I rejoice," "I suffer," have been said and felt many billions of times, and never twice the same. Every person who has ever lived has lived an unbroken succession of unique occasions. Yet the more one is aware of this individuality in experience (innumerable! innumerable!) the more one becomes attentive to what these disparate moments have in common, to repetitive patterns. As an artist (or listener or beholder) which "truth" do you prefer—that of the isolated occasion, or that which includes and resumes the innumerable? Which truth is more worth telling? Every age differs in this. Is the Venus de Milo "one woman"? Is the play *Macbeth* the story of "one destiny"? The theatre is admirably fitted to tell both truths. It has one foot planted firmly in the particular, since each actor before us (even when he wears a mask!) is indubitably a living breathing "one"; yet it tends and strains to exhibit a general truth since its relation to a specific "realistic" truth is confused and undermined by the fact that it is an accumulation of untruths, pretenses, and fiction.

All the arts depend on preposterous fictions, but the theatre is the most preposterous of all. Imagine asking us to believe that we are in Venice in the sixteenth century, and that Mr. Billington is a Moor, and that he is about to stifle the much-admired Miss Huckaby with a pillow; and imagine trying to make us believe that people ever talked in blank verse—more than that: that people were ever so marvelously articulate. The theatre is a lily that inexplicably arises from a jungle of weedy falsities. Yet it is precisely from the tension produced by all this absurdity, "contrary to fact," that it is able to create such poetry, power, enchantment, and truth.

The novel is pre-eminently the vehicle of the unique occasion, the theatre of the generalized one. It is through the theatre's power to raise the exhibited individual action into the realm of idea and type and universal that it is able to evoke our belief. But power is precisely what those nineteenth-century audiences did not—dared not—confront. They tamed it and drew its teeth; squeezed it into that removed showcase. They loaded the stage with specific objects, because every concrete object on the stage fixes and narrows the action to one moment in time and place. (Have you ever noticed that in the plays of Shakespeare no one—except occasionally a ruler—ever sits down? There were not even chairs on the English or Spanish stages in the time of Elizabeth I.) So it was by a jugglery with time that the middle classes devitalized the theatre. When you emphasize *place* in the theatre, you drag down and limit and harness time to it. You thrust the action back into past time, whereas it is precisely the glory of the stage that it is always "now" there. Under such production methods the characters are all dead before the action starts. You don't have to pay deeply from your heart's participation. No great age in the theatre ever attempted to capture the audience's belief through this kind of specification and localization. I became dissatisfied with the theatre because I was unable to lend credence to such childish attempts to be "real."

THE TORCH RACE

I began writing one-act plays that tried to capture not verisimilitude but reality. In *The Happy Journey to Trenton and Camden* four kitchen chairs represent an automobile and a family travels seventy miles in twenty minutes. Ninety years go by in *The Long Christmas Dinner.* In *Pullman Car Hiawatha* some more plain chairs serve as berths and we hear the very vital statistics of the towns and fields that passengers are traversing; we hear their thoughts; we even hear the planets over their heads. In Chinese drama a character, by straddling a stick, conveys to us that he is on horseback. In almost every No play of the Japanese an actor makes a tour of the stage and we know that he is making a long journey. Think of the ubiquity that Shakespeare's stage afforded for the battle scenes at the close of *Julius Caesar* and *Antony and Cleopatra.* As we see them today what a cutting and hacking of the text takes place—what condescension, what contempt for his dramaturgy.

Our Town is not offered as a picture of life in a New Hampshire village; or as a speculation about the conditions of life after death (that element I merely took from Dante's

Purgatory). It is an attempt to find a value above all price for the smallest events in our daily life. I have made the claim as preposterous as possible, for I have set the village against the largest dimensions of time and place. The recurrent words in this play (few have noticed it) are "hundreds," "thousands," and "millions." Emily's joys and griefs, her algebra lessons and her birthday presents—what are they when we consider all the billions of girls who have lived, who are living, and who will live? Each individual's assertion to an absolute reality can only be inner, very inner. And here the method of staging finds its justification—in the first two acts there are at least a few chairs and tables; but when she revisits the earth and the kitchen to which she descended on her twelfth birthday, the very chairs and table are gone. Our claim, our hope, our despair are in the mind—not in things, not in "scenery." Molière said that for the theatre all he needed was a platform and a passion or two. The climax of this play needs only five square feet of boarding and the passion to know what life means to us.

The Matchmaker is an only slightly modified version of *The Merchant of Yonkers* which I wrote in the year after I had written *Our Town.* One way to shake off the nonsense of the nineteenth-century staging is to make fun of it. This play parodies the stock company plays that I used to see at Ye Liberty Theatre, Oakland, California, when I was a boy. I have already read small theses in German comparing it with the great Austrian original on which it is based. The scholars are very bewildered. There's most of the plot (except that our friend Dolly Levi is not in Nestroy's play); there are some of the tags; but it's all "about" quite different matters. Nestroy's wonderful and sardonic plays are—like most of Molière's and Goldoni's—"about" the havoc that people create in their own lives and in those about them through the wrong-headed illusions they cherish. My play is about the aspirations of the young (and not only of the young) for a fuller, freer participation in life. Imagine an Austrian pharmacist going to the shelf to draw from a bottle which he knows to contain a stinging corrosive liquid, guaranteed to remove warts and wens; and imagine his surprise when he discovers that it has been filled with very American birch-bark beer.

The Skin of Our Teeth begins, also, by making fun of old-fashioned playwriting; but the audience soon perceives that he is seeing "two times at once." The Antrobus family is living both in prehistoric times and in a New Jersey commuter's suburb today. Again the events of our homely daily life—this time the family life—are depicted against the vast dimensions of time and place. It was written on the eve of our entrance into the war and under strong emotion, and I think it mostly comes alive under conditions of crisis. It has been often charged with being a bookish fantasia about history, full of rather bloodless schoolmasterish jokes. But to have seen it in Germany soon after the war, in the shattered churches and beer halls that were serving as theatres, with audiences whose price of admission meant the loss of a meal and for whom it was of absorbing interest that there was a "recipe for grass soup that did not cause diarrhea," was an experience that was not so cool. I am very proud that this year it has received a first and overwhelming reception in Warsaw.

The play is deeply indebted to James Joyce's *Finnegans Wake*. I should be very happy if, in the future, some author should feel similarly indebted to any work of mine. Literature has always more resembled a torch race than a furious dispute among heirs.

The theatre has lagged behind the other arts in finding the "new ways" to express how men and women think and feel in our time. I am not one of the dramatists we are looking for. I wish I were. I hope I have played a part in preparing the way for them. I am not an innovator but a rediscoverer of forgotten goods and I hope a remover of obtrusive bric-a-brac. And as I view the work of my contemporaries I seem to feel that I am exceptional in one thing—I give (don't I?) the impression of having enormously enjoyed it?

Wilder's Use of Staging

Allan Lewis

Allan Lewis, author of *The Contemporary Theatre*, reports that Wilder once "recalled longingly the time when, at the first performance of Euripides' *Medea*, 'strong men fainted and several children were prematurely born.'" In this essay from his book *American Plays and Playwrights of the Contemporary Theatre*, Lewis examines how Wilder has used very different forms of staging in his various plays in his attempt to restore theater to a commanding role in society. While neither the bare sets of *Our Town* nor the exuberant displays of choreography, song, and costume of the musical *Hello, Dolly!* are likely to make strong men faint, in each case the trappings (or lack thereof) deliberately fit—and enhance—the message of the individual play.

Thornton Wilder and William Saroyan are grouped together as prophets of optimism, a rare commodity in the serious theatre of today. Though ordinarily one would hardly pair the quiet dignity of Wilder with the undisciplined rebellion of Saroyan, the two playwrights are alike in an affirmative response to life. Neither has been too active in the theatre of the past decade, but the first signs of an upswing against the theatre of negativism have given new impetus to revivals of their plays and to a reconsideration of their influence. Both write of simple human beings surrounded by the mystery and enjoyment of life. Saroyan is more instinctive, responding on the immediate emotional level. Wilder coats his small-town folk with philosophic overtones. Both come close to the sermon of a Unitarian minister who has had his fling in Greenwich Village. They seek to break with the "box set" of conventional realism, and are unabashed at giving full lyric expression to the homespun message of heartwarming faith in man.

Wilder is the more careful craftsman, planned and deliberate. After painful analysis, he arrives at the awe and wonder
of the simple things in life. Saroyan is reckless and impulsive
and responds to life's beauty instinctively. Wilder revises
painstakingly: "I constantly rewrite, discard, and replace. . . .
There are no first drafts in my life. An incinerator is a writer's
best friend."[1] Saroyan appeared on a motion picture set in
London with the first line of a screen play and informed those
present that the rest of the story would unfold from combined
improvisation, while they were shooting. Wilder is the leisured
writer with financial means for intellectual detachment;
Saroyan is headline sensationalism, dissipating energies and
money—yet both have consistently refused to conform to the
demands of the commercial theatre.

AN ACTIVE DECADE IN THE THEATRE

In the theatre, Wilder has been the more active in the past
decade. *Plays for Bleecker Street* was presented at the Circle
in the Square Theatre in 1962. Only the first three of a projected series of fourteen one-act plays were offered by the
off-Broadway Bleecker Street Theatre, for which they were
expressly written. *Hello, Dolly!* (a musical play based on
Wilder's *The Matchmaker*) was the outstanding box-office
success of the 1963 season and gives every indication of
equaling the sustained record of *My Fair Lady. A Life in the
Sun,* based on the Alcestis legend, was performed at the
Edinburgh Festival in 1955, was retitled *The Alcestiad,* and
then became the libretto for an opera by Louise Talma, produced in Frankfurt in 1962. Paul Hindemith wrote the music
for *The Long Christmas Dinner,* which Wilder revised for the
premiere in Mannheim in 1961. Leonard Bernstein, com-
poser and director of the New York Philharmonic Society,
has indicated his interest in writing the score for a musical
play of *The Skin of Our Teeth.*

Wilder's reputation was first earned as a novelist with *The
Cabala* (1925), *The Bridge of San Luis Rey* (1927), and *The
Woman of Andros* (1930). He has written only four full-
length plays: *Our Town, The Skin of Our Teeth,* and *The
Matchmaker* (*The Alcestiad* is still unpublished and unper-
formed in this country). Like many European writers, particularly the French and the Russian, he turns to the theatre
for an immediate relationship with audiences and for a

1. *New York Times,* November 6, 1961

definitive summation of his philosophy in human terms. His admiration for the theatre is based on his belief that

> in the great ages it carried on its shoulders the livest realiza-
> tion of public consciousness. The tragic and comic poets of
> Greece, Lope de Vega, Corneille, Racine, Shakespeare, were
> recognized by their contemporaries as expressing what every
> citizen felt dimly and rejoiced to hear concretely.[2]

The theatre should stir the passions and direct the mind. In a recent interview Wilder recalled longingly the time when, at the first performance of Euripides' *Medea*, "strong men fainted and several children were prematurely born." The theatre can be restored to its commanding position if it pursues its role as a critic of society and becomes "the art form by which a nation recognizes its greatness."[3]

OUR TOWN

Our Town, first produced in 1938, achieved this mission. It has come to be considered the most typically American play— a classic of our time. The plot need not be repeated, for the play is known to every high school student, performed by every community theatre, and regarded as an essential element in the repertory of most professional groups. It is a miracle of theatrical magic. By eliminating the usual techniques of realistic representation, and avoiding all pretense, greater illusion was achieved. Wilder is interested in people and ideas, in "reality not verisimilitude." He merged form and meaning in a rare example of artistic unity.

The absence of scenery and elaborate costumes or props, other than a few chairs, a stepladder, and similar simple physical devices, may invite production by budget-conscious producers, but Wilder regards the physical accessories as the least necessary of the theatre's demands. The inner reality of each individual is unique, and imagination is preferable to mechanical devices to achieve it. "Our claim, our hope, our despair are in the mind, not in things, not in scenery," he wrote in the preface to his published plays, and insisted that since the play is a parable of modern times, the language which conveys the meaning should be "heard, not diverted." Such statements by any playwright are usually more theory than fact. *Our Town* appeals to the eye as well as to the ear, and audiences are amused by the bare upstage brick wall.

2. *Ibid.* 3. *Ibid.*

Wilder substitutes a different "scenery"; in *The Skin of Our Teeth* it becomes elaborate at times. Brecht was equally anxious to put an end to the Belasco era, but he used the complementary theatre arts for his purpose, to overwhelm through multiple sense appeals—music as well as words, props as well as costumes, reading as well as hearing. Wilder is likewise not recounting an anecdote or telling a story, which proscenium stage encourages. The unencumbered set reaches into "the truth operative in everyone. The less seen the more heard."

Wilder's departure from the staging of the well-made play was not original. He knew the work of Pirandello and the German expressionists. He had translated André Obey's *Le Viol de Lucrèce,* and *The Merchant of Yonkers* (later *The Matchmaker)* was an adaptation of a work by the nineteenth-century Viennese playwright, Johann Nestroy. More influential, perhaps, was his admiration for the Oriental theatre, which he knew well from his many years in the Far East when his father served in the diplomatic corps. A platform and a passion were the only indispensable ingredients; reducing the theatre to its skeletal requirements made it free to reach beyond the immediate. But no recital of influences can diminish Wilder's originality. All writers take from others. Wilder was skillful enough to add new touches, which, in turn, were seized upon by his European contemporaries—Brecht, Duerrenmatt, and Max Frisch in particular. His techniques made a deeper impression abroad; his story received wider acceptance in his own country.

The Stage Manager, who acts as narrator, commentator, and judge and participates in the action in several roles, is a genial creation. It is he who unites the play, disarms the audience, speaks for the author, and breaks the limitations of time and space. He is Greek chorus, Laudisi of Pirandello's *Six Characters in Search of an Author,* the poet in many guises of Strindberg's *Dream Play,* and Thornton Wilder. Narrators have been used with increasing frequency ever since, as in *The Glass Menagerie, After the Fall,* and *The Ballad of the Sad Cafe.*

Our Town summarizes the totality of life in a small New England village. The first act is labeled "Daily Life"; the second, "Love and Marriage"; the third, obviously, "Death." Grover's Corners is a community set against all of time. The characters are not specific individuals, psychologically revealed, but types. The Webbs and the Gibbses are representative of American middle-class life. Emily and George are young boy and young girl. They have already become legendary, ingrained in the myths of a nation. The method Wilder employs is quickly apparent. The smallest daily chores, the most repeated of living action, the local events—doing homework, listening to the Albany train, watching the boy down at the stable, ironing a dress—are magnified to equality with the movement of the stars. Whatever *is*, belongs to an intricately connected and meaningful system. Just as the earth is a speck in an endless succession of planetary units, so each moment of breathing is part of the history of man. Timelessness and pancakes are discussed in the same everyday language.

Most of the scenes could be inserted into a realistic play. Even the dead talk as though they were gathered around a New Hampshire cracker barrel. Pain and suffering are tolerable, for what we endure is both unique and common to all. Emily's early death in childbirth touches our hearts, but she is still with us in death. Her final statement is the lesson we never learn:

> We don't have time to look at one another . . . Oh earth, you're too wonderful for anyone to realize you . . . Do any human beings ever realize life while they live it—every, every minute?

Simon Stimson, the local drunk, now with the deceased, answers:

> That's what it was to be alive . . . to spend and to waste time, as though you had a million years.

Middle-class life is given dignity by relating it to the cosmos. Wilder objected to the theatre which arose in the nineteenth century with the domination of the merchant. "They wanted their theater soothing . . . they distrusted the passions and tried to deny them." The rules that developed for the situation play which did not disturb deprived the theatre of vitality. Wilder, resenting middle-class domination, broke all the rules and wrote the most complete middle-class play.

THE SKIN OF OUR TEETH

The Skin of Our Teeth uses the same technique, but carries it to the logical conclusion of relating the seemingly unimportant to the grandiose. Mr. and Mrs. Antrobus, of Excelsior, New Jersey, are Adam and Eve, Renaissance figures, and also the suburban neighbors next door. All history is merged with the present, picturing the rise from primordial ignorance to the continuing problem of survival. In the first act, man is pitted against the destructive forces of nature. The audience is called upon to help, Prometheus-like, by passing up chairs to keep the home fires burning during the glacial age. In the second act, man is ranged against the moral order, and in the third, against himself. A typical American family is the Human Family. The allegory borders upon the fantastic and the incredible—Mr. Antrobus' arrival on time at his office is as important as the invention of the wheel and the alphabet.

Wilder's use of composite historical characters was similar to that in *Finnegans Wake.* He had lectured on the work of James Joyce at the University of Chicago, and was taken to task for not indicating his sources. Wilder dismissed the charges by adding to the preface of the published version of the play:

> I should be very happy if, in the future, some author should feel similarly indebted to any work of mine. Literature has always more resembled a torch race, than a furious dispute among heirs.

The play is a brilliant example of expressionistic theatre. Unities of place and action are abolished. Man's fate is compressed into a circus satire in which burlesque and vaudeville antics combine with tightrope-walking on the razor edge of despair. Like Max Frisch in *The Chinese Wall* and Bertolt Brecht in *Mother Courage,* Wilder indicates that man has learned little from experience, but must go on laughing and striving. He cannot renege now and permit chaos to triumph. Somehow or other, he will survive. At the end of the play, when Antrobus has lost "the most important thing of all: the desire to begin again, to start building," Sabina, who is Vice and Virtue, Sex and Self-interest, Love and Deception, admonishes him, as she prepares to go to the movies, that she will work with him if he has any ideas about "improving the crazy old world." Antrobus adds:

> I've never forgotten for long at a time that living is struggle ... all I ask is the chance to build new worlds and God has always given us that ... we've come a long way.

As Sabina comes downstage to tell the audience good-night, she reassures all that as far as Mr. and Mrs. Antrobus are concerned, "their heads are full of plans and they are as confident as the first day they began."

Though hailed in Europe, the play had a mixed reception in New York. Many regarded it as a silly extravaganza, a sophomoric lampoon of history. Brooks Atkinson was enthusiastic, terming it "one of the wisest and friskiest comedies." The play won for Wilder his third Pulitzer Prize, his second for a dramatic work. It ranks with the best of Brecht—an example of historical realism in which the accumulation of evidence permits audiences to pass judgment.

THE MERCHANT OF YONKERS/ THE MATCHMAKER/HELLO, DOLLY!

The Merchant of Yonkers was Wilder's only failure, despite the fanfare that attended a production by Max Reinhardt, with an all-star cast headed by Jane Cowl and June Walker. Wilder refused to let the material die. He was determined to pull it through to survival, in the manner of Antrobus with mankind. Rewritten as *The Matchmaker* and directed by Tyrone Guthrie, the play did prove a success sixteen years later. The retired and professorial Wilder had become the maverick with three consecutive triumphs.

A libretto by Michael Stewart and music and lyrics by Jerry Hyman transformed *The Matchmaker* into *Hello, Dolly!*—the outstanding musical play of the 1964 season. The production was a triumph of the theatre arts, a vindication of the major trend in musical theatre. Choreography, costumes, design, and songs were interrelated with plot. Gower Champion, the director, exercised an overall control that fashioned a unified experience in the tradition of *Oklahoma!* Wilder's play gained in the process. As an acted piece, it was handicapped by reliance on verbal appeal. The musical version gave fuller scope than Wilder's original prose to the joyous sensation of being alive. The appeal to the eye, which Wilder had discounted, the multiple appeal to the ear, the evocation of unheard songs, enhanced a mediocre work and achieved a refreshing reiteration of "Isn't the world full of such wonderful things?" Sentimental and nostalgic, *Hello, Dolly!* restates the trite maxims that love conquers all, that woman is the greatest work of God, and that money is good only when it becomes "manure to be spread around to help young things grow." Despite Wilder's efforts to convert the middle-class theatre from its devotion to the soporific and its ignoring of the

> questions about the nature of life which seem to be sufficiently answered by the demonstration of financial status and by conformity to some clearly established rules of decorum,

the hit musical inspired by Wilder's work is a *soothing* play.

WILDER'S AMAZING THEATRICAL GIFT

This raises the question of Thornton Wilder's amazing gift. He deals with the most commonplace, the most trivial, relationships and gives the impression of being exceedingly profound. Remove the deceptive overtones, and his work all winds up with a simplistic philosophy—live every moment of your life, for life is beautiful; the tragedy is human wastefulness. Such nostrums, as in the case of Saroyan, fall short of revelation. The arts of the theatre, skillfully employed, can cover dross with an alluring sheen.

A defense of Wilder can be based on his similarity with Camus. Both explore consciously the absurdity of man's plight, reject irrational remedies, and end by asserting that at least one can live by not adding to the suffering of mankind. Both recognize the anxieties that plague the world, but rather than welcome defeat, they rely on man to effect solutions as he always has. Optimism is better conveyed in song and dance. *Hello, Dolly!* may be Wilder's most explicit statement.

PLAYS FOR BLEECKER STREET

Plays for Bleecker Street is an attempt to express in dramatic terms a definitive summary of Wilder's beliefs. The cycle of one-act plays will constitute a morality of the twentieth century. The theatre, Wilder feels, can be strengthened to achieve its role as the "signature of an age."

The overall title, *Plays for Bleecker Street,* is added proof of Wilder's opposition to the picture-frame stage, which "militates against belief" and squeezes the drama into a "removed showcase." A precondition for a revitalized theatre is to "kick the proscenium down." Wilder enjoys reminding us that in the great theatre of the past the audience encircled the acting area on three sides. The plays were entrusted to the Circle in the Square Theatre, a pioneer in the growing arena theatre movement. Though Wilder can afford artistic independence, his action was a courageous defiance of Broadway commercialism and its reluctance to experiment. He gave a boost to the struggling little theatres of New York by proving his willingness to have his work seen first at a small, off-Broadway organization.

The cycle consists of two series of seven plays each, entitled respectively *The Seven Ages of Man* and *The Seven Deadly Sins.* The first will be for five actors, the second for four. Eventually, when completed, all fourteen will be presented in sequence on several successive evenings in the theatre. The only ones available so far are *Infancy* and *Childhood*, the first two of *The Seven Ages of Man*, and *Someone from Assisi* or *Lust*, number four of *The Seven Deadly Sins*.

Infancy deals with two children in perambulators being taken for a walk by their parents. The parts of the children are played by grown actors dressed in baby clothes, who comment on the world situation, the adult world, and their own growing pains. Their highly imaginative response to their environment is reminiscent of Wordsworth's "The child is father to the man." *Childhood* reveals the gulf that separates the inner worlds of children and adults, no matter how wholesome and loving their relationship may be. In both plays, the child's struggle for improvement is thwarted by those who are older. "The reason why the world is in such a sloppy state," Wilder has remarked, "is that our parents were so stupid." The third of the plays deals with a fictionalized incident in the life of St. Francis of Assisi, when he was seized with desire for the beautiful Mona Lucrezia.

On the basis of but three examples of a large undertaking, judgment can be only tentative. *Infancy* is in the gay mood of *The Skin of Our Teeth*, and is by far the most effective on stage. *Someone from Assisi* is a disappointment. It lacks purpose and gives the impression of being removed from context. It is a serious sermon about the nature of lust, and Wilder is much more comfortable in the comic vein. The total concept of the cycle, however, is on a grand scale—the use of the theatre to crystallize views about "our lives and errors" from birth to death.

> I am interested in the drives that operate in society and in every man. Pride, avarice, and envy are in every home. I am not interested in the ephemeral—such subjects as the adulteries of dentists. I am interested in those things that repeat and repeat in the lives of millions.[4]

With this statement, Thornton Wilder, at seventy, becomes the youngest of our playwrights.

4. ibid.

An Unfashionable Optimist

Gerald Weales

Gerald Weales is an author and editor of several books on drama and film including *American Drama Since World War II, Religion in Modern English Drama,* and *Canned Goods as Caviar: American Film Comedy of the 1930s.* In this selection, Weales contends that Thornton Wilder's work presents a refreshing optimism. Most "serious" playwrights place the dignity of man well in the background of their darker subjects, Weales comments, and seem to feel it is more intellectually profound to be despairing than sunny. Wilder has shown the courage to be upbeat. Even his minimal stage sets reflect his belief that human reality is a quality of the mind, Weales points out, not dependent on "realistic" staging.

Thornton Wilder's recently issued *Three Plays* might have been called *The Collected Plays.* Except for two early books of short plays, the unpublished *A Life in the Sun* and the new one-acters that are presumably scheduled for production at the Circle in the Square,[1] the three plays—*Our Town, The Skin of Our Teeth* and *The Matchmaker*—comprise the bulk of Wilder's work for the theater. In the introduction to his first book of short plays, *The Angel That Troubled the Waters* (1928), Wilder spoke of "the inertia that barely permits me to write." Whether because of that inertia or a fondness for tinkering with already completed works (*Our Town* grew out of two early one-acters; *The Matchmaker* is a revision of a 1939 play, *The Merchant of Yonkers*), his theatrical output is small. Yet, he is one of America's most important playwrights.

Playwrights have a way of marking their work with the signature of personal mannerisms. A play of Tennessee

1. an off-Broadway theater in New York City

Williams or Eugene O'Neill, for instance, is easily identifiable. Wilder's three plays, unmistakably his, are dissimilar on the surface—one an essay in regionless regionalism, one an expressionistic comedy, one a traditional farce. In their manner they share only a distaste for conventional naturalistic staging; it is their matter that points an insistent finger at the author. Each of the plays embodies Wilder's concern with, admiration for and love of human life at its most ordinary, which is, for him, at its most consistent preoccupation with love, death, laughter, boredom, aspiration and despair.

AN OPTIMIST BY INSTINCT

Malcolm Cowley, in his introduction to *A Thornton Wilder Trio,* the re-issue of Wilder's first three novels, wrote, "He is optimistic by instinct, in the fashion of an older America." One of the remarkable things about Wilder's plays is that they—like his novels—have declared his optimism with a directness that is unusual on the American stage, at least among serious playwrights. The dignity of man is apparent behind the cosmic and familiar sufferings of O'Neill and behind the political and social uncertainty of Clifford Odets and Arthur Miller, perhaps even behind the sexual nervousness of Tennessee Williams, but in Wilder it is in the foreground. The emphasis, however, is not so much on dignity as it is on man; the one implies the other. Nor is his optimism the kind of adolescent enthusiasm that seems to be the stuff of William Saroyan's plays (Saroyan's cry of love, love, love has become so shrill that one suspects that he has not yet convinced himself); it is a recognition that pain, cruelty, death and failure are part of living, but that they can never completely define life. All of Wilder's plays say, with Chrysis in his novel *The Woman of Andros,* "that I have known the worst that the world can do to me, and that nevertheless I praise the world and all living."

There is an uncomfortable attitude around today that the clichés of despair are more profound than the bromides of optimism; it is intellectually proper to talk about the dark night of the soul, but only a popular song would be willing to walk on the sunny side of the street. Every man must decide whether he is a "lone, lorn creetur" with Mrs. Gummidge or whether, like Mr. Micawber, he lives on the expectation that something is about to turn up. At the moment the vote seems to be with Mrs. Gummidge, and Wilder's reputation has suffered as a result. People talk of outgrowing Wilder, as they talk of outgrowing Shaw, but they mean simply that even if one does believe in the ultimate value of human life, one does not say so, except obliquely. Wilder once told a reporter from *Time,* "Literature is the orchestration of platitudes." Wilder has chosen the unfashionable platitudes of the optimist; he has repeated them in his plays even though he knows, like Captain Alvarado in *The Bridge of San Luis Rey,* that "there are times when it requires a high courage to speak the banal." It is his distinction as a playwright that banality emerges as—what it is—one kind of truth.

A Passion for Life—and to Learn What Life Means

All three of Wilder's plays grow out of "the passion to know what life means to us." *Our Town* is an "attempt to find a value above all price for the smallest events in our daily life." The play is concerned, for the most part, with the ritual of daily tasks; the major actions in the play (Emily Webb's marriage to George Gibbs and her death in childbirth) celebrate those basic commonplaces that Sweeney expected to find on his cannibal isle: "Birth, and copulation, and death." Each of the events, the ordinary and the special (which is special only to Emily and George and those close to them), is seen as part of a continuing stream of life from which it grows and into which it will be absorbed and finally forgotten. The play is, in one sense, antitheatrical; instead of enlarging a moment until it bursts, throwing its significance into the audience, it cherishes the small and the everyday (whether it be cooking breakfast or dying). If the perspective is long enough, the individual and the general become one. For one kind of mind, such a long view might reduce life to inconsequence; for Wilder, it gives to the simplest action and the simplest emotion not cosmic value (the dead forget), but human value.

As *Our Town* is a play about the significance of the routine of living, so *The Matchmaker* is about man's attempt to dress that routine in the fantastic and the exciting; it is, as Barnaby says in his curtain speech, "about adventure." Adapted from a nineteenth century German farce, which was in turn taken from an English source, the play makes happy use of a stageful of stock farcical situations and devices. There is an elopement that must wait for parental (here, avuncular) approval. There are two innocent young men, loose in the wicked city. There are mistaken identities, assumed names, disguises. There is the final gathering and forgiving of all the erring characters in the play, an occasion for three marriages and a healthy helping of material and spiritual rewards. Picking its way among the farcical furniture of the play is Wilder's theme, the insistence that life cannot be embraced with care and hedging. "Is this an adventure?" asks Barnaby in Act Two, and Cornelius answers, "No, but it may be." Dolly Levi, the matchmaker, Wilder's wonderful addition to the German play, elbows her way through the action, like an edited echo of Cornelius' words: it not only may be, it can be, it must be. "My play," says Wilder, "is about the aspirations of the young (and not only of the young) for a fuller, freer participation in life."

The Skin of Our Teeth is Wilder's best play and his most ambitious one. It is a history of man under crisis. In Act One, the Antrobus family survive the ice age; in Act Two, they escape the deluge; in Act Three, they live through a world war. After each near destruction, Antrobus—falling back always on the words of the great prophets, thinkers and poets—begins to build again. The power of the play lies in the four main characters—Mr. and Mrs. Antrobus, their son Henry, and the maid-mistress Lily-Sabina. Antrobus is man, the creator (in the play he invents the wheel and the alphabet), and Henry (Cain) is man, the destroyer. These two are not only at war with one another; each is at war within himself. Antrobus' enthusiasm drains off easily into despair and his mind readily wanders from the alphabet to the maid; Henry not only wants to destroy his family, he wants to join it. Mrs. Antrobus and Sabina also form a contrast, that between Eve and Lilith, between woman as wife, mother and home-builder and woman as sexual object and home-wrecker. The play is often broadly funny, often sidetracked by its delight in intellectual jokes, but the warring qualities that go to make up man are always in evidence in the four characters, who, with the daughter Gladys (on hand to have a baby in Act Three), must be saved together if they are to be saved at all. The family, including Henry-Cain, always comes through; man is saved by the skin of his teeth, but with his evil as well as his aspirations intact.

UNCONVENTIONAL STAGING

All of Wilder's plays avoid conventional staging. They either attack it head-on, using the weapons of expressionism, as in

Our Town and *The Skin of Our Teeth*, or they join it with a
vengeance, as in *The Matchmaker*, and try to laugh it off the
stage. His attempt to splinter the box-set [proscenium stage,
which separates the audience from the play] or to treat it as
though it were a farceur's mask (the fight was pretty well
won when he got into it) grew out of his belief that plays
begin in generalization; the correct teacups on the correct
table in the correct drawing room have a way of reducing
universals to the tiresomely specific. Even in his novels, as
Cowley has pointed out, the settings are relatively unimportant. He is concerned with the recurrent human predicaments at the expense of the immediate surroundings. *The
Skin of Our Teeth* brings the ice age, Noah's flood, the invention of the wheel and Homer (singing "Jingle Bells") to contemporary New Jersey; *Our Town* can be identified as
Grover's Corners, New Hampshire, but it is also to be our
town wherever and at whatever time we live, as Editor Webb
implies when he says of ancient Babylon, "every night all
those families sat down to supper, and the father came home
from his work, and the smoke went up the chimney,—same
as here." The immediate references for the characters of *The
Matchmaker* are the stock figures of farce—the irate father,
the reluctant maiden, the drunken servant, the interfering
vice. The strength of the play lies, however, in the fact that,
even while they retain the force of philosophical generalization, the characters and the situations take on dramatic individuality; audiences identify with individuals not with
abstractions.

For all its importance to the themes of the plays, Wilder's
non-naturalistic structure gives too easy entrance to his
chief dramatic fault, a tendency to be overly didactic. He
seems afraid that apparent points will be missed. The stage
manager in *Our Town* explains too much and points up too
many morals. The long asides in *The Matchmaker* (although
I admire Mrs. Levi's, as Ruth Gordon read it) too often do
what the action has already done. The most obvious example is the emergency rehearsal at the beginning of Act Three
of *The Skin of Our Teeth;* although there are funny things in
it and although it is there, too, to emphasize Wilder's belief
that human reality is a quality of the mind and not the result
of realistic staging, it sounds as though the author were half-
afraid that the audience would not understand the passing of
the hours that speak the words of the philosophers. These

are minor blemishes, however; they weaken the plays without undermining them.

Wilder, as he says in his introduction, is not an innovator. He is not the kind of playwright who gathers disciples or inspires copyists. He is simply a man who has gone his own way, finding or borrowing the forms in which he could say what was on his mind. He has published only three full-length plays, but they are all good plays and that—on the American stage, or any stage—is an achievement.

CHAPTER 3

Pulitzer #1:
The Bridge of San Luis Rey

The Factual People and Places Behind *The Bridge of San Luis Rey*

Linda Simon

The Bridge of San Luis Rey is based on the collapse
of an actual bridge in Peru, writes Linda Simon, and
several of the main characters were drawn from people Wilder knew. These real-world influences are all
pulled into the service of what she calls "the literary
enthusiasms and personal obsessions that occupied
Thornton at the time." No less than Brother Juniper,
the Franciscan friar who studies the lives of the victims to find God's hand at work, Wilder is curious to
know whether those who died in the bridge's collapse were victims of destiny or circumstance. But
despite Brother Juniper's convictions, Simon notes,
Wilder's own conclusions are ambiguous. Linda
Simon is the author of *The Biography of Alice B.
Toklas* and editor of *Gertrude Stein: A Composite
Portrait.*

"I write first as if I were writing about people we know,"
Thornton Wilder once said. "Then I do my research after I
write—not before."[1] The basis for *The Bridge* was not so much
in historical research as it was in the literary enthusiasms
and personal obsessions that occupied Wilder at the time. But
of course there was a kernel of historical fact in his tale. There
had been a bridge, described as being "two hundred paces"
long, made of cables hand-twisted from the fibers of the
maguey plant. In heavy wind, it swung frighteningly over a
dark abyss, above threatening waves that thundered against
the rocks. It had been built across the Apurímac River in Peru
in about 1350 and had lasted for hundreds of years, support-

1. Boston *Traveler*, December 14, 1955

ed on either side by stone pillars. It was a much used thoroughfare, and every two years the cables were renewed and the wood planking replaced. But when the wheel came into common use among the Indian population, the bridge was allowed slowly to decay. It collapsed, and the few travelers upon it were plunged to their death.

Like many before him, Wilder asked, "Why? Why were those particular travelers chosen to die? Or were they chosen at all?" But his questions came from another source as well, a passage from the Bible [Luke 13:4] that continually rang in his mind:

> Or those eighteen, upon whom the tower in Siloam fell,
> and slew them, think ye that they were sinners above
> all men that dwelt in Jerusalem?

The passage set the theme; the characters were drawn from many sources.

The book is divided into five parts, with the central three describing the lives of the victims: the Marquesa de Montemayor and her servant Pepita, Esteban, Uncle Pio, and a young boy, Don Jaime. It is the self-imposed task of a Franciscan monk, Brother Juniper, to investigate their deaths and determine if "we live by accident and die by accident, or we live by plan and die by plan." For Brother Juniper there is no doubt: the accident must have been an act of God, and therefore the life and death of each person involved must have some meaning.

THE MARQUESA AND PEPITA

He tells us first about Doña María, the Marquesa de Montemayor, known through legend and her letters to her daughter. Doña Maria was inspired by Wilder's fascination for Madame de Sévigné, an enthusiasm he could not fully explain. "She is not devastatingly witty nor wise," he admitted once. "She is simply at one with French syntax."[2] So, too, the Marquesa frequently blunders in her dealings with others, but her letters are full of unleashed passion and "flamboyant" language. Doña María, like Wilder's early St. Zabett, rebels against marriage. But she is forced into a mismatched union by her mother and eventually has a daughter, the haughty Doña Clara. Doña María suffers unrequited love for

2. Richard Goldstone, "Thornton Wilder," in Malcolm Cowley, ed., *Writers at Work*, p. 108

her daughter, and her suffering gives her insight into the isolation of other humans. "She saw that the people of this world moved about in an armour of egotism, drunk with self-gazing, a thirst for compliments, hearing little of what was said to them, unmoved by accidents that befell their closest friends, in dread of all appeals that might interrupt their long communion with their own desires." Yet she, too, becomes blind to love and fails to appreciate the singular spirit of her young maid, Pepita, who despite her unhappiness serves her mistress in good faith.

Contrasted with the Marquesa is an Abbess, Madre María del Pilar, loosely modeled on Wilder's aunt Charlotte, his father's sister, then chairman of the International Committee of the YWCA and a woman Wilder admired and respected. The Abbess is an ardent feminist who wants only "to attach a little dignity to women." She realizes, of course, the futility of her goal in eighteenth-century Peru. Yet like a swallow who tried to build a mountain by adding a single pebble to a pile every thousand years, the Abbess perseveres. She sends her protégé, Pepita, to the Marquesa because she knows that not even the suffocating existence of that life will damp the girl's spirit.

Indeed, it is Pepita who ultimately shows Doña María that her life spent in pursuit of her daughter's affections has been wasted; Doña María realizes that she was a coward in both living and loving and resolves to start anew. "'Let me live now,' she whispered. 'Let me begin again.'" But two days later, she and Pepita die crossing the bridge.

ESTEBAN AND MANUEL

The characters in the next section are closer to Wilder's own life. Esteban and Manuel are orphaned twins, raised by the Abbess, who, despite her generalized hatred of men, grew fond of the two boys. The duality of personalities is treated more emotionally here than it was in *The Cabala,* where Samuele and James Blair are contrasted. For Wilder, the idea of being a twin, of living with a double, was almost an obsession.[3] His dead brother often haunted him; he carried within him the image of an identical likeness.

Esteban and Manuel are so close in spirit that "love is inadequate to describe their profound identity with one

---

3. Thornton Wilder's twin brother died within hours of birth.

another." They invent their own language and find that telepathy often occurs between them. No matter what they do or where they go, they are certain of one thing: "All the world was remote and strange and hostile except one's brother."

But their bond is broken when Manuel becomes infatuated with a beautiful actress, known as the Perichole. His brother feels estranged and once threatens to leave. There is a crisis, however: Manuel cuts his knee and is badly wounded. Esteban nurses him, but the infection worsens and his brother becomes delirious. Suddenly he begins to curse Esteban for coming between him and the actress. For several nights Esteban suffers under his brother's raving; on the third night, Manuel dies.

Esteban's grief causes near-madness. At first he pretends to be Manuel, and no one is the wiser. But he meets a sagacious sea captain, Alvarado, to whom he tells the truth, and his confession seems to relieve him somewhat. Alvarado invites him to join his crew. Esteban agrees, provided he can take on the hardest work. He knows suicide is proscribed, he tells Alvarado, but clearly he is seeking death in life.

Just before sailing, however, Esteban changes his mind, vacillates, and tries to kill himself. He cannot bear to leave Peru. He cannot bear to live alone. Alvarado tries to comfort him, but he knows how meaningless his words must sound to the young man. "We do what we can," he tells him. "We push on, Esteban, as best we can. It isn't for long, you know. Time keeps going by. You'll be surprised at the way time passes." Esteban, calmed, leaves with the captain and is killed when the bridge collapses.

THE PERICHOLE AND UNCLE PIO

The Perichole and her benefactor, Uncle Pio, are met again in the fourth section. Uncle Pio is a sympathetic character, a lonely man who discovered the actress when she was the waif Micaela Villegas and transformed her into an idolized figure. Uncle Pio decides early in his life that he will try to fulfill three aims: independence—keeping emotionally detached from people while able to act as "an agent" in their lives; proximity to beautiful women who would depend on him when they were in trouble, though they would not, he thought, love him; involvement with those who loved Spanish literature and its masterpieces, especially in the theater. His life with the Perichole seems on the surface to fill all three, but gradually it becomes evident that Uncle Pio is hardly detached from the young woman. He realizes that the world may be divided into two groups, "those who had loved and those who had not." His devotion to the actress places him among the former.

Though Uncle Pio's attachment to the Perichole tran-scends a mentor-student or father-daughter relationship, it never implies sexuality. Instead, Uncle Pio understands the rare communion between the two, and does not want to lose it. When the Perichole retires from the stage and finds a position in Peruvian high society, he urges her to return with him to Madrid and to the theater. But she refuses, mocking his dreams, and turns him away. Uncle Pio does not give up, however. Even when the Perichole contracts smallpox, he tries to see her, and one day comes upon her accidentally unveiled, her scars revealed as she tries to cover them with make-up. Enraged, she throws him out of her house. Still he persists. Finally he implores her to allow him to take her young son and raise him for a year. He will edu-cate the boy as he did her; and the child will be his new companion. She relents and sends her beloved Jaime to Uncle Pio. The next day the two leave for Lima—and cross the bridge.

AMBIGUOUS LESSONS

Despite Brother Juniper's dogged efforts, the author is not convinced that the collapse of the bridge was a deliberate and meaningful act of God. Surely there are lessons to be learned from the close examination of any life, but what these lessons teach are ambiguous. Each in a different way, the victims sought love; each was the victim of love. The dead live in the memory of the living until they, too, die and are forgotten. "But the love will have been enough; all those impulses of love return to the love that made them. Even memory is not necessary for love. There is a land of the liv-ing and a land of the dead and the bridge is love, the only survival, the only meaning."

CRITICAL ACCLAIM

Hardly anyone—least of all Wilder—was prepared for the accolades bestowed upon *The Bridge of San Luis Rey* when it appeared in late fall. "A new talent, and a very distinguished one, has appeared in American letters," Lee Wilson Dodd declared in the *Saturday Review.* While *The Cabala* had hinted at promise, Thornton's full talent was not yet evident. "It grows clear with his second book . . . ," Dodd saw,

that Mr. Thornton Wilder is not just another literate and sophisticated young man. *The Cabala,* his first book, had distinction, passages of genuine insight and beauty; yet there was about it an air of the tentative, the experimental. One felt that Mr. Wilder had wings, that they would prove to be good wings—and even enchanted wings; but one felt, also, that he was merely trying them out a little before they were fully fledged. There was a general atmosphere of flutter eddying round the whole charming performance.

But *The Bridge,* Dodd thought, was "a tale which I am grievously tempted to call a masterpiece. . . . This book is a poem, if you will, a romantic poem—for its true matter is human love." [4]

Wilder was heralded also in *The New Republic,* where Malcolm Cowley found that the book "without pretense to greatness is perfect in itself. . . . In *The Bridge of San Luis Rey,* the texture is completely unified; nothing falls short of its mark; nothing exceeds it; and the book as a whole is like some faultless temple erected to a minor deity." [5]

By the end of the year, praise for the book had appeared in most newspapers and magazines across the country. And in February an important review appeared in London's *Evening Standard.* Arnold Bennett wrote that he had been "dazzled" by the unsurpassed writing in the novel. "The author does not search for the right word. He calls, it comes." [6] Like his fictional Cabalists, Thornton had found that "to wish is to command." Yet he read each review in hope of some instruction, some advice. He wanted to be evaluated, and though he was more than pleased by the praise he was receiving, he was thankful, too, for less favorable assessments. [7] One of these came in March, 1928.

"And Then the (Bridge) Failed" was John Herrmann's review in *transition,* the Paris-based literary journal.

Now that it is definitely established that *The Bridge of San Luis Rey* by Thornton Wilder is a classic (Burton Rascoe), a work of genius (William Lyon Phelps), a little masterpiece

4. December 3, 1927, p. 371 5. December 28, 1927, p. 173 6. February 28, 1928 7. TW to Henry Blake Fuller, May 12, 1928

and of course a contribution to literature (Isabel Patterson), unsurpassed (Arnold Bennett), a great success for the discriminating (Henry Seidel Canby), and able to refresh such a jaded reviewer as Harry Hansen (Harry Hansen), I will horn in with two fingers and point out that the old bunkum is still the cat's eyebrows.

Herrmann thought the plot was "founded on a trick, a chain of feeble attempts at character sketching." The theme was inconsequential, he went on, and the descriptions "beatific." It would be a best seller only "because there is nothing new about it and readers have gotten used to it." But Herrmann scored the critics for heaping undeserved praise on what was, in his view, a failure.

Fortunately, Herrmann's view was in the minority. . . . On May 7, 1928, [Thornton Wilder] won his first Pulitzer Prize.

The Bridge of San Luis Rey: A Christian Novel

M.C. Kuner

Although Brother Juniper, the Franciscan friar who narrates The Bridge, misses the point of God's purpose, the book is built on Christian themes, declares M.C. Kuner, an associate professor of English at Hunter College in New York. In this excerpt from her book Thornton Wilder: The Bright and the Dark, she traces such Christian principles as the significance of suffering and the acceptance of the will of God. In The Bridge, Wilder examines every kind of love, she notes, but the impure human loves are finally filtered out to lead the bridge's victims to agape, the kind of love God has for people.

The Bridge of San Luis Rey can most correctly be characterized as a Christian novel in that it deals with themes and ideas that are part of the Christian faith. For example, what might be regarded as failure in the eyes of the world may, in fact, be success in the judgment of God. Suffering, which so often seems pointless, may have a significance, although we apprehend it only "through a glass, darkly." Thus Part One is entitled "Perhaps an Accident"; Part Five, "Perhaps an Intention." What looks like happenstance may indeed have a design to it, but one cannot be sure; hence the "perhaps." As Wilder himself has explained it, it is the "magic unity of purpose and chance, destiny and accident, that I have tried to describe in my books."

Other traditional Christian themes abound. There is value in suffering as a means of transforming character and ennobling it. Not, it must be added, the passive kind that turns a human being into an unthinking slave, but rather the willingness to recognize that pain and death are threads in the tapestry of life. We cannot avoid them, but we can use

From *Thornton Wilder: The Bright and the Dark*, by Mildred Kuner. Copyright © 1972 by Mildred Kuner. Reprinted by permission of HarperCollins Publishers, Inc.

them to enrich the pattern of our existence. . . . Wilder stands midway between those writers of the past who accepted their religion more or less unquestioningly ("Whatever is, is right") and those of his own day who relegated faith to the junk-heap of superstition. Perhaps Arthur Koestler, in his novel *The Age of Longing*, summed up the problem best [the italics in the quotation have been added]:

> Some people suffer and become saints. Others, by the same experience, are turned into brutes thirsting for vengeance. Others, just into neurotics. *To draw spiritual nourishment from suffering, one must be endowed with the right kind of digestive system.* Otherwise suffering turns sour on one. It was bad policy on the part of God to inflict suffering indiscriminately. It was like ordering laxatives for every kind of disease.

By and large, the people who most interest Wilder and the characters he most favors in his books are those with "the right kind of digestive system." Possibly it is his concentration on this category of human being (as contrasted, say, with such writers as François Mauriac or Graham Greene, who focus on those who have turned sour) that sometimes makes Wilder's philosophy seem too Pollyana-ish and his work too bland. Certainly the serenity of his point of view is in sharp conflict with the kind of novel that was being written in 1927, an age deeply preoccupied with the "lost generation."

DEATH AND ISOLATION

If suffering, however, is to be seen in its positive aspects, another element must accompany it: resignation, the acceptance of the will of God. Consequently, although death comes to the leading characters of *The Bridge* (in fact, death occupies the foreground of all Wilder's novels and plays), suicide seldom makes its appearance. For death belongs to the natural order of things, whereas suicide, the final act of defiant despair, disturbs the pattern. (Marcantonio of *The Cabala* is one of the few who takes this route.) Although the characters have known despair that has brought them to the brink of self-destruction, when death finds them on the bridge they have overcome their agony and look forward to a new and better life. Having discovered the noblest portion of their natures when they were under stress, they really have, artistically speaking, no further reason to survive. They have fulfilled their destiny.

Because so much of the novel deals with the theme of suffering, it necessarily explores its concomitant, loneliness. All the characters in *The Bridge* are, in one way or another, isolated: from God, from society, from relatives, from friends, from lovers. Even when they are most surrounded by groups of people, they are most conscious of their alienation. The Marquesa is abandoned by her daughter, whom she loves; Esteban and Manuel, twin brothers, are orphans who have neither family nor friends; Pepita, who dies with the Marquesa, is also alone in the world; and Uncle Pio and the little boy, Jaime, have little beyond each other. Like Christ, praying alone in the Garden of Gethsemane, forgotten by disciples who were too tired to keep watch with Him, those on the bridge live out their days forgotten by their fellows. But when they understand and accept the fact that loneliness is the natural condition (in the words of a character in T.S. Eliot's *The Cocktail Party,* "Hell is oneself, Hell is alone, the other figures in it merely projections. . . . One is always alone."), they begin to appreciate their common humanity. And at the same time they learn the name of the only cure for their loneliness—a love that transcends self.

A Useful Technique for Serious Themes

Though Wilder, when he wrote this novel, was only thirty, he had already developed a technique that was going to prove increasingly useful in giving shape to his major ideas. In such widely divergent future novels as *Heaven's My Destination* and *The Ides of March,* in plays like *Our Town* and *The Skin of Our Teeth,* he simply refines what he is doing in *The Bridge.* The themes in *The Bridge* are serious, transcendental. The content is religious, philosophical. From a practical point of view, these elements are not going to send the average reader rushing to buy the book. So Wilder's style becomes simple, unadorned; more important, he juxtaposes theological problems with everyday activities. For example, he spends some time describing the bridge physically: how well it is built, of what it is made, how proud the people are of its fame. It is quite important as a utilitarian object. We are so lulled by the ordinary, it seems so much part of our own lives, that we look no further. And when we have become comfortable with its familiar things, suddenly they turn into something else and become metaphysical symbols. That is why *Our Town,* which has a great deal to say about abstract subjects, is so convincing in its concentration on detail. And again, in *The Ides of March,* where Wilder raises questions that go far beyond the world of Julius Caesar, he surrounds these questions with the trivia of gossip, domestic intrigue, all the petty considerations of our daily routine had we been Romans. But this is not a mere literary device that Wilder employs to popularize his work: it springs from a belief that is characteristic of his temperament. One's immortal soul and one's laundry *have* to be considered simultaneously.

BROTHER JUNIPER

Like *The Eighth Day,* written forty years later, *The Bridge* opens with a calm recitation of a disaster—the death of five people caused by the collapse of a bridge. Significantly, the day on which it happens is Friday, Passion Day; the time is exactly noon—both hands of the clock pointing up. The faceless narrator tells us that everyone is deeply upset by the tragedy, though he cannot understand why, since people have accepted all sorts of other misfortunes with equanimity: tidal waves, earthquakes, crumbling towers. But there was something different, something special about this bridge, and so a little Franciscan friar, who "accidentally" happened to be in Peru at that time converting the Indians and who has witnessed the misfortune, decides to investigate the reason for it. It is Brother Juniper who initiates the first part, "Perhaps an Accident," for by discovering why those particular five people were the victims he believes he can prove that the universe operates according to a plan. Rather delightfully, Wilder gives us a brief sketch of the little Franciscan, who sees no reason why theology cannot be an exact science, like mathematics. . . .

As he is described, Brother Juniper hardly seems an Italian Catholic: he sounds much more like Wilder's analysis of an American Protestant: "There is no limit to the degree with which an American is imbued with the doctrine of progress. Place and environment are but décor to his journey. . . . He is what he is because his plans characterize him." This evaluation, made by the author twenty-five years after *The Bridge* was written, is still correct. Despite the general corruption, the economic inequities, the political ignorance, and the military tragedies to be found in certain Asiatic countries, the simple act of getting the population to vote—

whether or not it understands what it is doing—proves to many Americans that democracy is at work. (It was precisely this simplistic view of life that exasperated Charles Dickens a century before in *Martin Chuzzlewit.*) Few American writers, however severely they criticize their native land, do it as subtly, as gracefully, and as ironically as Wilder.

He has a little more fun with Brother Juniper in another capacity. Since the Franciscan looks upon it as his life's work to "justify the ways of God to man," he is forever keeping records, like a schoolteacher giving his students grades. He has, for instance, "a complete record of the Prayers for Rain and their results" (Americans are nothing if not pragmatists!). When the pestilence destroys a large number of peasants, he "secretly drew up a diagram of the characteristics of fifteen victims and fifteen survivors. . . . Each soul was rated upon a basis of ten as regards its goodness, its diligence in religious observance, and its importance to its family group." The only trouble is that after Brother Juniper finishes adding and subtracting and juggling his figures and statistics, he estimates "that the dead were five times more worth saving" than those who lived! He is badly shaken by the knowledge that "the discrepancy between faith and the facts is greater than is generally realized." George Brush is going to be shocked by the same discovery in *Heaven's My Destination.*

Yet while he has been busy collecting all the data about those who perished, Brother Juniper, a kind of eighteenth-century human computer, never really learns much about the five people he has studied. He gathers all the proper information, but what evades him is the central passion of their lives. At this point the narrator intrudes on the story and asks: "And I, who claim to know so much more, isn't it possible that even I have missed the very spring within the spring?" For the truth is, all human existence is a mystery, and no one can know everything about everyone. And even if one could, one could never understand the clockwork complications of the soul. The narrator concludes the first part:

> Some say that we shall never know and that to the gods we are like the flies that the boys kill on a summer day, and some say, on the contrary, that the very sparrows do not lose a feather that has not been brushed away by the finger of God.

THE VICTIMS

. . . The next three parts of *The Bridge* take up the lives of the people who were killed. The Marquesa de Montemayor, a middle-aged woman who has made an unhappy marriage, turns to her daughter, Doña Clara, as substitute for her lost emotional life and pours all her love out on the girl. Doña Clara, like James Blair in *The Cabala,* is a frigid young person with no love to give; further, she despises her mother's excessive demonstrations of affection. As quickly as she can she marries a Spanish grandee and returns with him to his home in Spain, leaving her mother in Peru. The Marquesa has only one outlet for her feelings: she turns to writing letters to her daughter as a means of binding them together, for literature "is the notation of the heart.". . .

Because of the Marquesa's loneliness the Abbess Madre Maria del Pilar sends a young girl, Pepita, to keep her company. Pepita loves the Abbess, suffers at leaving the convent, is unhappy with the Marquesa, and longs to return. She goes so far as to write a letter to the Abbess begging that she be allowed to come back—but she never sends the letter, for she knows that the best proof she can give the Abbess of her love is to do as she is bidden. In Pepita's love there is both self-discipline and self-sacrifice. The Marquesa, coming upon the letter "accidentally," understands for the first time how selfish her love for her daughter had been, how strong an element there was of a wish to dominate, to impress. . . .

The next section concerns the twin brothers Esteban and Manuel, who were abandoned as babies at the convent run by the Abbess. As they grow up they become more and more isolated from the world, more and more dependent on each other. They even have the knack of anticipating each other's wishes and wants without the need for speech. Between them there exists the bond that is lacking between the Marquesa and her daughter. But while the Marquesa is gradually moving in the direction of unselfish love, the love between the brothers, already too extreme, is tarnished by the intrusion of La Perichole, who arouses the passion of both brothers and for the first time awakens jealousy in their breasts.

Though Manuel and Esteban sincerely love each other, it is Manuel who feels more deeply. Recognizing that Esteban is suffering (La Perichole favors Manuel largely because he is a scribe who writes letters for her), Manuel gives her up.

Before long he has an accident, contracts a fever from an infected foot, and in his delirium cries out his love for La Perichole. Although Esteban has profited from his brother's sacrificial gesture of renunciation, he is plagued by guilt; when Manuel dies Esteban's collapse is so total that he refuses to be himself any longer and pretends that he is Manuel. . . . Esteban's moment of illumination comes when he realizes that self-destruction is not the answer. And at that moment of grace he crosses the bridge. . . .

The last section dealing with the other two victims is perhaps the least interesting, partly because of the characters, partly because Wilder has already made his point clearly enough and here simply repeats himself. Uncle Pio, alone in the world, has taken La Perichole into his profession and made a great actress out of her. She is a coarse, ignorant, vulgar woman; love, for her, is defined exclusively through sex. After a successful stage career and an interlude as the Viceroy's mistress, by whom she has three children, she leaves the stage. At the same time she suddenly discovers a craving for virtue and becomes more pious and proper than the most dedicated churchwoman. Finally she wearies of even this pose and embarks on a series of futile, furtive affairs.

Over the years Uncle Pio has learned something from his life and his amours: he never again "regarded any human being, from a prince to a servant, as a mechanical object." But not so Camilla, La Perichole. When he tells her of his devotion and wishes they could go away to some island where "the people would know [her] and love [her] for" herself, she laughs at him. "There is no such thing as that kind of love and that kind of island. It's in the theatre you find such things." La Perichole has never known real love. But she *has* known real art. And that, too, is a bridge.

Camilla and Uncle Pio drift apart until he discovers, again "accidentally," that she has been stricken with smallpox, and although she survives the disease, she loses all her beauty, of which she had been so vain. With its passing she knows that love will also die, for she had never been able to separate her beauty from the responses it evoked in her admirers: who could love her now that she was ugly and disfigured? And here the narrator interrupts to define the limitations of passion:

> Though it expends itself in generosity and thoughtfulness,
> though it give birth to visions and to great poetry, [it] remains

among the sharpest expressions of self-interest. Not until it has passed through a long servitude, through its own self-hatred, through mockery, through great doubts, can it take its place among the loyalties.

Uncle Pio, recognizing Camilla's complete spiritual shipwreck and anxious to salvage her little boy, Jaime, pleads with her to give the boy to him for a year. He loves Jaime, he wants to teach him, to raise him. And for the first time Camilla has an unselfish emotion: she consents to give the child up for his own good. Jaime will make a fresh start, Uncle Pio can renew himself in the boy, the future seems bright. As they draw near the bridge Uncle Pio tells Jaime that when they cross it "they would sit down and rest, but it turned out not to be necessary."

At the end of the novel Brother Juniper, having amassed all the necessary facts, which only baffle him since the key to the puzzle is missing, writes his book. The inferences he draws are confusing. Pepita was a good child, so was Jaime. Therefore the accident called the young to Heaven while they were still pure. On the other hand, Uncle Pio had led a dissolute life and the Marquesa was an avaricious drunkard. Therefore the accident punished the wicked. But how could the same accident perform two such different functions? In the midst of the friar's bafflement his book catches the eye of certain judges, who decide poor Brother Juniper is guilty of heresy because he has presumed to explain God's plan. As he sits in his cell awaiting punishment in the flames, he ponders over the riddle, anxious to find some meaning in his own demise, which would not be unwelcome if it brought some illumination. But he never finds the answer he is seeking; he simply calls upon St. Francis (feeling too inferior to invoke God at the moment of death), and leans upon a flame and dies, smiling.

FINDING THE MEANING

The funeral of the victims on the bridge brings together all those who were left behind. The Marquesa's daughter visits the Abbess, showing her mother's last letter and her transformation. La Perichole visits the Abbess and tells her of Esteban, Pepita, Uncle Pio, and Jaime. Before their deaths the five characters had, in Catholic terms, entered a state of grace, and by their deaths they have transformed those whom they loved. It does not matter that in a little while no one will remember them. For the Abbess knows:

. . . soon we shall die and all memory of those five will have left the earth, and we ourselves shall be loved for a while and forgotten. But the love will have been enough; all those impulses of love return to the love that made them. Even memory is not necessary for love. There is a land of the living and a land of the dead and the bridge is love, the only survival, the only meaning.

Every type of love is scrutinized in this novel: primitive sexual love, exaggerated fraternal love, one-sided mother love. All are, in one way or another, impure. But all pass through a kind of filter that drains off the dross, and what is left is the Christian *agape*—people loving each other in the same way God loves them. . . .

So, although Brother Juniper did not prove to his satisfaction that there was any design in the fall of the bridge, or in the deaths of the five who were present, those who read the book know that there was a meaning in these events, after all. By laying the story before us, the narrator enables us to see further than Brother Juniper, even as God, the Narrator, can see beyond us. It is safe to say that those with religious beliefs feel buttressed by *The Bridge of San Luis Rey;* those without them remain politely skeptical. For this is the final lesson of the novel: that faith has nothing to do with reason. If Brother Juniper had accepted instead of trying to prove, he would never have needed to write his book. And so need never have died.

QUESTIONING NIHILISM

It makes small sense, then, to quarrel with the book's theology, as some critics have done, a few arguing that every incident tries so hard to pile up proof of the "intention" that the book collapses, like the bridge, under such an artificial weight of evidence. . . . On its own terms *The Bridge* works; its very timelessness, its suspension in space, may in fact allow it to endure longer than other works of a different cast published during the same period—for example, the once-relevant, newspaperlike novels of John Dos Passos. It is almost as though Wilder had examined the exiles inhabiting the universe of Ernest Hemingway's *The Sun Also Rises,* the idle and the sybaritic who waft through F. Scott Fitzgerald's *The Great Gatsby,* the poor and the outcast who populate Sidney Kingsley's *Dead End,* and said, "Yes, there is death; yes, there is boredom; yes, there is poverty and despair. But are you quite sure there is nothing else?" While most

American writers of the time were busy showing the reading public an earth cut off from the light by a moral or economic eclipse, Wilder was gently reminding us that the sun was still there and that the darkness would have to pass for the simple reason that Nature had so ordained it. *The Bridge of San Luis Rey* remains a tribute to its author's particular vision, his uncompromising integrity as an artist, and—a peculiarly American virtue—his rugged individualism.

Wilder's Intent in *The Bridge of San Luis Rey*

Malcolm Goldstein

Malcolm Goldstein has written on drama and theater subjects ranging from Restoration drama to George S. Kaufman; he is also the author of *The Political Stage: American Drama and Theater of the Great Depression.* In this excerpt from his book *The Art of Thornton Wilder*, Goldstein discusses *The Bridge of San Luis Rey*, including the reasons Wilder set it in eighteenth-century Peru. He finds that *The Bridge* offers a philosophy that focuses on the individual—one that he says has been missed by those readers and critics who see in it a presentation of Christian themes.

The history of *The Bridge of San Luis Rey* . . . has included two Hollywood productions, a television adaptation, and continuous availability in a variety of hardcover and softbound printings, in addition to the Pulitzer Prize. From the outset, it has been a popular favorite.

Turning away from the modern world for the time being, Wilder set his new novel in eighteenth-century Peru. The setting is so distant from the areas explored by most of the established writers of the 1920's that Wilder's reasons for choosing it have frequently come under question. This was, after all, the decade when Willa Cather's tough-minded novels of the prairies and the Southwest were achieving the status of minor classics as soon as published, when Sinclair Lewis, for all his roughness of style, reached the best-seller lists with each novel of the Midwest, and when even the expatriates Ernest Hemingway and Gertrude Stein wrote with a patently deep attachment to their homeland. In attempting to account for Wilder's neglect of America in his fiction, Malcolm Cowley has suggested that, unlike his famous contemporaries, he has never lived long enough in any one region to put down roots in American soil.[1] He had spent his formative years not in one or (like Willa Cather) two places, but in Wisconsin, California, China, and California again, and having so many homes, he has none so distinctly his that it could serve as a base upon which to erect a fictional image of his country. . . .

MAKING USE OF HIS LEARNING

Of nearly equal consequence in the making of *The Bridge* was the range and continuity of Wilder's learning. As both an instinctive and academic scholar, he was inevitably persuaded by his researches to give them shape in his fiction. His recent study in Romance languages at Princeton makes itself apparent in *The Bridge*, through allusions to Spanish literature of the Golden Age, through his fashioning of one character, the Marquesa de Montemayor, upon the personality and literary pursuits of Mme. de Sévigné, and through the borrowing of another, Camilla Perichole, from Prosper Mérimée's *La Carosse du Saint Sacré*, which also provides the setting. The desire is always present in the scholar to make extensive use of his learning. With Wilder it manifested itself in fiction and drama, not, as with most academic men, in biographical, philological, or critical essays, though the initial impulse is the same for all. Considering this root quality in the scholarly personality, it is reasonable to say that the civilizations which Wilder had studied were as vivid to him as the life of his own time and place. That he had not traveled to Peru was of no consequence to him. Three decades later he remarked to an interviewer from the *Paris Review* that "the journey of the imagination to a remote place is child's play compared to a journey into another time. I've often been in New York, but it's just as preposterous to write about the New York of 1812 as to write about the Incas."[2]

Another influence, apparent in *The Cabala* also, was the humanistic criticism of More and Babbitt.[3] It manifests itself in two aspects of Wilder's art: the absence of violence and squalor and the acceptance of Christian values. In the first and second episodes of *The Cabala* Wilder describes the exotic col-

1. Malcolm Cowley, introduction, *A Thornton Wilder Trio* (New York: Criterion Books, 1956), p. 4.   2. Richard H. Goldstone, "Thornton Wilder," in *Writers at Work: The Paris Review Interviews*, ed. Malcolm Cowley (New York: Viking Press, 1958), pp. 104–105. 3. Paul Elmer More (1864–1937), U.S. essayist and critic, and Irving Babbitt (1865–1933), U.S. educator and critic, were the founders of the modern humanistic movement, which holds that human interests, values, and dignity are paramount and rejects the importance of a belief in God.

oration given to life by troubled belief; although he is sometimes scornful of or impatient with the wrong-headed characters of that novel, his tone is for the most part only mildly
ironic. He treats this subject again in *The Bridge*, but in a quite
different mode. We should note that the setting is a place
where the relationship of God to man made itself felt in all the
details of life, as it does not in twentieth-century America.

FINDING THE SPRING WITHIN THE SPRING

Structurally as well as thematically, *The Bridge of San Luis Rey*
resembles *The Cabala*. Wilder again employs a sketchy fram-
ing story to bring unity to three tales which are only partially
related in content. There are, however, certain differences in
the use of this device in the second novel, but not such as work
to Wilder's advantage. In the frame of *The Bridge*, the function
of Samuele goes to a young, earnest Franciscan friar, Brother
Juniper, who resembles Samuele in his presumptuousness,
but does not narrate the events and does not take part in them.
His presence is little more than an excuse for the three
episodes, and that little serves only to establish his own interpretation of them, which eventually Wilder overthrows in
favor of a superior interpretation. When Brother Juniper, on a
day in 1714, sees an old slat-and-vine bridge near Lima break
and send five travelers to death in the gorge below, he begins
a search through the history of their lives for pieces of evidence that God purposely let them die, for he is certain that the
event is no accident. The five are an old man, a middle-aged
woman, a young man, an adolescent girl, and a little boy.
Unlike the characters of *The Cabala*, they have not all played
important roles in one another's lives, and none has known
the young man who now takes a surpassing interest in them.
Compared to Samuele's old-maidish fussing over the
Cabalists, which in itself contributes abundantly to the theme
of the narrative, Brother Juniper's presence is an ungainly
expository contrivance, and his by-the-book religiosity, weigh-
ing so much good in each victim of the fall against so much
evil, is too obviously unavailing in the search for the meaning
of the disaster.

"Yet for all his diligence," the omniscient author says,
"Brother Juniper never knew the central passion of Doña
Maria's life; nor of Uncle Pio's, not even of Esteban's. And I,
who claim to know so much more, isn't it possible that even I
have missed the very spring within the spring?" Thus taking

the reader into his confidence with the suggestion that any system for measuring the quality of a life is certain to fail, Wilder begins the three short episodes which lead the five travelers up to the fatal moment. He himself does not give a direct interpretation of the event, but leaves it to the reader to discover what common concerns of all five have caused them to walk simultaneously over the bridge to death. In the last pages of the novel the alert reader's findings are given voice by Madre Maria del Pilar, Abbess of the Convent of Santa Maria de las Rosas, the one character who has knowledge of the entire group of victims:

> "Even now," she thought, "almost no one remembers Esteban and Pepita, but myself. Camila alone remembers her Uncle Pio and her son; this woman, her mother. But soon we shall die and all memory of those five will have left the earth, and we ourselves shall be loved for a while and forgotten. But the love will have been enough; all those impulses of love return to the love that made them. Even memory is not necessary for love. There is a land of the living and a land of the dead and the bridge is love, the only survival, the only meaning."

By this time the "spring within the spring" of each life has come to light, and for each it is the same: the desire for love. The episodes demonstrate that the fall of the bridge is actually a spring *into* love; on this point the deliberations of Brother Juniper, as well as the brief first-person comments of the author, are dust thrown into the reader's eyes, as though purposely to make difficult the analysis of a novel which is by no means complex. . . .

In review, the victims of the bridge are these: an old woman whose daughter spurns her affection, an adolescent girl who lives only for the affection of an older woman, a young man whose sole object of love is dead, an old man whose sole object of love has rejected him, and a child whose mother is too self-involved to give him the affection he requires. For one reason or another, each stands apart from human society: two because they are old and unkempt; two because they are orphans; and the fifth because he is chronically ill. And with the exception of Don Jaime, each has added to the barrier between himself and society by failing to respond to any activity which does not involve his beloved. Pepita is at only slightly greater odds with the rest of humanity than Don Jaime, but even she must think constantly of the one person she loves in order to sustain herself, and it is not until she begins to recognize the selfishness inherent in her distress in the Marquesa's household that she is allowed to escape through death. Perhaps it is a flaw in the novel that Don Jaime's life so poorly fits the pattern set by the other characters; yet he resembles them in part by agreeing to leave his mother, the only person whom he adores, and to go down to Lima with Uncle Pio. But, for that matter, Wilder flatly asserts that it is difficult, if not impossible, to find patterns in existence, and Brother Juniper is burned as a heretic for trying to do so.

WHAT MOST READERS—AND CRITICS—MISS

Although *The Bridge of San Luis Rey* is imperfect, its faults are not ruinous. Whatever they may be, they are not caused by such deficiencies in taste and wisdom as are evident in most American religious fiction—the novels of Lloyd C. Douglas provide suitable examples for comparison. *The Bridge* is not sentimental; it offers no promises of earthly rewards and no overestimation of the worth of the characters. Nor does it speak out against active participation in this life in favor of patient waiting for the life to come. Yet, noting that many persons have misunderstood his intention, Wilder has himself remarked: "only one reader in a thousand notices that I have asserted a denial of the survival of identity after death."[4] While it is true, as this comment suggests, that many find the book "inspirational" and read it precisely as they read Bishop Fulton J. Sheen's *Peace of Soul* or Rabbi Joshua Loth Liebmann's *Peace of Mind*, it is difficult to understand how they could be misled. For, far from recommending a narcotic contemplation of the afterlife, Wilder speaks out for the vigorous pursuit of purely human relationships. If the five characters are tragic, they are so not because they die suddenly, or simply because they die, but because they have not truly lived, and at no point are we led to think that they will win the reward of an eventual reunion in heaven with the recipients of the love that for so many years enchained them. Threading through the narrative is the career of the Abbess, whose closeness to the life of Lima and attentiveness to everyday events are a reminder of the indifference of the others to such matters in their pursuit of a single goal. None of the victims escapes the measurement of his personality against that of this very vital woman. The consecration of her life to a program of work for the good of all humanity, involving her in the sacri-

---

4. Wilder to Paul Friedman, undated letter, in Friedman, "The Bridge: A Study in Symbolism," *Psychoanalytic Quarterly*, XXI (Jan. 1952), 72.

fice of Pepita, Manuel, and Esteban, puts to shame the selfishness of the others as it is reflected in their indulgence in the anguish of love. In *The Bridge*, as in *The Cabala* and the major works which followed, Wilder insists that the life that is a rush of unanalyzed activity is as nothing when compared to the life in which the participant allows himself to become fully aware of the meaning of each experience.

Unhappily, Wilder's latter-day critics have served him no better than his most naive readers. Impatient with the slow-moving, aphoristic style and the historical setting, they have looked back on *The Bridge* as a kind of sport among the popular novels of the 1920's and mention it as such if they mention it at all. It is true that this work contrasts bleakly with the naturalistic novels which now seem to be the sum of the literature of the decade, but to admit that fact is not to deny its quality. However much it may differ in technique from the fiction of, say, Hemingway, Fitzgerald, or John Dos Passos, it does not display a soft attitude toward the human condition. At the time of its publication it offered a considerable change in tone from the fast-paced novels of the age, and obviously a welcome change in view of the sales record, but it did not offer easy lessons in contentment.

CHAPTER 4

Pulitzer #2: *Our Town*

Our Town's Big and Little Wheels

Winfield Townley Scott

As *Our Town* begins, writes Winfield Townley Scott, the playwright sets in motion the little wheel of everyday activities in Grover's Corners. The town's inhabitants are interesting and touching because of—rather than in spite of—their symbolic nature. The narrator, who is not bound by time, intersperses his descriptions of the ordinary activities of the scene onstage with mentions of future events, so the audience becomes aware of the turning of the big wheel—time itself, carrying the weight of births, marriages, deaths. At first, Scott points out, only the narrator and the audience are privy to this split view. But when Emily returns from the dead for just one day—"the least important day" in her life—every detail of that day stands out in poignant recognition of the need to live life fully as it happens. Winfield Townley Scott, a reviewer and poet, was literary editor of the *Providence (R.I.) Journal.*

Perhaps the germination of *Our Town* is in the legend Chrysis tells her young men in *The Woman of Andros,* that slender novel of the dying Grecian spirit which Wilder published eight years before his play. Chrysis tells of a dead hero for whom Zeus interceded with the King of the Dead and to whom it was permitted "to live over again that day in all the twenty-two thousand days of his lifetime that had been least eventful; but that it must be with a mind divided into two persons,—the participant and the onlooker: the participant who does the deeds and says the words of so many years before, and the onlooker who foresees the end. So the hero returned to the sunlight and to a certain day in his fifteenth year."

From "*Our Town* and the Golden Veil," by Winfield Townley Scott, *Virginia Quarterly Review*, Winter 1953. Reprinted with permission.

" 'My friends,' continued Chrysis, turning her eyes slowly from face to face, 'as he awoke in his boyhood's room, pain filled his heart,—not only because it had started beating again, but because he saw the walls of his home and knew that in a moment he would see his parents who lay long since in the earth of that country. He descended into the courtyard. His mother lifted her eyes from the loom and greeted him and went on with her work. His father passed through the court unseeing, for on that day his mind had been full of care. Suddenly the hero saw that the living too are dead and that we can only be said to be alive in those moments when our hearts are conscious of our treasure; for our hearts are not strong enough to love every moment. And not an hour had gone by before the hero *who was both watching life and living it* called on Zeus to release him from so terrible a dream. The gods heard him, but before he left he fell upon the ground and kissed the soil of the world that is too dear to be realized.' "

At *Our Town* the audience is the resurrected hero.

Birth; marriage; death: these are the respective keynotes of the three acts as they are of most lives. In Act I, birth is used only as a momentary tone and for its symbolic sake: Dr. Gibbs is on his way home at dawn from delivering, "easy as kittens," Mrs. Goruslawski's twins. Wilder extends the symbol of birth to compose an innocent picture of ordinary daily life, the seemingly unimportant trivia of the middleclass at school, at its jobs, at church, and in its homes in a New England small town. Here are a group of people and their relationships. He gives us, in Robert Hillyer's phrase, the "pattern of a day." It is not, on its obvious level, impinged upon by the great—and ordinary—ceremonies which mark Acts II and III.

It is a specific day. The Stage Manager sets it as he will continue to arrange and comment upon everything to follow. It is May 7, 1901. Nearly dawn. We are given the idea of what size and sort of town this is—"Nice town, y' know what I mean?"—and its rhythms begin. The 5:45 to Boston whistles through. Joe Crowell, Jr., starts his rounds delivering Editor Webb's newspaper. Howie Newsome's milk wagon appears—Mrs. Gibbs thinks Howie is a bit late today, which he is: "Somep'n went wrong with the separator." Both Mrs. Webb and Mrs. Gibbs are soon calling upstairs to their youngsters—Wally and Emily Webb, and George and Rebecca

Gibbs—to get a move on, hurry to breakfast and to school: as, one is sure, Mrs. Webb and Mrs. Gibbs holler up every schoolday in the year. And Dr. Gibbs, as I say, is just coming in from delivering Mrs. Goruslawski's twins. With his appearance on stage the scheme of *Our Town* quietly clicks into action. The scheme is hinted, even revealed, a moment or so before; now it really begins.

THE LITTLE WHEEL

As *Our Town* literally begins, Wilder sets in motion the little wheel of daily doings. This is the only wheel there is in most plays and fictions; it turns upon the events presented. So here, it spins with normal activities, the comings and goings and the conversations, weaving a special era and place and a particular people (though by the way I think Mrs. Gibbs and Mrs. Webb should not be stringing beans in early May in New Hampshire); and on through a gentle afternoon to the great moonlighted night of that May 7 and the ladies strolling chattering home from choir practice

This is the realism of the play and, superficially at least, it is very good. That is, these folk may not be deeply imagined but they are typically imagined; it is as types of Americana that they and their Grover's Corners interest us and touch us. They and the town are unremarkable: we are told so and we see that it is so; and this of course is the point. The youngsters with their twenty-five cents spending-money and love of strawberry phosphates and their schoolday affairs, the fathers absorbed in jobs and bringing up these young, the wives similarly absorbed though perhaps a little wistfully aware of larger worlds and startled at just this era that an old highboy might fetch $350 as an antique; yes, we are convinced that this must have been the way it was, and in most essentials still is fifty years later, in that kind of American town. For what the little wheel does in carrying these doings of realism is to give one a sense of changeless-ness from day to day, year to year: mothers and fathers waken early, they rouse children to breakfast and school, a Joe Crowell, Jr., always comes along with the newspaper and Howie Newsome with the milk; there is talk of weather which does change season to season but the changes are regular and assured. Far later in the play the Stage Manager remarks something we have known from the first, and known with an intimate feeling, and are not surprised as he said we would be—"on the whole, things don't change much at Grover's Corners."

Thus this little wheel gives us a sense of timeliness and also, oddly, of timelessness. We are transported back to May 7, 1901. At the same time we sense a certain universality about it; or we sense its *being* as a seemingly permanent thing. And this achievement is the one for which so much writing strives. Nevertheless, we are quickly aware of another dimension which begins to operate when Dr. Gibbs comes on.

We have learned a little earlier that though this is May 7, 1901, in Grover's Corners, New Hampshire, and though the townsman who appears to us as the Stage Manager is there presenting us with this scene and time, he is also existing in our time. He describes stores, streets, schools, churches in the present tense (and this forwards the feeling of changelessness within change as the newly discovered context is revealed), but he suddenly says, "First automobile's going to come along in about five years." And presently: "There's Doc Gibbs comin' down Main Street now. . . . Doc Gibbs died in 1930. The new hospital's named after him. Mrs. Gibbs died first—long time ago in fact. She went out to visit her daughter, Rebecca, who married an insurance man in Canton, Ohio, and died there—pneumonia . . ." and so on. "In our town we like to know the facts about everybody," he sums up matter of factly; and then: "That's Doc Gibbs." And Dr. Gibbs gets into a little gab with Joe Crowell, Jr., just as Mrs. Gibbs is seen entering her kitchen to start breakfast.

THE BIG WHEEL

The whole tone of *Our Town* is understatement. The colloquial run of the talk, its occasional dry wit, the unheroic folk, all contribute to this tone. So does the important admission that this *is* a play: we are not bid to suspend our disbelief in the usual way; and so does the bareboard, undecorated presentation. All is simple, modest, easy, plain. And so, in tone, the Stage Manager's revelation is utterly casual. But with it Wilder sets in counter-motion to the little wheel a big wheel; and as the little one spins the little doings, the big one begins slowly—slowly—for it is time itself, weighted with birth and marriage and death, with aging and with change. This is the great thing that *Our Town* accomplishes; simultaneously we are made aware of what is momentary and what is eternal.

We are involved by the Stage Manager in these presented actions and yet like him we are also apart; we are doubly spectators, having a double vision. We are not asked, as in the presentation of some philosophical concept, to perceive an abstract intellectualism. This is a play—this is art. So we are involved sensually and emotionally. Out of shirt-sleeved methods that would seem to defy all magic, and because of them not in spite of them, Wilder's play soon throttles us with its pathos; convinces and moves us so that we cannot imagine its being done in any other way; assumes a radiant beauty. And indeed we are not taken out of ourselves, we are driven deeper into ourselves. This, we say, is life: apparently monotonous, interminable, safe; really all mutable, brief, and in danger. "My," sighs the dead Mrs. Soames in Act III, "wasn't life awful—and wonderful." For what Wilder's art has reminded us is that beauty is recognizable because of change and life is meaningful because of death.

Later in Act I the Stage Manager deliberately and directly accounts for several future happenings. And again he sums up: "So, friends, this was the way we were in our growing up and in our marrying and in our doctoring and in our living and in our dying." This is the simplest way—and Thornton Wilder can be artfully simple—of saying what *Our Town* is about. It suggests why he chose a spare, documentary style as appropriate to his purpose. But the poetry, so to speak, comes from the juxtaposition of the points of view, human and superhuman, which combine, of course, to a fourth dimension. . . .

LACONIC YANKEE WIT

The wit is Yankee laconic; sometimes so wry you may ask if it is wit. Noting that lights are on in the distant farmhouses while most of Grover's Corners itself is still dark at six o'clock in the morning, the Stage Manager says, "But town people sleep late." It is funny—but is it funny to the Stage Manager? We have no way of knowing that the Stage Manager does not feel that people who don't get up till six-thirty or seven are late sleepers. This is a part of the charm.

The charm does not evade the big and the ephemeral troubles of life, the tears of youth and of age, and the terminal fact of death. As *Our Town* develops, it is more and more incandescent with the charges of change and of ending. There is not in it any of the ugliness present in the small town books I have likened it to: the violence and murder in *Tom Sawyer,* the meannesses and frustrations in *Spoon River Anthology* and *Winesburg, Ohio.* Yet these books also glow with a nostalgic beauty. True, the drunken, disappointed organist would be at home either in Masters' Spoon River or in Robinson's Tilbury Town; and in Act II, at the time of George's wedding, there is the bawdiness of the baseball players which, significantly, the Stage Manager quickly hushes. Brief touches: not much. Nevertheless, I would defend *Our Town* against the instant, obvious question whether Wilder in excluding harsher facts indigenous to life has written a sentimental play, by insisting Wilder would have warped the shape of his plan by such introductions. He was out not to compose a complete small-town history nor, on the other hand, to expose a seamy-sided one; his evident purpose was to dramatize the common essentials of the lives of average people. There are other colors, no doubt more passionate, but they would have deranged this simple purpose which, as I see it, is valid and has been well-served.

I do not know whether a great deal has been written about this play; I happen to have seen only a retrospective note by John Mason Brown. That is chiefly a paean of praise for the durable loveliness of *Our Town,* but Mr. Brown feels that Act III—the death act—loses the universality of the other two by being too colloquial and by serving forth "small ideas." I think this critic, and he is a fine critic, has hit to one side of a target which is there. It is not that Act III has a small idea; it has a very large one—the theory of death which the Stage Manager announces:

"You know as well as I do," he says, "that the dead don't stay interested in us living people for very long. Gradually . . ." and so on: readying us for the indifferent attitude of the dead and for the newly dead Emily's bewildered approach to it. This I would say is neither small nor too colloquial but too easy; it is too major a premise in the play to be tossed in casually. It cannot in itself carry conviction. The colloquialism of Act III, meanwhile, is proper to the tone of all that has gone before. We accept it and, presently, the conception of the dead because of the emotional power of the play's final passages. They throb with an accumulative and transcending strength.

The crisscross of feelings over the wedding in Act II starts the beat of an emotional pulse: the fear and love of the parents, the fear and desire of Emily and George, shudder in terror and wonder. Here is the new adult experience, central to most lives: marriage. It has its humor, for it is common; its pathos, for it is doomed. "No love story," Ernest Hemingway has remarked, "has a happy ending." By a leap of nine years we are plunged directly in Act III to the remaining enormous fact, death: Emily's death, while still young, in her second childbearing; Emily's death a matter of moments, so it seems, after her wedding.

"Things Don't Change Much"

It is twelve years since the literal time of Act I; it is the summer of 1913, and now the play vibrates with its full magic. Once again the Stage Manager sets the scene. He is in the Grover's Corners cemetery, but he lets us know that horses are rarer in the town, Fords frequenter, the youngsters avid for the movies. "Everybody locks their doors now at night. . . . But you'd be surprised though—on the whole, things don't change much at Grover's Corners." We now have the sense of knowing this town and its people a long while. "Here's your friend, Mrs. Gibbs," the Stage Manager says, pacing among the dead on the hill. "Here is Mr. Stimson, organist at the Congregational Church. And over there's Mrs. Soames who enjoyed the wedding so—you remember? . . . And Editor Webb's boy, Wallace . . ." and so on.

Now the "eternal" theme, counterpointed still to the little wheel, is carried by the dead; though with rural chatter. They talk of the weather, of George's barn on his uncle's farm; we discover from mention of Mrs. Gibbs' "legacy" of $350 to George and Emily that she must have sold that highboy she talked about in 1901 and that after all she did not persuade the doctor to travel on the money to Paris, France. Yes, we know them intimately, these emotionless dead and the grieving living townspeople who soon will come bearing young Emily to her grave.

Emily appears, to take her place with the dead. Already she is distant from the mourners, but her discovery that she can "go back" to past time seduces her despite the warnings of the older dead. The ubiquitous Stage Manager, too, can talk with Emily, and what he says to her introduces the summation scene with the keynote of the entire play: "You not only live it," he says, "but you watch yourself living it." Now

Emily, in the yet more poignant way of self-involvement, will achieve that double vision we have had all along; and now we shall be burdened also with her self-involvement.

"And as you watch it," the Stage Manager goes on, "you will see the thing that they—down there—never know. You see the future. You know what's going to happen afterwards."

Then perfectly in key comes Mrs. Gibbs' advice to Emily: "At least, choose an unimportant day. Choose the least important day in your life. It will be important enough." There sound the central chords of the play: the common day and the light of the future.

UNBEARABLE TENSION

Emily chooses her twelfth birthday and the magic begins to mount to almost unbearable tension. Now the Stage Manager repeats his enriched gesture as he announces that it is February 11, 1899, and once again, as we saw him summon it in the same casual way so many years before, the town of Grover's Corners stirs, awakens; a winter morning— Constable Warren, Howie Newsome, Joe Crowell, Jr., making their appearances along Main Street, Mrs. Webb firing the kitchen stove and calling Wally and Emily to breakfast. The little daily rhythms recur, now more touching for the big wheel has become vaster. Now *we* are taken back with Emily's double-awareness accenting our own. Though the then-living are unaware as always, now the golden veil [of nostalgia] shines everywhere, even all around us ourselves. It is a terrific triumph of dramatic method.

"Oh, that's the town I knew as a little girl. And, look, there is the old white fence that used to be around our house. Oh, I'd forgotten that! . . . I can't look at everything hard enough," Emily says. "There's Mr. Morgan's drugstore. And there's the High School, forever and ever, and ever." For her birthday young George Webb has left a postcard album on the doorstep: Emily had forgotten that.

The living cannot hear the dead Emily of fourteen years later, her whole lifetime later. Yet she cries out in the passion, which the play itself performs, to realize life while it is lived: "But, just for a moment now we're all together. Mama, just for a moment we're happy. Let's look at one another." And when offstage her father's voice is heard a second time calling, "Where's my girl? Where's my birthday girl?" Emily breaks. She flees back through the future, back to the patient and disinterested dead: "Oh," she says of life, "it goes so fast. We don't have time to look at one another."

Here if the play is to get its proper and merited response there is nothing further to say of it: one simply weeps.

It is thus, finally, that Emily can say farewell to the world— that is, to Grover's Corners. Night, now; the night after Emily's burial. The big wheel of the mutable universe turns almost alone. The Stage Manager notices starlight and its "millions of years," but time ticks eleven o'clock on his watch and the town, though there, is mostly asleep, as he dismisses us for "a good rest, too."

The aptest thing ever said about *Tom Sawyer* was said by the author himself and applies as nicely to *Our Town*. Mark Twain said his book was "a hymn."

A Contemporary Review

Mary McCarthy

Novelist Mary McCarthy (*The Company She Keeps, A Charmed Life*) was the radical *Partisan Review*'s theater critic–a job that was hers at first, she says, "because I had been married to an actor." In her review of *Our Town*, McCarthy says the play is innovative, intense, and poignant.

Mr. Thornton Wilder's play, . . . *Our Town*, like *Ah, Wilderness*, is an exercise in memory, but it differs from the O'Neill work in that it is not a play in the accepted sense of the term. It is essentially lyric, not dramatic. The tragic velocity of life, the elusive nature of experience, which can never be stopped or even truly felt at any given point, are the themes of the play— themes familiar enough in lyric poetry, but never met, except incidentally, in drama. Mr. Wilder, in attempting to give these themes theatrical form, was obliged, paradoxically, to abandon almost all the conventions of the theatre.

In the first place, he has dismissed scenery and props as irrelevant to, and, indeed, incongruous with his purpose. In the second place, he has invented the character of the stage manager, an affable, homespun conjuror who holds the power of life and death over the other characters, a local citizen who is in the town and outside of it at the same time. In the third place, he has taken what is accessory to the ordinary play, that is, exposition, and made it the main substance of his. The greater part of the first two acts is devoted to the imparting of information, to situating the town in time, space, politics, sociology, economics, and geology. But where in the conventional play, such pieces of information are insinuated into the plot or sugared over with stage business and repartee, in Mr. Wilder's play they are communicated directly; they take the place of plot, stage business, and

From *Sights and Spectacles, 1937–1956,* by Mary McCarthy (New York: Farrar, Straus & Cudahy, 1956). Reprinted by permission of the Mary McCarthy Literary Trust. Subheadings in this reprint have been added by Greenhaven editors.

repartee. Mr. Craven himself tells the biographies of the townspeople; he calls in an expert from the state college to give a scientific picture of the town, and the editor of the local newspaper to describe its social conditions. The action which is intermittently progressing on the stage merely illustrates Mr. Craven's talk.

RAISING THE DEAD

Mr. Wilder's fourth innovation is the most striking. In order to dramatize his feelings about life he has literally raised the dead. At the opening of the third act a group of people are discovered sitting in rows on one side of the stage; some of the faces are familiar, some are new. They are speaking quite naturally and calmly, and it is not until one has listened to them for some minutes that one realizes that this is the cemetery and these are the dead. A young woman whom we have seen grow up and marry the boy next door has died in childbirth; a small shabby funeral procession is bringing her to join her relatives and neighbors. Only when she is actually buried does the play proper begin. She has not yet reached the serenity of the long dead, and she yearns to return to the world. With the permission of the stage manager and against the advice of the dead, she goes back—to a birthday of her childhood. Hardly a fraction of that day has passed, however, before she retreats gratefully to the cemetery, for she has perceived that the tragedy of life lies in the fragmentary and imperfect awareness of the living.

Mr. Wilder's play is, in a sense, a refutation of its own thesis. *Our Town* is purely and simply an act of awareness, a demonstration of the fact that in a work of art, at least, experience *can* be arrested, imprisoned, and preserved. The perspective of death, which Mr. Wilder has chosen, gives an extra poignancy and intensity to the small-town life whose essence he is trying so urgently to communicate. The little boy delivering papers, for example, becomes more touching, more meaningful and important, when Mr. Craven announces casually that he is going to be killed in the War. The boy's morning round, for the spectator, is transfigured into an absorbing ritual; the unconsciousness of the character has heightened the consciousness of the audience. The perspective is, to be sure, hazardous: it invites bathos and sententiousness. Yet Mr. Wilder has used it honorably. He forbids the spectator to dote on that town of the past. He is

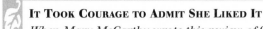

IT TOOK COURAGE TO ADMIT SHE LIKED IT

When Mary McCarthy wrote this review of Our Town, *she was, in her own words, "a young, earnest, pedantic, pontificating critic"—yet she was also unsure about her own feelings. She was taken aback by the fact that she enjoyed Wilder's highly successful play, as she explains here.*

It is the voice of a period, as well as that of a person. The period was 1937. The place was downtown, in the old Bible House on Astor Place, where *Partisan Review,* a radical literary magazine, had just opened its offices, after a break with the Communist Party over the Moscow Trials. The young men who were editing the new magazine, except one (the backer) were Marxists. I was not one, but I took my line, as well as I could, from them. We automatically suspected any commercial success, any *succès d'estime;* this, I fear, was my guiding critical principle. I remember how uneasy I felt when I decided that I *liked* Thornton Wilder's *Our Town.* Could this mean that there was something the matter with me? Was I starting to sell out? Such haunting fears, like the fear of impotence in men, were common in the avant-garde in those days. The safest position was to remain always on the attack.

Mary McCarthy, *Sights and Spectacles, 1937–1956.* New York: Farrar, Straus and Cudahy, 1956.

concerned only with saying: this is how it was, though then we did not know it. Once in a while, of course, his memory fails him, for young love was never so baldly and tritely gauche as his scene in the soda fountain suggests. This is, however, a deficiency of imagination, not an error of taste; and except in the third act, where the dead give some rather imprecise and inapposite definitions of the nature of the afterlife, the play keeps its balance beautifully. In this feat of equilibrium Mr. Wilder has had the complete cooperation of Mr. Craven, the serene, inexorable matter-of-factness of whose performance acts as a discipline upon the audience. Mr. Craven makes one quite definitely homesick, but pulls one up sharp if one begins to blubber about it.

CHAPTER 5

Pulitzer #3: *The Skin of Our Teeth*

Comparing *Finnegans Wake* with *The Skin of Our Teeth*

Joseph Campbell and Henry Morton Robinson

Joseph Campbell and Henry Morton Robinson had been working on a "key" to James Joyce's *Finnegans Wake* for three years when *The Skin of Our Teeth* opened in New York. They found many similarities in the two works, some of which they spelled out in articles in the December 19, 1942, and February 13, 1943, issues of *Saturday Review of Literature*. They stopped short of accusing Wilder of plagiarism, and indeed seemed unsure how to characterize their discovery at first, but the articles raised a storm of controversy that resulted in a flurry of essays and letters in several magazines. Wilder, like Campbell and Robinson, had been studying and lecturing on parts of *Finnegans Wake* for some time (he had delivered an hour-and-a-half lecture on seven pages of the book), but it is safe to say that few of those who joined the fray on either side had read more than a few sentences of that difficult volume. Campbell and Robinson's *Skeleton Key to Finnegans Wake* was published in 1961. Robinson also wrote a novel, *The Great Snow*, and *Fantastic Interim*, a look at recent American history. Campbell has written and edited many books on myth, religion, and philosophy, including *The Hero with a Thousand Faces* and *The Masks of God*.

While thousands cheer, no one has yet pointed out that Mr. Thornton Wilder's exciting play, *The Skin of Our Teeth*, is not an entirely original creation, but an Americanized re-creation, thinly disguised, of James Joyce's *Finnegans Wake*. Mr. Wilder himself goes out of his way to wink at the knowing one or two in the audience, by quoting from and actually naming some of his characters after the main figures of Joyce's masterpiece. Important plot elements, characters, devices of presentation, as well as major themes and many of the speeches, are directly and frankly imitated, with but the flimsiest veneer to lend an American touch to the original features.

The Skin of Our Teeth takes its circular form from *Finnegans Wake*, closing and opening with the cycle-renewing river-running thought-stream of the chief female character. The main divisions of the play are closed by periodic catastrophes (ice-age, deluge, war), devices which are borrowed from the cosmic dissolutions of *Finnegans Wake*. Furthermore, Mr. Antrobus, Thornton Wilder's hero, is strangely reminiscent of Joyce's protagonist, H.C. Earwicker, "that homogenius man," who has endured throughout all the ages of the world, though periodically overwhelmed by floods, wars, and other catastrophes. The activities, talents, and troubles of the two characters have significant resemblances. In both works they are Adam, All-Father of the world. They are tireless inventors and land-conquerors; both are constantly sending communiques back home; both run for election, broadcast to the world, and are seen in television. Moreover, their characters have been impugned. In each case the hero repudiates the charges against him, but the secret guilt which each seeks to hide is constantly betrayed by slips of the tongue. To add to the long list of similarities, both are seduced under extenuating circumstances by a couple of temptresses, and are forever "raping home" the women of the Sabines.

Sabine leads both authors to Sabina, the name of Mr. Wilder's housekeeper, who has been "raped home" by Mr. Antrobus from one of his war expeditions. Her prototype is the garrulous housekeeper of *Finnegans Wake*. "He raped her home," says Joyce, "Sabrine asthore, in a parakeet's cage, by dredgerous lands and devious delts." To this delicious Joycean line Mr. Wilder is apparently indebted for his rape theme and the name of the Antrobus housekeeper.

The conversation between Mrs. Antrobus and Sabina in Act I carries the lilt of the Anna Livia Plurabelle chapter, and rehearses some of its themes, notably the patience of the wife while younger love beguiles her husband; and again, the little feminine attentions lavished on the man while he broods in melancholy.

The wonderful letter which the wife of Mr. Antrobus throws into the ocean at the close of Act II—that letter which would have told him all the secrets of her woman's heart and would have revealed to him the mystery of why the universe was set in motion—is precisely the puzzling missive of *Finnegans Wake*, tossed into the sea, buried in the soil, ever-awaited, ever half-found, ever reinterpreted, misinterpreted, multifariously over-and-under interpreted, which continually twinkles, with its life-riddle, through every page of Joyce's work.

In Mr. Wilder's play, the wife's name is Maggy—which is one of her names in *Finnegans Wake*. She has borne innumerable children—again see *Finnegans Wake*. Her daughter aspires to powder and rouge and fancies herself in silks (*Finnegans Wake*). The two sons, Cain and Abel, the abominated and the cherished, supply a fratricidal battle-theme that throbs through the entire play, precisely as it does in *Finnegans Wake*. Cain in both works is a peeping-tom and publisher of forbidden secrets. In Mr. Wilder's work he spies on and speaks out about the love-makings in the beach cabana. In Joyce's, he tattles the whole story of the love life of his parents.

The ingenious and very amusing scene at the close of Act I in which Tallulah Bankhead turns to the audience and begs for wood—chairs, bric-a-brac, anything at all—with which to feed the fire that will preserve humanity during the approaching ice-age, is a clever re-rendering of a passage in *Finnegans Wake*. In Joyce's work, when elemental catastrophe has almost annihilated mankind, the heroine goes about gathering into her knapsack various odds and ends, to be reanimated by the fire of life. As Joyce puts it: "She'll loan a vesta (*i.e.*, borrow a light), and hire some peat and sarch the shores her cockles to heat and she'll do all a turfwoman can . . . to puff the blaziness on." Mr. Wilder here follows Joyce's lead even to the point of having his actress borrow a light with which to ignite the preserving hearth.

There are, in fact, no end of meticulous unacknowledged copyings. At the entrance of Mr. Antrobus, for instance: his terrific banging at the door duplicates the fantastic thumpings of Joyce's hero at the gate of his own home where he is arrested for thus disturbing the peace of the whole community. The great swathing of scarfs and wrappings, which Mr. Antrobus removes when he comes in, follows the mode of Joyce's hero who is characteristically enveloped in no end of costumery. In the famous passage [in *Finnegans Wake*], HCE is seen in heaped-up attire: "caoutchouc kepi and great belt and hideinsacks and his blaufunx fustian and ironsides jackboots and Bhagafat gaiters and his rubberized inverness." Perhaps the chief difference between the protean HCE and the rigid Mr. Antrobus is revealed when the latter's wrappings are removed, leaving only a thin reminder of Joyce's grotesque folk-hero.

Throughout the work there are innumerable minor parallelisms. The razzing which Mr. Antrobus endures at the Shriner's Convention repeats the predicament of H.C. Earwicker throughout Book II, Chapter III. "The Royal Divorce" theme of *Finnegans Wake* reappears in the wish of Mr. Antrobus to be divorced from his wife. Neither of the heroes achieves his end; the wish itself being liquidated by catastrophe. The fortune-teller in Act II plays the role of Joyce's heroine, A.L.P., who assigns to all at the Masquerade the tokens of their fate. Later Mr. Wilder's gypsy coaches the seductress of Mr. Antrobus, just as "Grandma Grammar" in *Finnegans Wake* teaches Isabelle how to "decline and conjugate" young men. Trivia-wise, the key-word "commodius" occurs in the second line of *Finnegans Wake* and within the first two minutes of *The Skin of Our Teeth.* Finally, at the end of Mr. Wilder's play, the Hours pass across the stage intoning sublime instructions. This is a device conspicuous both in *Ulysses* and in *Finnegans Wake.* Many further similarities could be cited.

It is a strange performance that Mr. Wilder has turned in. Is he hoaxing us? On the one hand, he gives no credit to his source, masking it with an Olsen and Johnson technique. On the other hand, he makes no attempt to conceal his borrowings, emphasizing them rather, sometimes even stressing details which with a minimum of ingenuity he could have suppressed or altered. But if puzzlement strikes us here, it grows when we consider the critics—those literary advisors who four years ago dismissed *Finnegans Wake* as a literary abortion not worth the modern reader's time, yet today hail with rave-notices its Broadway reaction. The banquet was rejected but the Hellzapoppin's scrap that fell from the table they clutch to their bosom. Writes Alexander Woollcott, "Thornton Wilder's dauntless and heartening comedy stands head and shoulders above anything ever written for our stage." And why not, since in inception and detail the work springs from that "dauntless and heartening" genius, James Joyce!

Editor's note: *When Campbell and Robinson wrote their first article on the similarities between* The Skin of Our Teeth *and* Finnegans Wake, *they had only seen Wilder's play in the theater. After the book version of the play was published, they were more easily able to study it for similarities to Joyce's novel. In this second article, published two months after the first, their disapproval verges on outrage.*

"There are certain charges that ought not to be made, and I think I may add, ought not to be allowed to be made" (*The Skin of Our Teeth*).

"There are certain statements which ought not to be, and one should like to hope to be able to add, ought not to be allowed to be made" (*Finnegans Wake*).

Several weeks ago we made charges. We indicated a relationship between Thornton Wilder's current Broadway play, *The Skin of Our Teeth*, and that big black book, *Finnegans Wake*. Our first article, based on a single evening at the play, no more than broached the problem of Mr. Wilder's indebtedness to James Joyce. But now the appearance of the play in book form[1] offers abundant evidence that Mr. Wilder not only vigorously adapted *Finnegans Wake* to the Broadway temper, but also intended that someone, somewhere, someday, should recognize his deed for what it is.

The author had good reason to expect that this would not happen immediately. He realized fully that *Finnegans Wake* has not yet been assimilated by the larger public, and that the chances of explicit protest during the run of the play were slight. For in Joyce's work the themes are multidimensional and queerly interwoven, developing bit by bit throughout the obscure text. Even the studious eye is baffled by their intricacy. Mr. Wilder, having mastered the elaborate web, has selected a few structural strands, reduced them in size and weight, and presented them, neatly crocheted to box-office taste. Many of the Joyce-Wilder correspondences are so subtle and extended that it would require a vast wall for their exhibition. Nevertheless, within the compass of a brief article it is possible to present a series of eye-openers even to the most languid observer.

These correspondences amount to much more than a mere sharing of great and constant human themes.

1. *The Skin of Our Teeth*, A Play in Three Acts. By Thornton Wilder. New York: Harper & Bros. 1942. 142 pp. $2.

Character by character, Act by Act, unmistakable re-renderings are evident. Both works have for setting, modern suburban homes not yet detached from the archaic past. The fathers of both families are about forty-five years old; they have both just survived election campaigns, during which certain charges have been made against their character—charges indignantly denied, yet not ill-founded. Mr. Antrobus pinches servant girls when he meets them in a dark corridor; H.C.E., too, is guilty of ungentlemanly conduct with maidservants. And they both indulge in extramarital sex adventures.

Such philanderings, it may be objected, are the common stuff of literature. But in *Finnegans Wake* and *The Skin of Our Teeth* the circumstances which surround them are *H*orrendous, *C*haracteristic, and *E*special. Mark what happens directly upon the husbands' stumbling into sin:—a thunder clap is heard. Barely has Antrobus entered the cabana with the seductress, barely has H.C.E. entered the bushes, when the thunder clap resounds and the hurricane signals go up. In both works this omen is a pronouncement of God's judgment on erring man, soon to be followed by deluge. The heroes' self-apologetic radio broadcasts to the world, describing their statesmanlike contributions to humanity, along with the worlds which they celebrate, dissolve in the engulfing catastrophe.

It is not enough to fob off this complex of themes, this curious telescoping of Adam and Noah, as "something out of Genesis." Quaintly enough, this merging of patriarchs does not occur in the Bible. It does occur, however, in *Finnegans Wake*—and now in *The Skin of Our Teeth*. Furthermore, Genesis 4 relates that the first son of Adam was Cain, the second Abel. But Joyce reverses this order in *Finnegans Wake;* so, oddly enough, does Wilder. Is our Broadway playwright deriving his themes from the Hebrew or the Irish?

Mr. Wilder's maid-seductress, Sabina, assumes the traits, at one time or another, of all the temptress masks of *Finnegans Wake.* She is the servant girl, fond of movies, the Napoleonic *fille du regiment,* the worn out soubrette, the popular beauty, the captive "raped home from her Sabine hills [all as in *Finnegans Wake*]. With Joyce she is "the rainbow girl": Sabina's costume in Act I suggests the colors of the rainbow. In *Finnegans Wake,* too, all these seductress traits play over the basic personality of a gossipacious maid.

The role of maid-temptress is counterbalanced by the wife-mother, whose function it is to rebuild and preserve the life fires which, through Sabina, have gone out. In the play, as in the book, the wife borrows the light with which she kindles the hearth; even further, she borrows the light from a character who is called the Postman in the Joyce work, and in the Wilder work, Telegraph Boy. In her speeches she recalls the times when there were "no weddings" (F.W., ST.). One of her manifestations in *Finnegans Wake* is a mother hen; as Joyce puts it, "she just feels she was kind of born to lay and love eggs." Mr. Antrobus calls *his* wife a "broken down old weather hen." The umbrella that the wife carries through Wilder's Act II is the famous umbrella of *Finnegans Wake.* Mrs. Antrobus re-echoes Mrs. Earwicker's railings against the candidate and scandalmongers who opposed her husband in the election.

The great letter that she throws into the sea is precisely the letter of *Finnegans Wake,* thrown away under identical circumstances. (Mr. Wilder's description of this letter is the most sensitive, most complete, most convincing interpretation yet to appear of this great Joycean theme.) The divorce which threatens the Antrobus household is the Royal Divorce of *Finnegans Wake.* The circumstances which postpone the divorce, and forever will postpone it, are those of *Finnegans Wake.* And again, as in *Finnegans Wake,* the mother's love for the evil, rejected Cain reconciles the male antagonisms within the family. With these parallels and the many more, it is not surprising that Mrs. Antrobus's name is Maggie,—written "Maggy" in *Finnegans Wake.*

So much for character comparisons; now for chronology. Skillfully and without essential dislocation, Mr. Wilder has adapted the four books of *Finnegans Wake* to the exigencies of a three-act play. Both works are composed in the form of a circle. Book I of *Finnegans Wake* and Act I of the play summon up the deepest past—the glacial age, dinosaurs, and mammoths (Joyce mentions both), as well as the dawn inventions of man—the alphabet, mechanics, and brewing. Book II and Act II take place in the present. Wilder's Act II is based specifically upon Book II, Section 3, of *Finnegans Wake;* Wilder simply transplants Joyce's Irish-tavern bacchanal to an Atlantic City convention. The last book of *Finnegans Wake* and the last Act of the play treat of the world's brave re-beginnings, following almost total catastrophe; they do not conclude, but circle back again to the start of all.

It is Book III of *Finnegans Wake* which would at first appear to have been omitted. But no. We find that this material has been telescoped retrospectively into the recitals of Mr. Antrobus in Act III, when he rehearses the fine ideals which he broodingly cherished during the years of struggle and war. These broodings and their return to the realities of peace correspond to H.C.E.'s dream for a future ideal and its dissolution into workaday fact. We cannot praise too highly what Mr. Wilder has here achieved in the way of re-creative interpretation. From these passages in his play a light goes back over great and very obscure sections of *Finnegans Wake.*

If the major correspondence are inescapable, minor similarities are numberless. Open the work to any page, and echoes vibrate from all directions. Some of them are highly esoteric and it is not improbable that Mr. Wilder is giving the wink of the fraternity to any Finnegan fan who may chance to be in the theatre. For instance, the play opens with an announcement that the sun arose at 6:32 a.m. Why precisely 32? This number, of all possible digits, is one of the ubiquitous puzzlers throughout the Wake: it appears during the course of the book some forty times in various combinations. Directly following the sunrise, we are shown three scrubwomen who have found Adam and Eve's wedding ring in the X Theatre. This literally reeks of Finnegan. No less than a dozen connotations spring immediately to mind: the scrubwoman theme, the entr'acte-scavenger theme, the "found article" theme, the ring theme, the wedding theme, the Phoenix Theatre theme, the "X" theme-complex (Xmas, Criss-Cross, Crucifixion-Resurrection, Crossbones, Crass-keys, XXX kisses, ex-wife, etc.), the Adam and Eve theme, etc.

An early stage direction bids Sabina to dust Mr. Antrobus's chair "including the under side." In Mr. Earwicker's tavern the man-of-all-work "dusts the both sides of the seats of the bigslaps." In Act I, in his conversation with the fish, Mr. Antrobus leans over the bowl and says, "How've things been, eh? Keck-keck-keck." When we try to remember where we have heard "keck" before, we recall the "Brekkek Kekkek" of the Aristophanes frog chorus in the diluvian passage of *Finnegans Wake.* In *The Skin of Our Teeth* "Keck" undergoes further Joycean development by appearing five times in the speeches of Esmeralda, fortune teller, who is called "Mrs. Croaker" by the convention delegates.

But why should Mr. Antrobus give special attention to a fish? Well, the fish is H.C.E.'s totem animal, as well as the giant Finn's Salmon of Knowledge.

Wilder's little girl, like Joyce's, is papa's darling, his "little star." Mr. Antrobus is revived from a mood of most desperate melancholy on hearing that she has recited Wordsworth's "The Star" in school. In *Finnegans Wake*, one of the daughter's principal manifestations is Stella (Stella— star) who revives life interest in the melancholy old man. When questioned by Mr. Antrobus, the daughter gives the exact dimensions of the ocean—a precocious knowledge suggestive of her "ocean origin" in *Finnegans Wake*.

To heap up resemblances: The message delivered by Mr. Wilder's Telegraph Boy has come by a wildly circuitous route, suggesting the peregrinations of the famous Finnegan missive. The children are called "little smellers" by Mr. Antrobus; the phrase "this little smeller" is remembered from *Finnegans Wake*. Among the refugees of the end of Act I, four old men, Doctor, Professor, Moses, and Homer, predominate; these are certainly the Four Old Men among the frequenters of Mr. Earwicker's hostel. The Antrobus inventions of beer brewing, alphabet, and mechanics are precisely those of the hero in *Finnegans Wake*.

Mr. Wilder is a man who has entered an uninventoried treasure cave and who emerges with a pouch full of sample sparklers. Only the lapidary who has himself paid a secret visit to the wonder-hoard is in a position to gasp at the authentic Joycean glitter of Mr. Wilder's re-settings.

As yet, Captain Wilder has not deigned to make public comment. But in the play itself he very cryptically pronounces as harsh an evaluation of his work as will ever be made. This pronouncement comes in Act I of *The Skin of Our Teeth*, when Mr. Antrobus comes home with his epochal invention, the wheel, which his son seizes with delight. Playing with the wheel, the son says: "Papa, you could put a chair on this." To which the father replies, broodingly: "Ye-e-s, any booby can fool with it now,—but I thought of it first."

The wheel is James Joyce's circular book of cyclewheeling history, "the Book of Doublends Jined"; Mr. Wilder has cleverly fixed a chair to it, wherein the public can ride.

Comparisons Between *Finnegans Wake* and *The Skin of Our Teeth* Have Been Exaggerated

Donald Haberman

Donald Haberman began his book *The Plays of Thornton Wilder: A Critical Study* as his doctoral thesis at Wilder's alma mater, Yale University. In this excerpt from his book, Haberman examines the relationship between *The Skin of Our Teeth* and *Finnegans Wake.* Although Haberman acknowledges that the Irish James Joyce was undoubtedly a rich source of inspiration, there were many others— including those who had originally inspired Joyce. What Wilder brought was his own way of looking at life; what resulted, Haberman declares, was not a bowdlerized version of *Finnegans Wake* designed for mass consumption, but a new and essentially American work.

Although the emphasis in his plays is on the narration, the sequence of events, Wilder has recognized the need of his audience for a story of some sort. The audience may create the story themselves, but Wilder has provided the clues. Any understanding of Wilder's style will depend, therefore, on the nature of those clues.

The anecdote in Wilder's plays is subservient to its meaning, but Wilder does not spin out ideas or philosophic systems. His abiding interest lies in human nature and its story. To explain what he intended by providing a work for the theater with significance, Wilder told the *Paris Review* interviewer:

> All the greatest dramatists, except the very greatest *one*, have precisely employed the stage to convey a moral or religious point of view concerning the action. . . .

I get around this difficulty by what may be an impertinence on my part. By believing that the moralizing intention resided in the authors as a convention of their times—usually, a social convention so deeply buried in the author's mode of thinking that it seemed to him to be inseparable from creation. . . . I say they injected a didactic intention in order to justify to themselves and to their audiences the exhibition of pure experience.[1]

Wilder is not a pamphleteer; his interest is not in social reform. For him the theater is the place where physical and emotional experience is arranged as effectively and precisely as possible.

In the introduction he wrote for Richard Beer-Hoffmann's *Jaakobs Traum,* Wilder explained how myth might resolve the differences between "didactic intention" and the "exhibition of pure experience."

A myth passing from oral tradition into literature, moves most congenially into poetry and particularly into the poetic drama. Even the most rationalistic reader consents to receive as given the elements of the supernatural and the incredible that are involved in these ancient stories. Their validity rests on the general ideas they contain. . . . The characters whom we have endowed with the life of significant ideas must be endowed with a different kind of life from the realistic—that of the recognizable quotidian.[2]

Characters from myth must be provided with a daily living that is ordinary and common to the audience. The advantage of employing a myth as the basis of a literary work is that it is already equipped with the substance of significant ideas. The anthropologist's and the psychologist's explanations of myth are dismissed as trivial and determined by detail of historical time and geographical place. More important to the artist is the problem of self-knowledge—individual and racial—which is enduring. The persistent elements of myth

are questions and not answers in regard to the human situation. In the majority of cases the questions seem to have to do with the mind disengaging itself from the passions of finding its true position in the presence of the established authorities, human or divine. They are concretizations of man's besetting preoccupation with the mind and mind's struggle to know itself; and each retelling requires that some answer be furnished to the question that infuses every part of the story.[3]

It is not sufficient to provide the myth with psychology or ordinary rational behavior. No amount of contemporary

1. Malcolm Cowley, ed., *Writers at Work* (New York, 1958), p. 109. 2. Richard Beer-Hoffmann, *Jacob's Dream* (New York, 1946), p. xvi. 3. *Ibid.,* p. xiii.

detail superimposed on the myth can make it significant. Its modernity must be inherent in its story, and the questions it raises must be answered, not finally for all time, but within the artist's comprehension of the world around him. His retelling will be judged by the questions he understands in the myth and the answers he provides to them, his separation of the eternal from the merely ephemeral.

MYTH FITS WILDER'S VIEW OF THE THEATER

Myth is well fitted to Wilder's idea of the theater, for it is peculiarly equipped to convey a generalized statement about human beings who seem themselves to be individualized. The writer need not bother to provide the characters of myth with details irrelevant to his idea in order to make the characters real. They are already in possession of a reality resulting from their existence throughout time. Neither does the plot concern the writer especially. Of greater importance is the large idea he sees illustrated in the story that is there. If, as Wilder believes, the anecdote matters only insofar as it illustrates that idea, then myth is the ideal anecdote because its general outlines are already known in some way to the audience. A myth is available to everyone. It is, as Wilder wrote in an essay on Joyce, "the dreaming soul of the race telling its story." Furthermore, he wrote that the "retelling of them on every hand occurs because they whisper a validation—they isolate and confer a significance."[4]

Wilder has really always used a myth as the anecdote for his plays. The story of Emily's return from the dead is not a classical myth, but Wilder had used it earlier in *The Woman of Andros* as though it were. Chrysis recounts it as a myth, and its adaptability to retelling is further evidence of its mythic quality. *The Merchant of Yonkers* is not a real myth either, but since its story is based on other works of literature, it is regarded by Wilder as a kind of myth. He, like Pound and Eliot, uses the writings of others as though they were part of the great body of ideas available to the entire human group, or in other words a myth: "Every novel for sale in a railway station is the dreaming soul of the human race telling its story."[5] *The Skin of Our Teeth* does use myth; furthermore, it employs history as though it were myth. The entire play is provided with coherence and additional mean-

4. Thornton Wilder, "Joyce and the Modern Novel," *A James Joyce Miscellany* (n.p., 1957), p. 15. 5. *Ibid.*

ing by its use of what Wilder would call a recent retelling of a myth, of many myths, *Finnegans Wake*.

CHARGES OF PLAGIARISM

Almost immediately after the opening of *The Skin of Our Teeth* two articles[6] by Joseph Campbell and Henry Morton Robinson in the *Saturday Review of Literature* linked the play with *Finnegans Wake*. The intent of these two men is not very clear; the tone they assumed, however, seems from this distance of time inexcusable, and a subsequent essay[7] by Robinson made evident his feeling, at least, that Wilder had been dishonest.

Campbell and Robinson wavered between assuming that the play was some sort of literary prank, the fun being able to recognize it, and stating baldly that it was something shoddy masquerading as first-rate. Perhaps this divided attitude indicates a division in the writers. Whatever their intent, when readers of the *Saturday Review of Literature* concluded that Wilder was a plagiarist, neither writer denied that the charge had been their idea in writing the articles. Perhaps the editorial policy of the magazine was at fault. The play, as a result of the two articles, for a while acquired the reputation of being at best unoriginal and derivative and at worst the unsavory work of thievery and plagiarism. Even today, reviews of its performance or comments on it display an uneasiness that can be traced to the *Saturday Review of Literature* articles.

Campbell and Robinson had been working on their *Skeleton Key to Finnegans Wake* and were in an unusually favorable position to recognize Wilder's debt to Joyce. Although they amassed all kinds of evidence to demonstrate the debt, they did not describe, or were unwilling to recognize, its precise nature. *The Skin of Our Teeth* is not, in fact, a dramatization of *Finnegans Wake*, as Edmund Wilson, who was not enthusiastic about the play, immediately recognized.[8]

Wilder never directly answered the two articles, which after all amounted to an attack, though he was painfully aware of them. His few simple and deceptively ingenuous remarks

---

6. Joseph Campbell and Henry Morton Robinson, "The Skin of Whose Teeth?," *Saturday Review of Literature*, XXV (December 19, 1942), 3–4, and "The Skin of Whose Teeth?: Part II," *Saturday Review of Literature*, XXVI (February 13, 1943), 16–19. 7. Henry Morton Robinson, "The Curious Case of Thornton Wilder," *Esquire*, XLVII (March, 1957), 70–71, 124, 125, 126. 8. Edmund Wilson, "The Antrobuses and The Earwickers," *Nation*, CXVI (January 30, 1943), 167f.

about Joyce and *The Skin of Our Teeth* have not supported his position very much. In 1948 he told an interviewer:

> I embedded one phrase of "Finnegans Wake" into the text as a salute and a bow of homage. . . .
>
> Sabina mockingly defending her employer, Mr. Antrobus who is also Adam and Everyman, says, "There are certain charges that ought not to be made and, I think I may say, ought not to be allowed to be made." This speech, with its feeble cadence and insecure indignation, is a wonderful example of Joyce's miraculous ear.
>
> "There are no other lines from Joyce?"
>
> "None," said Mr. Wilder.[9]

This clears up what was never in doubt really. The disturbing accusation of Campbell and Robinson was not that Wilder lifted lines from *Finnegans Wake*, but that he had adapted Joyce's inspiration and vision. They wrote, "Important plot elements, characters, devices of presentation, as well as major themes and many of the speeches, are directly and frankly imitated."[10] Wilder's statement is no answer to this kind of attack.

OTHER SOURCES

It is important first to be reminded that many of the devices and themes that Wilder found in his reading of Joyce he had come across earlier. The notion of circular time, for example, is as easily discovered in Vico's *Scienza Nuova*, where Joyce himself found it. But Gertrude Stein also had been fascinated with the possibilities in this idea, and Dreiser, a still earlier enthusiasm of Wilder's, was too.

In Dreiser's *Laughing Gas* a Doctor Vatabeel undergoes an operation which routinely should be simple, but grows more dangerously complicated as the play progresses. The anesthetic used is laughing gas, hence the title of the play; and it is while under the effect of the gas that the vision of repeated existing is revealed to Vatabeel. He dumbly considers: "In older worlds I have been, worlds like this. I have done this same thing. Society has done all the things it has done over and over."[11]

Vatabeel is pictured as an "endlessly serviceable victim— an avatar,"[12] with progress existing merely as an empty illusion. The urge to life, however, seems to work in him almost in spite of himself, as though it were a reflex action,

9. Robert van Gelder, "Interview with a Best-Selling Author: Thornton Wilder," *Cosmopolitan*, CXXIV (April, 1948), 120. 10. "The Skin of Whose Teeth?," p. 3. 11. Theodore Dreiser, *Plays of the Natural and the Supernatural* (New York, 1916), p. 107. 12. *Ibid.*, p. 109.

responding in defiance of his will to the stimulus of the operation. Various Voices urge him to try; he "senses some vast, generic, undecipherable human need."[13] At the same time the rhythm of the universe pounds a "sense of derision of indifference, of universal terror and futility."[14] Demyophon, one of the spirits of the Universe, tells him: "It has no meaning! Over and over! Round and round! . . . What you do now you will do again. And there is no explanation. You are so eager to live—to do it again. Do you not see the humor of that?"[15] And Vatabeel wakes from the gas laughing.

In Dreiser's grotesque play are two ideas that have remained with Wilder throughout his writing career. First and most apparent is the circular and repetitive nature of experience. Second and closely allied with the first is the existence in the individual, race, world, or evolution simultaneously of all experience. Vatabeel not only endlessly repeats experience; he is its avatar as well.

Of course, *Laughing Gas* is just barely literature, and Joyce's novel is one of the great if secret books of our time. Wilder, however, is one of the comparatively few men who have come close to deciphering the mysteries of *Finnegans Wake*, for he has spent hours and hours of his time, especially just before and after the war, reading it, and he possesses the knowledge and the languages to overcome its most obvious difficulties. In 1949 Wilder said at the Goethe Centennial celebration at Aspen, Colorado, that Joyce demonstrates that all the world at all times is one. He continued to say that Joyce did not use the work of others for "allusion, illustration, or ornament," but for "ambience."[16] Here, I think, Wilder has described his own attitude toward the work of Joyce and all his other "sources" as well.

"MAKE IT NEW"

The American writer has the disadvantage of being dependent on Europe (usually) for his culture and history, for the United States has provided relatively little of either commodity. Yet the artist requires both, and Henry James, Pound, Eliot, and Hemingway, to name only a very few, are American writers who made good use of what Europe had to offer without losing their distinctive American spirit.[17]

13. *Ibid.*, p. 110. 14. *Ibid.* 15. *Ibid*, p. 112. 16. Thornton Wilder, "World Literature and the Modern Mind," in Arnold Bergstraesser, ed., *Goethe and the Modern Age* (Chicago, 1950), p. 218. 17. Norman Holmes Pearson, "The American Novelist and the Uses of Europe," *Some American Studies* (Kyoto, 1964).

ANY PUBLICITY IS GOOD PUBLICITY?

Advertisement for the book version of The Skin of Our
Teeth *in the* Saturday Review of Literature *issue of April
10, 1943—less than four months after Campbell and
Robinson's first article and two months after their second one
(which referred to the book version of the play).*

THORNTON WILDER
THE SKIN OF OUR TEETH

No play in recent years has aroused such a torrent of discussion. Whether or not you've seen the play, read the book
and find out what the uproar is all about. "Screwy but exciting."—*Chicago News.*

Wilder has made just such use of Joyce, but he has each time
heeded Ezra Pound's command to Make It New, for Wilder
learned from Ezra Pound how to master the literary as well
as the historic past.[18] *Finnegans Wake* provided for Wilder's
play a myth of the historical and cultural environment
which created America. Its advantages to Wilder may be
summed up in his definition of the kind of story a myth is.

First, its "historical authenticity is so far irrelevant as to
permit to the narrator an assumption of omniscience in
regard to what took place."[19] The writer need not waste any
effort establishing the truth of his story. No matter how fantastic the events, they are accepted by the audience as having happened exactly as the writer reports them.

Secondly, a myth is a story "whose antiquity and popular
diffusion confer upon it an authority which limits the degree
of variation that may be employed in its retelling."[20] The
major outlines of the story must be retained to satisfy the
audience's pleasure in recognizing the familiar.

Finally, a myth is a story "whose subject matter is felt to
have a significance which renders each retelling a contribution to the received ideas of the entire community to which
in a very real sense it belongs."[21] Here is the most difficult
task for the writer. He must demonstrate his originality, not
in the plot, but in the meaning. He must create a significance
that does not overstep the limitations of the events that are
given, but a significance that is new and contemporary.

---

18. Ezra Pound is one of the two modern American writers whom Wilder admires and
to whom he feels indebted. See Cowley, *Writers at Work*, p. 115. 19. Beer-Hofmann,
Jacob's Dream, p. xi. 20. *Ibid.* 21. *Ibid.*, p. xii.

CAMPBELL AND ROBINSON WERE MISTAKEN

It is a serious mistake to assume, as Campbell and Robinson did, that Wilder's play is a rehash of Joyce's novel. Readers of Virgil who come to the *Aeneid* after Homer are inevitably disappointed in Aeneas and utterly fail to understand the Latin epic if they demand another Achilles or Odysseus. Just so puzzled and irritated were Campbell and Robinson when they did not find in Antrobus an exact copy of H.C. Earwicker. In spite of all the parallels between *Finnegans Wake* and *The Skin of Our Teeth* that Campbell and Robinson uncovered, it is careless to conclude, as they did, that Wilder merely collected and catalogued Joyce's discoveries into an adaptation suitable to the Broadway temper. That he had studied and comprehended Joyce's work is certain; but he also succeeded in pervading the whole of his play with his own optimistic and peculiarly American vision of the human animal and his experience through time.

It is not simple patriotism that locates Antrobus and his family in New Jersey. No matter if he is Adam or Noah or Everybody, he is America's version of Man, and unlike Joyce's heroes, he is not determined by his environment, whether it be cultural, physical, or moral. Antrobus is eternally extricating himself from his "ambience" or reinterpreting it or literally changing it. When the American confronts an ice age, he will invent a more efficient way to heat his house.

In 1928 Wilder told André Maurois, "In the whole of the world's literature there are only seven or eight great subjects. By the time of Euripides they had all been dealt with already, and all one can do is to pick them up again.... There is nothing new that a writer can hope to bring except a certain way of looking at life." [22] Wilder brought to the myths of *Finnegans Wake* precisely another way of interpreting them. He saw in Joyce's work another version of the Europe that has been so important to the American writer. Perhaps, as Professor Pearson suggests,[23] the actual experience of Europe has become too commonplace for American writers, but the secondary or literary experience is still available. Through Joyce's novel, Wilder reinterpreted Europe for the American. Antrobus is free to escape—though with the skin of his teeth only—and create a new independent future. It is more than

22. André Maurois, *A Private Universe*, tr. Hamish Miles (New York, 1932), p. 39. 23. "The American Novelist and the Uses of Europe," p. 18.

mere chance, in the light of what the Old World has always dreamed of the United States and perhaps during World War II more realistically expected from it, that *The Skin of Our Teeth* should have presented for a destroyed and to all appearances utterly debilitated Europe a promise for the future. Wilder's play is unquestionably an original work. It portrays the mythic American cheerfully and energetically progressing through a mythic Western civilization.

THE RELIGIOUS HERO

That the American has no sense of tragedy is perhaps a national flaw, but as Wilder has noted, it is just as surely a major source of national energy. The American has created a new kind of hero, distinct from the tragic hero, and this new hero offers a challenge to American writers for the theater. Using Abraham as an example, Kierkegaard described just such a hero, calling him the religious hero. . . .

Ethical standards may exist, but for the religious hero they are meaningless because he does not act for others, except as he acts for himself. The usual motives of the tragic hero are absent. . . . For [Wilder] the religious hero is the person who is most intensely alive, the person most intimately related with his everyday existence. The divine is simply that which is unknowable, and it is the unknowable that clarifies everyday living by forcing attention to it. This understanding is not unchristian, but it is more general than most traditional theology would allow.

Kierkegaard wrote also that the "tragic hero accomplishes his act at a definite instant in time."[24] The religious hero's act is performed in "an absolute relation to the absolute," which is not so impersonal as it might first seem, for he is justified by "being the particular individual."[25] The connection between what Wilder learned from Gertrude Stein and what he learned from Kierkegaard is probably most clearly perceptible here. The freedom of Kierkegaard's religious hero is the rootlessness described by Gertrude Stein as the moving in all directions, the absence of a beginning, middle, and end, characteristic of America and the Bible. It is Wilder's "abstract" American and another way of describing the validity of the individual in the face of all the millions who have lived, who are living, and who will live.

24. S. Kierkegaard, *Fear and Trembling,* tr. Walter Lowrie (Princeton, 1941), p. 91.
25. *Ibid.,* p. 93

The success of Wilder's theater, which has not been recognized because every attempt has been made to measure it against the old standards, is, in fact, that he has helped create new standards. Whether or not we derive pleasure from the theater he has so carefully developed will probably depend on whether or not we are happy about the political, social, and intellectual changes that have resulted in our time and country.

Archetypal Characters in *The Skin of Our Teeth*

Helmut Papajewski, translated by John Conway

The Skin of Our Teeth, which opened during World War II, uses archetypal characters to explore the question of whether humanity would change in the wake of the devastation it had brought upon itself, writes Helmut Papajewski, author of a German study on Wilder's works. Papajewski examines the major characters—the Antrobus family and Sabina—and the complex links to their biblical and mythical forerunners.

On October 15, 1942, in the little Shubert Theater in New Haven, Connecticut, *The Skin of Our Teeth* received its first performance. This out-of-town premiere was followed on November 18 by the New York opening at the Plymouth Theater. Wilder's new play—with its title indicating alarm, hope, and resignation—was an outgrowth of world events and literary experiences since his last work. The Second World War had entered its fourth year, and for almost a year America had been actively engaged. Wilder does not pose any specifically political questions concerning this war, but directs his attention once again to the anthropological-ethical problem connected with it: If man survives this war too, will he fundamentally change his ways? There were many political programs during this war, but Wilder had experienced too much disillusionment after World War One—when he was already at the age of awareness—for him to place very much credence in the new program; and he had too clear an idea of man's limited possibilities and the chance of relapse to be able to share the renewed easy optimism. Antrobus speaks of all this in down-to-earth language in Act Three: "When you're at war you think about a better life; when you're at peace you think about a more comfortable one." With all their stress on "reality," the politicians were bound to build their grand designs in a vacuum, because they did not take into account the really decisive thing, the world's anthropological substructure. . . .

Viewed in relation to previous drama, the Wilder play differs in the manner of its division into three acts, and in a way also in the kind of plot as given by the title. The title implies that man once again escapes from his current plight and that his personal behavior approximates that of characters in a comedy—a comedy, to be sure, with metaphysical overtones rather than a straight comedy of definite time and place.

The play's three acts do not represent one continuous action. Each culminates in a great world catastrophe: the Ice Age, the Deluge, and the World War. Out of each catastrophe man finds his way by dint of his enthusiasm for a new beginning, without fundamentally changing his ways, for the evil which drove him into the catastrophe remains immanent in him.

THE TWO ASPECTS OF MAN

Thus man is seen under two aspects: as a creature who is delivered up to these catastrophes, and as a creature who lives in the self-contained unit of the family. Wilder sets forth both of these aspects at the very beginning. In place of the usual prologue there are lantern-slide showings by the announcer, which are meant to give a graphic idea of the oppressive cold. This "prelude" alludes at the same time to the crisis within the family: a wedding ring is found with the inscription, "To Eve from Adam."

From these lantern-slide showings Wilder shifts to the Antrobus family, which has to cope with the threatening Ice Age. It is a deranged and topsy-turvy world that is presented to us. In the warmest month, August, the severest frost prevails. The walls of the house rise, sink, and lean to one side. The dinosaur lives with man, at one point drolly taking its place with Mrs. Antrobus and the children in a triangular tableau reminiscent of Raphael. The alphabet is invented, and the fact is announced by telegram. Antrobus discovers the arithmetic significance of tens, though the course of the proceedings shows that the concept has long been part of the currency of human thought. Instability appears to be raised to the level of a principle, and anachronism displaces the normal time pattern.

There is plenty of fun with this hyper-baroque theater. Many over-serious playgoers, on the other hand, have been irritated by such "nonsense." The sense of what Wilder is up to is disclosed only when it is remembered that the real world of our life in the here-and-now was strongly called into question: the reality of this world had proved to be only a seeming reality. . . .

In our everyday life we are not in a position to penetrate the sense-deception of the world around us. Wilder returns to this idea, in the course of representing each hour of the twenty-four with a philosopher, at the ninth hour in the evening, represented by Spinoza:

> After experience had taught me that the common occurrences of daily life are vain and futile; and I saw that all the objects of my desire and fear were in themselves nothing good nor bad save insofar as the mind was affected by them; I at length determined to search out whether there was something truly good and communicable to man.

Spinoza with nine o'clock represents the beginning of the intellectually reflective hours of the night. Before being followed by Plato and Aristotle, he called attention to the meaning of the "common occurrences of daily life." But what a role these "common occurrences" have played in Wilder's dramas! *Our Town* was completely geared to them—only to lead them finally *ad absurdum* in the life of Emily. Seen from this standpoint, then, *The Skin of Our Teeth* is a consistent continuation of the small-town play. Of course it does not begin with the "occurrences," not even when in the course of the First Act the view narrows from the wide-angle lens of the "announcer" down to the family circle.

A COMPOSITE FAMILY TREE

This Antrobus family lives in a dual system of categories, the one being in terms of nature and natural catastrophe, and the other being religious-eschatological. The name Antrobus is itself a hint of this; one thinks of the Greek word *anthropos*. Wilder represents him as the Chief of the mammals and president of their assembly. Antrobus speaks of the beginning of life billions of years ago, and he even gives a presentation of the polygenetic development of man.

But beside this there is another family tree and another chronology: here the span is not billions of years, but the 4,000 to 5,000 years of world history according to Biblical tradition. In this family tree, Antrobus becomes the Old Testament Adam, both figures merging to form a composite. From the statement of the "announcer," the provenance of Anthropos-Adam is clear: "He comes of very old stock and made his way up from next to nothing." Following Genesis, the "announcer" continues: "It is reported that he was once a gardener, but left that situation under circumstances that have been variously reported." Antrobus is the genius who invented such things as the wheel (which is not expressly mentioned in the Bible); but he is also the inventor of beer, and this suggests the Biblical parallel Noah.

This parallel becomes still clearer with the events of the Second Act. When the Deluge comes, Antrobus takes pairs of all species of animal aboard the Ark, two by two, and thus helps to save creation. All animals are represented, even the famous Biblical snake to which Gladys calls attention while embarking.

RACIAL AND RELIGIOUS PARENTAGE

The Biblical parentage is not limited to one meaning or one person, but, just as the natural racial parentage reflected all vital stages of development, so also the religious parentage has—if not all—many essential features in itself. Among these is the wounding of Antrobus that causes his limp: it is the wound he received in the fight over the absolute, the wound of Jacob. Sabina at one point characterizes him with mingled mockery and approval: ". . . An excellent husband and father, a pillar of the church, and has all the best interests of the community at heart. Of course, every muscle goes tight every time he passes a policeman."

All this sounds very bourgeois, but the analogies point beyond: Antrobus is not only the first man, Adam, but also the progenitor of the people and guardian of the community, Abraham. The Biblical analogy probably extends to David, whose sins of the flesh are reflected in Antrobus. It is interesting to see how the analogy is not always unequivocal. The Henry-Cain analogy is an example: Cain has killed someone with a slingshot, the typical weapon of David.

Wilder has discussed at length the use of this kind of literary technique in his lecture "Goethe and World Literature." Referring to Goethe's thesis that "national literature" now does not "say" much and that one must take into account mankind's "long memory"—Wilder is borrowing a phrase from Ortega y Gasset—Wilder takes up the subject of Goethe's employment of universal materials: "He did not shrink from anachronisms. He wedded his Faust to Helena; he grafted his Weimar on to Shiraz, the city of the Persian poet." It is not a question here of whether the examples Wilder has chosen from Goethe are, from the standpoint of tradition, entirely correct. What is much more important in the present connection is Wilder's reference to Goethe's mode of relating and integrating things of different cultures. . . .

The recourse to world literature is important for Wilder in another sense also. He sees in it the expression of the fact that man as an individual is in the millions—a view that may also have its significance in connection with his speculations about the soul's divestment of its individuality after death. . . .

HENRY-CAIN, THE EVIL ONE

From the beginning it is quite definite that Henry is Cain. Sabina gives it away at the beginning of the First Act. A tactful yet incautious question by Moses awakens Mrs. Antrobus' grief over the loss of Abel. It is she who tries again and again with her apron to rub away the mark of Cain from her son's forehead—but it remains. Cain, too, must remain. From a dramaturgic standpoint he is the recurrent type; from a metaphysical standpoint he is the Evil that must accompany man. His existence makes Antrobus despair and wish himself rid of this son who makes himself intolerable in all polite society. Evil is ordained for him as the curse of man's original Fall. Nor can it be domesticated. Wilder has included in *The Skin of Our Teeth* a number of contrast scenes by which he aims to show that man in a state of peril gives himself up to illusions. Thus we see Sabina in a bourgeois fashion doing the housework and dusting everything when the Ice Age is already close at hand. Thus we see Antrobus just before the Flood, planning to take his sweetheart to a hotel room. Above all there is the scene in which Antrobus, who should have no illusions about Cain's nature, sits at the family hearth drilling him in the multiplication table.

The essential element is the constant accompaniment of that which is evil, with which Antrobus must identify himself, as in the scene where Sabina breaks the news to him that Cain has killed the neighbors' son. At first Antrobus is extremely angry, and despite the approach of the Ice Age he wants to stamp out the life-preserving fire—on which everything constantly depends and which only Mrs. Antrobus is really competent to preserve—and in this way to put an end to everything. Then the sense of his own guilt returns: "Henry! Henry! (Puts his hand on his forehead.) Myself. All of us, we're covered with blood.". . .

Antrobus is the master of the house, who should give the family its solidarity, whereas Cain is increasingly the one without any ties, who wants no home and no solidarity. Even a total war with all its consequences cannot awake such desires in him. When Henry-Cain after the world war emerges a general from the air raid shelter, he rejects all shelter and all ties, to say nothing of order and subordination. His mother's wish that there be peace at last in the family as well as in the world, he brusquely rejects: "I don't live here. I don't belong to anybody."

Still stronger is his negation of his father: "You don't have to think I'm any relation of yours. I haven't got any father or any mother, or brothers or sisters. And I don't want any. And what's more I haven't got anybody over me; and I never will have. I'm alone, and that's all I want to be: alone." The man without any ties, the man who denies, is also the man who brooks no commandments: "Nobody can say *must* to me."

Henry-Cain is also the embodiment of the so-called new political principles, which equate youth with an unbridled striving for power. All contemporaries still remember the words, "What have they done for us?", and still more "When are you going to wake up?" Toward the play's end, however, Wilder does not see Cain as representing the revolt of youth, but as a representation of strong unreconciled evil, of whom it is said in the stage directions at the very end: "Henry appears at the edge of the scene, brooding and unreconciled, but present." When creation begins again, he is there, just as at the second Creation by Noah the serpent was also among those present.

THE TWO EVES

Among the female characters Mrs. Antrobus is Eve (Hebrew for "the maternal one") who guards the fire that keeps life. Opposed to her is Sabina as the other Eve, the temptress. Sabina appears in the play under various names which give clues to her identity. When the characters are introduced by the announcer, she is called Lily Sabina; she is also called the servant girl. She is the daughter of Lilith of Talmudic tradition; and Lilith is of the night, demonic: she is the evil female, the night-hag.

She has not come into the family by orderly process, but— as her name Sabina indicates—by rapine. In the first argument between the two main female characters of the play, Mrs. Antrobus gives the facts about Sabina's past: "O,

Sabina, I know you. When Mr. Antrobus raped you home from your Sabine hills, he did it to insult me. You were the new wife, weren't you?" But Sabina finally did not hold her place. She let the fire go out, and was demoted to the kitchen to be servant instead of guardian of the fire. In the next-to-last scene of the Third Act she says resignedly: "Kitchen! Why is it that however far I go away, I always find myself back in the kitchen?" For her, life has no other final solution than servitude.

In the Second Act it does appear for a time that her hour has come. Her name is enlarged to Sabina Fairweather, a reference to the time of her effectiveness. In crises she always fails; in fair weather she is able to achieve recognition, as when Antrobus becomes President. But it is President of a state full of illusions, where the "truth" is obtained from the fortune-teller and accomplice of prostitutes. Esmeralda the gypsy seems to have the power of regulating the action, but it is action that is altogether brittle and cannot last. The brief dream of Helen of Troy, about whom Sabina asks the fortune-teller, is finally over, and Sabina says naïvely: "I don't know why my life's always being interrupted—just when everything's going fine!" Esmeralda has just banished her to the kitchen: "Yes, go—back to the kitchen with you."

The Second Act not only marks Sabina's seduction of Mr. Antrobus and demonstrates his moral blindness in seeing in the prostitute the loved one; but also, in the Second Act, it is through Sabina that Antrobus becomes conscious of his own guilt. When he sees Gladys wearing the red stockings, the color of Man's Fall and of temptation, he realizes at once that the source of this is Sabina. His own guilt causes him to guard against his daughter's going wrong.

The four main characters—Mr. and Mrs. Antrobus, Henry, and Sabina—make up the world, in its good aspect as well as its bad. The one cannot be divorced from the other, and nothing can be made an absolute value. The human archetypes which these characters embody form the foundation on which being—for Wilder, Christian being—rests. In them Wilder's cycle of theological existence runs a full course: "The Fall as the result of sin, the dawning consciousness of what is sinful, the new beginning in excessive hope and in pride, and thereby the first beginning of a new Fall.". . .

THE LINK WITH "REALITY"

In this play Sabina is the one to whom Wilder assigns the task of establishing the link with "reality," as that term is understood by people generally. She repeatedly acts out of character. She does not understand the play or does not want to. Parts of it she does not want to play because a friend of hers is present in the theater and parts of it might shock her by recalling her own hard fate.

But Sabina's function is also that she must ironically play the play out. At one point she names the play by its title. As Miss Somerset, she says three times in the First Act: ". . . A few years ago we came through the depression by the skin of our teeth! One more tight squeeze like that and where will we be?" The audience receives a strong and sustained statement of the play's theme, but the words are in an ironical context, for this very statement is also a cue line and the prompter is unable to respond. Miss Somerset makes use of the breakdown to address herself to the audience.

Through her outbursts she establishes the link to the audience, and the stage manager has to bring her back into the action of the play. Thus the stage manager has a function somewhat the reverse of that in *Our Town*. In that play, within his technical limits, he let the people come forward; and he repeatedly bridged the gap between the transcendental area and the here-and-now. In *The Skin of Our Teeth* the transcendental is itself here, and the task of the stage manager is limited.

BREAKING CHARACTER FOR EFFECT

The startling effects are so increased in *The Skin of Our Teeth* that they bear upon the movement and the success of the play itself. Occasionally a minor character such as the telegraph boy makes a remark to this effect: "I . . . I can't do this last part very well." Antrobus too has trouble with his role. In a scene in which Sabina has created a sort of general chaos, he cannot get back on track right away. Antrobus: "Wait a minute. I can't get back into it as easily as all that."

Sabina is the one who, more than anyone else, puts everything in question. She seems to have certain intellectual difficulties. When it dawns on her that the crisis also brings the refugee problem, she briefly gives vent to her feelings. She tries to avert an ugly encounter between the angry father and the furious son by saying: "Stop! Stop! Don't play this scene," even reminding the players what happened when this scene was played in the previous evening's performance.

Sabina, the frivolous one, who in *The Skin of Our Teeth* does not see any eschatological event but only sees a threat, gives vent to her aversion to the play: "I hate this play and every word in it. As for me, I don't understand a single word of it, anyway—all about the troubles the human race has gone through, there's a subject for you."

Wilder even takes the opportunity to have Sabina make sarcastic remarks about him as a dramatist. Sabina, in a commedia dell'arte situation, had been told by the prompter to improvise something, at which she had only poor success. She now gives her opinion of the play's content, which is unclear and seems to have been insufficiently thought out: "Besides the author hasn't made up his silly mind as to whether we're all living back in caves or in New Jersey today, and that's the way it is all the way through."

A Visible Trend to Universality

Something of their double nature is still to be detected in the characters, their ephemeral quality bound by time and place, as well as their human universality. In the inclinations of the characters there is still the father-daughter and mother-son relationship—Maggie is concerned for Henry, Antrobus for Gladys—just as in *Our Town*. But by making the usual space and time relationships questionable from the beginning, Wilder manages to reach the sphere that encompasses the millions of living and dead. The play's entire design in this respect is anchored so firmly in the typological that in the nomenclature of persons as well as places there is a visible trend to universality, to the metaphysical comedy of types, and to the grand style.

In *The Skin of Our Teeth* there is no longer a Grover's Corners [of *Our Town*] that can be located by its degree of latitude and longitude, no Webbs and no Gibbses, but only the four basic human types, who are, to be sure, organized as a family, but whose significance is purely archetypical. Even when specific place names are still given, as in the brief listing of school, department store, etc., they are not meant to play any role in the play, but represent certain human necessities: education, divine worship, satisfaction of one's daily wants. They will remain, according to Wilder's view, as will also the primeval types of good and evil in a world of recurring catastrophes. "Oh, anyway," Sabina exclaims, "nothing matters! It'll all be the same in a hundred years." It is Sabina, too, who closes the play, shuffling the levels of reality as she refers simultaneously to herself, the audience, and humanity: "This is where you came in. We have to go on for ages and ages yet."

A Powerful Study of Humanity's Ability to Survive

David Castronovo

Wilder's jumble of theatrical styles helps support the universal themes in *The Skin of Our Teeth*, explains David Castronovo. Comparing *The Skin of Our Teeth* with *Our Town*, Castronovo declares the former play both more penetrating and more satisfying. Castronovo argues that Wilder assimilated influences from world theater, particularly the works of Pirandello and Brecht, to produce a play that simultaneously deals with everyday American life and "the churnings of the universe." Castronovo is also the author of works on Edmund Wilson and Richard Yates, and of *The English Gentleman: Images and Ideals in Literature and Society.*

Measuring Wilder's progress as a dramatist inevitably involves placing *The Skin of Our Teeth* beside *Our Town:* the works invite comparison not only because of their ambitiousness but more importantly because of strong thematic affinities. Both concern American families struggling with implacable fate and their own smallness: Emily and George and their parents and Mr. and Mrs. Antrobus and their children experience joy and dread as they contend not only with the localized social problems of American life, but more importantly with the churnings of the universe. The macrocosmic references in both plays—to planets, vast numbers, ideas that hover around mortal lives—are an unmistakable sign that Wilder remains obsessed by the ways ordinary lives in Grover's Corners or Excelsior, New Jersey, take their place in a universal design. But for all this similarity in cosmic subject matter, there is a very considerable difference in the dramatic visions of the plays. The last act of *Our Town* takes place in a graveyard—its epiphanies are tragic, but its affirmations about stars and striving are so much inauthentic rhetoric grafted onto a great play. Unfortunately for those who seek easy contrasts with *The Skin of Our Teeth,* the later play—for all its brio and broad humor—is not essentially comic, although a wide variety of comic and humorous strategies are used in the very serious, emotionally wrenching drama about the struggle to transcend the disasters of nature, human society, and the warped human self. Act III situates the family in a war-ravaged home with Gladys as an unwed mother, Henry filled with fascistic rage, and Sabina anxious to become a good self-absorbed American citizen ready for a peacetime prosperity of movies and fun. Mr. Antrobus is ready to start putting the world together again, but he is old and tired and has had many setbacks. This is hardly comic—and in its matter-of-fact look at what men and women wind up with, it is hardly the complacent vision that repelled Mary McCarthy when she reviewed the play.[1] *The Skin of Our Teeth* is not about the fat of the land: what's in view for man is grinding struggle, close calls with total destruction, and the permanent fact of human violence and selfishness.

SHATTERING DRAMATIC CONVENTIONS

This theme of human struggle and limited achievement comes to us in the form of three loosely constructed, elliptical acts. Never a writer of well-made plays, Wilder has now brought his own episodic technique to a pitch of dizzy perfection. From his *Journals* we learn that Wilder considered that he was "shattering the ossified conventions" of realistic drama in order to let his "generalized beings" emerge.[2]

Act I, set in Excelsior, New Jersey, has about as much logic and verisimilitude as a vaudeville skit. Using the Brechtian strategy of screen projections and announcements, Wilder surveys the "News Events of the World." Mostly the reports concern the extreme cold, the wall of ice moving south, and the scene in the home of George Antrobus. It is six o'clock and "the master not home yet"; Sabina—the sexy maid who sometimes steps out of her part to complain about the play—is parodying the chitchat that often opens a realistic well-made

---

1. Mary McCarthy, *"The Skin of Our Teeth,"* in *Sights and Spectacles* (New York: Farrar, Straus and Cudahy, 1956). 2. *The Journals of Thornton Wilder 1939–1961.* Selected and edited by Donald Gallup. (New Haven: Yale University Press, 1985).

play: "If anything happened to him, we would certainly be inconsolable and have to move into a less desirable residential district." The dramatic movement—never Wilder's strong point—involves waiting for Antrobus, contending with the cold, disciplining a dinosaur and a mastodon, receiving Antrobus's messages about surviving ("burn everything except Shakespeare"), and living in a typical bickering American family; Maggie Antrobus—unlike her inventive, intellectual, progressive husband—is instinctual and practical. Her children, Henry and Gladys, are emblems of violence and sexuality: the boy has obviously killed his brother with a stone; the girl has trouble keeping her dress down. When their father arrives home—with a face like that of a Keystone Cop, a tendency to pinch Sabina, and a line of insults that sounds like W.C. Fields, the plot moves a bit more swiftly. He asks the dinosaur to leave and receives Homer and Moses into the house. As the act ends, the family of man is trying to conserve its ideas and knowledge—including the alphabet and arithmetic; it has also accepted "the refugees"—the Greek poet and the Hebrew lawgiver. The fire of civilization is alive, and members of the audience are asked to pass up chairs to keep it going.

Act II has the glitz of Atlantic City and the continuing problem of Mr. Antrobus dealing with the disasters of terrestrial life, the fact of his own sexuality, and the gnawing obligations of a father and husband. Once again, in the style of Brecht's epic theater, an announcer comments on screen projections—"Fun at the Beach" and the events of the convocation of "the Ancient and Honorable Order of Mammals." The plot is jumpier than ever—Miss Lily Sabina Fairweather, Miss Atlantic City 1942, tries to seduce Antrobus; a fortune-teller squawks about coming rains; Mrs. Antrobus bickers with the children, champions the idea of the family, and protests against Antrobus's breaking of his marriage promise; Antrobus, ashamed of himself at last, shepherds his flock and an assortment of animals into a boat.

THE INEVITABLE BUSINESS OF ENDURING

Dealing with the effects of war, Act III is a powerful ending to this play about surviving. The wild and often inspired stage gimmickry of the first two acts has given way to the darkened stage and the ravaged Antrobus home. The emotions become more concentrated, the actions and efforts seem less scattered, the people's situations reach us as both tragedy and the inevitable business of men and women enduring. A play that seemed to be in revolt against realistic character representation, psychological probing, and the fine shadings of nineteenth-century drama, explodes into a moving exploration of personalities as they face the modern world. Deeply affected by the suffering of the war, the family members come into focus as human beings rather than emblems. Henry, the linchpin of this act about war and violence, explains himself for the first time and becomes more than a stick figure. Resentful about having "anybody over me" he has turned himself into a fascist as a way of mastering the authorities—his father, especially––who oppressed him. His truculence, fierce selfishness, and horrible individualism make him both a believable neurotic and a distillation of brutal resentment. Sabina, the temptress who has competed with Mrs. Antrobus for the attention of George, also comes alive as an individual. Driven to depression and cynicism by the hardship of the war, she pronounces that people "have a right to grab what they can find." As "just an ordinary girl" who doesn't mind dealing in black-market goods to pay for a night at the movies, she represents Wilder's honest appraisal of what suffering often does to people. Antrobus—the principle of light, reason, and progress in the play—also has his moments of depression. He yearns for simple relief: "Just a desire to settle down; to slip into the old grooves and keep the neighbors from walking over my lawn." But somehow a pile of old tattered books, brought to life by passages from Spinoza, Plato, and Aristotle delivered by stand-in actors, rekindles the desire "to start building." Self-interest, complacency, despair, and violence coexist with intellectual aspirations and energies to begin again: although outnumbered by ordinarily self-involved and extraordinarily violent people, Antrobus can still go on. Despite the fact that the play ends, as it began, with "the world at sixes and sevens," there is still the principle of the family in Mrs. Antrobus's words and the desire to create the future from the past in Mr. Antrobus's reverence for Plato and technology.

A JUMBLE OF DRAMATIC STYLES

The styles of this play are as various as modern literature and the twentieth-century stage. Not at all austere or carefully crafted, the drama is a brilliant jumble of Pirandello, Joyce, and epic theater.

Once again Wilder employs the manner, and the basic outlook, of *Six Characters in Search of an Author.* Sabina and Henry, particularly, make us aware that they are performing, that their parts are not entirely to their liking, and that they want to convey something about themselves that the theater does not have the means to express. Just as Pirandello's actors distort the story of a tragic family, Wilder's script does not always allow Sabina to tell about her truths or Henry to explain his real-life motivations. Like Pirandello's agonized daughter-figure, Henry insists on the brutal truth of his situation and interrupts the flow of the action to cry out against the false representation that he is given by the playwright. The management of the stage business in *The Skin of Our Teeth* is another reminder of Pirandello's theater. The awkward, clumsy matter of props and their arrangement leads us back to *Six Characters* and its arguments about where people should stand, what a room was like, and how people should look. Wilder delights in offering us not only a drama of survival, but also the laborious process of making a play—the scaffolding of a work of art is just as much his subject as the work itself. The stops and starts, the interruptions and localized quarrels of the actors, the puncturing of the whole theatrical illusion by the reality of actors who have become sick from some food and need to be replaced: such ploys carry through Wilder's theme of struggle and endurance, but also suggest the impact of Pirandello's artfully disordered dramas. Wilder's debt to Pirandello does not end with stage technique. The vision of the play—Antrobus beginning again and the family ready "to go on for ages and ages yet"—has most often been traced to Joyce's *Finnegans Wake:* Wilder himself acknowledged this partial debt in the midst of the brouhaha about his "plagiarism." Other influences were overlooked. Pirandello's tragic and tormented family in *Six Characters* goes offstage only to find another theater in which to play out its drama: in a mood of guarded optimism, this is precisely what the Antrobus family is about to do. Sabina reports that they are on their way.

The Skin of Our Teeth also becomes a more enjoyable and intelligible theatrical experience when it is placed beside Bertolt Brecht's epic-theater works. The staging, character presentation, themes, and generalizing power bear an important relationship to Brecht's experiments in the

1930s.[3] Without having to argue for direct influences, one still can see a great deal about Wilder's techniques and idea by placing them in apposition to a work like *Mother Courage.* Since both plays take place in time of war, employ epic exaggeration, explore violence and selfishness, and take an unadorned look at what suffering does to people, it is not unreasonable to view them together. *Mother Courage* was also written three years before *The Skin of Our Teeth,* a fact that is not without significance considering Wilder's close touch with the currents of twentieth-century literature. Yet whether he was influenced directly or not, the affinities are strong. As pieces of stagecraft, both plays employ a large historical sweep and present material in a nonrealistic manner; Brecht's play of the Thirty Years War and Wilder's play of civilization's disaster both reach for large generalizations about man's durability and defects. The works do this essentially didactic job by means of screen projections, announcers, jagged episodic plots, and characters who are often stereotypical or emblematic. Wilder's third act overcomes Brecht's relentless detachment from his characters, but even here—as we sympathize with Sabina and Henry—we are not in a theater where the individual psyche is the main concern. Wilder is more involved with the process of learning, the hope of progress, and the impediments in human nature and culture than with the individuality of his people. In this he is one with Brecht, a writer who studies the harshness of civilization and the brutality of ordinary folk. Sabina's selfish, compromising, essentially amoral view of the human struggle for survival is like nothing so much as Mother Courage's matter-of-fact attitude toward suffering and willingness to hitch up her wagon and do business after her children are dead. Wilder has humanized and intellectualized this savage world, but he essentially works with its terrifying ingredients. Even Antrobus, the beacon light of the three acts, is tainted by the lust, a cynicism, cheapness, and hypocrisy that Brecht saw as the central features of bourgeois life. While Antrobus brings his noble and selfish impulses into a unity, he is still like Humanity as described by Brecht in *Saint Joan of the Stockyards:*

3. See also Douglas Wixon, Jr., "The Dramatic Techniques of Thornton Wilder and Bertolt Brecht," *Modern Drama,* XV, no. 2 (September 1972). This informative essay gives special attention to the anti-illusionist theater of Brecht and Wilder; it argues that Wilder employed Brechtian techniques from 1931 onward. The article does not explore the thematic affinities of the two writers.

Humanity! Two souls abide
Within thy breast!
Do not set either one aside:
To live with both is best!
Be torn apart with constant care!
Be two in one! Be here, be there!
Hold the low one, hold the high one—
Hold the straight one, hold the sly one—
Hold the pair![4]

During the period when Wilder was working on *The Skin of Our Teeth,* the influence of *Finnegans Wake* was also taking effect on his vision. In his correspondence with Edmund Wilson in 1940 and 1941 Wilder gave his own version of the Joyce connection and offered a perspective on his imagination that is more wide-ranging than Robinson and Campbell's detective work. Wilder explained to Wilson that the *Wake* was a book with "a figure in the carpet": the design, he argued, was to be discovered in Joyce's anal eroticism; the great conundrum of modern literature was all about "order, neatness, single-minded economy of means."[5] Whether or not this is a reductive interpretation of Joyce, the "discovery" tells us something about Wilder's mind, points to his own career as a preserver of other people's motifs, and suggests a possible explanation for his constant borrowings in *The Skin.* Wilder claimed that he felt a joyous "relief"[6] as he understood Joyce's psychic and literary strategies; each interpreter of these remarks (and of Wilder's *Wake* obsessions) will have to decide what they are revealing. But the present study of Wilder's imagination offers this material as another example of his loving accumulation of ideas and patterns. The letters are a way of coming to terms with his own nature.

Writing to Wilson, Wilder spoke of the *Wake* as embodying "the neurotic's frenzy to tell and not tell."[7] Tell what? the reader might ask. Once again, this remark might be turned on Wilder's own work-in-progress: there are at least two of Wilder's recurring anxieties in the new play—resentment and guilt felt by a son *and* fear of civilization's destruction. His play, Wilder told Wilson, was meant to dramatize "the end of the world in comic strip."[8] On one level the description matched Joyce's remarks that *Finnegans Wake* is "a farce of destiny." But Wilder's readers cannot help recalling

4. *Seven Plays* (Brecht), ed. Eric Bentley (New York: Grove Press, 1961). 5. Letter to Edmund Wilson (January 13, 1940), Beinecke Library. 6. Letter to Edmund Wilson (June 15, 1940), Beinecke Library. 7. Ibid. 8. Letter to Edmund Wilson (June 26, 1940), Beinecke Library.

the disaster of *The Bridge,* the end of the patrician world in *The Cabala,* the declining pagan world in *The Woman of Andros. The Skin of Our Teeth* may be seen as both a Joyce-burdened work and the latest version of Wilder's anxieties about violence and the collapse of Western culture.

The folk-style of *Our Town,* the social parable of *The Merchant of Yonkers,* and the rich suggestiveness and borrowing of *The Skin of Our Teeth* are three forms of expression that Wilder developed to convey the struggle of people enduring the churnings of the cosmos and the conflicts of civilization. The three plays offer guarded affirmations about man's strivings: growth and insight are abundantly available in Wilder's theater and make it altogether unlike the visions of other major American playwrights.

CHRONOLOGY

1897

Thornton Niven Wilder is born in Madison, Wisconsin, on April 17. His identical twin dies within a few hours of birth.

1906–1911

Father, Amos P. Wilder, is appointed American consul general to Hong Kong; the family accompanies him to his new post, where Thornton attends a German school. After only six months, Isabella Wilder, Thornton's mother, takes the children to Berkeley, California, where they reside until 1911.

1911

The family rejoins their father in Shanghai, where he is now posted. After a short stint at another German school, Thornton attends the China Inland Mission Boys and Girls School at Chefoo.

1912–1915

Back in California, Thornton attends school in Ojai and Berkeley, graduating from Berkeley High School in 1915.

1914–1918

World War I; the United States enters the war in 1917.

1915–1917

Wilder attends Oberlin College in Ohio; some of his earliest works are published in the *Oberlin Literary Magazine*.

1917

Transfers to Yale University in New Haven, Connecticut.

1918

Yale Literary Magazine publishes several of his short plays and essays.

1918–1919

After a summer working for the War Industries Board in Washington, D.C., tries to enlist, but several armed services reject him for poor eyesight. Accepted by the Coast Artillery Corps, he serves for a few months as a corporal in Rhode Island, after which he returns to Yale.

1920

After serving for a year on the editorial board of the *Yale Literary Magazine* (which publishes his play *The Trumpet Shall Sound* as a serial), he graduates with a bachelor of arts degree. F. Scott Fitzgerald publishes *This Side of Paradise;* Sinclair Lewis publishes *Main Street;* Nineteenth Amendment grants women the right to vote.

1920–1921

In Rome, at the American Academy, Wilder studies archeology and begins writing *The Cabala*. After a year abroad, he returns to the United States to teach French at Lawrenceville, a boys' school in New Jersey.

1922

Fitzgerald publishes *The Beautiful and Damned;* James Joyce publishes *Ulysses;* T.S. Eliot publishes *The Waste Land.*

1924

Takes a leave of absence to attend graduate school at Princeton University.

1925

Receives M.A. in French literature from Princeton; spends the summer at MacDowell Colony in New Hampshire. Begins writing *The Bridge of San Luis Rey,* continuing to work on it in Europe that fall. Fitzgerald publishes *The Great Gatsby.*

1926

The Cabala is published. Ernest Hemingway publishes *The Sun Also Rises.*

1927

Wilder returns to Lawrenceville; *The Bridge of San Luis Rey* is published.

1928

Receives Pulitzer Prize for *The Bridge of San Luis Rey*. Publishes *The Angel That Troubled the Waters*. Resigns from Lawrenceville and goes to Europe, where he works on *The Woman of Andros*.

1929

William Faulkner publishes *The Sound and the Fury*.

1929–1937

Great Depression follows the stock market crash of October 29, 1929.

1930

Wilder publishes *The Woman of Andros*. Begins lecturing in comparative literature at the University of Chicago.

1931

Publishes *The Long Christmas Dinner and Other Plays*.

1933

President Franklin Roosevelt introduces his New Deal, programs intended to end the depression.

1935

Wilder meets Gertrude Stein, beginning a long, warm friendship. Publishes *Heaven's My Destination*. Italy invades Ethiopia.

1936–1939

Spanish Civil War.

1937

Japan invades China.

1938

Germany annexes Austria. *Our Town* opens in New York, receives Pulitzer Prize. *The Merchant of Yonkers* opens in New York.

1939

John Steinbeck publishes *The Grapes of Wrath.*

1939–1945

World War II. The United States enters the war in 1941, after the December 7 Japanese attack on Pearl Harbor.

1942

Wilder writes movie script *The Shadow of a Doubt* for Alfred Hitchcock. Enlists in the air force, where he is commissioned a captain. *The Skin of Our Teeth* opens in New York.

1942–1943

Serves in Africa. Receives his third Pulitzer Prize in 1943 for *The Skin of Our Teeth.*

1945

Leaves the air force in September.

1948

Publishes *The Ides of March.*

1950–1951

Awarded the Charles Eliot Norton Professorship of Poetry at Harvard University, where he lectures on "The American Characteristics in Classic American Literature."

1952

American Academy of Arts and Letters awards him its gold medal for fiction.

1963

Awarded the Presidential Medal of Freedom.

1964

Hello, Dolly!, based on *The Matchmaker,* first produced for the stage.

1965

Awarded the National Medal of Literature.

1967

Publishes *The Eighth Day.*

1968

Awarded the National Book Award for *The Eighth Day.*

1973

Publishes *Theophilus North.*

1975

Thornton Wilder dies December 7.

FOR FURTHER RESEARCH

Martin Blank, ed., *Critical Essays on Thornton Wilder.* New York: G.K. Hall, 1996.

Jackson R. Bryer, ed., *Conversations with Thornton Wilder.* Jackson: University Press of Mississippi, 1992.

Edward Burns, Ulla E. Dydo, and William Rice, eds., *The Letters of Gertrude Stein and Thornton Wilder.* New Haven, CT: Yale University Press, 1996.

David Castronovo, *Thornton Wilder.* New York: Ungar, 1986.

Malcolm Goldstein, *The Art of Thornton Wilder.* Omaha: University of Nebraska Press, 1965.

Richard H. Goldstone, *Thornton Wilder: An Intimate Portrait.* New York: Saturday Review Press, 1975.

Richard H. Goldstone and Gary Anderson, *Thornton Wilder. An Annotated Bibliography of Works by and About Thornton Wilder.* New York: AMS Press, 1982.

Bernard Grebanier, *Thornton Wilder.* Minneapolis: University of Minnesota Press, 1964.

Donald Haberman, *The Plays of Thornton Wilder.* Middletown, CT: Wesleyan University Press, 1967.

Gilbert A. Harrison, *The Enthusiast: A Life of Thornton Wilder.* New Haven, CT: Ticknor & Fields, 1983.

M.C. Kuner, *Thornton Wilder: The Bright and the Dark.* New York: Crowell, 1972.

Paul Lifton, *Vast Encyclopedia: The Theatre of Thornton Wilder.* Westport, CT: Greenwood Press, 1995.

Elizabeth Barron McCasland, *The Philosophy of Thornton Wilder.* New York: Carlton Press, 1976.

Helmut Papajewski, *Thornton Wilder.* Trans. John Conway. New York: Ungar, 1968.

Linda Simon, *Thornton Wilder: His World.* Garden City, NY: Doubleday, 1979.

Amos Niven Wilder, *Thornton Wilder and His Public.* Philadelphia: Fortress Press, 1980.

Mary Ellen Williams (Walsh), *A Vast Landscape: Time in the Novels of Thornton Wilder.* Pocatello: Idaho State University Press, 1979.

THE WORLD WIDE WEB

There are a variety of Wilder resources on the Internet; the editors direct interested readers to a website being developed by the Columbia University Graduate School of the Arts, in honor of Wilder's centenary, as a promising starting point for research. Find the website at **www.columbia.edu/cu/arts/wilder/index.html.** Its "wilder.net" link on the Education Resources page claims it will link to "every on-line resource with a connection to Thornton Wilder."

Works by Thornton Wilder

Novels

The Cabala (1926)

The Bridge of San Luis Rey (1927)

The Woman of Andros (1930)

Heaven's My Destination (1935)

The Ides of March (1948)

The Eighth Day (1967)

Theophilus North (1973)

Plays

Our Town (1938)

The Merchant of Yonkers (1939)

The Skin of Our Teeth (1942)

The Matchmaker (1955)

The Alcestiad (1955)

The Drunken Sisters (1957), (a satyr play, published with *The Alcestiad)*

Collections of Short Plays

The Angel That Troubled the Waters and Other Plays (1928)

The Long Christmas Dinner and Other Plays (1931)

Essays

"Some Thoughts on Playwrighting," in *The Intent of the Artist,* edited by Augusto Cereno (1941)

American Characteristics and Other Essays (1979) (published posthumously)

Journals

The Journals of Thornton Wilder, 1939–1961. (1985) Selected and edited by Donald Gallup, with two scenes of an uncompleted play, *The Emporium* (published posthumously)

Index